4·29·77

GOING TOO FAR

BY ROBIN MORGAN

GOING TOO FAR

THE PERSONAL
CHRONICLE OF
A FEMINIST

by ROBIN MORGAN

 RANDOM HOUSE, New York

Since this copyright page cannot accommodate all acknowledgments, they can be
found on the following pages.

Library of Congress Cataloging in Publication Data

Morgan, Robin.
    Going too far.

    1. Feminism—United States—History—Addresses, essays, lectures.   2. Morgan,
Robin.   3. Feminists—United States—Correspondence.   I. Title.
HQ1426.M84   301.41′2′0924   76-53507
ISBN 0-394-48227-1

Designed by Anita Karl

Manufactured in the United States of America

9 8 7 6 5 4 3 2

First Edition

ACKNOWLEDGMENTS

1955068

"Rights of Passage" first appeared, in an earlier version, in *Ms.* magazine.

"Women Disrupt the Miss America Pageant" and all three of the articles included here on WITCH were originally published in *Rat*, and subsequently reprinted by *Liberation News Service*.

"Take a Memo, Mr. Smith" and "How to Freak Out the Pope," in earlier versions, first were published in *Win* and *Liberation* magazines, respectively.

"The Media and the Man" first appeared, in slightly altered form, on the Op-Ed Page of the *New York Times*, December 22, 1970. Copyright © 1970 by The New York Times Company. Reprinted by permission.

"Barbarous Rituals" is reprinted from *Sisterhood is Powerful: An Anthology of Writings from The Women's Liberation Movement*.

All but one of the articles in Part III of this book first appeared in the Women's *Rat*. "Goodbye to All That," in addition, has been widely reprinted in both alternative and mass media, appearing in such varied publications as *The Berkeley Tribe, The Chicago Seed, The Old Mole, It Ain't Me Babe, Everywoman, Goodbye to All That,* KNOW, Inc.'s *Feminist Classic Pamphlets Series, Liberation News Service, The Great Speckled Bird, The Nickel Review, Leviathan,* and in such anthologies as *Voices from Women's Liberation* (Tanner, ed., Signet/New American Library, 1970) and *Masculine/Feminine* (Roszaks, eds., Harper & Row, 1972). "Goodbye to All That" also has been translated into French, Spanish, German, Danish, and Japanese, and has been published in feminist journals in those countries, as well as in England, Australia, New Zealand, and Canada.

"On Women as a Colonized People" first appeared in *Circle One: A Woman's Beginning Guide to Self-Health and Sexuality*, and was reprinted in *The New Woman's Survival Sourcebook* (Grimstad and Rennie, eds., Knopf, 1975).

"Lesbianism and Feminism: Synonyms or Contradictions?" was published in *The Lesbian Tide, Amazon Quarterly,* and *The Second Wave,* and is available as a reprint from KNOW, Inc., the feminist publishing house.

The article on Women's Studies, herein entitled "The Proper Study of Womankind," first appeared in transcript form in the book published by KNOW, Inc., *Report on the West Coast Women's Studies Conference.* The version I reprint here has been edited for length.

For
the Snow Queen
and the Robber Girl,
but especially for Little Gerda.

CONTENTS

PREFACE

The contents of this book tell a story which covers the last decade and a half. In selecting the pieces assembled here I have chosen those which seemed best to represent my own evolving political/personal thought of a given period. These writings were map notations in the journey of an individual woman through uncharted territory, via the intertwined roads of daughterhood, artistry, marriage, motherhood, radicalism. The interior terrain was one of ambivalent love, of dreams and fantasies, an exploration of "madness," and an affirmation of the artistic process. The exterior reality was of the 1960's: reform and then revolutionary politics, militant tactics (and rhetoric), and the emergence of feminist consciousness. The progress is revealingly reflected, I think, in that basic measure of human communication: language.

By 1962, I was a professional writer, one who loved and was addicted to words—and the subsequent changes in content and consciousness would be shown most clearly in the changes of style. Sand, Koestler, Camus, de Beauvoir, Sartre, and Fanon are only a few of the many writers who have explored the problem of style for the artist who is also an active political person of her/his time. Does one retain (indeed, strive to heighten) the subtle and elegant possibilities language has to offer in one's work, even at the risk of appearing dense, elitist, or irrelevant perhaps to the very people one wants most to reach? Does one dare write "down" for the sake of accessibility? If so, how far can the words be simplified before the ideas themselves begin to lose the integrity of their own complexities? How do urgencies of the time, pressures by one's political peers, feelings of guilt for a private joy found in the so-called individualistic act of writing—how do all these affect one's work? The essays in this book show, I think, part of the effect on one such writer's development. My "pre-political" respect for words was driven underground, so to speak, not so much by the civil-rights movement beginning in the late 1950's, as by the New Left in the 1960's; the very tools which were my best offering to the politics of my own generation were often regarded with contempt. Right and Left anti-intellectualism united when middle-class guilt drove my contemporaries into rebellion not only against educational institutions (which highly deserved such a revolt), but against education itself. Television had replaced books for many; rhetoric, in time, replaced thought. Or is this last an occupational hazard of all dedicated idealogues, an expedient if tragic inevitability?

I myself, then in my twenties, careened between my own fierce and often melodramatic individuality and a surrender to the intense pressure we radicals mutually exerted upon one another—all of us eagerly conforming to the dogma of non-conformity. I remember more than one demonstration of revolutionary sisters and brothers standardized in the regalia of psychedelic splendor and chanting in unison some slogan that conveyed our rejection of a society which processed people into identical robots. Irony (perhaps alone) still lives.

As feminist consciousness trickled into my life, however, another shift in my attitude toward language came about. It was not mere coincidence. Many of us began to recognize that we as women were trying to communicate hitherto unspeakable truths about our condition in the very language and concepts of the patriarchal culture (of the Left *or* Right) which caused that condition. Alma Graham and other feminist lexicographers and linguistic scholars explored the biased usage of everyday language, and began to devise new ways of freeing our speech. Synchronistically, an awkward but intrepid feminist culture was born, making it possible, among other things, to use in a poem words previously considered unpoetic, such as *menstrual, dishcloth, diaper.* Meanwhile I was finding my own way, as these essays reflect, back to that original concern for language, but a concern informed and transformed by the political consciousness gained in the interim. No revolution has yet dared understand its artists. Perhaps the Feminist Revolution will.

. . .

Some words are necessary on the structure of this book. I have collected these "documentary papers" in sections corresponding to their period and to my outlook at that time. Accordingly, I have restricted my editing of content to two areas: clarification of original intent and some unavoidable cutting to lessen redundancy. A selective process was necessary; there are articles that belong in this book which cannot be included, for legal and other reasons—their place is in a future volume. Only time can make definitive such a documentary record. Nevertheless, I have tried to be as comprehensively—and representatively—inclusive as possible of the years covered herein.

Each section, or part, has an introductory note placing the pieces that follow in their proper context. In many instances, an individual article required its own prefatory comments as well, providing background detail or explanation vital to the full comprehension of that essay. In most of these cases, I found a dialogue emerging between my voice today and my voice at the time of the piece's writing. At first this dialogue between present and past selves unsettled me, but I have come to respect and learn from it, and so have left it to be shared with my readers. If the present voice sometimes seems overly judgmental of the past one, defensive for her, amused by her, or pitying of her, I can only trust that from this public conversation across the space of my own private growth something will emerge recognizable to other women and, I hope, of use.

Robin Morgan
New York City, 1977

GOING
TOO
FAR

INTRODUCTION:
RIGHTS OF PASSAGE

THE WOMAN is a writer, primarily a poet. She is thirty-five years old, a wife, mother of a seven-year-old son. She is white, apostately Jewish, and of that nebulous nonclass variously referred to as "artists" or "intellectuals": words of floating definition meant to describe those persons possessed of intense vocations, educational riches, and financial insolvency—a study in contradictory classlessness. And she is a radical feminist. In fact she is an "oldie"—one of the women who helped start this wave of feminism back in the Pleistocene Age of the middle and late 1960's—a rare species characterized by idealism, enthusiasm, and round-the-clock energy. It is a species now endangered: often burnt out, weary, cynical, embittered, and prone to seizures of matronizing advice for younger sisters. Yet this particular specimen is still active, hopeful even, and the face that looks out from beneath a few more proudly exhibited gray hairs each day, the face is almost—good grief—*mature*.

The face looks out from a mirror. It is my face, and I am that woman.

I wanted to write this Introduction as a sort of "personal retrospective" on the Women's Movement: where we've been, where we are, where we might be going—all this in a classically theoretical style, preferably obscure, yea, unintelligible, so that people would be unable to understand what in hell I was saying and would therefore label me A Brilliant Thinker. But the risk-taking, subjective voice of poetry is more honestly my style, and so, to look at the Women's Movement, I go to the mirror—and gaze at myself. Everywoman? Surely a staggering egotism, that! I hardly believe *"Le Mouvement, c'est moi."* I *do* still believe, though, that the personal is political, and vice versa (the *politics* of sex, the *politics* of housework, the *politics* of motherhood, etc.), and that this insight into the necessary integration of exterior realities and interior imperatives is one of the themes of consciousness that makes the Women's Movement unique, less abstract, and more functionally *possible* than previous movements for social change.

So I must dare to begin with myself, my own experience.

Ten years ago I was a woman who believed in the reality of the vaginal orgasm (and had become adept at faking spiffy ones). I felt legitimized by a successful crown roast and was the fastest hand in the East at emptying ashtrays. I never condemned pornography for fear of seeming unsophisticated and prudish. My teenage rebellion against my mother had atrophied into a permanent standoff. Despite hours of priming myself to reflect acceptable beauty standards, I was convinced that my body was lumpy, that my face was possessed of a caterpillar's bone structure, and that my hair was resolutely unyielding to *any* flattering style. And ten years ago my poems quietly began muttering something about my personal pain as a woman—unconnected, of course, to anyone else, since I saw this merely as my own inadequacy, my own battle.

I've thought a lot recently, while assembling the essays in this book, about that intervening decade and the startling changes it brought about. *Going Too Far* is more than a collection of my prose writings on feminism dating back to the early 1960's; it is also a graph of slow growth, defensiveness, struggle, painful new consciousness, and gradual affirmation. My decision to leave each piece in this book unretouched—warts and all—has necessitated an editorial self-discipline as redolent with embarrassment as nostalgia, the two alternating in waves, like chills and fever.

There were the years in the New Left—the civil-rights movement, the student movement, the peace movement, and their more "militant" offspring groups—until my inescapably intensifying woman's consciousness led me, along with thousands of other women, to become a refugee from what I came to call "the male-dominated Left" and what I now refer to as "the boys' movement." And it wasn't merely the mass epidemic of bursitis (from the continual cranking of mimeograph machines) which drove us all out, but the serious, ceaseless, degrading, and pervasive sexism we encountered there, in each man's attitude and in every group's structure and in the narrow political emphases and manhood-proving tactical styles themselves. We were used to such an approach from the Establishment, but here, too? In a context which was supposed to be different, to be fighting for all human freedom?

That was the period when I still could fake a convincing orgasm, still wouldn't be caught dead confronting an issue like pornography (for fear, this time, of being "a bad vibes, uptight, un-hip chick"). I could now afford to reject my mother for a new, radical-chic reason: the generation gap. I learned to pretend contempt for monogamy as both my husband and I careened (secretly grieving for each other) through the fake "sexual revolution" of the sixties. Meanwhile, correctly Maoist rice and vegetables filled our menus—and I *still* put in hours priming myself to reflect acceptable beauty standards, this time those of a tough-broad street fighter: uniform jeans, combat boots, long hair, and sunglasses worn even at night (which didn't help one see better when running from rioting cops). And my poems lurched forth guiltily, unevenly, while I developed a chronic case of Leningitis and mostly churned out political essays—although Donne and Dickinson, Kafka, Woolf, and James were still read in secret at our home (dangerous intellectual tendencies), and television was surreptitiously watched (decadent bourgeois privileges).

For years my essays implored, in escalating tones, the "brothers" of the "revolution" to let us women *in*, to take more-than-lip-service notice of what the women's caucuses were saying, especially since "they" (women) constitute more than half the human species. Then, at a certain point, I began to stop addressing such men as "brothers," and began (O language, thou precise Richter scale of attitudinal earthquakes!) to use the word "we" when speaking of women. And there was no turning back.

The ensuing years can seem to me a blur of joy, misery, and daily surprise: my first consciousness-raising group and the subsequent groups I was in; the guerrilla theater, the marches, meetings, demonstrations, picketings, sit-ins, conferences, workshops, plenaries; the newspaper projects, the child-care collectives, the first anti-rape squads, the earliest seminars (some women now prefer the word "ovulars"—how lovely!) on women's health, women's legal rights, women's sexuality. And all the while, the profound "interior" changes: the transformation of my work—content, language, *and* form—released by this consciousness; the tears and shouts and laughter and despair and growth wrought in the struggle with my husband; the birth of our child (a radicalizing occasion, to say the least); the detailed examinations of life experience, of power, honesty, commitment, bravely explored through so many vulnerable hours with other women—the discovery of a shared suffering and of a shared determination to become whole.

During those years we felt a desperate urgency, arising in part from the barrage of brain-boggling "clicks" our consciousness encountered about our condition as females in a patriarchal world. We were also influenced, I must confess, by tendencies of the male movements, which were given to abstract rhetoric but ejaculatory tactics; that is, if the revolution as they defined it didn't occur in a meretricious spurt within the next week, month, five years at the maximum—then the hell with it. Depression. Impotence. If radicals wouldn't be alive, anyway, to see it, then we might as well die for it. This comfortably settled the necessity for any long-range planning.

Today, my just-as-ever-urgent anger is tempered by a patience born of the recognition that the process, the form of change itself, is everything: the means and the goal justifying each other.

There are no easy victories, no pat answers—and anyone who purveys such solutions alarms me now. But when I look back from my still-militantly rocking chair, or sit at my ultimate weapon, the typewriter, I see the transformations spiraling upward so rapidly and so astonishingly that I feel awe and gratitude at being a part of such change.

We were an "American phenomenon," they said—a symptom of the untreated neurosis and stridency of spoiled American women. ("They" were the patriarchal Left, Right, and Middle, the media, most men, and some women.) They overlooked certain little facts: that women had been oppressed longer than any other group, this subjugation having stood as the model for all subsequent forms of oppression; that women were a majority of the world's population; that specific commonalities of biology, attitude, and certainly treatment potentially united us across all the patriarchally imposed barriers of race, age, class, sexual preference, superficial politics, and life-styles. Now, as I write, this potential is vibrating throughout the globe—among Women's Movements in Thailand and Tanzania, Japan and Australia, China and South America and all across Europe, New Zealand, Algeria, Canada, Israel, Egypt, and the Indian subcontinent.

We were "a white, middle-class, youth movement," they said. And even as some of us wrung our hands with guilt hand lotion, we knew otherwise. Because from the beginning there were women involved who were of every class and race and age, even if the media did focus on a conveniently stereotyped "feminist image." Today, the National Black Feminist Organization—to name only one such group—has chapters in many major cities and has had two national conventions; Native American feminist activism is blossoming in the Southwest; Chicana, Puerto Rican, and Asian-American women are publicly affirming the feminist consciousness they have known all along. Grandmothers and grammar-school feminists are organizing, in everything from OWL (Older Women's Liberation) groups to Little League assaults. The Coalition of Labor Union Women is making waves within the male-controlled labor movement; and domestic workers, secretaries, hospital employees, welfare mothers, waitresses, and hundreds of thousands of other women—too long a list to name here—are fighting for their/our rights.

They said we were "anti-housewife," though many of us *were* housewives, and it was not us, but society itself, as structured by men, which had contempt for life-sustenance tasks. Today, too many housewives are in open participation in the Women's Movement to be ignored—and many are talking of a housewives' union. (Not to speak of the phenomenon of "runaway wives," as the news media call them in articles which puzzle over the motivation of women who simply have picked up one dirty sock too many from the living-room floor.)

They said we were "a lesbian plot," and the carefully implanted and fostered bigotry of many heterosexual feminists rose eagerly to deny that, thereby driving many lesbian women out of the movement, back into the arms of their gay "brothers," who promptly shoved mimeograph machines at them. What a choice. But the process did continue, and so the pendulum swung into its tactically tragic but expectable position, a reply-in-kind from some lesbian-feminists who created the politics of "dyke separatism," the refusal to work with or sometimes even speak to women who could not prove lesbian credentials. This was sometimes accompanied by the proclamation that lesbians were the only true feminists, or were the feminist "vanguard," and the accusation that all heterosexual women were forever "sold out" to men (leaving lesbian mothers, by the way, in a no-woman's-land). In some parts of the country it was called "the lesbian-straight split"— or even the "lesbian-feminist split"—with a terrifying antagonism on both sides. Yet most serious feminists continued to work together across sexual-preference labeling, and the process endured (through many tears), and we survived.

More and more, every day, that "split" is healing, from both sides: a changing attitude on the part of so-called straight women—about our own sexuality, about the necessity and joyousness of loving other women *and* ourselves, whether emotionally or physically, about the commitment and support our lesbian sisters require and deserve of us. And a changing attitude on the part of lesbian feminists—about *our* own sexuality, about the self- and sister-destructive compartmentalizing of women in roles *or* vanguards *or* self-affirmed ghettos. During that struggle, many an anti-lesbian woman conquered feelings of threat, of terror, and "came out" in fact, learning proudly to love another woman. Many lesbian women came to a more earnest feminism: a realization that we each need all women to survive—and that no woman's life-style, whether apparently chosen or seemingly forced upon her, could be held in contempt for the sake of some abstract "correct line." Because the Women's Movement *is* a plot of women who are lesbians—and a plot of women who are virgins, heterosexuals, celibates, and bisexuals. And we conspirators are all unlearning the absurd prefixes to the word "sexual" and beginning to discover, create, define ourselves as *women*.

They said we were "anti-motherhood"—and in the growing pains of certain periods, some of us were. There were times when I was made to feel guilty for having wanted and borne a child—let alone a male one, forgodsake. There were other times when we "collectivized" around children, and I found myself miffed at the temporary loss of that relationship unique to the specific mother and specific child. So much of the transition is understandable now. Since the patriarchy commanded women to be mothers (the thesis), we had to rebel with our own polarity and declare motherhood a reactionary cabal (antithesis). Today a new synthesis has emerged; the concept of mother-right, the affirmation of child-bearing and/or child-rearing when it is a woman's *choice*. And while that synthesis itself will in turn become a new thesis (a dialectic, a process, a development), it is refreshing at last to be able to come out of my mother-closet and yell to the world that I love my dear wonderful delicious child—and am not one damned whit less the radical feminist for that.

None of the above-mentioned issues is simple. None is "solved." Struggle, experimentation, and examination of each of these differences (and new ones yet to come) will continue, must continue, for years. And we can expect these divisions to be exploited as *diversions* by those who would love to see us fail. But that no longer scares or depresses me, despite the enormity of the job ahead. The only thing that does frighten me is the superficial treatment of any such issue, the simplifying of complexities out of intellectual laziness, fear of the unknown, or rigidified thinking. Yet despite the temptation to fall into such traps of "nonthought," the growth does continue and the motion cannot be stopped.

They said we were "going too far." Perhaps this has been their most frequent and basic accusation, phrased in a thousand different ways. Never mind that we are forced to act, or react, by the pain of our status itself (even as the young woman responding to relentless pressure in the back seat of the car nevertheless gets blamed for the result, enduring a cliché situation only to acquire a reputation for "going too far"). No, it's our fault, always. The vote? "This time the ladies are going too far." An end to foot-binding? "That goes too far." Abolishing slavery, wife-buying and -selling and -beating, rape, clitoridectomies, butcher-abortions, suttee—attacks on such issues were all radical, "extremist" notions in their time (in some parts of the world, radical and extreme to this day). A woman working outside the home? In other than volunteer jobs? You mean for *pay?* Surely that takes things too far, undermines the very foundations of family and therefore state (unless of course she is a "lower-class" woman who has always been permitted menial jobs—in which case her demand for a *decent* living would be seen comparably as, naturally, going too far). More recently, perhaps: "Well, equal pay for equal work, yes, but a woman learning karate, a woman raising a child with her lesbian lover, a woman brain surgeon or priest or astronaut or architect or President—now *that's* going too far."

At last. At last we seem to be understanding that there *is* no "too far," that *as* we grow and change we expand the categories themselves, that we create new space, that our just expectations and visionary demands for ourselves and our children bear us forward on an inexorable tide past all the fears and clucking tongues (even our own)—much too wonderfully far for even our own senses to realize, in this, our historical present. And there is never any turning back.

I call myself a radical feminist, and that means specific things to me. The etymology of the word "radical" refers to "one who goes to the root." I believe that sexism is the root oppression, the one which, until and unless we *up*root it, will continue to put forth the branches of racism, class hatred, ageism, competition, ecological disaster, and economic exploitation. This means, to me, that the so-called revolutions to date have been coups d'états between men, in a half-hearted attempt to prune the branches but leave the root embedded—for the sake of preserving their own male privileges. This also means that I'm not out for us as women to settle for a "piece of the pie," equality in an unjust society, or for mere "top-down" change which can be corrupted into leaving the basic system unaltered. I think our feminist revolution gains momentum from a "ripple effect"—from each individual woman gaining self-respect and yes, power, over her own body and soul first, then within her family, on her block, in her town, state, and so on out from the center, overlapping with similar changes other women are experiencing, the circles rippling more widely and inclusively as they go. This is a revolution in consciousness, rising expectations, and the actions which reflect that organic process.

In the past decade I have seen just such methods give birth to hundreds of alternate feminist institutions, created and sustained by women's energy—all concrete moves toward self-determination and power.

There are the Feminist Women's Health Centers proliferating in cities and towns around the country, proving that the speculum may well be mightier than the scalpel; the Rape Crisis Centers and the Centers for Battered Women; the Women's Law Centers; the expanding feminist media—books and newspapers and newsletters and magazines and pamphlets, literary and scholarly and how-to practical journals, as well as film groups, videotape collectives, radio and television and cable TV programs; the record companies; the Feminist Federal Credit Unions, begun only a few years ago (Detroit was the first) and now spreading to other cities—with assets approaching one and a half million dollars in women's control. There are the child-care centers which differ radically in tone, function, and cost from the "Kentucky-fried children" chains. There are the women's-studies programs which range all the way from that first "token" course to full-fledged departments, some of them allowing a minor, a major, or complete graduate work. There are the small feminist businesses—trusting enterprises in the face of a national depression—somehow managing to stay afloat while serving the women's community and at the same time providing salaries for the women who work there. Restaurants, craft shops, self-defense schools, employment agencies, bookstores, publishing houses and small presses—the list goes on and on.

Whenever I hear certain men sonorously announce that the Women's Movement is dead (a prediction they have been promoting hopefully since 1968), I am moved to an awkwardly unmilitant hilarity. I know, of course, that they mean we seem less sensational: "Where are all those bra-burnings?" (none of which ever took place anyway, to my knowledge). Such death-knell articulations are not only (deliberately?) unaware of multiform alternate institutions that are mushrooming, but unconscious of the more profound and threatening-to-the-status-quo political *attitudes* which underlie that surface. It is, for example, a grave error to see feminists as "retrenching" when the reality is that we have been maturing beyond those aforementioned "ejaculatory tactics" into a long-term, committed attitude toward *winning*. We are digging in, since we know that patriarchy won't be unbuilt in a day, and the revolution we are making is one on *every* front: economic, social, political, cultural, personal, public, sexual, biological, and even metaphysical.

The early ultra-egalitarianism and guilt-ridden "downward mobility" motifs of certain radical feminist groups, for instance, have modulated into a realization that women deserve to have credit for what we accomplish, whether that be the author's name signed to her article (after centuries of being "Anonymous"), or the right to be paid a living wage for her work at a feminist business (instead of falling prey to a new volunteerism—this one "for the revolution's sake"). The early antipathy toward any and all structure has given way to a recognition that we must evolve totally new ways of organizing ourselves, something other than chaotic spontaneity *or* masculinist hierarchy. The early excesses of collective tyranny have shifted into an understanding that there is a difference between individualism and individuality—and that the latter is admirable and to be cherished. The emphasis on women's studies reflects the welcome end of anti-intellectual trends (again picked up from male movements—a "line" created by privileged men who already had their college educations along with their charisma points in SDS or the counter-culture). We are daring to demand and explore the delights of hard intellectual work, both as personal challenge and shared necessity. All the jargon exhorting us to "seize power" won't help if we "seize" the labs, for instance, and stand ignorantly gaping at the test tubes. We are daring to research our own cleverly buried herstorical past, even to develop new and radical teaching methods as joint odysseys between teachers and students, without deification—or degradation—of either. Beneath the expansion of presses and magazines is an explosion of women's culture so energetic and widespread that it has not only given voice to women as a people but shows signs of rescuing art itself from the necrophiliac modernism of the Establishment, making poetry and music and drama and visual art and dance once again relevant, passionate, accessible, something to be integrated into all of our daily lives.

Underlying the visible activity of the women's health movement are political implications which could shake society's assumptions to the core: the reviving profession of midwifery; the research into menstrual extraction done by the Feminist Women's Health Centers (a technique allowing a woman to reduce her five-day period into one of five minutes' duration); abortion and contraceptive research done *by* women; new and humane means of giving birth with the mother in control of the choice and procedure of method; and feminist research into orgasm and women-run therapy sessions, with a 90 percent success rate, for "pre-orgasmic" women (who were formerly labeled "frigid" by male therapists). There are also the beginnings of feminist research into fetology and genetics, cloning and extra-uterine birth techniques— which *could* be tools of liberation if women controlled the means of such reproduction, but which would be agents of a science-fiction nightmare if the present medical establishment maintains its hegemony over this research. All these "ripple effects" circle out from the reclaiming of our most basic right, our own bodies, for our own purposes.

But the developments have not been limited to the physical and material sphere. A spiritual hunger is being expressed by women. I do not mean the hunger for an "opiate of the people" or escapism or a fad like the one which gooses frantic followers into chasing after a plump, rich, teenage boy for the truth and the light. On the contrary, this new spirituality transcends all such simplicities. It is the birth of a genuine feminist metaphysics. It is as if women were realizing that, to paraphrase Mary Daly, the ultimate degradation foisted on any oppressed people is a thievery of the right "to name"—to name ourselves, and our relation to the universe. And so, while some sisters continue to batter away at the discrimination from within patriarchal religions (those dear uppity nuns, those intrepid women ministers and rabbis and priests), many other women are researching the original matriarchal faiths and philosophies which most anthropologists now agree predated patriarchal ones—and there is an accompanying revival of interest in Wicce, or the Craft of the Wise: witchcraft (as the highly sophisticated and lyrical nature philosophy it is—not the satanic weirdo fringe that the patriarchy would have us *believe* it is).

Most important, all these psychic and religious explorations are part of a process of affirming the complexity of the universe and the divinity in each of us. How different from dogmatic pronouncements, from the centuries-old misogyny which still blames Eve for "the fall," and which burned millions of her daughters at the stake! How refreshing and fitting to be able to conceive of the life force as a *creatrix*, one which our own female creative bodies reflect! The possibilities opened up by such thought are tremendously exciting. Oh, I have my "mother of us all" moments when I stir the chicken soup and worry that these concepts can be too easily trivialized, reduced into excuses which might sound like, "Oh, goody, now we can pray to the Mother Goddess for freedom, and it will fall like womanna from heaven—so we don't have to organize or work to bring it about." But I also know that the process is a tempering one, and for every woman who gets mired in *spiritualism* as an excuse, there will be many more who will be strengthened, affirmed, and energized by *spirituality*—"Praise the Goddess and pass the petition," as it were. Which is fortunate, because I assume that the Goddess is a feminist who would not feel amusement at being expected to pick up after others' messes.

And where, my dear reader may well ask, does this Pollyanna writer see the dangers, the failures, the losses? Or is she so blind, the woman in the mirror, that she thinks we've really come a long way, baby? Hardly.

These arms have held the vomitous shudderings of a sister-prostitute undergoing forced jail-withdrawal from her heroin addiction. These eyes have wept over the suicide of a sister-poet. These shoulders have tightened at the vilifications of men—on the street, in the media, on the lecture platform. These fists have clenched at the reality of backlash against us: the well-financed "friends of the fetus" mobilizing again to retake what small ground we have gained in the area of abortion; the rise in rape statistics (not only because more women are daring to *report* rapes, but also because more rapes are occurring). This stomach has knotted at the anonymous phone calls, the unsigned death threats, the real bombs planted in real auditoriums before a poetry reading or speech, the real bullet fired from a real pistol at the real podium behind which I was standing. (Those who have power over our lives recognize the threat we pose—even when we ourselves do not.)

And yes, these fingers have knotted versions of "correct lines"— to strangle my own neck and the necks of other sisters.

I have watched some of the best minds of my *feminist* generation go mad with impatience and despair. So many other "oldie" radical feminists have been lost, having themselves lost the vision in all its intricacy, having let themselves be driven into irrelevance: the analytical pioneer whose "premature" brilliance isolated her into solipsism and finally self-signed-in commitment for "mental treatment"; the theorist whose nihilistic fear of "womanly" emotion led her into an obfuscated style and a "negative charisma"—an obsessive "I accuse" acridity corrosive to herself and other women; the fine minds lost to alcohol, or to "personal solutions," or to inertia, or to the comforting central-committeeist neat blueprint of outmoded politics, or to the equally reassuring glaze of "humanism," a word often misused as a bludgeon to convince women that we must put our suffering back at the bottom of the priority list. Some of these women never actually worked on a tangible feminist project—storefront legal counseling or a nursery or a self-help clinic—never had or have now lost touch with women outside their own "feminist café society" circles. Such alienation from the world of women's genuine daily needs seems to have provoked in some of my sister "oldies" a bizarre new definition of "radical feminist"; that is, one who relentlessly assails any political effectiveness on the part of other feminists, while frequently choosing to do so in terms of personalities and with scalding cruelty. After so many centuries of spending all our compassion on men, could we not spare a little for each other?

I've watched the bloody internecine warfare between groups, between individuals. All that fantastic energy going to fight each other instead of our opposition! (It is, after all, safer to attack "just women.") So much false excitement, self-righteousness, and judgmental posturing! Gossip, accusations, counter-accusations, smears—all leapt to, spread, and sometimes believed without the impediment of facts. I've come to think that we need a feminist code of ethics, that we need to create a new *women's* morality, an antidote of honor against this contagion by male supremacist values.

I've watched the rise of what I call "Failure Vanguardism"—the philosophy that if your group falls apart, your personal relationships fail, your political project dissolves, and your individual attitude is both bitter and suicidal, you are obviously a Radical. If, on the other hand, your group is solidifying itself (let alone expanding), if you are making progress in your struggle with lover/husband/friends, if you have gained some ground for women in the area of economics, health, legislation, literature, or whatever, and if, most of all, you appear optimistic—you are clearly Sold Out. To succeed in the slightest is to be Impure. Only if your entire life, political and personal, is one plummet of downward mobility and despair, may you be garlanded with the crown of feminist thorns. You will then have one-upped everybody by your competitive wretchedness, and won their guilty respect. Well, to such a transparently destructive message I say, with great dignity, "Fooey." I want to win for a change. I want us *all* to *win*. And I love, support, and honor the courage of every feminist who dares try to succeed, whatever the realm of her attempt: the woman who sued her male psychiatrist for rape—and won; the woman who ran for governor—and won; the young girl who brought suit against her school for enforced home-economics classes (for girls only)—and won. There are a million "fronts" to this feminist revolution, and we *each* of us need *each* of us pluckily fighting away on every barricade, *and* connecting her victories to the needs of other women.

I would say to those few dear "oldies" who are burned out or embittered: you have forgotten that women are not fools, not sheep. We know about the dangers of commercialism and tokenism from the male Right, and the dangers of manipulation and co-optation from the male Left (the boys' Establishment and the boys' movement). We are, frankly, bored by correct lines and vanguards and failurism and particularly by that chronic disease—guilt. Those of us who choose to struggle with men we love, well, we demand respect and support for that, and an end to psychological torture which claims we have made our choice only *because* of psychological torture. Those of us who choose to relate solely to other women demand respect and support for *that*, and an end to the legal persecution and attitudinal bigotry that condemns freedom of sexual choice. Those of us who choose to have or choose *not* to have children demand support and respect for *that*. We also demand respect for our feelings, and for the desire to forge them into art; we know that the emerging women's aesthetic and women's spirituality are lifeblood for our survival—resilient cultures have kept oppressed groups alive even when economic analyses and revolutionary strategy fizzled.

We know that serious, lasting change does not come about overnight, or simply, or without enormous pain and diligent examination and tireless, undramatic, every-day-a-bit-more-one-step-at-a-time work. We know that such change seems to move in cycles (thesis, antithesis, and synthesis—which itself in turn becomes a new thesis . . .), and we also know that those cycles are not merely going around in circles. They are, rather, an *upward spiral*, so that each time we reevaluate a position or place we've been before, we do so from a new perspective. We are *in process*, continually evolving, and we will no longer be made to feel inferior or ineffectual for knowing and being what we are at any given moment.

Housewives across the nation stage the largest consumer boycott ever known (the meat boycott) and while it may not seem, superficially, a feminist action, *women* are doing this, women who ten years ago, before this feminist movement, might have regarded such an action as unthinkable. The campaign for passage of the Equal Rights Amendment does continue to gain supporters (like those fine closet feminists Betty Ford and Joan Kennedy) despite all the combined forces of reaction against it. Consciousness-raising proliferates, in groups, in individuals, in new forms and with new structures. The lines of communication begin to center around content instead of geography, and to stretch from coast to coast, so that women in an anti-rape project, for example, may be more in touch with other anti-rape groups nationally than with every latest development on the Women's Movement in their own backyards. I think this is to the good; it's a widening of vision, an exercising of muscle.

Once I would have sneered at what I then called "the reformist wing" of our movement—groups like the National Organization for Women, Women's Equity Action League, the National Women's Political Caucus. But my own individual process has led me to a more pluralistic tolerance of other women's life-styles *and* politics. At the same time (miracle of the spiral), there has been substantial change taking place in such groups. As a radical feminist, I still disagree with some of the politics operating there, but I'm forced to reevaluate what I now call, respectfully, the "civil-rights front" of the movement. How can I not do so when, for instance, Karen DeCrow's acceptance speech after her election in 1974 as national president of NOW expressed authentically radical concern with those issues that had discomfited the national board in the past: rape, lesbianism, self-help health techniques, the representation and priorities of minority women? What else can I do but heartily applaud the moves toward genuine democracy in NOW, via ballot-by-mail and chapter rights? How can I not burst with pride when my "average American" sister-in-law in Seattle takes up feminist cudgels, braving ridicule at her job for doing so? How can I not chortle with glee when in one week I read the following two quotes in national newsmagazines: "I'm tired of being a martyr. When we got married Chuck expected that I'd work, but that I'd also be the chief one to have lunch money ready in the morning and take the kids to the doctor. Men need to volunteer more. . . . We've got to get some help for this job."—Lynda Johnson Robb, speaking at a Boston symposium on "The American Woman." And this: "Sisters, we must bury Dr. Spock and assert equal rights for women!"—Margaret Trudeau, at a Canadian women's seminar. Well! Am I to dismiss such courageous converts as "ruling-class women"? Am I to throw a stone at the mirror in a defeatist desire for seven years of purist bad luck? No way, no more.

I've changed too much for those games, and I'm in this process for good. I've learned that the "either/or" dichotomy is inherently, classically patriarchal. It is that puerile insistence on compartmentaliza-tion (art *versus* science, intelligence *versus* passion, etc.) that I abhor. We needn't settle for such impoverished choices. Reason without emotion is fascistic, emotion without reason sentimental (cheap feel-ing which is, in turn, fertile ground for the fascistic). Science and art budded from the same stem—the alchemist poets, the Wiccean herb-alists, the Minoan and Druidic astrologer-mystics and mathematician-musicians. The integration of such crafts was assumed, we now know, in the early matriarchal cultures, but a love of excellence, a devotion to skill, a thirst for wisdom, and a sense of humor are still great unifiers, capable of overcoming the current binary pigeonholing of people, ideas, vocations. The point is, we are all part of the problem *and* the solution— rhetoric to the contrary. And it is the inclusiveness of the feminist vision, the balance, the *gestalt*, the refusal to settle for parts of a completeness, that I love passionately.

This process is metamorphic. Today, my sexuality unfolds in ever more complex and satisfying layers. Today, I can affirm my mother and identify with her beyond all my intricate ambivalence. I can confront ersatz "sexual liberation" and its pornographic manifestos for what they are—degrading sexist propaganda. And I can confess my pride at an ongoing committed relationship with the husband I love and have loved all along, whose transformation by feminism I have watched over and struggled with and marveled at. This process has given me the tools, as well, to affirm the women I love, to help raise the child I love in new and freer ways. I have now curled round another spiral, and can admit that I *like* good food and enjoy cooking it (when that's not assumed to be my reason for existing). I have found my own appearance at last. No more "uniforms," but clothes that are comfortable, pleasant, and *me*: hair that I cut or let grow as *I* choose, unconforming to fashion as dictated by V*ogue* or its inverse image, *Rolling Stone*. And this process, most of all, has given me the tools of self-respect as a woman artist, so that I am reclaiming my own shameless singing poet's voice beyond the untenable choices of uninvolved "ivory-tower" pseudo-art or polemical "socialist-realist" imitation-art.

This reclamation of my own art (and unapologetic affirmation, indeed, of art itself) is inseparable from what I have lovingly named "metaphysical feminism"—the insistence on "going too far," the refusal to simplify or polarize, the insatiable demand for a passionate, intelligent, complex, visionary, and *continuing* process which dares to include in its patterns everything from the scientific transformation which stars express as they nova, to the metaphorical use of that expression in a poem; a process which dares to celebrate contradiction and diversity, dares to see each field-daisy as miraculous, each pebble as unique, each sentient being as holy.

And also, more humbly, this process, this Women's Movement, has given me the chance to travel through it, to witness the splendor of women's faces all over America blossoming with hope, to hear women's voices rising in an at-first fragile, then stronger chorus of anger and determination. Pocatello, Idaho, and Escanaba, Michigan, and Lawrence, Kansas, and Sarasota, Florida, and Northampton, Massachusetts, and Sacramento, California, and Portales, New Mexico—and how many others? It has exhausted me, this Women's Movement, and sometimes made me cranky and guilty and gossipy and manipulative and self-pitying and self-righteous and sour. It has exasperated me, frustrated me, and driven me gloriously crazy.

But it is in my blood, and I love it, do you hear? I know that women's consciousness and our desire for freedom and for the power to create a humane world society will survive even the mistakes the Women's Movement makes—as if feminism were a card-carrying nitsy little sect and not what it *is*, an inherently radical and profound vision of what can save this planet. There is no stopping the combined energy potential of Norma Kusske and her daughters and Joann Little and Jan Raymond and Morgan McFarland and Jane Alpert and Audre Lorde and Joan Nixon and Jill Johnston and Connie Carroll and Maria Del Drago and Linda Fowler and Kathleen Barry and Diane Running Deer and Mallica Vajrathon and Antonia Brico and Billie Jean King and Jean Pohoryles and Nancy Inglis. There are millions of us now, and the vision is enlarging its process to include us all.

I trust that process with my life. I have learned to love that Women's Movement, that face in the mirror, wearing its new, wry, patient smile; those eyes that have rained grief but can still see clearly; that body with its unashamed sags and stretch marks; that mind, with all its failings and its cowardices and its courage and its inexhaustible will to try again, to go further.

I want to say to that woman: we've only just begun, and there's no stopping us. I want to tell her that she is maturing and stretching and daring and yes, succeeding, in ways undreamt until now. She will survive the naysayers, male *and* female, and she will coalesce in all her wondrously various forms and diverse life-styles, ages, races, classes, and internationalities into one harmonious blessing on this agonized world. She will go splendidly "too far." She is so very beautiful, and I love her. The face in the mirror is myself.

And the face in the mirror is you.

PART ONE

Letters from
a Marriage

PART I:
INTRODUCTORY NOTE

Women are only now discovering how many great literary treasures of our history lie buried—in diaries, journals, letters sent and unsent, folk songs and lullabies never written down, poetry scribbled on the flyleaves of old pioneer-family Bibles and recipe books, aphorisms scratched on the walls of prisons and asylums, published volumes whose authorship was attributed to husbands and fathers and brothers and lovers, meditations written around the margins of cloister prayer books, unforgettable tales woven by the grandmother who never learned to read or write. For each woman of genius who was permitted minimally to consider herself a writer, to publish, to be acknowledged (albeit patronizingly), and to pay the enormous and at times even fatal price for this privilege—for each of those desperate and intrepid few, there were literally thousands of others who went to their graves unheard and unacknowledged. "Anonymous" herself, it would appear, was most frequently a woman, forced into secret writing when she could not be silenced altogether.

Although I have wanted consciously to be a writer from the age of four, and although I have worked seriously at my craft from the age of fourteen and published professionally from the age of seventeen, I too have written an entire body of work "in secret"—so strong is the message of female literary history. I don't mean that work which I wrote with an eye to publication but which simply has not been published. I mean, rather, other work, including the letters in this section of Going Too Far.

"Letters from a Marriage" were written on the dates they bear, to myself or my child, and mostly to my husband. They were almost all written before any feminist consciousness had touched my life, although in my ongoing fight for equal treatment I had fallen into the trap of thinking I must be an "exceptional woman" to be taken seriously. When my attempts to live up to such an image still didn't produce the desired result, I thought I was at fault, or perhaps (rarely) the individual man or situation was to blame—but I always saw the *problem as unique, not universal or political. And I was in continual psychic pain about this: I had grown so used to that pain, in fact, that it seemed an integral part of myself.*

These letters span a period of eleven years. I was twenty-one years old when I wrote the first one, thirty-two when I wrote the last. The first was written before I was married, the last when my child was four years old. The bulk of the letters, those to my husband, Kenneth Pitchford, herein referred to as "K.," were written out of those thoughts and feelings I feared I could never actually speak aloud to him. I thought of them as diary leaves—written mostly for my own sake, with the remote possibility of someday perhaps being able to show them to him. Beyond that, I admit that I secretly hoped the letters would be found after my death, and then could be seen by the whole world, should it care. I confess this last because to do otherwise would be hypocritical; the driving, voracious, irrepressible, and brazen desire of a writer is, after all, to write, and yes, to be read.

As becomes evident in the later letters, I did eventually let K. read them, and that reading opened up new channels in our relationship. Publishing them is another step altogether. They are, to say the least, embarrassing. They reveal both pleasant and unpleasant truths about myself, K., and our marriage, which inclinations toward complacency would rather leave unsaid, or at least unprinted. I know that there will be those who will be surprised that we remain together; those men who will wonder why K. never left me, and those women who, from a superficially "correct" feminist position, will have only contempt for me, for not having left him. Some readers will be voyeurs and some will be judges. There will even be some, perhaps, who disbelieve the validity of the letters; who will insist that I wrote them all recently, specifically for publication in this book, as some sort of gimmick.

One cannot require that the world understand one's actions. One can only try to proceed honorably, and to explain those actions one feels it necessary to clarify. The letters are real, and were written at the time of their dates. I publish them now because I feel they are an important part of my life, and because I am convinced that they name truths, trace patterns, and expose attitudes which in one way or another every woman who has ever lived under patriarchy has experienced.

The sharing of that experience is at the heart of the feminist metamorphosis—and for every reader who willfully misunderstands the letters there will be more women who will recognize this voice as their own. That would be sufficient reason for making myself vulnerable. Indeed, it is merely a measure of residual patriarchal identification in me that I still feel embarrassed about this at all. But such are the ironies inherent in the process.

"Love is more complex than theory," I wrote once in a poem. The letters are ultimately about love, in its various and terrifying and life-sustaining forms—and about the griefs that accompany it, today, for a woman, although I could at the time of writing most of them give no name yet to those griefs. But I could not know what I know now, however little that is, had I not dared to begin at that point.

Awkwardly, then, I affirm these letters, claim them for my own, and send them forth on their own. And I affirm the woman who wrote them, the man who finally read them and later courageously supported the idea of their publication, and the relationship which so far has endured and which continues to pay the costly price of growth.

The personal is political, I know as a feminist. The personal is also the pure ore to be mined for literature, I know as an artist. There is no way, then, that I cannot dare publish these letters.

1

The first letter in this series is both naïve and prophetic; it was written to myself one week before I married Kenneth Pitchford. He and I had met almost four years earlier, when I was seventeen; we met through a poetry anthology in which we each were represented by some poems. The relationship deepened and intensified during the following years, when we formed a poetry workshop together. There are references in this letter to various friends' and relatives' opposition to our marriage; indeed, my mother was greatly upset, as were most close family friends. Surprisingly, most of K.'s friends—a supposedly less conventionally minded circle of artists—were also opposed. Hardly anyone saw much of a future for such a couple: the man a poet and an unashamed homosexual (this, years before Gay Liberation), the woman a virginal former child actress ten years his junior who claimed she wanted to be a writer.[1] Such a marriage, buzzed the consensus, in traditional, or Freudian, or even bohemian terms, was going too far.

12 September 1962

So I am, after all, going to marry K. And for my own benefit, I want to put into words below what that—and the very living of my life entirely, which only really begins now—will entail:

I will learn to love him even as he loves me, from knowledge and not abstraction. I will use him to find more of myself, and be at his hand for the same purpose. I will not lie to him, or deceive him, no matter what the cost. I will insist on mutual honesty between us, whatever it discloses. I will not be subject to his life or work, be beset upon by him or any other; neither will I ask that of him. I will assert my selfness, my work, my desires and hours, not at the cost of his but to bring about between us a separate wholeness, threatening neither, reinforcing both. I will not play the girl-child to his father, nor will I

---

[1] I had been working, primarily in theater and television, since the age of two, managing to extricate myself from this busy precocity when I was sixteen.

patronize him, emphasizing his impracticalities or awkwardness in technicalities of this world. I will work toward becoming a woman rather than a wife, knowing that the latter need not include the former, but rather the former can with ease and a whole graciousness bring about the latter. I will remain me. I will fight all images that sprout between us of unconscious making. I will find the strength to be with him, or without him, as the case may be. I will try never to hurt him, within the bonds of loving or awareness. I will try to make him love me more each day, surprising his own limitations. I will not be overly dependent upon him, his potential as an artist, or his opinions—nor allow him to be tricked into leaning overly much on me. I will respect his actions all, his motives all, his ideas all, reserving that individual right of persons to differ.

I will survive my mother's hurt and horror, until such time as she can know me—and him—again. I will never stop a barrage of love toward her that must someday break her hatred and despair, and bring her to me. I will watch her always and be there when she needs me. I will find the strength and humor to cope with friends and acquaintances and their shock or disapproval. I will not let them touch me deeply, where I dwell, but will retain a compassion, with action, toward those I care for. I will not be ashamed of what I am doing, but will compel acceptance on my own terms. I will not justify, excuse, explain, or plead. I am what I am, in pride and excitement.

I will follow him into any paths he chooses, however alien or dark, or blinding, and at the same time seek my own paths. I will respect myself and my work, alone and to his face. I will strive to enjoy his bed truthfully, his work critically, and our life, with all the endurance, passion, and honesty I, as a separate me, can bring to them.

And I will love him enough, and more. And that will make everything possible.

R.M.

2

At the time of this letter's writing I had given up hope of reconciling my mother to my marriage, and had not spoken to her for over a year (it would be two more years before we resumed knowing one another). During the middle sixties, K. was working at a publishing house as a lexicographer, and I was doing free-lance editing and proof-reading, as referred to in this letter. The reference to my father stems from my not having met him until I was eighteen years old—and then infrequently, and disappointingly; my parents had been divorced when I was born. My maternal aunt, who had lived with my mother and me until I was twelve years old, was dying of cancer in Florida when this letter was written.

13 July 1965, Midnight

Dᴇᴀʀ K.:

This will be the first in a series of letters I've been wanting to write you for a long time. I shrink somehow from keeping a diary; it seems solipsistic or self-conscious, at least the way I would go about it, I know. And so many times I want to say things to you that I don't. Not because I can't—I really think we have an extremely rare ability and will to communicate with one another—but because the time isn't right, or the mood, or simply because the thought doesn't actually form itself until flowing out on paper. It's absurd to begin a one-sided correspondence to the person with whom one is living, I know, seeing every day, lying beside every night. Especially absurd since we so often sit and talk, long and animatedly, about everything important or unimportant, talking just as we did before we lived together, with the same earnest desperation as if one of us had to leave in a few hours. But whatever the real reason, which may only become clear to me later on, I write to you instead of to a diary or journal. Perhaps it's just the pompous thought that this medium will be more interesting to posterity. I wouldn't put it past me.

Tonight, you are sleeping, and since we're on slightly different schedules, I'm wide awake, not quite alert or detached enough to really write or read; not lazy enough to watch television or goof off. But my mind is teeming with ghosts and realizations and ideas, unbidden and not quite welcome. That's why I write this, instead of the first draft of a poem.

I've finished proof-reading the Jo Mielziner memoir for Atheneum, which was filled with recollections of his having done the set for *Death of a Salesman*. This sent me back to the play, of course, which I've just now reread for about the fifth time, weeping again like a fool. The terrible love between Biff and Willy makes me realize how desperately I want to work with that subject matter I so fear and so desire: the awful love and struggle and noncommunication, and that same hopeless *belief* in one another—despite all the awareness of the heavy embroidery of lies that makes it possible—between my mother and myself. I think, too, of my Aunt Sally, dying slowly in Florida between her pitiable letters to me, trying to love me in some compromise between the way she knows how to love (possessiveness, gifts, guilt, harangues) and the way she somehow glimpses I want to be loved and to love (honestly, communicatively, with respect and some honor—oh, impossibly, I guess, with everyone in my life until you). I love and pity her in her little dying, and can do nothing. Nothing but go down and live with her and wait on her and love on her terms, be possessed and give up all that I have fought to learn and be. And even that would be nothing, because I couldn't give it up or hide it successfully, so that she would soon be disillusioned about the person she thinks she loves but could never understand.

Why is there still this interminable ache in me, in all of us, cut the bonds as we may, to try to love and know those of our own blood? I mourn my living mother tonight, for the more than a year we have lost of each other. I mourn my living father for the twenty years we never had of each other. I mourn myself as a torn child and adolescent, still trying feverishly to act upon that love and understanding and forgiveness that I am now wise enough to put only in a letter which may never be seen, or a poem which will. How many years do we go on using against ourselves the same knives our parents have bequeathed to us, still red with our own blood that they drew early in our lives?

You've just awakened and trotted out past my desk, naked, in that sleep-potty summery way of yours that is so foggy and bewildered at being awake, and so endearing. And for the thousandth time, your presence in the room, simply as that, all unaware, drives old ghosts back to their graves, your love for me wrapping me round in itself as protection against all their haunting cries, all my failed loves.

So I will speak of another realization I had tonight, which has rocked me somewhat. I don't know yet whether it's good or bad, but it's frightening. That same silly Mielziner book (such petty things can set off *such* thought processes) rambled on about the *theatah*, and actors and rehearsals and the comradliness of it all and the nervousness before openings, etc., all so familiar to me, both from the cliché of it and the actual knowledge of having done these things for so long, that I was deeply shocked to find it all totally foreign to me. I mean, simply, that although I could remember those experiences and even recall those very feelings, I suddenly knew as an absolute fact that I could never know them again. I don't believe I can act any more. I don't mean this as a rehash of all the old disillusionment I went through when I first left acting, which I've since coped with by looking at it simply as a job. I mean I know I can never really act again. Nor does having been away a long time explain it. I don't think I can perform a character before an audience any more. That schizophrenic temperament—the weirdness of being onstage or before a camera, speaking, and *meaning*, mind you, lines—and still knowing that you are yourself, at least partly, aware of both in the same instant, is now . . . not incomprehensible quite, but foreign, alien, impossible to me. I'm too much myself, too integrated, to exorcise myself from my own body successfully. The thought terrifies me, as if I were a schoolgirl afraid of standing in front of people to say my piece. And all the techniques and tricks that I can still call up to aid me don't help if, in that moment, a real and a fictional character strive for existence in the same body. The real one wins, the performance is false, the tricks are just tricks. I really don't think I can ever act again. This has nothing to do with wanting or not wanting to, it's quite beyond both. Does this mean I've become realer as a human being, more vivid in my own personality, more introspective as a person or a better poet? I think not, but don't know. I've lost one thing, and don't know if I've gained another in its place or, to be more exact, don't know what has thrust the first thing out. Perhaps I've indeed lost the world, but gained my own soul.

This letter—or entry—has served its purpose and comforted me. Sometimes I think that all writing is just an expression of frustrated love, but at least I've learned to turn (most of the time) that frustration on thinking of the past into something constructive in the present, or at least something self-revealing, or even merely sedating, to the pain. Strange that I should write this first letter tonight. So many times I've been about to start it, either in a mood of great mushy Schubertian love and yearning, or simply to number in writing the one hundred reasons why you should go to hell. Neither, tonight, but calmly, confidentially, as to a friend. My dear, my dear, you're still the only *friend* I have.

R.

On rereading this, I feel I should add that I don't intend to polish these letters (if I ever write another one), but just let the thoughts come as they will in what language they will. Hence the striking lack of immortal prose. With all my secret hopes that you, or posterity, will read this, for the sake of truth—and my own sanity—I had better assume nobody ever will.

3

This letter refers to the writing of the first draft of K.'s novel, *The Beholding*, which was ultimately completed in 1976. "Killing off Leonard Porterfield" is a reference to his writing the death scene of one of the major characters in the novel. Hektor, the cat mentioned throughout this letter, was born on the day we were married. One of a circle of cats all named for Homeric characters, he is at present alive and well, thirteen years old, and extremely dignified at such a venerable age.

27 July 1965, 1:00 a.m.
(actually 28 July)

Dear K.:

Tonight you are killing off Leonard Porterfield at last, and before I set to work myself I thought I would put down the "Leech Dream" we've so often discussed—probably the most beautiful and terrifying dream I've had.

It's been almost a year since the dream, but I still can recall it quite vividly, partly from our many talks about it, and partly from the clarity of its symbolism.

I was in a small stone cottage in a tiny clearing, in the midst of dense, almost jungle-like woods. You, already my husband, were away, on a space mission actually, although it was not so much for the government as a private, personal expedition to some planet—Venus, I believe. I was confident of your safe return, and I lived quietly, without fear, despite my solitude. My only companion was Hektor, our orange tiger cat, still young and lean and affectionate. He didn't live in the tiny cottage, but in the woods just beyond. He visited me daily. It was summer, the sun was warm, and I took a mat outside (just beyond the house, in the little clearing) to lie on and enjoy the sun. Hektor came up as I was doing this, and after I had taken off my shoes (which, for some reason, were brown loafers—the kind kids put pennies in) and set them a little away, at the edge of the woods, he lay down beside me to sleep. Somehow he was much larger stretched out beside me, reaching from my breasts, where he nestled his head, to below my knees.

As he lay there, a strange snake-like creature, part lizard, with a head like a snake but with squat legs and claws, and a long tail, appeared from out of the surrounding growth. (I somehow knew, in the dream, that he was a leech, although an actual leech looks much different.) He hissed out a warning to us, saying that he hated us and would destroy us.

In the passage of time in the dream, this scene seemed to have occurred a number of times. Then, one day, as Hektor and I lay in the sun, both thinking of you with confidence and love, we began to shift positions. He now lay on top of me, long, silky, luxuriant, and quite without hurting or clawing, he entered me. As we made love, it was somehow an offering, a tribute to you away on your planet or star. But the leech appeared, more malevolent than ever, and sidled over to one of my shoes, hissing that whatever he touched became poisoned, and that he would destroy us now. He said that the instant one of us moved off the protective mat, he would sting or even just touch us, and we would die. He said that he would avenge you for our unfaithfulness.

I asked Hektor if the leech didn't know, didn't understand what this scene meant, that our love was part of you, that you would have approved, that in some way you were even participating in our lovemaking yourself. I began to move toward the shoes to explain, to make the leech see this. But Hektor would not let me. He said, in a terrible voice, that others will see evil where they will, through their own distorted view of good; that one can never assume any act, no matter how pure, will not be misunderstood—nor should one then, knowing that, cease to act.

Overhearing this, the leech expanded in anger to half again his size, left my shoes, and approached us. He said he would touch us even *on* our protective mat, killing us and freezing us in our sexual position so that the proof of our infidelity would be there for you to see when you returned.

"But he will not care!" I cried. "He would not feel betrayed, don't you understand? He would not see evil in this, he would understand the love we have for him, expressed in the love we have for each other!" The leech still approached, and then Hektor sprang at him. I fled to the safety of the cottage, but looked out the window to see their battle. It was over almost instantly, the leech dead, and Hektor alive but frozen in a horrible, crouched position: mouth open, fangs bared, claws spread, muscles straining in rage, terror, agony. I knew now I could not touch him either, so infused was he with the poison. His paralyzed eyes looked back into mine through the window, as if to warn me away.

Then I had left the cottage and the woods, still dark and overgrown around the sunny clearing, and I was in a spaceship hurtling through the star-splashed black to join you. Somehow, I felt that Hektor would survive the poison, and would join us, too, in time. But I also felt that the leech was not really dead either, that he would crawl back into the jungle to recover, let his poison fill his veins again, and then emerge to cry his evil morality against the world once more.

Whatever else the dream meant, I really believe that Hektor's words are a profound truth. He seemed to be a symbol for you in the dream (I've often commented that I think you and he look alike!), and he spoke with your voice, I remember. The feeling was that he, being an animal, albeit a tame one (not completely so; remember he lived in the woods, too), could understand the true nature of the leech more quickly and thoroughly than I, and could do battle against it with some hope of survival. Perhaps it is the civilized element, the moral element in the human being that is more easily converted to evil without recognizing it, that thinks sex is wrong, that sets up mores and then lives in terror of them. Certainly people are more "bestial" than any beasts which have ever existed. We are the only creatures who kill for pleasure, beyond food or survival.

In any case, before I dig this line of reasoning into a Rousseauean trap for myself, I will stop here and get to work. Dreaming, I survived the leech, and went off to join the other part of Hektor (you) on a distant star. But awake, I have not forgotten the leech's eyes, or his hiss, or what that hiss said.

R.

4

"The rains came" refers to a Swiss-cheese leaky roof in our apartment which, during one particular rainy season, left us vulnerable to the deluge and to a consequent indoor flood. We were months repairing the damage. "D." was a neighbor, one of those persons who are overly generous about music—he played Puccini operas ceaselessly on his phonograph, and at a volume which made it all but impossible for anyone within hearing distance to work. Fortunately, he finally moved away. "T." was a male acquaintance who seemed to think he was Tristan and Don Juan in one miraculous combination.

1 August 1965

D<small>EAR</small> K.:

Tonight I must write you, as tonight is an Occasion.

You sit at your desk now (ten in the evening, August first, a Sunday), finishing the last chapter of your first full-length novel. Wearing only white undershorts, the broad expanse of your back, slightly tanned from our two times at the beach so far this summer, hunches over your typewriter. You sit with your chair tipped back but your body leaning forward (that funny old oak desk chair!), and you're typing very fast now and not even smoking and I love you.

Later a few close friends will come over and we will celebrate and you will type the last period with a flourish, like a ritual, a ceremony. Oh, yes, and there's much revising to do but the main body of the work, the foundation, will be done as of tonight. You began the novel before we were married, and began it in your mind years before that. And that first summer of our marriage, you worked on it, and I worked, quietly, happily, before "the rains came" and then D. began his assault with sound. And now, just about a month ago, you picked up again, and it will all be completed in a matter of minutes now, a short while. So much struggling, this past year and a half, so much *angst* and unnecessary suffering, while that novel lay gathering dust in its uncompleted state. Some of the first pages of the manuscript are slightly yellowed already, as you write the final pages now. (T. just called and would adore to come by, but could he bring a new girlfriend, one of the Radio City Rockettes, with him?—God, novels get finished after all, but some things never change!)

And it's a good novel, by God, it's right and good. It frightened me sometimes, reading it hot off the typewriter, chapter by chapter, even in rough state, by its power and rightness and painful lyricism. Dear God, it makes me proud. And having just completed a six-months' affair with Faulkner, every one of his novels, and having just a day or so ago finished reading *The Rainbow* and tonight completed *Women in Love*, I'm *not* merely rhapsodizing about my husband. *The Beholding* will stand up. It will be around for a long time.

But very soon now you will be finished and then people, albeit dear friends, will be here. I wanted to say in this letter what I may not have time to say, shortly, to you, though God knows I will try (despite Rockettes). How deeply happy I am, how gratified, how worth it it all has been, how this seems only the beginning—but if it were the end, tonight, even so, we have lived more and crammed more life and work and spirit into our days and nights so far than most people have in whole lifetimes; how remarkable a man you are, dancing a little jig of excitement in your undershorts just before beginning the last chapter, lying above me last night in our bed, straining now over your writing; how stunningly free our relationship seems (especially after *Women in Love*), a clean, frank, uncompetitive, comradely working together, loving each other's work more than each other, loving our own work more than each other's, proudly, strongly. All fine, so fine.

About five years ago in a chrome luncheonette on Third Avenue, a funny, plump young girl, with dyed blond hair fizzing over the mink collar of a pearl beaver coat, told you earnestly (while ripped to shreds of despair internally, since you were something she could never have, somthing denied to her forever) that she loved you because you were a great writer. Tonight, I sit in our lovely dark-beamed study, walled round with books, pools of light encircling our two huge desks. And my hair is natural, a dark green-gold, and my body is inhabited by me in every limb and pore, supple and light, your touch still warm upon it under my white summer shorts and avocado sweater, and I look across at your back and neck and proud head, and I bless this night, this moment, and that long-ago despair that brought me here. I bless this study, I bless our bed, I bless the past year of anguish that proved we would endure, I bless the absurd sound of our typewriter keys clacking together, I bless myself for my courage and wisdom in fighting for all this, I bless you, oh, I bless you for all that you are.

But one thing has not changed, the seed of my salvation years ago and the flowering of my pride tonight. I know that you are a great writer.

R.

5

The phrase "We have a conflict of life-styles here" and, indeed, this entire letter could serve as a classic example of the confused search of a woman, in pre-feminist consciousness, to find a personal solution for those problems she thinks of as uniquely her own. The pain is not yet recognized as being *political*; it is felt as individual, *her* problem, *her* fault. Guilt, self-contempt, and feelings of unworthiness—all inevitable responses of the depressed oppressed person—are stunningly manifest in the accompanying Various Failures of Me list. This was written, of course, before most women, myself included, knew that the vaginal orgasm was a myth, that housecleaning and cooking standards did not after all have to bear a Good Housekeeping Seal of Approval, and that being a size five (while standing almost six feet tall) did not necessarily constitute being beautiful. The self-loathing so evident here was at its peak during the very periods when I thoroughly cleaned house twice a week, baked quiche Lorraine and whipped up soufflés, and also dieted furiously—none of which made any difference to my self-hatred. Something else would be needed to give me glimpses into my own real worth. Something else would be needed to give me the tools by which to struggle with the man I loved.

1955068

1 July 1966, 1:00 a.m.

Dear K.:

I've just reread the previous letters and noted, with interest, that it has been almost a year now since I've written another. I do so tonight out of a very different spirit than that which prompted the others. Again, you are out, gone on a summer walk and to get something to eat and read the *Times*, because you are angry and depressed and want to get away from me. Fine. There's a peace in the house at the moment because only one depressed and angry person is here—not two, competing in their misery.

And quite a year has passed. Sally dead; three months of my

intensely renewed existential duel with that death, any death; your revising and typing of your novel; your second book of poems sold; the big party in celebration; our redoing the bedroom and painting the downstairs and putting finishing touches on the apartment; our month-long joint poetry-reading tour; and our return—to this.

And now all at once it seems that the weaknesses in our personalities and our relationship appear more exposed than ever before. No one thing new, all problems we know and have talked about and worked on and even joked about. But not now, not this time, not with this sudden weariness and hopelessness we both seem to feel on being confronted with them. Last night we had the long talk I had so longed for and then begun not to care about, after almost two months of being dazed, rather than depressed, and quite depersonalized about my immense failings. We hadn't talked earlier because of the exhaustion of the trip; then your fall from the library-ladder and the pain-killing drugs which put you out for weeks, it seemed; then because it appeared to be too late to talk. But it wasn't. Or was it? Because we didn't "solve" or really get to a damned thing. We sort of faked a solution, a communication, an understanding, but we have after all had the real thing in the past with each other, and we both know the difference. And now, tonight, your inevitable delayed reaction has set in, further prompted by what I meant to be a short, casual, practical talk about money affairs earlier today.

My, but you plummeted quickly. A bad headache, a sick feeling, a hostile depression, total noncommunication. I went and did errands, housework, felt that I had (for the first time in days) accomplished something practical, felt refreshed by the manual labor, returned to find you worse. Sleeping on the floor in the study, huddled by the air conditioner, a reproach (or so I take it) that I have not managed the money well, haven't saved enough for the bedroom air conditioner we had planned. And you're right, too. Oh, always right. That supposedly is what we talked about last night. Various failures of Robin Morgan, listed on the attached sheet which I made up for my own sick amusement. You had reassured me, oh, yes, and explained that you criticize only to urge further improvement on my already astounding successes. Then today you went and huddled by the air conditioner. Today you looked at me out of eyes that, far back, said "You are destroying me." Now just where does my guilt come from? Yes, yes, we know I have a pattern of it from having lived with my mother, we know I have (your words) an acute "critical faculty" where my work and my life are concerned, but does no one encourage this? Does no one play into it? I asked if I could get you anything, help somehow, cook something, or should we take a walk together. You went out alone. Ah, does no one play into it?

Well, and are *you* destroying *me?* More, that is, than any person living with another does, than any human being inevitably tries to do to another. You try not to, God knows, I try not to, we talk about it sensibly all the time. We are aware, perceptive, articulate. And if I make you pay for my guilt, don't you perpetuate the cycle with more criticism? I don't mean ordinary criticism, I mean the myriad tiny reproaches every day, said and glanced and subtly communicated.

Something, at any rate, has gone wrong. How irreparably? I don't know. I do know that for some weeks now we have not been really sexually attracted to each other. Sex has been mechanical. I half-dread it, half-hope for it on the chance that this time things will really come off successfully. Nobody's really getting any work done. You wrote a few poems. I wrote one. You are behind on final revisions for the novel and the book of poems, behind on your office work (two weeks to write the synonymies you do in thirteen hours), behind in your correspondence. Your desk is a holy mess. You always tended to work in this belated, procrastinating manner (I remember snowdrifts of uncorrected papers on your desk when you used to teach, and that was before we were married), and you know it. But it is more convenient to say that my moods, or my household interruptions, or my *something* is responsible.

Yes, I'm reeking with self-pity, my dear, as I plod through laundry and cleaning and cooking and bills and bank accounts and insurance and ordering books and theater tickets and keeping up with your correspondence as well as mine and running the errands and making the telephone calls. Yes, I seem to fuck them all up. Yes, I am filled with self-loathing as well as self-pity. Poor K., what did he ever do to deserve this? Of course he shares the burden, does his part, except that there are hundreds of little things he doesn't even think of, doesn't foresee, couldn't care less about if he did. But this daily business of living is a full-time job and has to be seen to.

We've got a conflict of life-styles here. I know that I work best when my life is cleared away, things in order, no bills or errands or laundry on my mind. So I do them. It's not easy when I'm also trying to drift along with your schedule instead of ignoring or fighting it, and am therefore up all night and sleeping all day. You, of course, also work best when things are in order, except it will never be you who orders them, by God.

I'm tired of all this, K. Tired of doing the things I actually love to do: cook, clean, etc. Tired of your constant criticism, tired of failing and feeling it myself *and* from your alternating condemnation and condescension. Tired of your god-like manner, all the while you're complaining that people cast you as an oracle. Tired of your equality-in-our-marriage talk, which I've always heartily seconded, silently planning the dinner or how to get to the bank on time meanwhile. Tired of *your* moods, which you indulge in freely (mine, of course, are unfortunate—you can't help being sensitive to them, and they upset you and you can't get your work done). Tired of the way you come to a mutual project late, reluctantly, and then take it over completely. Tired and ashamed that I so pled my unworthiness before you last night, until you had to concede it—a little. My God! Has the fight been broken out of me completely? If so, then you, not meaning to, have succeeded where others, meaning to, have failed.

I like our home, our life together. It's the two of us I can't stand. I feel I'm giving more, far more, to this marriage than you are, and such self-pity combined with guilt that I'm still not giving *enough*: I feel, shall we say, uncomfortable. Oh, Christ, I'm tired of this letter, too. I'm tired of waiting for you. I'm tired of *you*.

I'm going for a walk.

R.

Various Failures of Me

EDUCATION	Don't know my own field, literature, sufficiently.
WRITING	Ignorant of basic, classic terms, let alone complexities.
SEX	With ease clitorally, with more difficulty vaginally; perhaps basically asexual? An indifferent, unexciting partner.
HOUSEKEEPING	
Cooking	Some things decently, not very adventurous, fairly unchallenging.
Cleaning	Sporadic, undisciplined yet obsessive, never quite "on top of things"; laundry usually late, buttons unsewn, etc.
Sewing	Zero, and hopeless about learning.
House repairs	Have learned to do some things, but ridiculously incompetent.
SWIMMING	Learned, sort of tries, pretends to, can't *well*.
FRENCH	" " " " " " " "
PIANO	" " " " " " " "
DRIVING A CAR	" " " " " " " "
EXERCISE	Sedentary.
BUSINESS	Officious but not very efficient, bad in math, procrastinates.

MONEY

Panics when overdrawn, low, or when bills mount up, yet irresponsible and lives high (cabs, etc.) when money is there. Unplanning. Unrealistic. Unprepared.

APPEARANCE

Overweight, short; hair never quite in a neat or flattering style for the round, rather low-foreheaded face. Eyelids puffy, nose too large for features. Dresses more fashionably than used to but due to height and weight often still looks out of place or "dowdy."

CONVERSATION

Voice too loud generally, shouts when excited. Overbearing, nervous, talks in clichés and often about subjects which expose terrific ignorance. Calls people darling, sweetie, etc. Feels one must be smiling or laughing a great deal. Plays very sexy. Feels inferior and uneasy when someone else is in control, but blind to own faults, statements, etc., when in control myself. No wit. Little spontaneous humor, except when in a bitchy mood; otherwise, borrows that of others. Jealous of chic or brilliant women, or those quietly self-possessed. Likes women who are bright, but young or naïve or in some way flawed enough for feeling superior to, or for mothering. Pretty much the same toward men. An extrovert in classically insecure manner.

6

"Jim A." was a man with whom I tried—and failed—to have an affair, thinking, as so many women have, that such an affair would solve the difficulties in my marriage one way or the other. In my case, it was also a rebellion against any implicit (though denied) double standard in my marriage, and an attempt to "get with" the swinging morality of the sixties. God forbid I should be square, un-hip, puritanical, prudish. The "sexual revolution" which we now know never really occurred for women certainly wasn't going to leave *me* behind.

"Father James" was a Catholic priest who, oddly enough, was a close friend of my rather apostate Jewish family when I was a child. He served as a powerful surrogate for the father I had not known. Years later I realized that he had his own erotic reasons for loving to be around children—especially little girls. "Your onion skin" refers to a poem of K.'s from his first book;[1] the refrain is "peeling, peeling the onion skin/down to the nothingness within." The reference to "that memorable day in Pippin's" recalls a landmark conversation over Sunday brunch in a small neighborhood restaurant, during which I told K. that I had actually faked orgasm with him many times. I was convinced I was the only woman in the world sick enough to have done this.

27 November 1966
3:00 a.m. next morning

Dear K.:

Well, one thing is for certain from now on—I'm never going to reread the previous letters before starting a new one. It's too depressing, and also makes me feel I have to "fill in" what happened since. I guess I got one good poem out of that last letter's crisis, though, "Satellite,"[2] and we survived. Survived not only the deadlines, and severe money pres-

---

[1] *The Blizzard Ape: Poems* by Kenneth Pitchford in the Poets of Today Series (Scribner's, New York, 1958), p. 83.

[2] *Monster* (Random House and Vintage Books, New York, 1972), p. 7.

sures, but also the Jim A. crisis. The week of almost solid talk we suffered through saved us from, I somehow know, really dangerous shoals. Yet even now, understanding each other's positions so much better, and having tried to be honest as much as one ever can be (which is bloody little), I still sense a treacherous undercurrent. About Jim perhaps, because I'm still, despite everything, strongly attracted to him, despite my own self-disgust and fear and plain irritation at the whole mess. Maybe it would have been easier if he and I had just had a toss in the hay before all this got started—layer over layer of emotion and meaningful glances. Christ. Then the whole thing might not occupy so much of my precious thought time, which really annoys the hell out of me. Except that that's a lie, too—I enjoy it.

Ah, K., I'm scared, I'm scared. So much that I thought I'd won out over in myself is blossoming forth again like some parasitical evergreen. I don't mean that I thought I'd conquered forever; not quite that naïve or self-deluding. But that I'd learned to watch for, to combat, to deal with and not submit to in a delicious indulgent loosening of mind and spirit. And not because of Jim himself. Poor guy, he's really fairly simple, and very confused by you, me, and us together. I mean by the situation: his "love" for me, my entrapment of him, your reaction to both. And suddenly, slowly, steadily, it is easier to tell a half-truth, or to exaggerate again, though I have so far stopped this side of an outright lie. And suddenly, slowly, steadily, the sado-masochistic fantasies return. And the nightmares. And the plotting: how I will sit, what I will wear, what expressions my face will speak while my words speak other, innocent meanings. And dear god, how can I even use my poems: to lure him, reassure you, and lull myself into thinking I'm really being honest in my work? Even that.

I dreamt a little while ago that Jim who, as you know, once wanted to be a priest, was Father James as a young man, except that he took the path away from where poor *Father* Jim wound up. And in my dream, I tore open Jim/James' flesh with my nails and lifted out his heart, still trailing veins and arteries, and gave it to my mother, who neatly clipped off the dangling lines and hung it on a chain around her neck with other charms. She thanked me for it, and said he (both J.'s, I assume) was grateful, too. I tried to believe her, but I didn't, I didn't. I can't remember the rest. Mercifully blocked.

Obvious enough, I suppose. And I had made a conscious connection between the two J.'s earlier. Sort of getting my own back at the nympholeptic Franciscan who was such a surrogate father in my non-Catholic girlhood. But what I hadn't connected was the role my mother played in the whole Father James thing, and my own actions in the present situation. So she rises, again and again, with her flirtation and her lies and her hoarded guilt and her martyr's revenge. And I play her out to the full of my ability. Except that even that's a lie—nobody rising like some hidden personality in me—no hereditary or even environmental traits working in me that I'm powerless to control. Lie upon lie. Like your onion skin.

K., I've been more honest with you than with any other person in my life, including, at times, myself. Yet I've lied to you, as you know (that memorable day in Pippin's), and I'm prevaricating now, in some way. I don't even know how. I do know this: that though I've finally begun to believe you're a human being, not a god, that you're a hypocrite and you're intolerant, lazy, weak, and vulnerable as the rest of us, you somehow do try and do trust and do commit yourself on some level I've yet to reach, and I never will without you.

We've both said that if we were to break up tomorrow we'd each walk away having gained something. The only thing I'd have gained would have been a glimpse of what I'd lost. I used to think that what I'd learned living with you had cleansed me of many, if not all, of the old crawly cunning patterns that clothed me like tattoos. These last weeks, and my behavior over Jim, have taught me differently. Even knowing this, I am not able to say firmly to myself how I will proceed now. Perhaps even deeper back into the old ways. Perhaps into fresh, more cunning, slimier ones. Perhaps to some kind of freedom from all of them.

But whatever happens, and despite our having settled all such questions in our long talks—having vowed to stick to each other no matter what, now, now, in the middle of the night with you asleep and my nightmare still flashing on and off in my brain; now, when I sit here wanting to wake you up to hold me and at the same instant am thinking about when I'll next see Jim—some corner of my mind plotting, never dormant, planning, exulting; now, when everything clean and healthful seems impossible for me to even approximate; now, in the mocking quiet of our study where I'm crying without noise as I type, afraid that any sobs will echo back to me as the staged hypocrisies even they somehow are; now, I have one prayer to pray to no one: that you will not leave me, that I will not lose you. Because my only hope for even an attempt at truth lies with you, living with you. Because your love and trust blesses my twisted life like the hands of a healer on a sick body. Because I have been able to love you as I want to love. And because I feel, too, that it is a hopeless prayer, one that is doomed somehow not to come true.

Or is that hypocrisy, too? The easy way out? Because the prayer is answerable and is, in fact, even addressed to someone. No god, anthropomorphic or mystical, and not to you, either. But to the only person who can possibly grant it. Myself.

I guess I'm finally very tired, and I won't reread this letter on the suspicion that despite all its pretense at searing honesty it's just another onion-skin layer. Maybe I can get to sleep now. There're errands tomorrow. Sometimes I think that "telegrams and anger" and bank deposits and grocery shopping are what really keep us alive, despite all our bitching at them. At any rate, I can understand those people who choose to live wholly within that world in complacent comfort, without attempting the difficulties we choose to face—even to lie about—in our lives. Forgive me, my darling, for this letter—and what I never did say in it.

R.

7

The schizophrenic quality of internal emptiness expressed in this letter seems endemic to a woman in a not-yet-struggle relationship with a man. The strong sense of identification with the work and life of Sylvia Plath interests me, particularly since I was so resistant to admitting it. Interesting, too, the tenacity of love in the marriage, and my refusal to give up on what seemed to be an all-but-hopeless situation. Within a few months I was to attend my first consciousness-raising meeting which, in time, would explain the identification with Plath, the tenacity of love, and the refusal to give up—among other things.

2 December 1966
8:10 p.m.

Dᴇᴀʀ K.:

This will be the final letter in this "series"—by which I mean the group of letters I wrote you thinking they would not be read for some years, if at all. This very letter, in fact, is not a proper companion to the previous ones, as I already know that you will read it, soon, tonight perhaps, because on finishing it I will place the entire folder on your desk, for you to read when you wish. So a new element enters into the writing of it, inescapably.

Since I first told you about these letters and you wanted immediately to see them, feeling saddened and hurt by their secrecy and wanting a chance to reply—not years later, but closer to the time of their having been written—I've feared that my knowing they'd be read, truly knowing it as a certainty, would inhibit the writing of them. I've really used them so far as a diary, or journal, or what-have-you, except that they have always, in a very real way, been meant for you. From here on in, I don't know what form they'll take: will I be able to write them at all? will I write them hypocritically? use them as ploys? be able to be honest in them? perhaps be able to be more honest than before in them? I really can't say. I do know that this, the first of the new batch, is very difficult for me, and feels like gobbledegook even as it's coming out on the page.

Rereading the other letters in this folder touches me, not only letter by letter, but as a progression—toward nowhere, I could feel, if I let myself. Each letter brings back its intense mood so vividly, but enhances my present kind 'of schizophrenic state of mind by doing that very thing. It would appear from the progression that it sure as hell has been a struggle to love you, one that has rewarded me well more often than not—and more, a struggle to love myself, with lesser, or false, self-deluding rewards.

Interesting, that The Leech Dream is in here, and that the reason I'll be showing you these letters tonight is partly brought about by our still not having learned that dream's lesson. Interesting that the letter just before this one is like the wail of a child for help; a pathological liar-child, in fact, with fantasies and mother-problems and all the old boring shit. Interesting that I'm writing almost a poem a day and fantasizing about suicide, only to be infuriated by the cliché of self-pity of *that* Plath-y role, unable to enjoy even the fantasies or take them seriously, mocking my own depression, my own secret filthy boring self. Mocking even that last bit of melodrama in the previous sentence.

I'm sure it all is really very funny. In fact, I think I'll dig up and place at the beginning of this folder the letter I wrote myself before we were married. Might as well include the whole grandstand gesture, and round it out. I won't reread that one, though, because I know from the last time I did that I almost hate it, and its writer, for such smugness, such naïve I-can-lick-the-worldness, such humility, such simple-minded unawareness of what I felt even then: resentments, hurts, hostilities, all "unimportant" and unexpressed, buried under that rosy glow of positive thinking. God knows I admire the courage, though, and am touched by the rather trusting innocence, icky as that sounds and ironic as it is, because I thought, at that time, that of course I wasn't innocent but on the contrary very aware: of you, me, the way the relationship worked. More complex than that, dears. I'll include it anyway.

So what else do I say before I turn these over for your perusal? Worse—or better—for your replies. Will those replies make it easier, or harder, for me to write more letters? I wonder. We'll soon find out, I guess, and I'll be interested to see—although at this moment my curiosity, spontaneity, and general "negative capability" seem at a record low ebb.

But since I don't know, I must make this letter an end, to this series at least, hoping it will be followed by others more, not less, sincere. Notice I say sincere and not honest, as I don't know that I possess one fiber of the latter quality, but I will allow myself at least the former.

A farewell letter of sorts, then, from that secret letter-writer to her unknowing, unreading reader. There were more things I wanted to say in these letters than I ever got around to saying. I don't know if the new writer will be able to write such things to her new reader.

Where from here? Tonight, coming home on the bus together, we saw a beautiful mother and baby, wonderful, free with each other, obviously healthy and rare and commonplace, utterly lovely. I want to have your child. Unsure again, afraid again, now it seems a fantastic dream. Still, still, I want that, want us together, raising it and writing and talking for twelve-hour stretches and making love.

This moment, when I am numb and tired and want only to sleep and know you are lying in bed a few feet from my desk, one thin wall between us, waiting for me to finish this—have you an idea that I'm writing the final letter of this group?—waiting for me to lie down beside you, hating, desiring, fearing, and loving me at this moment when I've no heart for it, for anything but to finish this, bring it to a close, place it on your desk and sleep, this moment when to feel even hopelessness is impossible, let alone hope—this is like being at the center of some simple emptiness that has lain in wait for me longer than you have lain in wait in that bed. There's nothing grandiose about it, or dark-night-of-the-soul; on the contrary, it's a rather light-headed and silly, obvious feeling. A quarter of a century it took me to reach this! I should've stopped when I was four and first had inklings!

Ah, well, my dear, nothing matters, after all, so how dare we care or pretend that it is otherwise? Except that, before this letter dwindles off and ends, and before I learn that that is only a new beginning, perhaps I should tell you one thing that I meant once to write a whole letter about: the most beautiful moment of my life, when I lay naked on the earth under your naked body, and saw only redwood-filtered sunlight, heard only the buzz of insects and your breathing, watched only cypresses bend to a breeze that swept over, not on, us, and felt only you. Something beneficent in the universe, after all—you and I, that moment? Perhaps only that, nothing else, only that worth holding on to somehow, somehow.

The letter, the series, is ended now. Goodbye, my darling. I'll try to write again.

I love you very much.

R.

8

The following is not a letter but a short entry from my journal, which I kept at that time unevenly but which I knew enough to thrust into my shoulderbag the bitter cold December night when I left K.

Talks, tears, argument, thick silences—the pain had been constant between us for weeks, broken only long enough to give us each a faint, desperate, renewed energy sufficient to prolong the agony still further. The sour residue we both felt over my abortive affair; his anguish over a publisher's cowardly and devious rejection of his already-contracted-for novel (an early version of what was to become *The Beholding*); blame of the self, blame of the other; my despair at his ever *hearing* what I could not manage to say—these were some of the reasons. But the underlying theme, of course, was our love for each other, spoken in two enforcedly different languages, a woman's and a man's. There was yet no technique of translation available to us.

Still, we hung on somehow. Our proposed four-month separation turned out to be one night long. When I came back home later the following day, to formally collect a few clothes and books (I had stormed out of the house with nothing but my purse), I was grateful for the excuse of seeing him again. He, meanwhile, had done a huge grocery shopping, and filled the house with homey temptations—food, wine, candles, flowers. None of which, even so, would have tempted me. His face, his loud tears and quiet voice, the *words* he said, however, met my own longing at least halfway—and I stayed.

That night, both of us utterly spent with emotion, we went to a small New Year's Eve gathering at a friend's house. I remember that the genial level of moronic conversation there served to unite us, reminding each of us of the value of the other. But what I remember most is our standing together on the front stoop of that New York brownstone before we rang the bell to our friend's apartment. The bells of the city were announcing midnight, the breaking of the new year, and the wind cut so punishingly that neither of us could have said whether we were crying because of the cold or because of the moment. Both, naturally. The clouds of our warm breath formed a misty screen between our faces, as if we were swimming toward each other through fog. We stood there a long time, like figures on a stele, looking into each other's eyes. I remember thinking with a sense of outrage what a pathetic waste it would be if we were to lose one another, what a failure of nerve. I think we kissed, then; I think we told each other that we loved; I think we said "Happy New Year" to each other. Then we went on in to the other people.

There were days of talking after, of sorting things out, still without the aid of translation (which would not be available for three more years), but with renewed will. There would be more bitterness as well, more pain, more sign language. Yet I never again left K., nor he me.

In the years since, one or the other of us has spent time away from home, giving poetry readings in distant cities, lecturing, traveling around the country in a political context. There have also been those nights when, both of us home and in the same bed, we were hoarding each our separateness, not speaking, not touching out of anger or hurt. But the night before this journal entry was written is still the only night we have ever really been apart.

Day #1, 8:00 a.m., 31 December 1966

THE LAST DAY of the old year, at Micki's, in her bedroom. She generously insisted on sleeping on the couch, giving me the privacy of a closed door.

I'm still numb. Haven't eaten since Wednesday night (today is a Saturday). I went off tranquilizers on Thursday, but took two last night, to sleep. Dropping off like a stone at eleven, I'm surprised to find myself up now, wide awake, unable to sleep any more. That's a disappointment—I had hoped, given the exhaustion, that I'd sleep much longer, all day perhaps. I'd like to be unconscious for days, weeks, to escape feeling anything.

Numb, bitter, injured, self-pitying, self-righteous, scared. A little excited, too; curious as to how K. is taking it. I'm not lonely yet, although last night, after having left the apartment, I felt horribly alone and very cold. I had too little money on me for cabs, and the long, aimless bus rides were like trips through hell, a surly Charon for a driver, my few companion-passengers the tired night-shift workers of the city and the late-night drunks who huddle for temporary warmth into the yellow fluorescence of a bus, not caring where it takes them.

I had nowhere to go. Too many friends who would have received me with unabashed glee, Job's comforters who would underestimate what K. and I mean—together *or* separately. To their hospitality I could not sink. My mother, out of the question. And so forth. So I rode the buses of New York for hours, finally winding up at Times Square and Forty-second Street, where the movies run all night. Except that most are pornographic and sado-masochistic flicks, the audience filled with middle-aged men hunched over the secret in their laps, with young gay male hustlers taking a break from their cold rounds on the winter streets, with more drunks loudly sleeping off their stupor. Only one movie was acceptable: Godard's *Masculine–Feminine*—ha! Which I ignored while staring at the screen, thinking about K. and me, and phoning Micki every fifteen minutes until she returned home. Not the ideal hostess, Micki, for such a guest as me, but I knew she would at least sympathize, shut up mostly, and leave me alone, as well as let me spend the night.

At last she answered the phone, and so I left Godard without finding out how his film ended—ha *ha!*—and came here.

Now: resentful, worried, yet strangely relieved. I can't believe the separation is other than a trial one, can't believe it will take as long as planned, until April. My eyes are swollen with crying. My body aches. I feel like I used to after big-scene-fights with my mother, needing to sleep, to heal, to be comatose for days afterward.

I have actually left K.

I can't help being stunned that things have gone even *this* far, for *us*, we who were going to be different.

But I have hope.

Why do I have hope?

I have hope because there's nothing else for me to have.

9

My pregnancy and childbirth were "natural," the Lamaze method, wherein the mother is awake and the father present throughout labor and delivery. In the early stage of labor, before we left for the hospital, I carried out a plan I had contemplated for some months: I sat down at my typewriter and wrote two letters. The actual writing was punctuated, therefore, by a labor contraction every second paragraph or so, K. meanwhile timing the length of the contractions, Lamaze style, with a stopwatch. At my request, he did not read either this letter or the one following until he returned home alone from the hospital, after the birth, some fifteen hours later.

We had been active in "New Left" politics, demonstrations, and actions for some years at this point, and had not infrequently feared for our lives. Though active in "Women's Liberation," I was not yet a feminist, but as any woman with her first childbirth, I was prey to deep, almost archetypal feelings that I must be ready for the possibility of losing the child—or of dying, myself, in childbirth. No matter how "modern" we become, it will take still more time and consciousness and change in medical procedure before the imprint of a million ghosts dead in childbirth will be erased from the secret thoughts of a pregnant woman. This letter was written, as was the following one, out of an acute awareness that these might be the last words I would ever write.

Wednesday, 9 July 1969

DEAREST K.:

It's almost six o'clock in the afternoon now and we know we definitely are in labor because of the bloody mucous plug having loosened, and we've had our baths and are all ready, just playing hide-and-seek now with the irregular contractions. And you're running about crazy loon with our color Polaroid camera taking pictures of me typing this very letter to you—images of images—visual of verbal—as we each try to reach and make permanent contact with and of and for each other.

And all I really wanted to say in this letter was and is and will be that I love you very much and am very happy at this second of our absurd existence. These last days have been so beautiful, as we finally seemed to find some way of growing closer out of all the difficulties we've been having these past months. I want you to know that I feel these days have been so perfect *because* of you—how you've tried (and how I know it) so hard, so very hard. I feel very sad because of the previous months—when I did fail you in your own crisis, out of which by sheer will you seem to have pulled yourself (and me) to make this birth a beautiful thing.

Maybe the ways we have failed each other in the past are no longer relevant, except to look back upon and learn from a little, like people after a revolution reminiscing about the old, corrupt system only enough to stay aware of its ways not creeping into the new.

We're an odd pair, odd enough to have changed shape many times already in our living together, but only now, I feel, somehow to be really challenged—not just by this new person living with us but by the objective reality of our planet and species in what could be birth- or death-throes—to build whole new previously unimaginable miraculous forms, with our flesh and genes and words and light-screen colors and tape recordings and politics and will and blood and love.

Even if some inverse miracle should occur; should anything that people other than you would be silly enough to consider negative or tragic or whatever; I mean if anything should happen to the baby or to me, I know that we still have—in truly remarkable ways—each other, and that the years I've lived with you have taken me in directions I've so wanted to go, since I can remember wanting anything. What I'm trying to say, rather badly, is that it's already been worth it, after all, you see, even if there isn't any more. I know you, and know that you'll always find your art and your politics, know as certainly as I knew years ago in that dumb chrome luncheonette that what shines in you is irreplaceable and irrepressible and inevitable. It's that in you that I can never help fighting for and against, because it sustains and threatens me—challenges me—almost unendurably.

But our time for psychic analytical indulgence of a certain type is over. We have begun to act, separately and together, in response to a challenge that will test us in new ways. I'm less afraid now than I've ever been, although with more reasons to fear for us all. Not that any of this matters, as acid has taught even me.

But for the time left to us—you and me and our child—and for the work and play we have ahead of us to do, for whatever illusory, arbitrary, exquisitely insane reasons that we choose to believe are our purpose, I think we've only begun to surprise each other, only begun to live.

I love you, K.

                                                                    R.

10

We had chosen together a "genderless" name for our child, whether it was to be a girl or a boy: Blake, because the name means "bringer of light" or "illumined one," and also for William Blake, the eighteenth-century poet and mystic who knew and was deeply influenced by Mary Wollstonecraft, as well as by Catherine Boucher, the artist whom he married.

I am touched, now, by the innocent false consciousness of this letter, the simple-minded views on oppression, revolution, sexuality, parenthood. Some of the language reflects a striving to be "hip," although a tug toward careful articulation is also present. Mostly, though, I am surprised at how deeply this letter still moves me, how much I recognize its sense of urgency, and how intensely I still validate what was happening there—in that woman's body, and on that woman's page.

Wednesday, 9 July 1969
6:38 p.m.

DEAR BLAKE:

I've written you no poems or letters while carrying you these past nine months, and somehow feel I can write you now only because we know, K. and I, that our labor with you has definitely begun, and so you seem finally very real, beginning your own struggle into the conscious universe.

First, I ask you to forgive us for having coalesced you via our genes from that whirling matter and energy that you were before. A planetary famine is likely within ten years; nuclear, biological, gas, and chemical warfare are all possibilities; our species is poisoning what little is left of the air, water, and soil that is our natural Edenic heritage, and it is moving out later this very month to land on (explore? contaminate?) our satellite, the moon. You are part of a population explosion which may well be alone responsible for the destruction of life on earth. Overbreed and overkill begin to be common everyday phrases.

Yet we have conceived you from our sex and love, from the blending together of our brief tissues, K. and I. I could cite excuses, some of which I believe and some of which I don't: our own egos, our curiosity about what our genes would produce, our callousness, our desire to make an ongoing revolution in our own lives, on and on. Perhaps none is the truth, or all are. Perhaps none is really relevant.

The fact is that you are now being born, a woman or a man, but mostly yourself, Blake for now (later you might want to change that name to one nobody has a right to give you but yourself), into a dimension we are all struggling to space out, to make freer, until we are ultimately free from it, into some new life or death—some meaningful way of living, or dying at least, in ecstasy.

Some people are arming themselves—for love.

Some people are refusing to bear arms—for love.

K. and I will be trying to find new ways to save ourselves and our sisters and brothers from suffering and extinction under the greedy powers of a few madmen, and you will be involved unavoidably in that struggle. But on your own terms, as soon as you know them and make them known.

We have no claims on you. We are your genetic mother and father, and beyond that, and more important, merely two people who will take the responsibility of you while you are still small and helpless, who will love you to the best of our ability, provide you with whatever tools of knowledge, skill, humor, and emotional freedom seem to interest you, respect your own individuality, hope you dig us as people but hardly dare insist on that (only try to earn it)—and let go.

Of course, I already envy you. Despite the horrors that oppress people around the world, those people are rising up to fight for their freedom. You are born into the age of worldwide revolution. You will be thirty-one years old in the year 2000. You may well travel to other planets. More prosaically, you have one hell of a groovy father, which I never had, and in some ways I trust him more with you than I do myself. I know you two will have crazy beautiful fun together. I have to get my ass in gear so I can join in.

If you are a woman, you will grow up in an atmosphere—indeed, a whole Movement—for women's liberation, so that your life will be less reflective of sexual oppression than mine, more human.

If you are a man, you will also be freer; you will not need to live a form of stereotyped masculinity which is based on the oppression of the other sex.

If you are a woman, you will be free to think—unlike so many women today. If you are a man, you will be free to feel—unlike so many men today.

K. and I are trying to be humanly unisexual, or pansexual. Join us?

If any of us survive these next decades on this planet, you will live to make a society where people share and love and laugh and understand each other. If none of us survive, it won't matter, because then we'll be free. Meanwhile, we can play with each other, and create poems and colors and songs and orgasms together, and learn to fight not so much for what we believe in as for what we love.

Dear Blake, I love myself right now.

Dear Blake, I love K. so very much.

Dear Blake, I love you, even though we've not been introduced.

Dear Blake, leave my body behind you quickly. K. and I together, throughout labor and delivery, will work hard to aid you in your struggle toward light and air and independence.

Dear Blake, welcome to the universe.

Dear, dear Blake, goodbye.

R.

11

The period following Blake's birth seemed like a violently upward-rushing vertical curve of frantic activity. Not only the staggering changes in living habits wrought by the arrival of a baby, but the fact that, after more than a year of "exterior" involvement in the Women's Movement, I finally "brought the struggle home" three months after our child was born. Feminist consciousness began to function as an "interior" force, and that process, in the months and years since, has transformed our life together. The struggle with K. became more verbal; the grievances did not have to be written down secretly anymore. They could be stated calmly, or shouted angrily, or even put openly into poems. That process has had an incalculable influence on both our lives, and on our writing. Of other letters that followed (for another book, another time, perhaps), and of the letters I have written Blake during my political travels, this last one seems a most fitting close to the present series.

Friday, 13 April 1973
(A good day for us Witches!)

D<small>EAR</small> B<small>LAKE</small>:

Here I am, in a BIG plane again, way up above the clouds and the snow-covered Rocky Mountains. I just ate some supper on a tray, and then went to the Flying Bathroom (remember that?), and now I'm drinking some coffee and thinking about you and dearest K.

Do I ever miss you! I miss you so much it hurts like a toothache.

This morning, very early, before I got on the plane in Rochester to fly to California, I went with some other women to see the home of Susan B. Anthony—who was a wonderful woman who fought some bad men very hard and for very long, many years in fact. She lived a long time ago (not *so* long ago, actually—although it would seem a lot of time to you, I bet, even though you are, as you often remind us, four whole years old). Well, she is dead now, so we also went to see where she is buried.

We stood by her small grave very quietly in the cold spring dawn, and we thought about her, and we cried because she was so brave and we love her and wish we had known her. It was something to remember.

Now I am going on (like she did—she traveled a lot; her own worn and battered little suitcase still rests in her bedroom)—on to see some more women and talk with them about ways in which we can all fight some of the things that come from the bad men. I'll have a lot to tell you about all that when I get home next week. And I'll tell you all about Susan B. Anthony's house, too, and her walls covered with photographs of women from all over the world, and her odd old typewriter, and the locks of her hair that are displayed curled up in a glass case, and lots of other things. I am so glad you are interested in these stories about brave women (like the stories about Emmeline and Christabel Pankhurst, remember?), because that means to me that you are already fighting hard to grow up and not be like the bad men who are mean to women. I am so proud of you for being interested and helpful and brave.

I am sending you the drawing you asked me for, of the tree and the singing bird—but I have only two colored pens with me, black and green, so I hope you won't mind that the picture isn't *very* colorful, okay? Also, the plane sort of bumped once while I was drawing it so there's one wavy line that's not supposed to be wavy. But trees are mostly like that, anyway.

Take care of K. for me (and also of Hektor, of course). I love you more and more every day and can't wait to come home and tell you all the adventures that happened to me, and hear your adventures, too.

Tell K., who will help you read this letter, that I am no longer afraid of what I must do, not at all, not after this morning. Greatness is neither a blessing nor a curse, as they would have us believe. It is simply a way of life, and it must become so for everyone—that is what revolution really means. K. will explain that to you.

He will also explain what I mean when I say that you are the honey in my life—and he the salt.

I love you both,

R.

PART TWO

The Emergence of Women's Liberation

PART II:
INTRODUCTORY NOTE

The private landscape of the previous letters coexisted in some multi-dimensional space with the public, general, shared realities of our time. There were periods when it could have been said, perhaps, that K. and I stayed together for the sake of the revolution—especially since the so-called revolution during the sixties was rarely defined as a struggle seriously inclusive of "women's issues." We might have rejected splitting up as a time-wasting bourgeois self-indulgence at certain points—at least that would have been a convenient argument for staying together (how ingeniously creative can the shared delusion of lovers be!). The Women's Movement, ironically, would present at once the most serious threat to our relationship (as it then stood) and the most hopeful possibility for our relationship (as it would change).

Meanwhile, we continued, both of us, to write. I took on a defense of "the woman question" even as I dived into groups and meetings and actions. The articles in this section were part of a flood of writing I produced during the middle and late sixties—mostly for Leftist journals such as Liberation, Win, Rat, The Guardian (and its ostensibly more radical spin-off, The Liberated Guardian). I know that even today there are some misguided pseudo-feminists who believe it possible to reach millions of American women—including housewives, secretaries, and other such sane folk—by spewing rhetoric onto the pages of magazines with names like Red Star over the Bible Belt or Hammer, Sickle, and Breadbasket.

But this was still the sixties, remember, and the Women's Movement embodied startling new concepts: the Miss America Pageant was considered a fixture of popular American culture—a vulgar fixture perhaps, but a harmless one all the same; even to speak of reforming abortion laws was shocking to many—and the idea of repeal was outright seditious; furthermore, for such issues to be discussed seriously in the pages of the New York Times was seen by some as proof that the Times no longer knew what was fit to print.

The distance we've traveled seems less astounding, though, upon considering that the Equal Rights Amendment is still a controversial issue. One could relax into despondency if not rescued by a sense of the ridiculous.

Meanwhile, my own private landscape lay buried beneath the writings in this section. It can be glimpsed erupting between the lines, or blurring and merging in outline with some abstract political concept referred to in a tone quite different from any in the "Letters from a Marriage." Toward the end of the sixties there would be no keeping the two terrains apart any longer; like a time-space warp they would impinge, alchemize each other, and simultaneously surface in my writing— the superimposition has begun irresistibly in the last piece of this section, "Barbarous Rituals." I was to learn that when one has been fragmented ever since one can remember, the state of integrity—in all the meanings of that word—is an exhilarating but astonishingly uncomfortable one.

Each part of this book seems to inflict an embarrassment on me peculiar to its own content. In this, Part II, I find myself discomfited at the Patient Griselda attitude I had toward men; younger feminists today, assuming at least a minimal lip service consciousness on the part of most men, might find themselves irritated by what may strike them as my shuffling. Yet I am much more embarrassed—mortified, in fact— at having clung for so long to Leftist analysis and jargon. I should not include some of these pieces at all, were there not still some sisters addicted to the same nonthought and nonlanguage. Perhaps it will help them to make some of the connections if they are able to watch another woman's gradual withdrawal. For it must be acknowledged that I did not come to feminism from a suburban kitchen or a classroom or factory or office: I did come from the New Left, with all its faults and failures and foolishness—and virtues. I came to feminism already with a radical view of society's ills, with the burn of tear gas still smarting in my eyes, the bruises from nightsticks still livid on my flesh, and the determination and vision of a generation whose ideals were originally strong, sensible, and beautiful. I should not have wished to be anywhere else in this country during the sixties than where I mostly was: on the streets in protest against war, racism, and poverty, and at my typewriter, in protest against these same evils.

The right to criticize is earned fairly only through love. And when I hear anyone, even today, attack the Left from a Rightist viewpoint, my blood begins to simmer. A reactionary dismissal of unions, for example, or a sweepingly insensible statement like "After all, welfare recipients do cheat the taxpayer," or "Socialism must inevitably produce a society of ants"—and I feel La Pasionara rise in me again and march hand-in-fist with the spirit of George Sand to the barricades.

For me, the task was never one of retrenching from the radical *analysis of the New Left; it was simply to go further. "Too far," said Leftist men, for obvious and shameful reasons unable to admit the failure of their politics and practice in recognizing the very center of the problem: sexism—because that recognition would in turn uncover the very heart of the revolution: feminism. What remains of the Left still seems unable to admit this. Naturally the weary rhetoric has been stretched a bit to include a new "constituency," and what was called "the woman question" is granted the pretense of an answer, albeit an answer laughable to feminists.*

Yet if one is to acknowledge fairly all the factors in one's growth, and to attempt doing so with love (since to do other is merely to have contempt for one's own past self, an unnecessarily severe judgment which can only embitter one's present) then it is important for me to say that I, arch-critic of the sexist American Left who take back not one breath of my denunciations of that masculinist movement, nevertheless preserve in my heart an honorable loyalty to what we all—women and men alike—hoped to stand for then, and to our courage and idealism and innocence. We changed something in this country, in this world, for the better. And if I feel ashamed of how that movement perforce failed because of its narrowness, its sexism; and if I feel righteously justified, as a woman and a feminist, in its consequently inevitable failure; I can still feel proud at having been "a child of the sixties," at having shared in all the tantrums—and in all the outrageous beauty.

WOMEN DISRUPT THE MISS AMERICA PAGEANT

The following piece is based on an article of mine which appeared in various New Left publications. I made no pretense at being an objective journalist (if such an animal ever existed); I had been one of the organizers of the demonstration, and so my article was a perfect example of what then was called proudly "participatory journalism."

The 1968 women's demonstration against the Miss America Pageant in Atlantic City was the first major action of the current Women's Movement. It announced our existence to the world, and is often taken as the date of birth of this feminist wave (as differentiated from the nineteenth-century feminist suffrage struggle). If it was the birthdate, conception and gestation had been going on for a long time; years of meetings, consciousness-raising, thought, and plain old organizing had taken place before any of us set foot on the boardwalk.

It was out of that first group, New York Radical Women, that the idea to protest the pageant developed. Almost all of us had been active in the civil-rights movement, the student movement, or some other such wing of the New Left, but not one of us had ever organized a demonstration on her own before. I can still remember the feverish excitement I felt: dickering with the company that chartered buses, wangling a permit from the mayor of Atlantic City, sleeping about three hours a night for days preceding the demonstration, borrowing a bullhorn for our marshals to use. The acid taste of coffee from paper containers and of cigarettes from crumpled packs was in my mouth; my eyes were bloodshot and my glasses kept slipping down my nose; my feet hurt and my neck ached and my voice had gone hoarse—and I was deliriously happy. Each work-meeting with the other organizers of the protest was an excitement fix: whether we were lettering posters or writing leaflets or deciding who would deal with which reporter requesting an interview, we were affirming our mutual feelings of outrage, hope, and readiness to conquer the world. We also all felt, well, *grown up*; we were doing this one for *ourselves*, not for our men, and we were consequently getting to do those things the men never let us do, like talking to the press or dealing with the mayor's office. We fought a lot and laughed a lot and felt very extremely nervous.

Possibly the most enduring contribution of that protest was our decision to recognize only newswomen. There was much discussion about this, and we finally settled on refusing to speak to male reporters *not* because we were so naïve as to think that women journalists would automatically give us more sympathetic coverage but rather because the stand made a political statement consistent with our beliefs. Furthermore, it would raise consciousness on the position of women in the media—and maybe help more women get jobs there (as well, perhaps, as helping those who were already there out of the ghetto of the women's pages). It was a risky but wise decision which shocked many at first but which soon set a precedent for almost all of the Women's Movement. Today most networks, wire services, and major newspapers across the country know without being reminded that newswomen should be sent to cover feminist demonstrations and press conferences. And this has perceptibly helped to change the heretofore all-but-invisible status of women in media.

We also made certain Big Mistakes in our protest. Not so much the tactical ones: we had women doctors and nurses there, and women lawyers and stand-by emergency phone numbers and local "turf" to which we could strategically flee if the going got too ugly. Our mistakes were more in the area of consciousness about ourselves and other women—who we really were and who we wanted to reach. For example, our leaflets and press statements didn't make the point strongly enough that we were *not* demonstrating against the pageant *contestants* (with whom, on the contrary, we expressed solidarity as women victimized by the male system). Too many of our guerrilla-theater actions seemed to ridicule the women participants of the pageant rather than the pageant itself. The spontaneous appearance of various posters sprouting slogans like "Miss America Goes Down" and certain revised song lyrics (such as "Ain't she sweet/making profit off her meat") didn't help matters much.

Still: we came, we saw, and if we didn't instantly conquer, we learned. And other women learned that we existed; the week before the demonstration there were about thirty women at the New York Radical Women meeting; the week after, there were approximately a hundred and fifty.

A year later, there was another demonstration in Atlantic City; I went as a reluctant "old organizer"—to help those who were putting it together that year out of my experience from the previous year. I had given birth less than two months earlier and was breast-feeding the baby, who was clearly too young to hack an all-day and most-of-the-night demonstration. Thus my memories of the protest in 1969 tend to focus on my worrying that the child would accept my husband's bottle-feeding, and on my own keen discomfort with milk-full breasts —which I regularly emptied via a tiny breast pump I had brought along for that purpose, quitting the picket line every two hours or so to dash to the nearest ladies' room and pump myself out. Such are the vicissitudes encountered by a feminist activist.

The protests have continued, becoming an annual event in themselves. Meanwhile, the pageant gets sillier and draws less of an audience each year. The time will come when feminists automatically gearing themselves up for the Miss America protest will have to remind themselves that there is no longer anything there about which to protest.

N O MATTER how empathetic you are to another's oppression, you only become truly committed to radical change when you realize your own oppression—it has to reach you on a gut level. This is what has been happening to American women, both in and out of the New Left.

Having functioned "underground" for a few years now, the Women's Liberation Movement surfaced with its first major militant demonstration on September 7, 1968, in Atlantic City, at the Miss America Pageant. Women came from as far away as Canada, Florida, and Michigan, as well as from all over the Eastern Seaboard. The pageant was chosen as a target for a number of reasons: it is, of course, patently degrading to women (in propagating the Mindless Sex Object Image); it has always been a lily-white, racist contest (there has never been a black finalist); the winner tours Vietnam, entertaining the troops as a Murder Mascot; the whole gimmick of the million-dollar Pageant Corporation is one commercial shill-game to sell the sponsors' products. Where else could one find such a perfect combination of American values—racism, militarism, capitalism—all packaged in one "ideal" symbol, a woman. This was, of course, the basic reason why the protesters disrupted the pageant—the contestants epitomize the role all women are forced to play in this society, one way or the other: apolitical, unoffending, passive, delicate (but drudgery-delighted) *things*.

About two hundred women descended on this tacky town and staged an all-day demonstration on the boardwalk in front of Convention Hall (where the pageant was taking place), singing, chanting, and performing guerrilla theater nonstop throughout the day. The crowning of a live sheep as Miss America was relevant to where this society is at; the crowning of Miss Illinois as the "real" Miss America, her smile still blood-flecked from Mayor Daley's kiss, was also relevant. The demonstrators mock-auctioned off a dummy of Miss America and flung dishcloths, steno pads, girdles, and bras into a Freedom Trash Can. (This last was translated by the male-controlled media into the totally invented act of "bra-burning," a nonevent upon which they have fixated constantly ever since, in order to avoid presenting the real reasons for the growing discontent of women.)

Most picket signs proclaimed solidarity with the pageant contestants, while condemning the pageant itself. An *active* solidarity has possibly been at work for that matter: it has been rumored that one of the contestants decided to function as an infiltrator and was responsible for the scrambling of Bert Parks' cue cards, temporarily melting his perfect plastic smile. At night, an "inside squad" of twenty brave sisters disrupted the live telecast of the pageant itself, yodeling the eerie Berber Yell (from *The Battle of Algiers*), shouting "Freedom for Women!" and hanging a huge banner reading WOMEN'S LIBERATION from the balcony rail—all of which stopped the nationwide show cold for ten blood-curdling seconds. One woman was arrested for "emitting a noxious odor"—spraying Toni hair-conditioner (a vile-smelling sponsor of the pageant) near the mayor's box, although the sister-traveler among the contestants who shuffled Bert Parks' cue cards was never apprehended. The upshot: the show may have to be taped in the future, possibly without an audience, and the action, widely covered in the press, brought excited new members pouring in to the Women's Movement. Who knows? There just might be two *thousand* of us liberating women from the Miss America image some year.[1] Women's Liberation immediately set up a Legal Defense Fund for those busted in Atlantic City—bread and supportive letters piled in to help these sisters. One groovy by-product from the action is a film *by* women, to be used for organizing purposes. All along, Women's Liberation has demanded the use of women reporters—much to the annoyance of the male-dominated media under- and over-ground, which like to keep "news chicks" covering flower and fashion shows.

Some of the press were put through considerable changes by this insistence of the demonstrators on recognizing only women reporters, but the press as a whole weren't prepared for anything as "heavy" as arrests; most of them had assumed that the protesters wouldn't be taken that seriously. This assumption came from reading too much Marcuse, and from not realizing that the real soft white underbelly of the Ameri-

---

[1] In September of 1974, more than two thousand women demonstrated against the pageant, marching intrepidly in front of Convention Hall; this, according to the wire-service stories and the *New York Times*. The prophecy was not an empty rhetorical flourish, after all.

can beast was being socked in Atlantic City. So seriously were the women taken, in fact, that the original disorderly conduct charge for the militant use of hair-spray was later escalated to an indictable offense with a possible two-to-three-year sentence (ultimately, the sentence was suspended). Reports are also coming back that the fears of the pageant officials are not completely lulled by the idea of taping future events without an audience—since what will they do for contestants, when they no longer can trust even "their own"? It would appear that the demonstrators were taken quite seriously by the Man.

Nevertheless, some male reactionaries in the Left still think Women's Liberation "frivolous" in the face of "larger, more important" revolutionary problems. But what is "frivolous" about rapping for four hours across police barricades with hecklers, trying to get through to the women in the crowd who smile surreptitiously but remain silent while their men scream vilifications? What is frivolous, for that matter, about a woman who isn't rich enough to fly to Puerto Rico for an abortion and so must lie on some kitchen table watching cockroaches on the ceiling articulate the graph of her pain? What is frivolous about the young black woman, proud and beautiful and militant, whose spirit cracks when she hears Stokely Carmichael say that "the only position for women in SNCC[2] is prone"? What is frivolous about the welfare recipient who must smuggle her husband or boyfriend out of the house when the worker arrives, denying her own sexuality or risking the loss of her sustenance (to say nothing of having her children taken away from her)? What is frivolous about the migrant-worker mother who must be yet one step lower than her oppressed husband, must let him beat her up a bit, impregnate her just after she's dropped her seventh child, and maybe disappear for a year now and then so that he, at least, can feel a little of his "manhood"? And what is frivolous about the women in Fayerweather Hall at Columbia last spring, new-minted revolutionaries ready to be beaten and busted as well as anybody (and they were), ready to form a commune that would reflect alternative life-styles to this whole sick culture, only to hear a male SDS leader ask for "chicks to volunteer for cooking duty"?

Sexual mores lie at the heart of a society. Men will not be liberated until women are free—truly free, not tokenly equal. The Women's Liberation Groups, already becoming a Movement, take on this task of liberating themselves and their society on a new (although the oldest) front. Their plans include twenty-four-hour storefronts providing everything from birth-control and abortion information to child-care services, crash pads for women "running away from home," English lessons for Spanish-speaking women (and vice versa), judo lessons for all

---

[2] Student Nonviolent Coordinating Committee.

women, free food and coffee and liberation rapping. They are plotting actions against cosmetic and fashion empires for perpetuating ludicrous beauty standards, against male-supremacist No Women Allowed public eating places, against debutante balls and the conditions in decrepit women's houses of detention.

The death of the concept of Miss America in Atlantic City (which was celebrated by a candlelight funeral dance on the boardwalk at midnight) was only the beginning. A sisterhood of free women is giving birth to a new life-style, and the throes of its labor are authentic stages in the Revolution.

October 1968

TAKE A MEMO, MR. SMITH

During the late sixties, when I was writing article after article for Leftist journals, it seemed I was saying the same thing in a hundred different ways. The message was earnest, desperate; a trustful and patient eagerness to *convince* those men that women were oppressed. *Don't you see*, I said over and over, *women's liberation is a valid part of "the larger Movement," too, just like black power and student rights and all the other acknowledged aspects of the revolution. Let us in, let us in*, we cried, pounding our newly-calloused-from-karate-practice fists on the doors to the pot-smoke-filled rooms of the Left. *We suffer, we are in pain, we are angry, we are ready to fight. Only let us fight with you. Let us fight together.*

This article has that same intense plea not very well concealed beneath its tough approach. In it, I make an analogy we women were to rely on frequently: between the oppression and consciousness of black people and that of all women. This was done with the fragile hope that white radical men, at that point finally in support of the Black Movement, would realize that they were still making the same patronizing comments about women which they had made a few short years earlier about blacks. I was not yet ready to see that the analogy works the other way: that racism stems *from* sexism; that, as black feminists have pointed out, black men were "womanized" in the process of their oppression—long before women began to claim we had been "niggerized." The model for an oppressed people, in the eyes of the oppressor, has always been his first victim: woman.

This article ends on what seems to me now a poignant note. I was still calling the men who ridiculed us, who broke up our meetings, who purged us from their groups, who snarled that we were divisive, bourgeois, selfish, dumb, and reactionary for daring to speak our own feelings—brothers. I had been in the Women's Movement for two years, and I was still calling such men brothers.

TAKE A MEMO, MR. SMITH: Madame Nguyen Thi Binh leads the Vietnamese National Liberation Front delegation to the Paris peace negotiations; Indonesian women demonstrate to demand a legal voice in their husbands' taking of second wives; Sweden passes a law creating enforced shorter work hours for men, providing that this extra time is spent in child-raising and household duties; Chiang Ch'ing seems to be more in evidence than Mao; the Episcopal Church considers admitting women to the priesthood; and on and on. And in the United States, the Women's Liberation Movement is becoming more vocal, visible, and active every day.

Women's Liberation in the United States is composed mostly of women from the larger Movement, veterans of civil-rights summers, peace demonstrations, and college sit-ins who became fed up with being handed the same old second-class status *in* the Movement as *out* of it. Women's Liberation has sometimes been accused of more often attacking male chauvinism among Movement men than among Establishment males. But surely even a male reactionary on this issue can realize that it is *really* mind-blowing to hear some young male "revolutionary"— supposedly dedicated to building a new, free social order to replace this vicious one under which we live—turn around and absent-mindedly order his "chick" to shut up and make supper or wash his socks—*he's* talking now. We're used to such attitudes from the average American clod, but from this brave new radical?

In September of 1968, Women's Liberation was ready for its first major action, zapping the Miss America Pageant at Atlantic City. Not resting on any laurels after that, Women's Liberation gave birth to WITCH (Women's International Terrorist Conspiracy from Hell). Aware that witches were the original guerrilla fighters against oppression, and that any woman who was intelligent, articulate, nonconformist, aggressive, or sexually liberated was usually burned at the stake, WITCH took off on, of course, Halloween. WITCH would seem to be the striking arm of the Women's Liberation Movement, and as such is firing women's imagination in totally unrelated places where covens have sprung up and witch guerrilla actions have occurred.

Meanwhile, back in the ghetto-harem of our society, all sorts of different women are digging the Women's Movement. College women are organizing to protest patronizing dorm rules, and to demand courses in women's history. High-school women are demanding the right to take "shop" instead of or as well as "home ec" if they choose, to wear slacks to school, to have an equal voice in high-school student politics. Pacifist women are getting weary of the delicate-smiley-flower image—

Grace Paley[1] was the first woman to burn a draft card—and of functioning only as "support groups" for men in the Movement. Women in The Resistance[2] have formed a Women's Liberation group; they've had it with typing and groundless coffee-making, and with being used as sex-object bait for GI's. Black women don't dig the male-supremacy trend in their struggle—black women's liberation groups are forming out of SNCC as well as the Panthers, spurred on, one hears, by Eldridge Cleaver's new jokes about "Pussy Power." Welfare women are already making their voices heard loud and clear.

Like any young movement, we have our problems, and not only the usual ones, like lack of bread, like police harassment; we must also cope with the derision of our oppressors as well as their anger. Yet we know that the sexual mores of this culture dehumanize both men and women. We have energy and ideas and dedication and a double knowledge: that women alone cannot be free unless the system itself is destroyed, freeing *all* people. But we know, too, that no revolution can succeed unless once and for all women can call their bodies their own, unless all our minds are liberated from sexual stereotypes, unless each life is self-determining—truly, not tokenly, free. Join us, sisters!

And a word to the brothers.

You few "male radicals": Civilize your own "communities" (other men); as blacks said to whites, rap with your brothers about the so-called petty ways they continually make women suffer. You're beautiful, and we need you, and you need us. *The revolution begins at home.*

"Male liberals": Watch that you practice what you preach about "digging Women's Liberation." We see through that bullshit when your Hemingway mystique of super-maleness begins to brutalize us.

And you smug "male reactionary" bigots: Dig it—women are *not* inherently passive or peaceful. We're not inherently anything except human.

Take a memo, Mr. Smith: Like every other oppressed people rising up today, we're out for our freedom—*by any means necessary.*

November 1968

---

[1] One of the few public women leaders at that time in the peace movement (which was comprised in the rank and filing cabinet mostly of women), and herself a distinguished writer.

[2] The Resistance was a working coalition of anti-war groups, primarily those concerned with supporting draft resisters.

THREE ARTICLES
ON WITCH

WITCH was a child of New York Radical Women. After the first Miss America demonstration, NYRW meetings were attended by more women than we could handle. Not everyone could speak in one evening, thus making impossible the techniques of consciousness-raising, where the "testimony" goes around the room with each woman contributing in turn. So we decided to split up into small groups, coming together in the "umbrella group" once a month for information exchanges, business meetings, and continued communication. The splits were actually political divisions, though. Out of this mitosis came Redstockings, founded by those women who declared themselves radical feminists; a number of small, nameless groups which fell somewhere in the middle politically; and WITCH, founded by those women who were self-styled "politicos"—women's liberationists who still strongly affirmed a Marxist analysis and a hip Left style. I was a founder of WITCH, of course, and I was proud that we were not "man-haters" like those dreadful Redstockings women. While they quietly went about doing steady consciousness-raising and writing papers which were destined to become new feminist classics ("The Politics of Housework," "Resistances to Consciousness," "Techniques of Consciousness-Raising," "The Personal is Political," "The Redstockings Manifesto," and "The Pro-Woman Line," to name only a few[1]), WITCH became an action group.

All this time later, and even given all my regrets about the way we squandered WITCH, I still must admit that the group had something going for it. For one thing, its insouciance was undeniable. For another, we were on to a valid theme— identifying with the witches—although it is only now, eight years later, that women are taking up that theme with the serious

---

[1] Regrettably, the original large Redstockings group no longer exists. Even more distressing are the recent attempts of a few women to wear the honorable name "Redstockings" while initiating patriarchal-style attacks against a number of feminists and feminist groups.

study it warrants, recognizing it as a part of our entombed history, a remnant of the Old Religion which pre-dated all patriarchal faiths and which was a Goddess-worshiping, matriarchal faith. We in WITCH always *meant* to do the real research, to read the anthropological, religious, and mythographic studies on the subject—but we never got around to it. We were too busy doing actions. We also meant to have more consciousness-raising meetings—but we were too busy doing actions. We meant to write some papers of theory and analysis—but we were too busy doing actions.

Our frantic activity was the result of a number of goads. We were women who identified politically with the confrontative tactics of the male Left and stylistically with the clownish proto-anarchism of such groups as the Yippies. Dense as we were in our persistent identification with such disastrous models, we were also, in all fairness, newly aroused and angry about our own oppression as women—and we wanted to *move*. It seemed intolerable that we should sit around "just talking" when there was so much to be done. So we went out and did it.

Except that, not having raised our own consciousness very far out of our combat boots, we didn't know what we were doing, or why. In our Halloween action for example, described in the first of the three following pieces, we emphasized the class struggle between the rich and the poor, with little mention about the class struggle between the class of *men* and the class of *women*. We demanded an audience with Satan, our superior, at the Stock Exchange—an ignorant *faux pas* which now makes me cringe: the members of the Old Religion never worshiped Satan. They were followers of a tripartite Goddess; it was the Christian church who invented Satan and then claimed that witches were Satanists. We had bitten the patriarchal bait on that one, and on so many others. We called the Samhain Sabbat (one of the four Cross-Quarter Days of the Wiccean lunar calendar) by its patriarchally given name—Halloween. We didn't even know that the word witch had its roots in *wicce*, Anglo-Saxon for "wise one" or "wise woman." We were plain dumb.

But we were dumb with style. The wordplays, the theater, the sheer audacity of our image caught on. WITCH covens began to spring up around us, spreading across the country. The anagram was a convenient one; originally Women's International Terrorist Conspiracy from Hell, it became in other groups and at other times: Women Incensed at Telephone Company Harassment, Women Indentured to Traveler's Corporate Hell (a coven who worked at the insurance company); Women Inspired to Commit Herstory; Women Intent on Toppling Consumer Holidays, and further variants. In Portland, Oregon, a WITCH group hexed Mrs. Pat Nixon when the then

First Lady appeared there (as if the poor soul had any power of her own); in Washington, D.C., WITCHes had a spell-in at United Fruit Company (for oppressing South American peasants and North American secretaries); in Chicago, another coven hexed the Transit Authority. In New York, Berkeley, and Boston, WITCH groups disrupted commercial horrors such as Bridal Fairs, and college covens took to zapping those gross fraternity mixers and homecoming-queen contests.

Leftist men began to approve of us because we were getting media attention (therefore useful for bringing more women into *their* groups, as if the movement were a body count), and because they "dug" our style. Some other feminist groups quite understandably did *not* "dig" our style, and there were heated arguments at those umbrella meetings of NYRW. We in WITCH joked to conceal our discomfort, telling each other that we should rename ourselves "The Pantyhose" because we were "more together" than Redstockings.

The factionalism peaked during the Washington, D.C., counter-Inaugural demonstrations in January of 1969, described in the second article of this trio. I wrote this piece for circulation among women's groups, with a thought to publishing it in *The Guardian* (a vomitously dull Leftist newspaper which everyone Took Seriously), but I never went ahead with publication. I print it here precisely because the chart of a changing consciousness, including detours, should be presented without convenient revisionism. The article is an excellent example of where we "were at," in our language, our defensiveness against feminism, and our general zaniness. In it, I calculatedly make fun of what was a sincere tactical disagreement between the other women (over whether or not to burn voter-registration cards). I defend our rip-off of their materials. I proclaim my contempt for a feminist slogan which was effective in its very simplicity. I play the wounded innocent when it turns out the feminist women are mad at us. I try to make us seem enchantingly good, funny, militant, and lovable—while making everyone opposed to us appear dreary at best and obnoxious at worst. And I wriggle away from dealing with any of the real political differences which caused the split in the first place. Yet a confession is in order: I think I do all the above with a certain skill and wit; I still chortle with pleasure in realizing that. (This is probably why political movements distrust artists—we tend to appreciate satisfactory work even when its content is abysmally "incorrect.")

The inauspicious scene in Washington ought to have taught us in WITCH something, but we had a way to go before we would bring ourselves up short and look at what we had been doing. In February of 1969, we organized the Bridal Fair protest—again with such catchy sloganeering and Harpo-Marxist *joie de vivre* that young women all over began zapping Bridal Fairs in their local communities in the WITCH manner. We were obviously doing something right—but we were doing it wrong.

The Bridal Fair protest was a new low for us in our pattern of alienating all women except young, hip, Leftist ones like ourselves. We wore black veils and sang "Here come the slaves/off to their graves" at the prospective brides. This did not win them over to the cause. Plastering stickers all around the city which read "Confront the Whore-makers at the Bridal Fair" wasn't helpful, either—although we really meant well twice-over on that slogan: (1) we were punning on the anti-war movement's slogan "Confront the Warmakers," and (2) we thought it would be clear that this time we were blaming the *men* who forced women into the institution of marriage, not pillorying the *women*. We might have realized that brides-to-be don't like being called whores. We then compounded our exercise in How Not to Stage a Demonstration by releasing live white mice inside Madison Square Garden—which of course scared and consequently humiliated the brides and their mothers, not to mention the extent to which it scared and humiliated the mice.

In fact, we did very little *right* at that action; serving free hot cocoa was a nice idea, and distributing "shop-lifting bags" was clever, but that just about took care of the plus side. Our leaflet was mindlessly against marriage without taking the trouble to explain why, or to differentiate between the patri-archal *institution* of marriage and what "marriage" as a committed bond of love might mean. The same leaflet was crystal clear, however, on what we thought was wrong with imperial-ism, consumerism, and capitalist corporate power. The entire action was a self-indulgent insult to the very women we claimed we wanted to reach.

After this, WITCH retrenched. We *were* serious about our commitment to a revolution, and we *were* capable of self-criticism. Besides, various individual women in our group had been having nervous breakdowns, marriage breakups, and hive breakouts—all without any support from their group sisters, because we had very little time for such "personal" things. We had been too busy doing actions. At this stage, though, we finally settled down to talking, listening, and even reading (a lot of those feminist tracts). The original WITCH group, our group, the "mother coven" as it came to be called, stayed together for almost another year, doing—at last—consciousness-raising.

During that year, I began putting together the anthology *Sisterhood is Powerful*, an experience which, combined with the birth of a child and the initial "engaging of the struggle" with my husband, created a triple-play of events which would conspire to drag me, kicking and screaming all the way, closer to radical feminism.

I: WITCH HEXES WALL STREET

Oɴ ᴛʜᴇ ᴛʀᴜᴇ Underground's Holiest Day of the Year, All Hallows' Eve (known to mortals and Woolworth's as Halloween), at the stroke of High Noon, a Coven of WITCH (Women's International Terrorist Conspiracy from Hell) emerged from the Underground Gates of the IRT at Wall Street to pit their ancient magic against the evil powers of the Financial District—the center of the Imperialist Phallic Society, the enemy of all witches, gypsies, guerrillas, and grooves.

WITCH, the child of the Women's Liberation Movement, first surfaced aboveground (aptly enough) at the recent HUAC witch-hunt hearings, and is motivated by the awareness that witches have always fought oppression (of women, and men as well) down through the ages. A fourteenth-century Church tract refers to witches as "politically dangerous," and it becomes more and more obvious all the time *why* they burned at the stake people who were joyous, creative, scientifically minded (the study of early medicine via herbs and potions) or actively rebellious (witches were the first to disseminate birth-control information, the first abortionists, the first Heads and Friendly Dealers).

So to liberate the daytime ghetto community of the Financial District, the Coven, costumed, masked, and made up as Shamans, Faerie Queens, Matriarchal Old Sorceresses, and Guerrilla Witches, danced first to the Federal Reserve Treasury Bank, led by a High Priestess bearing the papier-maché head of a pig on a golden platter, garnished with greenery plucked from the poison money trees indigenous to the area. Bearing verges, wands, and bezants, the WITCHes surrounded the statue of George Washington on the steps of the building, striking terror into the hearts of Humphrey and Nixon campaigners nearby, who castigated the women for desecrating (with WITCH stickers) the icon of the Father of our Country (not understanding that this was a necessary ritual against a symbol of patriarchal, slave-holding power). The WITCHes also cast a spell rendering the hoarded gold bricks therein valueless—except for casting through windows.

Proceeding to the New York Stock Exchange, the women sang (to the ancient melody of "Tisket-a-Tasket"): "Wall Street, Wall Street, Crookedest Street of All Street / Foreign Exchange / Student Exchange / Wife Exchange / Stock Exchange / Trick or Treat / Up Against the Wall Street!" When the guards resisted their entrance, the

WITCHes demanded a check with their superiors, claiming they had an appointment with the Chief Executor of Wall Street himself—the Boss, Satan. The guards tried to phone for help—but the line went mysteriously dead. (Dig it: these are *guerrilla* witches.) The frightened serfs, anxious to gain the WITCHes' good will, forced the guards to cease their persecution of the women long enough to beg stock quotations from the Coven, and then over two hundred local vassals watched in fascinated delight as the WITCHes formed a Sacred Circle (joined by two "normal" women from the crowd who were eager to round out the Holy Thirteen—undercover witches, no doubt). With closed eyes and lowered heads, the women incanted the Berber Yell (sacred to Algerian witches) and proclaimed the coming demise of various stocks. (A few hours later, the market closed 1.5 points down, and the following day it dropped 5 points.) One businessman, when asked if the bombing "halt" and peace move were responsible for the market drop, naturally denied the connection vehemently, shrugging that it must have been the witches. He had obviously read the article in *Business Week* describing a case in President-elect Nixon's law office involving the suit of General Cigars against labor organizers in Puerto Rico, charging the latter with using witchcraft in a labor dispute.

The WITCHes then wended their way toward One Chase Manhattan Plaza, the glass erection abhorrent to their sister witches in South Africa, Bolivia, and elsewhere, who know damned well they Have A Fiend [*sic*] At Chase Manhattan. They encircled the building mumbling an elaborate curse containing references to Jericho, and allusions to a future insurrection involving buglers.

The Coven next manifested itself in the lobby of Manufacturers' Hanover Dis-Trust, informing the guards there that they had an appointment with the Devil on the Thirteenth Floor. Elevating themselves accordingly, they haunted the investment house of Bache & Co., leaving the dreaded letters WITCH stenciled ineradicably on the carpet, and echoes of a curse to drive the Dow Jones Index down. In the bank itself, the WITCHes Trick-or-Treated the tellers' windows; unTreated, they vanished, having magically cast WITCH and Women's Liberation stickers against various marble surfaces and nameplates. (The same hex stickers also appeared in subways across Virginia Slim and Diet Jello ads—WITCHes are not co-optable.)

At dusk, the WITCHes came into their own element, and also their own turf. They alighted on the Lower East Side, beginning with a siege at McSorley's (a men-only bar), and moved on to exorcise two girlie burlesque houses (mortifying one uptown-type customer who was trying to sneak in inconspicuously—he even asked for his money back, was refused by the cashier, and fled in misery). They descended on a beauty parlor singing: "What's the Factor, the Factor in Max / Dirty old man with the Hollywood tan / Fact you, Factor, Hex on Max." Upon their invasion of a discotheque on St. Marx Place, four bouncers rushed the women, hitting and pounding until two women were thrown downstairs. Noting that male physical violence employed against women is always at the heart of a repressive society, the WITCHes retaliated on two fronts—some, who are trained in judo and karate, landed a few lumps on their attackers, and then they assembled on the street in front of the building and blew the minds of the bouncers (who were black) with a rap about the temptation to sell out to the Man. This went down well with the indigenous crowd of black guys hanging around the street, who joined in the WITCHes' calls to "desert to our side." The bouncers, utterly freaked by this, fled back through the bosses' portals.

At Max's Kansas City (an "in" restaurant with The Would-Be-Beautiful People), the Coven distributed garlic cloves and cards reading: We Are Witch We Are Women We Are Liberation We Are We, chanted "Nine Million Women, Burned as Witches" (historical fact), and questioned women customers about selling themselves like pieces of meat for the price of a dinner. One woman said, "My god, it's true, it's true," and began to cry. Her escort was amused.

The wind-up of the Sabbath peaked when the Coven trooped over to the Theater of Ideas where the usual group of chic liberals were klatching, this night about the subject of Media. Witches being the original Mediums, and therefore the original Message, the women simply walked in and took over the meeting, passing a small cauldron for contributions to the Women's Liberation Legal Defense Fund (under the helpful prodding by a guerrilla WITCH of a broom and a—toy?—machine gun); and creating a genuine discussion on theater, media, ideas, women, the revolution, and other topics relevant to Halloween.

A fund-raising celebration the next night included spells, fortune-telling, apple-bobbing, solemnization of a Pact toward the Unholy Undoing of the Fillmore theaters and their cock-rock assault on women—exotic herbal smoking rituals, and a stunning light show. The WITCHes then went temporarily underground again until their next (secret) action, leaving behind a trail of zapped stocks and bonds, broom straws, and torn Humphrey/Nixon/Wallace/ and Nudie posters. Further evidence included WITCH stickers on burlesque houses, in men's rooms, and on the front doors of known male supremacists. Little old Ukrainian men are still crossing themselves furiously on Second Avenue. In the Holiest Names of Hecate, Isis, Astarte, Hester Prinn, and Bonnie Parker, *we shall return!*

November 1968

II: WITCH AT THE
COUNTER-INAUGURAL

BY NOW, many people know what WITCH *is*. This statement will attempt to say a few things about what WITCH is *not*. There appears to be a necessity for this in light of recent unfortunate occurrences during the counter-Inauguration demonstration in Washington, D.C.[2]

A group of people from New York Radical Women had decided to go to Washington some time in advance; WITCH as a coven had decided not to go, since many of our people had flu, and since we are generally bored by marching and would prefer to demolish things— by magic, of course. At the last minute, quite unplanned and unbeknownst to each other, it happened that about six individual WITCHes, on a whim and a broom, turned up in Washington.

Congratulating ourselves on our synchronicity, we proceeded together to the center of women's activities, of all places the Institute for Policy Studies. We figured that was a pretty bizarre place to meet, but never ones to carp, we walked on in.

We entered squack into the middle of some very bad-vibe internecine power struggles between the New York and Washington women: who would give which speech and when; what "image" to present; to burn voter-registration cards in solidarity with the draft-card burners, or not to burn; to tear up voter-registration cards or not to tear; to chew up and swallow voter-registration cards or not to chew. WITCH was freaked by all this, so on the synchronized signal (the right foot of each of us falling asleep), we rose and mysteriously split for the basement of the Instrument for Palsy Sturdies [*sic*], to try and regain a feeling of sisterhood from each other, if not from those in the above-world.

Lacking a complete coven, we put ourselves together as best we could—spontaneity being one of our strong points. We unearthed a local broom, quickly made our own posters and headbands, found some chest-banners printed with the yawn-provoking slogan "Feminism Lives" and reversed them, crayoning WITCH, which sounded a lot less pompous, on the other side. We also threw together some songs and chants to make the marching endurable, and lugged along a seven-foot-tall mock tube of Vote toothpaste one of us had made, as a possible prop for an unplanned, play-it-by-ear theater action at the end of the march. Happily humming "You'll wonder where the power went/when

---

[2] A general convocation of all Leftist groups, to protest the Vietnam War and to solidify the male "Movement."

you cast your vote for President," we made for the rally to join our other sisters who were to speak there.

On our arrival at the tent, we found we were excommunicate, anathema, and also not welcome—by those same sisters. They had obviously been united by our presence, and had resolved to chew us up instead of those divisive voter-registration cards. We were gratified that our existence seemed to unify and give meaning to theirs, but we didn't understand why. We wished only to join them near the stage, to help form an honor guard around the women speakers, and to cheer and shake our tambourines at the appropriate places.

But they barred us from getting near them (employing a line of male Mobe[3] marshals, who looked like bouncers, to help). They screeched various epithets over the pony-tailed heads of their smug male accomplices, such as: WITCHes should be burned, You're going to try and disrupt our speeches, We know you've been planning this for months, You're thieves (a reference, we presume after much analysis, to our use of the leftover banners they had been selling each other at a quarter each), You're undignified freaks (a patent untruth—we are dignified freaks), and other vilifications.

They would not listen to our protestations (or those of a Boston women's group who had joined with us—and who were promptly accused of being dupes in our conspiracy), and they ignored the one woman on the platform who tried to allay their paranoia and vouch for our good intentions.

We stayed and cheered anyway, since WITCHes are good sports even when listening to dull, overlong speeches. And we marched near those sisters, but far enough away to be protected from their bell-book-and-candle glares. Then we split and grooved together over food and good talk, regrouping at the tent that night to hear rock bands dedicate "Season of the Witch" to us at the counter-Inaugural Ball.

The point of all this is simply that, although a small and we feel unrepresentative group were horrified by everything we did or didn't do, many other people loved us. We rapped with women on the march, with high-school kids and children and plain folks (even with some *brothers*—so there). They liked our style, our humor, our tone of militance, fun, revolution. If this same style disturbs some people, we are sorry, but as we do not try to liven up their comatose tactics neither should they try to de-, re-, or op-press ours. There is room in the Women's Movement for all of us, and the more styles, tactics, and approaches the better. We can't be monolithic in our thinking or paranoid in our relations, especially with each other.

---

[3] Mobe: Mobilization Against the War—umbrella group of the demonstration.

This is not the first time that a small group has attempted to inflict their will on us, or to insist that they alone represent all women. Our positions vary widely, which is fine, since the goal—freedom for women—is the same for all of us. Why not hit on every front then, with every available style and strategy? This, we would hope, is the way our other New York and Washington sisters would also feel, and we felt it necessary to get our side of the story to them through this paper— since at present none of them are speaking to any of us.

We heard that they think we wanted to hex them. Given the general conception of what we mean by a hex, we can understand their terror. But WITCHes do not hex their sisters. We are irrepressible, mythic, action-oriented, guerrilla-theater, *and* plain *guerrilla*—and we *are* dangerous. But only to those who have reason to fear us.

January 1969

III: WITCH HEXES THE BRIDAL FAIR

ON SATURDAY, February 15, 1969, the first New York Bridal Fair was held in Madison Square Garden. A rather tacky, motorboat-showtype extravaganza-commercial, this fair was sponsored by radio station WMCA, and boasted exhibitors from the "Bridal Industry"—manufacturers and marketers of gowns, wedding pictures, caterers, furniture, appliances, honeymoon trips, etc.—the biggest daddies being Chase Manhattan Bank (where you get the loan in order to buy all the things you don't need), International Coffee, American Telephone and Telegraph, Blue Cross/Blue Shield, and J. P. Stevens.

Appalled at the notion of the Bridle Un-fair, as they termed it, and smelling the corporate rats behind such an American tradition, members of WITCH issued a call to other groups in the Women's Liberation Movement to join them in a demonstration at the Garden on the opening day of the fair. The slogan of the action was "Confront the Whoremakers"—and ten thousand stickers appeared all over New York City two weeks earlier, issuing that call.

Accordingly, while the brides-to-be and their mothers shivered in the cold, waiting in line to get into the fair, the women demonstrators assembled, about a hundred strong, to leaflet, picket, perform guerrilla theater, and cast a hex on the manipulator-exhibitors. Some of the demonstrators carried signs reading: *Always a Bride, Never a Person, Coffee Causes Chromosome Damage, Ask Not for Whom the Wedding Bell Tolls,* and *Here Comes the Bribe.*

The women demonstrators were protesting not only the obvious chicanery of the buying ritual which insists one must have sixteen appliances and a matched bedroom set—all the commercial and legal trappings—before one can simply live with another person; they were also bent on exposing the Dracula face of capitalism behind all the orange blossoms, pointing out how Chase Manhattan enslaves and murders in South Africa, how International Coffee exploits the peasants of South America, how AT&T and Blue Cross oppress and control people at home. But the heart of their attack was aimed at the institution of marriage itself, and at the structure of the bourgeois family, which oppresses everyone, and particularly women. In a "WITCH Un-Wedding Ceremony," performed in the morning, the women made the following pledge of disallegiance:

> We are gathered together here in the spirit of our passion to affirm love and initiate our freedom from the unholy state of American patriarchal oppression.

> We promise to love, cherish, and groove on each other and on all living things. We promise to smash the alienated family unit. We promise not to obey. We promise this through highs and bummers, in recognition that riches and objects are totally available through socialism or theft (but also that possessing is irrelevant to love).

> We promise these things until choice do us part. In the name of our sisters and brothers everywhere, and in the name of the Revolution, we pronounce ourselves Free Human Beings.

Later, inside the fair itself, women disrupted the "question-and-answer" period for brides, and zapped the trousseau fashion show by releasing 150 live white mice (a permanent present to the Garden). There were no arrests, but fifteen women from Brooklyn College SDS were roughed up by cops and thrown down a flight of stairs. As they were being carried out through the audience, they cleverly co-opted their bouncers by screaming, "I *won't* get married, no, no, I *won't*."

A few days later, San Francisco women's groups disrupted a Bridal Un-Fair on the West Coast with almost the same tactics. Yes, Betty Crocker, a conspiracy *does* exist.

February 1969

BEING REASONABLE:
TWO LETTERS TO MEN

If considering some women sisters was trying to one's patience, considering some men brothers was trying to one's sanity. As each "movement man" came forth with *his* reasons why "the woman question" should not be seriously considered by radicals—or why it *should* be taken up and used to further the antiwar effort—I began to think that there was hardly a Leftist male alive able to chafe two brain cells together into the spark of a genuine thought.

I got angrier and more militant as a women's liberationist. But I hadn't yet stopped answering them. I replied, I shouted, I even *reasoned* with these jock "revolutionaries" whose intellect seemed to hover perilously near that of a drunken gnat.

It took a lot of time, adrenaline, and idealism. It also took a lot of rather touching stupidity.

DEAR *RAT*:

BARBARA GARSON'S[1] husband's article, "The Feminine Mistake," in your October 4th issue was a masterpiece of male supremacist liberalism combined with love-freakiness of the most nauseating type.

That Garson could ever assume Women's Liberation was a "joke, a lesbian conspiracy, or a Trotskyist splinter group" just shows where he's at, and he cops the Rennie Davis award of the year (for misogyny, subtle variety) for "hoping we will soon be finished with the phrase 'the women question.'" Dig it, Marvin: *More* than half of humanity are women—the only majority to be treated like a tiny oppressed minority.

Sure, the system oppresses men as well as women, which is why all of us must work to destroy the system together. But there's a sub-oppression, a "pecking order" that permits oppressed white people to take their rage and misery out on blacks, oppressed men to do the same

---

[1] Playwright; author of *MacBird, The Co-op,* and *All the Live-Long Day.*

to women, etc. A concrete example, small but enraging: how many "Movement couples" stagger home from a demonstration, or from jail, court, etc., so that he, exhausted, can collapse, while she, exhausted, fixes something to eat for them, *or* cleans up the pad, *or* picks up the kids, *or, or, or.* (If in certain cases there is cooperation between them on the gray shit of everyday living duties, is it because the guy has volunteered to do his part naturally, or because after hassling and pressure he is forced to cooperate, despite his inclination *and power* to do otherwise?)

Garson claims that "women oppress men as well." Sure, baby, and what else is new? The blacks were the white man's burden, eh? It's rough to be an oppressor, particularly when the oppressed begin looking around and see where they're at. *Then:* speak up for yourself and you're a castrating bitch. Plead for your rights and you're a nag. Refuse to be a sexual object and you're a tease. Shriek your rage and you're a hysteric. Articulate your anger quietly and you're a manipulator. Get disgusted with the whole bag and you're frigid, neurotic, etc. Sure, pity the poor oppressor "man-un-kind." Well, we want to free men from that role, too—and by any means necessary, no matter what we are called.

Garson's reaction to the "sexual electricity" that can make political meetings where women are present "unproductive" is a symptom of his being unable to see the person for the woman. And his description of the Movement "sexual code of freedom" (whatever the hell that is) I deplore for different reasons than he does. For one thing, it doesn't exist—for women. Sexual freedom still operates on a double standard among radicals as everywhere else. For another thing, sex is *not* at the heart of women's liberation (unless you're a male liberal who still sees women in terms only of their genitals). The same issues are at stake here that are moving all oppressed people to rebel—we will not be dehumanized any longer!

And a new "revolutionary" society that carries with it contaminating stereotypes about more than half the human beings alive today is doomed, brother, doomed.

October 1968

DEAR *LIBERATION*:

DESPITE THE trepidation felt (so I understand) by certain fair-minded male editors of *Liberation* who wished to afford me the chance of replying to a letter attacking my article on the women's movement, but who were afraid I'd "savage this man in true Amazonian fashion"— despite this reaction, which in itself is instructive, I prefer to draw attention to the ironies implicit in reading "blacks" for "women" in his statement, "In my opinion, women are a lower form of life that has not yet evolved to the human level." I doubt that even *Liberation's* fair-minded white male editors would ask any black leader to answer such a statement, so rephrased. Such a denial of my humanity makes any attempt to "be reasonable," or indeed reply at all, unnecessary.

Actually, what is less simple and more insidious than this blatantly bigoted letter is one published last month in *Liberation* (November 1968) by Allen Ginsberg—a brother who, one might think, should know better. It was a gentle, loving missive which degraded women far more than any statement calling us "a lower form of life." Allen, dear Allen, would never say that, and he's too well-read to quote imaginary biological facts which every finding of modern science refutes. Yet he proposed busing hundreds (or better yet, thousands) of "calm girls" to Fort Dix and other military installations, to talk with the soldiers (not about politics, God forbid), to sing and look pleasant and give the boys a good time and not be hostile—all this as the "best strategy" for "transforming" the boys in uniform. Strategy it may be, and even a shrewd one, but at the cost of again presenting women as sexual bait, albeit in a subtle new "hip" disguise. It is interesting, too, how uninvolved and *un*empathetic Ginsberg allows himself to remain, as a declared homosexual, to the suffering of another oppressed people.

Look, Virginia, look. See the stereotype live. Color the A scarlet for Revolution. See how girls are calm, passive, unpolitical bait-objects to lure unsuspecting males in ways unavailable to other males who wish to manipulate both groups. See how the women are shamed by this misuse of their own political convictions. See how the soldiers are taken in by the ploy and then resent it. This destructive attitude— evinced by the leading gentle soul of our day—is precisely what I am fighting against. Ah, give me the equivalent of a Southern redneck like your other correspondent any time, rather than such a Northern liberal; with the former at least I know where I stand.

In any event, I propose a dialogue-duel between the two—Allen's weapons being bells, flowers, candles, and a loaded hookah, and his twin adversary fighting with a volume of the Nazi Party's theories on evolution. The two deserve each other. Please do not misunderstand the suggestion—it is hardly because I wish to return to the days of gentlemen fighting over ladies. It is rather that I think both parties might benefit from such an exchange, and besides, it really is their problem, just as racism is something whites, not blacks, have to "work through." And although it's a confrontation I personally would love to witness, nevertheless we in the struggle for the liberation of women—and men— have more important things to do with our time.

December 1968

HOW TO FREAK
OUT THE POPE

When this piece was written, the Supreme Court decision on abortion and the liberalizing of abortion statutes in many states (including New York) seemed a far-off dream. I was doing secret abortion referrals, as were many other women in and out of the Women's Movement.

The reference in this article to some women beginning to withdraw their support of Bill Baird is an understated forecast of what was to come. Baird turned out to be one of the more male-supremacist men around, despite his years of having fought for legalized abortion and contraceptives. (Men frequently support these issues in the hope that abortion reform and more easily available birth control will make women "come across" better and more often—a very different reason from that of women's support in these areas, obviously.) Whatever Baird's reasons had been, he came to feel martyred. He tried to crash various all-women conferences, and when he was turned away, he denounced the women therein as "ungrateful." He thought of himself, it was said, as the leader of Women's Liberation—a concept which not surprisingly offended many of us. We *had* been working on these issues, after all, and our bodies were the ones at stake. Yet Baird must have fallen into the trap which had closed around so many white radicals during the civil-rights movement in the early sixties: the arrogance of expecting oppressed people you claim to support to feel gratitude that you are doing only what you *should* have been doing all along, given your position of relative power and any sense of decency.[1]

I, in my chronic confusion, was at least clear about being for outright repeal of all abortion laws, not their reformation.

---

[1] The *New York Post*, May 5, 1976, reported that Baird recently said he resented being told by women's groups to get out of their movement. "Since when did it become their movement?" said Baird as quoted by the *Post*, which further claimed he added the warning that this may be his last year fighting for the people's (*sic*) right to abortion; he may go into ecology crusading, the article concluded.

That was one of the few things I *was* clear about. In other respects, I compartmentalized, carefully refusing to make the connections which would have raised that specter of genuinely *feminist* politics.

Thus I could, in this article, speak reverently of the Catonsville Nine (Catholic pacifist anti-war activists) and conveniently ignore the fact that no major Catholic Leftist—male or female, priest, nun, or lay person—had taken a public stand differing with their church on the issues of abortion or even contraception. On "politics" they were radicals, but on Faith and Morals they were Catholics. Unfortunately the church feels that a woman should be the repository of Faith and the carrier of Morals, as if these were a kind of gene, like that for hemophilia. We do not qualify—once more—as "political." Simone de Beauvoir's bon mot, that the church has always reserved its uncompromising concern for humanity to life in the fetal form, is still true. The Catonsville Nine, one might say, had an uncompromising concern for human life everywhere except in the female form.

Still another pitiable example of my unconnected insights is obvious in my blaming Ethel Kennedy for having so many children—simply because she's wealthy. Labor contractions are labor contractions, and morning sickness is morning sickness, no matter how much money you have. Furthermore, had I stopped to think for a moment, I might at least have wondered whether there wasn't a wee possibility of family pressure on this woman to further extend the line of succession in a political dynasty. I hadn't even got to the point of affirming that if she was my "class" enemy, she was my "caste" sister, *as a woman*. I was too busy praising the male-Left-approved model of Madame Binh. Consciousness dawns slowly.

Legislative change approaches even more slowly. The Supreme Court decision and the abortion reforms that now exist in the United States came in late and remain insecure. Friends-of-the-Fetus types all over the country have been mobilizing day and night to roll back state reforms and to get a national referendum that would overthrow the Court's decision. (Right-to-Lifers are my special favorites in their revealing inconsistency: in between mobilizations against abortion, they frequently demonstrate in favor of greater military spending and the revival of capital punishment.) We can't afford to sit back and think of this issue as settled. It will be settled when *no abortion laws at all exist* on the books (where they have about as much place as tonsillectomy laws). Most of all, it will be settled when inexpensive, simple, safe contraception is available everywhere in forms which won't give a woman blood clots, weight gain or loss, cancer, *or* a baby (such reliable contraception thus making abortion itself, always less desirable, also less necessary). It will be settled when we at last have self-determination over our own bodies.

D URING THE WEEK of November 11, 1968, the Roman Catholic Bishops of the United States wrestled with the Coil and the Loop and came up with a "Pastoral Letter" on the issue of birth control— a document so diplomatically evasive and theologically Machiavellian that it is worthy of the Borgia popes (who were also against birth control, albeit for rakishly different reasons). Nevertheless, the present pope, not one to have his miter pulled over his eyes, may just declare even this double-talk document invalid, adhering rigidly to a policy created by celibate septuagenarians like himself: a policy powerful enough to influence world population growth to the crisis point we now face—not in the distant future, but tomorrow—with a world famine now a ghastly probability which will make Biafra seem commonplace. How difficult it is to relate this attitude to that of the Catonsville Nine and their commitment to the preservation of human life!

Boston, Massachusetts, famous for Crispus Attucks and notorious for the Kennedys, is a heavily Catholic city. Massachusetts, in fact, has the alarming distinction of being somewhere to the *Right* of the Catholic Church on the issue of birth control. For example, in that state it is illegal to disseminate any information about any kind of birth control: the church itself breaks the law, since the Catholic Information Center displays books on the rhythm method (the scientific name for people who practice this form of contraception is "parents"). Forget about the pill, the diaphragm, IUDs, etc.—even foam can be purchased only by prescription from a regular pharmacy, and only married women can get such a prescription. So reads the law, which then adds the final touch: it is illegal to inform a woman that she can go to a doctor to *get* the prescription. Again, we have good old American race and class distinction—the wealthy know about the doctor anyway, and can afford not to have children they don't want (or, à la Ethel Kennedy, to *have* those they do). The poor, however, who don't know where to go or how to obtain relief—from dropping a child every year, from an incredibly high infant mortality rate *(in the United States)*, from more dull-eyed, swollen-bellied hungry babies—for such people birth-control information is *verboten*.

The related issues of birth control and abortion have been of obvious major concern to the Women's Liberation Movement. In our society men legislate what women may do with our own bodies. *Ten thousand women die each year from illegal abortions in the United States.* Each death is an execution by the State.

Protesting this bondage, more than one hundred women held a demonstration in Boston on October 18. Their specific reason for being there was to support Bill Baird of Parents' Aid Society on the anniversary of his original conviction for (1) having given a young, unmarried woman a can of foam, and (2) having publicly displayed a contraceptive device (the Pill). (Baird has already been convicted in the lower courts, and has now appealed to the State Supreme Court.)

The demonstrators, some of whom were from Women's Liberation and from National Organization for Women in New York, some from Mothers for Adequate Welfare, and some unaffiliated women from the Boston area, gathered at the Boston University Student Union and marched up Commonwealth Avenue to the State House, joined by considerable numbers of young women from junior colleges along the route. On reaching Governor Volpe's offices, the women picketed and held up cans of foam, a symbolic gesture identical to that for which Baird had been convicted. Women in the watching crowd eagerly snatched up leaflets, and when the foam was distributed, there was almost a crush as desperate women grabbed for a can and scurried away with their booty hidden under their coats. Yet the police averted their eyes; no one was hassled or busted.[2]

On November 4, a follow-up demonstration was staged at the courthouse where everyone thought Baird's appeal would be taking place. (The case was postponed at the last minute.) This second group of women (who earlier that day had attended and supported the MIT sanctuary for a draft refuser), picketed, sang reworded nursery rhymes, and leafleted campuses as well as the streets.

Both seemed rather humble demonstrations: no surges, no guerrilla theater, no mace, no arrests. But one must remember that this is *Boston*, where to be a premenopausal woman at all is to invite suspicion, and where to whisper anything about sex is to acknowledge being a commie pinko pervert.

There were some women in the Women's Movement, nevertheless, who while sympathizing with Baird and his stand felt that the period for functioning as another "support group" was past. They said it was time to break the conditioning of "letting a man do it," and urged women to challenge these depraved laws on their own. In fact, the best way to "support" anyone is to take up the issue yourself, especially if it is your own to begin with.

Out of this thinking come plans for workshops in ghetto areas by

---

[2] The foam fuss is pathetic. Foam is almost as ineffective as toothpaste.

the October 17th Group[3] (a "cell" of women who recently split from the more conservative NOW), the blueprint being penetration into areas where women's oppression is multifold. Black, brown, Spanish-speaking, spied on by the (perhaps reluctant) welfare worker and kept in ignorance of her rights to her own body, the woman in the ghetto has always been lowest on the totem pole—her man was allowed his concept of *machismo*, often at the cost of her health or even life. And now there's yet another turn of the screw: the feeling among (mostly male) militant blacks that birth control aimed at black communities is a form of attempted genocide. While it is imperative to understand the partial truth inherent in this accusation, it is even more imperative to reach our sisters whose bodies are being destroyed by that eighth child, and whose minds and souls are barred by such sexual stereotyping from participation in their own lives, let alone in the revolutionary restructuring of our whole society. Many women's groups are already at work disseminating birth-control and abortion information, and WITCH has been investigating a challenge through Abortion Ships—small, well-equipped, professionally staffed boats to sail just outside "legal waters" and perform abortions in a clean, competent manner for about twenty-five dollars. (If there can be floating gambling parties for high society just outside the twelve-mile limit, well?)

It's too late, Pope Paul. Over half the couples who seek help from Planned Parenthood are Roman Catholics. Many of your own nuns and priests have rejected your fallibility, choosing instead to follow the figure of a revolutionary agitator named Christ. Mary Wollstonecraft, Sojourner Truth, Margaret Sanger, Rosa Luxemburg, Harriet Tubman, and many, many others right up to Madame Nguyen Thi Binh—they all have something to do with it, and they're bringing down a male-dominated system of oppression, rapacity, and egotism—crashing down right about your ears.

January 1969

---

[3] Later to become The Feminists, an important New York group which made interesting contributions to feminist theory.

THE MEDIA
AND THE MAN

This article was written for the Op-Ed page (Opposite-the-Editorial page) of the *New York Times*, where it appeared in December of 1970. Despite promises to the contrary, the editor of the Op-Ed page at that time—a male—made certain cuts which were politically expedient. This was done without my permission, and in addition to other cuts I had agreed on because of space limitations. The version included here is my original one.[1]

My attack on the Equal Rights Amendment in this piece was part of a general opposition I took at that time to the ERA—out of my leftover Leftism. My criticism was unfair and willfully misrepresentative of the proposed Amendment. To reply to myself, then: (1) One of the aims of ERA supporters is to get protective labor legislation *extended* to cover men, too—so that it will not be thrown out for anyone. (2) The ERA would not necessarily make it more difficult for women to get alimony: it could hardly be more difficult than it already is. In half of all the cases where the wife is awarded alimony the husband stops payments about two years later. The woman usually does not have the time, money, or energy to take him back to court repeatedly, so she lets it slide, having already got herself a (rotten) job to bring her income up to subsistence level. (3) The ERA might have made women eligible for the draft (there was some disagreement among lawyers and legislators about this), but it would have been for noncombatant service in any case. The question is now academic, of course, since the draft itself has been abolished for everybody.

I support the ERA today, although as a radical feminist I don't believe it is The Answer, and I wish the document were stronger and more inclusive. This is doubtless quixotic of me, since the Amendment even as it stands is having a difficult

---

[1] Even the version the *Times* did print was apparently feisty enough to require a rebuttal by Pete Hamill in the *Post* a day later; he devoted his entire column to satirizing my style, which was vulnerable, and my politics, which were not.

time of it passing some state legislatures. The Founding Fathers did not view women as whole human beings, and their male descendants in Congress and in Statehouses two hundred years later seem to be wooden-headed chips off the same old block.

O NE GLANCE at the masthead on the opposite page is sufficient to reinforce the irony of a feminist writing anything in the pages of the *New York Times*. When C. Wright Mills included the *Times* in his listing of the Power Elite, he neglected to say (although it ought to be obvious) that the *Times*, with its brother listees, was/is dominated by rich white heterosexual males. In the United States of Amanica [*sic*], if you are poor, non-Caucasian, homosexual, and/or *female*, you are by all past definitions less than human, and by all present ones, dangerous as well. (If you happen to be all those things combined, God won't even help you.)

The growing repression clearly shows the basic means by which white male imperialism intends to try to keep "those people" from a righteous rebellion. With women, however, we see the Man trying to use a special tactic in addition to the usual brutality: co-optation. (The *Times* can congratulate itself on the liberalism of permitting such dissent in its pages—and thus retain the ability to "permit" what is a human right.)

Women struggling for their liberation have always been good for a laugh. The history books snicker about those crazy old ladies in bloomers; but did you know that the news journal published by Susan B. Anthony and Elizabeth Cady Stanton in the late 1800's was titled *The Revolution?* Women have always been good for a patronizing smile and even a modicum of agreement—if we don't "go too far," if we ask for things like nice ladies should, and if our demands require no basic change and do not threaten the phallic imperialism that is out to destroy the entire planet. And this is where, today, the media comes in to manipulate, ridicule, and co-opt.

Like the *Times*, all mass newspapers and magazines, both general and "for women," are male-controlled. So is the electronic media; you sometimes see a token female reporter these days (frequently a Third World woman—two oppressions for the convenient price of one salary), but men still own the networks, write the news, determine the coverage and emphasis and analysis, and decide the programming, no matter how strong the rumblings of anger from the women themselves who work within those institutions.

This leaves the Women's Liberation Movement with a dilemma. Women *as women* do not even have the tactical advantage (from an organizing—and military—viewpoint) of a ghetto situation. We are isolated from one another by the nuclear family structure, by cultural conditioning, and by the barriers of race, class, economics, age, and sexual preference. How does a new movement cut through that isolation to raise consciousness around the fact that all women are viewed in the same basic roles (nurturer, sexual object, reproductive vessel, cheap or even free labor, etc.) across those barriers? Leafleting on New York's Lower East Side for ten years could not reach the housewife in Escanaba, Michigan, but thirty seconds on the six o'clock news would. We were forced to use a medium which we knew was in the control of an adversary, one we knew would distort, truncate, and ridicule our issues. Even now, I am writing this in the context of the *New York Times* in order to reach still more women. *By any means necessary* means just that.

But the Women's Liberation Movement has grown at a fantastic rate. We no longer need to get the word out that we exist. Welfare mothers, nuns, airline stewardesses, housewives, women in the military, Playboy Bunnies, professional women, prostitutes, high-school women, and grandmothers are moving against their oppression. We can afford to be more discriminating and demanding, and not only vis-à-vis the media. We can stop being grateful for crumbs of reform and tokenism being offered us (reform abortion bills instead of outright repeal of laws restricting abortion; government-run day-care centers instead of community-controlled free twenty-four-hour-available child-care centers, etc.). We can refuse to support an Equal Rights Amendment which would have (1) thrown away protective labor legislation, (2) made it more difficult for a woman to get "alimony" (i.e., reparations for unpaid labor), (3) made women eligible for the draft (when neither men nor women should be drafted to fight genocidal wars). We can, and must, build a movement that will *not* be based on gaining more privileges for those few women who already have some (white, upper- and middle-class and professional women—many of you, sisters, reading this) *at the expense* of poor white, Third World, and working-class women, but a movement which will fight for the needs of *all* women, the entirety of half the human population which has been subjugated and oppressed longer than any other people. It is not enough if *Mrs.* Sulzberger were to take over from Arthur but leave the *Times* structure intact, although even that admittedly might be refreshing.

And as we refuse absorption by a female Right, so we must reject manipulation by the male Left, which would create not a revolution, but a power-exchange between men. We are creating a *revolutionary feminist movement*, from the cooperative child-care projects in Detroit to the housewives' unions in California; from abortion referral, legal or not, everywhere, to the free karate lessons for women in Boston, and the organizing of factory-worker women in Louisiana. We are redefining our own political theory, our own sexuality, our own non-leadership-oriented structures. We are creating our *own* media: sisters, forget the "newspaper of (the Man's) record" and try reading some of these over breakfast instead: *Everywoman. It Ain't Me, Babe. Ain't I a Woman. Off Our Backs. A Journal of Liberation. Up from Under.* We are making films, books, tapes, newspapers, magazines, songs, theater—of our own. We are learning all forms of self-defense, because we know that any alternative medium and alternative institution is a stopgap survival measure until our total revolution frees not only ourselves but *all* people—from sexism, racism, and the hunger, war, and ecological disaster that results from the Man's competitiveness and greed. On that day, sister Charlotte Curtis of the *Times'* Women's Bureau, with, say, sister Beulah Saunders of the National Welfare Rights Organization might well assist in the liberating of the *New York Times* by a revolutionary women's collective, bent on replacing the male hierarchical form with a communal egalitarian structure, and not presuming to judge for the people what is fit (by imperialist male standards) to print.[2]

Emmeline Pankhurst, the English feminist, said it perfectly in 1888: "Remember the dignity of your womanhood. Do not appeal, do not beg, do not grovel. Take courage, join hands, stand beside us, fight with us."

December 1970

---

[2] Charlotte Curtis has not yet seized the *Times*, but as of 1974 she became the editor of the Op-Ed Page itself, a stimulating change from being head of the *Times'* Family Bureau (their euphemism for the Women's Page). In time, bits and pieces of one's prophecies do come true.

THE WRETCHED
OF THE HEARTH

This article was originally written as the token Women's Liberation piece for inclusion in an anthology representing all segments of the New Left. The anthology never was published
because the young male radical who was compiling it couldn't
get himself together to finish the job he had taken on. The
piece remains for me an interesting fossil of that period. Because I wrote it for a mass audience who might never have
read anything but *Time* magazine's definitions of the Women's
Movement, it contains more than a few points I had made
earlier in articles for Leftist media. Yet something has changed
in the tone; the author seems less driven to convince *herself*.

I still shrank from saying, in this piece, that women should
be the priority for women. I was grovelingly grateful to SDS
for having thrown a crumb of recognition to the Women's
Movement, and I refrained, like a good girl, from noting that
the practice of anti-sexism in SDS was all but nonexistent. I
still had a disgustingly missionary attitude toward Third World
women and remained fixated with guilt that there seemed so
few nonwhite women in the Women's Movement. I looked
for them in the unpromising Leftward direction of the Black
Panthers—myopically unable to foresee that the National Black
Feminist Organization might boast, as it does today, members
who are housewives, lesbians, college professors, welfare
mothers, poets, legislators, editors, businesswomen, *and* ex-
Panthers, among others. I referred to the "internalization" of
roles, the "brainwashing" of women, as if that act took place
once, like the insertion of an electrode into the skull, and as
if it were our own fault that we didn't just pluck the bug out.
(This shallow analysis denies the daily reinforcement of the
patriarchal message, shored up by a continual system of threat
and reward. Sexism is no one-time occurrence.) I still made a
rather superficial attack on the family, reflexively advocating
communes as the perfect alternative—despite the fact that my
own experience with even semi-communal "extended family"
living had been oppressive to me as a woman *and* as a mother

(this would not necessarily have to be the case, though it was so for me, in 1969). I still largely ignored the oppression of housewives and mothers, despite the title of the article.

But there are shifts in perception. I ventured a glimpse of the white, middle-class, educated woman as relatively powerless; I began to affirm her as a sister. I let myself glimpse her suffering and I was less guilty about saying that (even if I did solve her problems abominably by having her, in my article, drop out of college and reject the tools of power inherent in education). Most important, I had begun to *read* again, unashamedly: anthropology, history, the background of the suffrage movement—the stuff, in fact, of women's studies. I acknowledged lesbian suffering and supported lesbian pride. I affirmed the clitoral orgasm. I even advanced, tentatively, the need for an autonomous Women's Movement. I hinted that I was getting flashes about feminism being something more than even a major "front" of any male-defined or male-controlled movement.

I wish I could go back in time to where I sat writing this article. I wish I could embrace me and encourage me and tell me what a long way there was ahead.

After all, in this piece I still mostly referred to women as "they." But I was at least experimenting with the frightening word "we."

SHE IS WHITE, about nineteen, carefully made up with blush-on, adorned in the latest tights-and-miniskirt, her hair properly ironed for that long wild look. She wears a shy smile and a huge plastic ring on a nonengagement finger. She attends one of the Seven Sisters, the Ivy League colleges which originally were established as valid feminist institutions pledged to educate women—now dedicated to churning out the corporate wives of tomorrow's Big Business. She curls up in the corner of a sofa in her dorm lounge, and lights a Virginia Slim. Underneath her languor, she is angry. She knows she is insulated, but she reads the *New York Times:*

Twelve teen-age girls are in training to climb Mount Everest. A nineteen-year-old woman jockey braves rocks hurled at her by male jockeys defending their hegemony. A thirteen-year-old girl goes to court to desegregate an all-male public high school specializing in math and science, supposedly unfeminine subjects. Sarah Lawrence and Briarcliff students have seized buildings on their campuses.

These and certain other facts have penetrated her quiet campus and dented her consciousness. Although she seems far less politically awake than her sisters at a coed college, she still feels herself part of a generation pledged to radical change. Perhaps she's even more frustrated than her activist contemporaries, because she is so tightly leashed and because she cannot help but realize that she is undergoing a four-year packaging program especially aimed at manufacturing "a certain kind of woman." Any recognition, let alone admission, of this, no matter how oblique, humiliates and hurts, so she must defend her situation:

"But *I'm* not oppressed."

At the largest women's college in the United States, which has never had a woman president, and where there is no course in women's history, there is, on the other hand, a required course in "Basic Motor Skills"—how to enter and leave an automobile gracefully, how to pour tea, which foot to shift your weight to as you stand at a cocktail party. No birth-control information is disseminated, but students who become pregnant are expelled in disgrace. (This is not a finishing school, but a college with a proudly defended "academic standing.") At a nearby less social women's college where the dorm rules are just as absurd (no drinking, no smoking, no men, no door keys except to seniors, and weekly housemother chit-chats required) the emphasis is more on in-tellectual pursuits: a crypto-analysis course is good preparation for the CIA recruiters when they appear frequently on campus. At the more demure schools, women may not wear slacks to dinner or even to class. At the "swinging" schools, there are still courses (often required) in "Preparation for Marriage." Women are discouraged from going on to graduate school—the proportion of Ph.D. degrees awarded to women has *declined* in the past fifty years. The emphasis now is on glorification of Woman in the Home, the Creative Housewife, active (but not too active) in her community, focused on husband and children.

She knows all this. She finds forty such focused years yawning ahead of her unattractive. But she has been carefully conditioned, and out come the proper programmed defenses: "Woman's place is in the home. Aggressive women are emasculating. A clever woman never shows her brains. It is glorious to be the mother of mankind. Women like to be protected and treated like little girls. It's a woman's duty to make herself attractive. Women aren't really interested in sex. Women love to be dominated. Women are basically passive, intuitive, and simple. *It's inherent.*"

The subtlest and most vicious aspect of women's oppression is that we have been convinced we are not oppressed. We have been blinded so as not to see our own condition. But when a well-trained slave first encounters even the concept of injustice, let alone the notion of fighting against it, psychical sunbursts occur. How many of us have grown up with the lovingly nurtured fantasy of marrying the right guy and then helping him become great, powerful, famous, wealthy, or—the 1969 radical woman's version—a leader of the revolution? The initial jolt of consciousness-raising comes as a profound shock: always the power behind the throne, the hand that rocks the cradle, the face that launches those bloody ships. Where is the *sum* of my parts? Where did I get lost as a human being? What are my plans for myself? Who am I?

She begins to think for herself. She uncurls herself from her kittenish pose and stretches her legs. She checks some books out of the library. She starts to question just what *is* inherent in being "womanly." She talks with other women. She dares to disagree with men, even to argue heatedly. Perhaps her boyfriend wonders why she has become such an aggressive bitch all of a sudden. She gets depressed, fears she is becoming a "man-hater." She begins to *listen* to other women, to respect some of their ideas, to even *like* other women. Shocking. One day she wears slacks to dinner, mortally offending her housemother; she hadn't even thought about it, having become accustomed to the comfort of her new costume. She is less interested in make-up, but is still afraid of going too far and looking like a grind. She is also less interested in all the books available on women by men—an endless reading list of cultural assumptions by male psychologists, psychiatrists, historians. She starts turning on to anthropology, since it attempts to report cultural differences without value judgments; she notices that traits considered inherent in one culture need not even exist in another. She experiences pressure from family, friends, the man in her life, to cut out what they term identity confusion and to return to her former state of blissful ignorance. She gets angrier.

She realizes that she is being schooled in a nineteenth-century institution—what does one do with such an artifact? Get the hell out of it, or change it, or hurry the dying process along from within. She drops out of school and begins to organize other women on campus. She experiences a "freedom high." She begins to look at her own degraded position as related to that of others—blacks, poor people, the "underprivileged" and "underdeveloped" she has been taught to pity and despise. She undergoes a mutation toward something human.

This imaginary young woman is neither a stereotypical nor an atypical college student. She shares much in common with women at coed schools—even radical women—despite her wrapped-in-cotton-batting life. In fact, women in superficially freer atmospheres often take longer to realize their true situation.

At the time of this writing, in early 1969, when radicals all over the United States are in varying stages of depression, and when the most frequently asked and argued question is, "Where does the Left go from here?" it becomes progressively more apparent that the disheartened questioners are mostly white males. Black people are getting their thing together in a tight, organized way—they are moving, not theorizing. And now there is another group—this time not a minority (albeit treated like one). It is a potential revolutionary vanguard:

women. We have seen the consciousness which arises and the results which are born out of a growing awareness that race lines cut even deeper than class lines in a capitalist society—or that the two are inseparable. If we begin to think about *sex* lines and how these distinctions shore up the values of our culture, and begin to wake up to what could happen if these were challenged—the concept is mind-blowing.

First some historical background. The Women's Movement in the last century in the United States and England was originally a revolutionary movement (a little-known fact, since women's history, like that of black people, has been neatly edited away by white men). The winning of suffrage for women was more the compromise than victory of that movement. Women had been the first abolitionists, which struggle led them to relate their own oppression to that of the slaves. These women began to look around them, to see, denounce, and fight against the structure that had conceived such abominations; some denounced the concepts of private property, bourgeois marriage, and family structures, as well as expansionist foreign policy and domestic robber-baronism. And then the heavy stuff came down. Riots. Insurrections. Civil War. And finally, an early version of what Marcuse would later call repressive tolerance:

"See, we've freed the slaves (now we create segregation)."

"Look, we'll *give* you the vote (which will be meaningless anyway)."

So radicalism gave way to reformism, and the women bound up their wounds, as well as everybody else's, and were silent for a while. The first decades of this century saw the beginnings of what has been amusingly referred to as the sexual liberation of women—culminating in the frenzy of the twenties and collapsing in the gloom of the thirties. Men began to admit that maybe all women didn't detest sex; that maybe women could smoke and drink and even carry on an intellectual conversation—although, of course, they weren't quite "nice" if they did so. But with the Depression, the rise of the labor movement and then the coming of World War II, the issue of women's status again got shunted to second (or third, or tenth) place. Radicals in the thirties were even more puritanical and culture-bound than we are today—which is saying something. But at least during the war years, with the need for labor in factories, women achieved some economic standing and glimpsed some escape from the kitchen. Then, the war over—back to the stove. A lot of women wouldn't go. Some began to make inroads into professions hitherto considered male territory: medicine, publishing, scientific research, business, and law. We're not now speaking of the already enghettoed women's professions, for which read service professions, i.e., nursing, teaching, garment-making, waiting on tables, etc.—those jobs with little prestige, low pay, and back-breaking labor. Also, women could now be active in the arts without being marked as "fallen." But engineering, architecture, positions of corporate or military or political power—the positions that control our lives, remained, and still largely remain, sealed to all but the white male.

Nevertheless, even throughout the death-dull fifties and McCarthy the First's heyday (Joseph, remember him?), women kept trying for some modicum of economic, if not social or sexual, freedom. And when, in the early sixties, new political consciousness began to stretch liberals' minds, women began to relate the oppression of others, at home and abroad, to that of themselves. They poured into the civil-rights movement, the anti-war movement, and the student movement. Today they constitute more than half of what has become known as *the* Movement: a fact which simply mirrors basic population statistics— women are 53 percent of the country's population.

Women As Radicals: New Ideas, Old Roles

So now we're part of a growing number of radicals fighting for a just society, at first nonviolently, later on with whatever tactics necessitated by the nature of the enemy. And what are we, as women, doing? We are doing, to put it delicately, shit jobs: bolstering the boys' egos and keeping the necessities of existence functioning while the men go off to change the system. We're goddamn home-fire revolutionaries.

Most of all, women still and always end up "supporting." Good god, supporting McCarthy the Second or Bobby the Progenitor. Or moving past such expectable traps, supporting draft resisters, supporting (male-led) black groups, supporting (male-led) grape strikers, support-ing (male) deserters, (male) baby doctors,[1] (male) GI's. You'd think we were caryatids. Not that any of these actions were unimportant, ignoble, or wrong. On the contrary, they may have been valid tactics at the time, just as "Girls say yes to boys who say no" is a very clever and workable, if degrading, slogan. But each of these roles reinforce the stereotype of women as sub-citizens, even sub-radicals—defining women only as they relate to men.

Stereotypes are powerful things—as our black sisters and brothers have learned (and then unlearned). *The oppressor may, in fact, never really believe in the stereotype at all—what is important is that the oppressed do.* Women have internalized the image of themselves as weak, incompetent, emotional, unintellectual, dependent. Who wants to dare speak out at a meeting and risk the labels: movement harridan,

---

[1] A reference to Dr. Benjamin Spock, then active in the anti-war movement, and only as late as 1976 publicly criticized as a male supremacist by Jane Spock, his former wife and unacknowledged co-author.

castrating bitch, frigid neurotic, shrike, unfeminine pushy bitch? That's one extreme reaction, of course. The other extreme is that she will simply be ignored: The Invisible Woman, since whatever she has to say couldn't possibly be relevant anyway, the dumb cunt. If she does grit her teeth and try to speak out, she will be so uptight by this time that she will stutter, anecdotalize, and generally reinforce the image of her inarticulacy to everyone's satisfaction and her own torment. Naturally, a few women managed to overcome this, often at high personal and emotional cost, and in fact were accepted as equals—for public view, at least. The Movement has to have its tokens, too.

The upshot of more than five years of such frustration was that radical women, borrowing a leaf from the Black Movement, began to think about their own forced servility, their own fight, indeed their own *movement*.

Feminine Radicals Become Radical Feminists

Starting in 1966, small caucuses of radical women were formed at SDS conventions, at campus meetings, at nationwide actions such as the March on the Pentagon. (Later, in the 1968 Battle of Chicago, cadres of women would be into actions all their own.) In November of 1967, thousands of women participated in the Jeannette Rankin Brigade March against the Vietnam War in Washington. There, a group of radical women split off from the march and met to discuss the possibilities of a feminist movement. And over the next few months, brought into clearer focus by Women's Liberation meetings at the Columbia Liberation School during the summer of 1968, that movement began to come together. At present, there are women's groups in every major city in the United States. The Women's Movement, at first composed largely of white women, is becoming more representative, although there are still relatively few black, Puerto Rican, Mexican, and Native American women involved. Our militant Third World sisters seem to feel that their place at present is mostly in the Third World Movements—a difficult position to argue with; nevertheless, there are signs that the virulent male supremacy in *those* movements, too, is not safe from challenge. Some female Black Panthers in California, tired of being referred to as Pantherettes, have been discussing setting up a separate headquarters, perhaps starting a separate women's corps in the Panthers.

Women—black and white—are beginning to *act*. As one (woman) journalist wrote: "For some time the underground has been railing against 'plastic' or phony commercial cultural events. It took the Women's Liberation Groups to lead the way to action. They threw stink bombs in the auditorium at the Miss America contest, called the winner 'a military mascot, off to Vietnam'/to entertain the troops each year/ . . . The success of the venture has opened up new horizons in the Movement. Any film or rock festival is vulnerable."[2]

This, however, was only the beginning. NOW forced the *New York Times* to desegregate its help-wanted ads, while WITCH hexed Wall Street. Films, articles, guerrilla-theater skits began to be used by groups organizing on campuses and in high schools. All-male-public-accommodations establishments were hit with a rash of challenges and, in some cases, sit-ins or even bricks. The provision on sex in the civil-rights bill was inserted as a joke by a Southern congressman; the joke has proved a valuable loophole. Individual women, taking courage from the solidarity of a burgeoning movement, are becoming politicized and reporting discriminatory practices to Human Rights Bureaus, even going to court. As of this writing, the National Association to Repeal Abortion Laws has just been formed; meanwhile there are a number of abortion test cases in the docket. Actions are being planned against women's houses of detention as well as against debutante balls. Ironically, it is only now, with such furious challenge in so many areas, that one can really begin to see the extent of the oppression of women.

The Real Issues, the Real Constituency

On the surface, it seems easy enough to chronicle the process of de-humanization—even the most blatant male supremacist will agree that in the past women have been shunted aside—although *now* what do you people want? The male liberal on this issue will of course agree that birth-control and abortion laws created by men—pressured by a male celibate clergy, to boot—are horrendous, tsk tsk. The male liberal will tell you this earnestly, not even realizing that as he does so, he is interrupting "his" woman who is trying to say something from the depths of the sink where she is doing supper dishes. ("Not with *my* woman, you don't!")

But what about the real constituency? The one based on an op-pression that recognizes no class and economic lines, making the woman always lowest within each self-contained pecking order? What about the Puerto Rican girl who suffers all the indignities that the men in her family suffer, but who also bears knife scars on her body as testi-mony to the *machismo* in the rage those men feel for other men but direct against her? What about the laborer's wife who is brutalized by a slow procession of days in which the only relief is a television soap

---

[2] Ethel Romm, *New York* magazine, October 14, 1968.

opera? What about the knocked-up Italian Catholic kid who must fear for her immortal soul, feeling her screams aborted along with her child? What about the woman factory worker who does embittering, uncreative work all day, and then goes home to clean and cook, and to pamper her equally embittered husband, who can at least be a "king in his castle"? What about the young mother who spends all day with kids and housework and then is accused of being uninformed by her newspaper-leisure spouse? What about the middle-class woman whose family has died or grown up or moved away, whom society treats as a pitiable leper? What about the fourteen-year-old girl who is the victim of rape, and is then considered unmarriageable? And the single woman who is nothing, nowhere, unless she can find a man and thus her own identity? What about the few women in Congress, who are patronized despite the population proportions of their sex? And what about the female homosexual, who is even less socially acceptable than the male homosexual, although she is (reputedly) less harassed legally— because after all, whatever women do is less important than that done by men.

From Resistance to Revolution

Some radicals wonder how women can relate to the rest of the Movement, to the struggle that is taking place within America and against its tentacles of power all over the world. A few points seem obvious.

Women have been subjugated longer than any other people on earth. Empires rose and fell but one constant remained, except in a few civilized tribal pockets of the world—everyone could stomp on women. This knowledge is carried, even if only semiconsciously, by every woman, and accounts for a cumulative rage which, once released, will make demands for Black Power look by comparison not only suddenly reasonable but eminently desirable.

Blacks once told idealistic young Lord and Lady Bountiful whites back in the civil-rights movement to turn around and look at their own lives. By god, they *weren't* free, even nice middle-class college grad students—they were enslaved by the culture itself. And from this awareness was born the New Left. Now, women, who have been angels of mercy for so many other causes, have also become fully awake to their own cause. Radical women learned, from that same Black Liberation Movement, that mere empathy for the suffering of others is basically a liberal emotion—at least it never makes for revolutionary thinking or motivates a passionate desire for change.

Nevertheless, the chameleonic so-called revolutionist male in the Movement (who at first thought the Women's Movement ridiculous, later modified that to "frivolous in the face of larger issues," still later accepted it if only as an "organizing tool," and now nervously finds it "valid") has dreamed up a new hypocritical twist: isn't a drive for equality of women ultimately reformist, eminently co-optable?

Of course. So is Black Power—into Black Capitalism. So are the initial demands of any oppressed group. When slammed up against the wall, the Man will liberalize abortion and birth-control laws, and open up the professions to a few more token women, just as he once rigged up for us the already marked ballot. But we want something more—like freedom. "Equality in an unjust society is meaningless. We want equality in a *just* society."[3]

Students for a Democratic Society, until recently male dominated in action as well as male supremacist in attitude, passed their first resolution on the Women's Movement in December 1968, at their Ann Arbor National Conference. The statement, which takes almost no notice of the social, sexual, or emotional valences of women's oppression, nevertheless is very cogent on the economic aspects, and how they relate, ultimately, to revolutionary commitment:

> The inability of the most advanced, technologically developed, etc. capitalist society to provide equality to [more than] half its citizens not only exposes the thorough hypocrisy of all that society's words about "justice" and "equality." It also shows that the struggle for equality of women is a revolutionary task. . . . Male supremacy in the Movement mirrors male supremacy in the capitalist society. [This fact] raises the issue that although no people's liberation can happen without a socialist revolution in this country, a socialist revolution could take place which maintains the secondary position of women in society. . . . The fight for Women's Liberation is a concretization of the struggle of all peoples from oppression. . . . Therefore, the liberation of women must become a conscious part of our struggle.

We have, indeed, seen the erosion of women's position in the Soviet Union, and heard rumors of the same development in Algeria and even in Cuba. The day comes when women who fought and died on the barricades as bravely as men are told, "That phase is over, comrade. Back to the kitchen." Hell no, we won't go.

Meanwhile, back in the United States, the newly articulated demands of such a vast constituency are proving revolutionary. What we must all learn, this time, is *not* to repeat history, not to copy the ego-tripping of many male-movement "nonleaders," not to gain control in order to manipulate and exploit others as they have us, but rather to seize power over our own lives by any means necessary, including

---

[3] *Voice of the Women's Liberation Movement* (newsletter).

force of arms, and *then* to begin the Revolution—in our minds, hearts, guts, culture, daily lives. *That* is the difficult task: to create a truly free society. Imperialism begins at home. The Revolution begins at home.

"The Revolution Made Flesh"

How relatively simple the economics seem when compared to the cultural, psychological, emotional, and sexual problems. *Naturally* no one should lack medical care or food or shelter or the pleasures of challenging work (as opposed to debilitating toil, which technology is ready to assume).

But why are we ready to reject most values of a depraved society, while still clinging to others? How pervasive the puritanical conditioning must have been, to make us still afraid of our naked bodies, to still fear the mystery of the opposite sex, and to be even more terrified of the familiarity of our own sex in someone else's body! Movement men who in one breath declare that the whole political structure must be torn down, in the next breath will play their male-mystique roles to the full (cuff women, talk heavy, and *never* embrace another man except in a locker-room parody of affection). Movement women, especially those into women's rights, are used to having commie-dirty-punk-creep epithets thrown at them; they just chuckle. But whisper "lesbian" and they will cringe in agonized denial. And of what? Of the natural bisexuality in all of us? Intelligent people who have read their Freud and Jung and Norman O. Brown and Masters and Johnson as well as their Marx, Marcuse, Mao, and Guevara, still flinch at the thought of a revolution in sexual mores.

Surely no one dare call oneself a revolutionary unless a continual attempt is made to create a revolution in one's own psyche—the ongoing struggle toward the deepening of one's humanity. Any acid trip will teach you that, as it will prove the silly absurdity of emphasis on purely genitally oriented sex, and the natural order of what could only be termed omnisexuality.

Yet so basic a scientific revelation as that in *Human Sexual Response* (Masters and Johnson), talking about the *one* female orgasm—the clitorally based one—has hardly dented consciousness two years after the publication of the best-seller. Nor has Anne Koedt's feminist paper, "The Myth of the Vaginal Orgasm," had any greater effect, although it makes the ramifications of this revelation even clearer. "The myths remain," wrote Sue Lydon in *Ramparts* (December 14, 1968), "because a male-dominated American culture has a vested interest in this continuance. Before Masters and Johnson, men defined female sexuality in a way as favorable to themselves as possible." That is, a woman must receive her sexual satisfaction only as a concomitant of a man's seeking his.

While the myth of the vaginal orgasm managed to thoroughly frustrate generations of women up until Masters and Johnson's liberating discovery (because one cannot achieve what is physically impossible—so what's wrong with *you*), the earlier Victorians were at least honest about their sexual repression. Women weren't supposed to have orgasms at all—and one Dr. Isaac Brown Baker, suspecting that some women were getting uppity and daring to enjoy themselves, performed numerous clitoridectomies, claiming that sexual excitement in women led to insanity, catalepsy, and epileptic seizures.

Depraved, of course, yet no more so than modern legislators who refuse to change perverted laws about natural behavior. Food, shelter, medicine—these are inalienable rights, hardly revolutionary demands. Yet even as we require these obvious rights, we must also have truly revolutionary goals: for a whole new concept of sexuality, for a new definition of what a woman is, what a man is; for the gentle laying to rest of limiting monosexuality; for joy and fun and freedom.

An examination of the structure of the bourgeois family and the mental price it has extracted is causing many people to think more and more in terms of the communal family, where children are raised by men as well as by women, and by more than one pair; where parenthood is perhaps a biological fact but not a property-defined relationship. Where else do we first learn the dynamics of domination but in the family triangle of our culture in which the woman is treated as a distinct inferior? Therefore, to eliminate political and economic domination, we must simultaneously uproot sexual domination from that microcosm where the developing individual's view of human possibility is irrevocably formed. Marriage as a bourgeois institution is beginning to fade slowly but surely from the needs of the under-twenty-five-year-olds. No more need the bride be passed from her father to her husband in order to produce (let's face it) sons. No more need the mother possess her children to death, since she will have, in fact, something of herself to call her own.

Nor does this relate to the myth of the sexual revolution. There is no such thing yet—for women. Rather, the double standard exists more powerfully and hypocritically than ever, among radicals and hippies as well as straights. A sexually free girl is still a lay whom guys can exchange stories about, while a girl who might *not* "want to" with just any man is considered hung-up—she has the Pill, so what's stopping her? (Conceivably, a sense of distaste.)

Surely it is because women have for so long been regarded merely as objects for sex and reproduction that we have learned to scrutinize those areas of our culture with particular suspicion. It was Margaret

Mead (whose work was held for a period in disrepute by her male contemporaries, but is now being reexamined by younger anthropologists) who first studied how permissive sexual mores in "primitive" cultures informed those societies with unique strength and survival values. Morgan, Lévi-Strauss, Montague, and Benedict have also investigated this theme. Serious anthropologists (as opposed to reactionary popularizers of a pseudo-scientific ethology, like Ardrey, Fox, and Tiger) continue to turn up examples which prove that competitive, aggressive cultures are those in which sexual stereotypes are most polarized, while those social structures allowing for an overlap of roles and functions between men and women tend to be collectivist, cooperative, and peaceful.

As women, our past has been taken from us. Our present is confused, our future uncertain. The very semantics of the language reflect our condition. We do not even have our own names, but bear that of the father until we exchange it for that of the husband. We have no word for what we are unless it be an auxiliary term for the opposite: man/wo-man, male/fe-male. No one, including us, knows who we really are.

But we are now pledged to find out, to create new selves if necessary, in a process as revolutionary as giving birth to one's own soul. And that process is inextricably bound up with liberating our brothers, as well, from sick sexual codes and from the enslavement of *being* the master. It must begin now, this re-creation. No waiting until after the revolution.

Humankind has polluted the air and water and land of our planet; we have all but destroyed ourselves by the twin suicidal weapons of overkill and overbreeding. The famine is upon us, the cities are in flames, our sisters and brothers all over the world are locked in a struggle with the dragon that is imperialism. It is for us in America, the dragon's lair, to put *every* priority of oppression first, to fight on every front for human dignity, to burn our way out of the dragon's gut while our comrades hack away at its scaly exterior, until the beast is dead, and we rise in joy, a woman and a man, phoenix from its ashes.

Spring 1969

BARBAROUS RITUALS

During much of 1968, all of 1969, and most of 1970, I was preoccupied with compiling and editing *Sisterhood is Powerful:* the first anthology of writings from the Women's Liberation Movement. I wrote in the Introduction to *Sisterhood*: "This book is an action . . . all of us who worked on it in a variety of ways had to read and think and talk about the condition of women until we began to dream about the subject, literally. The suffering and courage and humor and rage and intelligence and endurance that spilled out from the pages that came in from different women! . . . The history we learned, the political sophistication we discovered, the insights into our own lives that dawned on us! I couldn't believe—still can't—how angry I could become, from deep down and way back, something like a five-thousand-year buried anger."

"Barbarous Rituals" was written out of that anger, as a shorthand encoding of some basic themes in the educational conditioning of a woman in Western "civilization." It was almost an afterthought to the anthology, a piece which nevertheless demanded inclusion. I wrote it as an outline of my own memories, fears, dreaded expectations, and fury, expanded to encompass the experiences of as many sisters' lives as I could imagine. I didn't sign the piece because (I claimed) it might look nepotistic; this excuse, because of a deplorable tendency on the part of some anthologists to allot themselves the lion's share of their own collections. But the real reason I assumed the cloak of anonymity was that I feared to own up to authorship of a piece which confessed such rage, such consciousness, such vulnerability about concrete details of my own life. Even when women's reactions proved the piece to be one of the most popular in the book, I kept my secret. Intellectually I knew my condition was shared by all other women; emotionally I just evaded acknowledging the article.

The time has come, I think, to claim the orphan for my own, in love and in pride. I reprint it here for that purpose and because the writing of it, even if I could not admit as much publicly at that time, constituted for me a major commitment to feminism. It seems to me now such an obvious little article. Why then has it taken me so long to sign my name to its truths?

After all, elsewhere in the same anthology I stated in a brave although still tentative voice, "More and more, I begin to think of a worldwide Women's Revolution as the only hope for life on this planet."

Indeed.

Woman Is:

—kicking strongly in your mother's womb, upon which she is told, "It must be a boy if it's so active!"

—being tagged with a *pink* beaded bracelet thirty seconds after you are born, and wrapped in *pink* blankets five minutes thereafter.

—being confined to the Doll Corner in nursery school when you are really fascinated by Tinker Toys.

—wanting to wear overalls instead of "frocks."

—learning to detest the words "dainty" and "cute."

—being labeled a tomboy when all you wanted to do was climb that tree to look out and see a distance.

—learning to sit with your legs crossed, even when your feet can't touch the floor yet.

—hating boys—because they're allowed to do things you want to do but are forbidden to—and being told hating boys is a phase.

—learning that something you do is "naughty," but when your brother does the same thing, it's "spunky."

—wondering why your father gets mad now and then, but your mother mostly sighs a lot.

—seeing grownups chuckle when you say you want to be an engineer or doctor when you grow up—and learning to say you want to be a mommy or a nurse, instead.

—wanting to shave your legs at twelve and being agonized because your mother won't let you.

—being agonized at fourteen because you finally have shaved your legs, and your flesh is on fire.

—being told nothing whatsoever about menstruation, so that you think you are bleeding to death with your first period, *or*

—being told all about it in advance by kids at school who titter and make it clear the whole thing is dirty, *or*

—being prepared for it by your mother, who carefully reiterates that it *isn't* dirty, all the while talking just above a whisper, and referring to it as "the curse," "being sick," or "falling off the roof."

—feeling proud of and disgusted by your own body, for the first, but not last, time.

—dying of shame because your mother makes you wear a "training bra" but there's nothing to train, *or*

—dying of shame because your mother *won't* let you wear a bra and your breasts are bigger than those of other girls your age and they flop when you run and you sit all the time with your arms folded over your chest.

—feeling basically comfortable in your own body, but gradually learning to hate it because you are: too short or tall, too fat or thin, thick-thighed or big-wristed, large-eared or stringy-haired, short-necked or long-armed, bowlegged, knock-kneed, or pigeon-toed—*something* that *might* make boys not like you.

—wanting to kill yourself because of pimples, dandruff, or a natural tendency to sweat—and discovering that commercials about miracle products just lie.

—dreading summertime because more of your body with its imperfections will be seen—and judged.

—tweezing your eyebrows/bleaching your hair/scraping your armpits/dieting/investigating vaginal sprays/biting your nails and hating that and filing what's left of them but hitting the quick instead.

—liking math or history a lot and getting hints that boys are turned off by smart girls.

—getting hints that other *girls* are turned off by smart girls.

—finally getting turned off by smart girls, unconsciously dropping back, lousing up your marks, and being liked by the other kids at last.

—having an intense crush on another girl or on a woman teacher and learning that that's unspeakable.

—going to your first dance and dreaming about it beforehand, and hating it, just *hating* it afterwards: you didn't dance right, you spilled the punch, you were a wallflower in anguish (*or* you were popular but in anguish because your best *friend* was a wallflower); you said all the wrong things.

—being absolutely convinced that you are a clod, a goon, a dog, a schlep, a flop, and an utter klutz.

—discovering that what seems like everything worthwhile doing in life "isn't feminine," and learning to just *delight* in being feminine and "nice"—and feeling somehow guilty.

—masturbating like crazy and being terrified that you'll go insane, be sterile, turn into a whore, or destroy your own virginity.

—getting more information any way you can, and then being worried because you've been masturbating clitorally, and that isn't even the "right way."

—swinging down the street feeling good and smiling at people and being hassled like a piece of meat in return.

—having your first real human talk with your mother and being told about all her old hopes and lost ambitions, and how you can't fight it, and that's just the way it is: life, sex, men, the works—and loving her and hating her for having been so beaten down.

—having your first real human talk with your father and being told about all *his* old hopes and lost ambitions, and how women really have it easier, and "what a man really wants in a woman,"—and loving him and hating him for having been beaten down—and for beating down your mother in turn.

—brooding about "how far" you should go with the guy you really like. Will he no longer respect you? Will you get—oh God—a "reputation"? Or, if not, are you a square? Being pissed off because you can't just do what *you* feel like doing.

—being secretly afraid that you'll lose your virginity to a tampon, but being too ashamed to ask anyone about it.

—lying awake wondering if a girl really *can* get pregnant by the sperm swimming *through* her panties.

—having a horrible fight with your boyfriend, who keeps shouting how *he's* frustrated by not "doing it"—it never occurring to him that *you* might be climbing walls, too, which you maybe don't even dare to admit.

—finally screwing and your groin and buttocks and thighs ache like hell and you're all wet and maybe bloody and it wasn't like a Hollywood movie at all but jesus at least you're not a virgin any more but is this what it's all about?—and meanwhile he's asking, "Did you come?"

—discovering you need an abortion, and really learning for the first time what your man, your parents, and your society think of you. Frequently paying for that knowledge with your death.

—finding that the career you've chosen exacts more than just study or hard work—an emotional price of being made to feel "less a woman."

—finding that almost all jobs open to you pay less, for harder work, than to men.

—being bugged by men in the office who assume that you're a virginal prude if you don't flirt, and that you're an easy mark if you are halfway relaxed and pleasant.

—learning to be *very tactful* if you have men working "under you." More likely, learning to always be working under men.

—becoming a woman *executive*, forgodsake, and then being asked to order the delicatessen food for an office party.

—finding out how difficult it is to get hold of "easily accessible" birth-control information.

—chasing the slippery diaphragm around the bathroom as if in a game of Frisbee the first time you try to insert it yourself, *or*

—gaining weight or hemorrhaging or feeling generally miserable with the Pill, or just freaking out at the scare stories about it, *or*

—going on a cross-country car trip in a Volkswagen, during which the Loop or the Coil becomes dislodged and begins to tear at your flesh.

—wondering why we can have live color telecasts of the moon's surface, but still no truly simple, humane, safe method of birth control.

—going the rounds of showers, shopping, money worries, invitation lists, licenses—when all you really wanted to do was live with the guy.

—quarreling with your fiancé over whether "and obey" should be in the marriage ceremony.

—secretly being bitched because the ceremony says "man and wife" —not "husband and wife" or "man and woman." Resenting having to change your (actually, your father's) name.

—having been up since 6:00 A.M. on your wedding day seeing family and friends you really don't even like and being exhausted from standing just so and not creasing your gown and from the ceremony and reception and traveling and now being alone with this strange man who wants to "make love" when you don't know that you even like him and even if you did you desperately want to just sleep for fourteen hours, *or*

—*not* getting married, just living together in "free love," and finding out it's just the same as marriage anyway, and you're the one who pays for the "free."

—playing the role to the hilt, cooking special dishes, cleaning, etc.— and knowing you'll *never* make it as *Good Housekeeping*'s "ideal," *or*

—"dropping out" together in a "hip, groovy" commune—and cooking brown rice instead of Betty Crocker.

—having menstrual cramps each month quite normally, cramps and/or headaches and/or nausea that would put a "normal" man out of commission for two weeks—and going on with your job or chores, etc., so no one will be inconvenienced.

—finding out that you're bored by your husband in bed.

—faking an orgasm for the first time: disgust, frustration—and relief (because he never even knew the difference).

—feeling guilty for not having an orgasm: *what* is wrong with *you?*

—finding out that *you* bore your *husband* in bed. Getting desperate— where have *you* failed?

—wanting desperately to know what special things he wants you to do to him in bed—and being afraid to tell him what you'd want him to do; or telling him hints that he promptly forgets for ever after.

—wanting to be the power behind the throne and finding out either that he's not a great man after all, or that he doesn't need your support.

—being jealous and hating yourself for showing it.

—hating certain books that you might have loved—all because he read them first and told you all about them. Feeling robbed. This goes for movies too.

—wanting to go back to school, to read, to join something, do something. Why isn't home enough for you? What's wrong with *you?*

—coming home from work—and starting *in* to work: unpack the groceries, fix supper, wash up the dishes, rinse out some laundry, etc., etc.

—feeling a need to say thank you when your guy actually fixes *himself* a meal now that you're dying with the flu.

—getting pregnant, hearing all the earth-mother shit from everyone, going around with a fixed smile on your terrified face.

—having men on the street, in cabs and buses, no longer (at least) regard you as an ogle-object; now they regard you as Carrier of the Species.

—knowing there must be some deep-down way to enjoy this that maybe women in some "primitive" tribe feel, but being elephantine, achy, nauseated—and *kvetched* at having to be cheerful.

—wanting your husband with you, or wanting natural childbirth, and either he won't, or the doctor or hospital won't—and you're on your own, *or*

—maybe you're lucky and he's not afraid or disgusted and the doctor approves and you go through it together and it's even beautiful—and you hear another woman screaming in solitary labor next door.

—feeling responsible for *more* lives—your kids' as well as your man's—but never, never your own life.

—learning to hate other women who are: younger, freer, unmarried, without children, in jobs, in school, in careers—whatever. Hating yourself for hating them.

—trying desperately not to repeat the pattern, and catching yourself telling your daughter one day that she "isn't acting like a lady," or warning your son "not to be a sissy."

—knowing that your husband is "playing around" and wanting to care, but not even being able to.

—being widowed or divorced, and trying to get a "good" job—at your age.

—claiming not to understand the "revolt" of your kids, but understanding it in your gut and not being able to help being bitter because you think it's too late for you.

—still wanting to have sex but feeling faintly ridiculous before your husband, let alone other men.

—being patronized and smirked over by your own children during the agonizing ritual of widowhood dating.

—getting older, getting lonelier, getting ready to die—and knowing it wouldn't have had to be this way, after all.

April 1970

PART THREE

Feminist Leanings:
Articles for
a Women's
Newspaper

PART III:
INTRODUCTORY NOTE

In the late 1960's, Rat was one of the major "underground" newspapers of the New Left and the so-called alternative culture. Although published in New York and focused partially on local issues, Rat had a national circulation and in fact an international list of subscribers. More serious at its inception than most underground papers, Rat was perhaps best known for having dared be the first to publish documents stolen by anonymous students from the administrative offices of Columbia University during the Columbia student rebellion. The documents seemed to implicate the university in the U.S. war in Vietnam, and Rat's "scoop" in publishing them created a sensation in both the mass and alternate media.

Yet despite its attempts at genuine muckraking journalism, Rat nevertheless had been created and sustained by and for men and male attitudes. As the gentle flower-children style of the middle sixties flared into the confrontation tactics of the late sixties, these male attitudes solidified themselves in Leftist consciousness—being tough, butch, "heavy," and "a street-fighter" were now prerequisites for being a radical, male or female. Not surprisingly, most men had a better chance at cutting such a figure than did most women. Rat reflected these changes, and began presenting as well a kind of "cultural nationalism" for young white males: rock music coverage, pornography articles, and sex-wanted ads (euphemistically called "Personals") began to clog the pages. As the women Rat staffers later wrote, "Rat has given the impression that [it] regards politics as that thing the Black Panthers and the Young Lords are into. White youth and non-Panthers/Lords (one would think after reading back issues) just lie back and groove on pornography, rock, dope, and movies."

In 1968 I had written some articles for Rat on the emerging "Women's Liberation Front"—a front, that is, of the real movement, the New Left. During the following year I had been inching my way toward a more feminist position, although my attitude of Marxism-über-alles *persisted. Still, even I could no longer tolerate the blatant sexism of Rat, and by the winter of 1969 I refused to write for the paper any longer. I had heard that the women who worked at Rat (none of them in any positions of power, naturally) were also angry and had been confronting the men about the paper's sexism and its hierarchy, which employed men as editors and feature writers, women as (usually volunteer) secretaries and bottle-washers who were sometimes permitted to write a short article. I had even warned one of the Rat men that women might take over the paper if there were no change forthcoming. But I was still unprepared for the delightful telephone call I received in January of 1970 from Jane Alpert, one of the Rat women, in the course of which she serenely informed me that the women on the paper had seized it and now needed ideas, support, and the physical presence of Women's Liberationists to sustain their action.*

We came from all parts of the then Women's Movement in New York: from Redstockings and WITCH, from what remained of New York Radical Women, even from NOW. There were lesbian women from Gay Liberation, Weatherwomen from the then-overground Weather Communes, women from various caucuses in male-Left organizations. Most of us knew precisely nothing about typesetting, layout, advertising, dealing with printers, or distribution. But we put out a paper. And the first "Women's Rat" became a reality.

A few feminist newspapers were already in existence, Everywoman, It Ain't Me Babe, *and* Off Our Backs, *among them. But this was the first time women had seized a male-run newspaper, and the action created ripples all over the Left, with women following suit in other cities and taking over their local underground media temporarily or permanently.*

It was not until after that first issue had been put together by women that we ourselves realized we weren't about to give the paper back. We intended to keep it, in fact, as a radical newspaper written and published collectively by women. And our Rat did continue, with a kind of core collective comprised of those women who stayed and worked regularly on the publication, and a larger group of women who for various reasons drifted in and out. I myself remained on Rat for a year, as did six or seven other women of the original collective. During that time the overall group kept shifting and changing; this had the salutary effect of refreshing our ideas and energy, but it also was expressed negatively in a lack of solidity or real knowledge of each other.

I wrote "Goodbye to All That" for the first issue of the Women's Rat. Sometimes I wonder how I could publish my parting statement to the male Left there—and then remain for a full year on such a Leftist newspaper. Yet I know the answer. In "Goodbye" I was saying farewell to working with men in the Left. I could not have foreseen that working

*with Leftist women on those same male-Left-defined issues of impor-
tance would be little different. These were, after all, women. Besides, I
myself was not that free from a Marxist analysis; my own political
priorities were largely defined by guilt for whatever I was not doing at
any given moment.*

*Rat's priorities were never clarified either. We put out a paper by
women, but we didn't want it to be "only" for women. In fact, we
wanted to show all those men who thought we couldn't do it that we
could—and so we had to keep the coverage of subjects interesting to
them, to win their approval. We never openly admitted this last, of
course—even among ourselves—but it was pathetically true. And as
Leftist women joined the collective in greater numbers during the ensuing weeks that tendency became more noticeable. New York feminists
were not without blame, however; many began to stay away out of a
sense of disdainful purism instead of coming around and helping to turn
Rat into the feminist paper they claimed, accurately, it had not yet
become.*

*The double guilt suffered by those of us who remained was ulcer-
ating then, if humorous now. We came to be called "the feminist
caucus"—a small group of women who dared to be more and more concerned with women, but who still functioned within a larger group
which was concerned with "the real revolution." We tried frantically
to cover all bases. I myself had a six-month-old baby, and I was involved
in a union-organizing effort in the publishing house where I had an
editorial job. Yet I wrote for and worked at Rat most evenings; in addition, I took part in a separate weekly consciousness-raising group (with
non-Rat women of a more feminist stripe); was involved in the founding of the Women's Center (more feminist points on my chart); helped
organize two demonstrations in support of the Panthers (Leftist points);
carried the Manual of an Urban Guerrilla or The Golden Notebook to
different meetings (double points) and actually read both; salivated
every time the bell rang that a Weatherperson had been busted and
rushed out to be rent-a-body at the ritual riot (Leftist points plus a red
star); and struggled with my husband (feminist points—although these
stung more than being tear-gassed).*

*During this same period I was finishing Sisterhood is Powerful, a
task which in itself involved a considerable amount of work. It was that
work, perhaps more than anything else, which gradually drew me closer
and closer to radical feminism. It became harder every day to put other
oppressions first when my brain was barraged with objective facts, figures, statistics, and analyses—and subjective anguish—all on and of
women. The anthology transformed my own views at least as much as
it has those of other women, thousands of whom have told me it
wrought drastic shifts in their attitudes and in their daily realities. The*

statistics came alive vividly in my daily realities, too, when I found my-self suddenly unemployed and soon after in jail for political reasons.

Meanwhile, back at Rat, the contradictions certainly were becom-ing clearer. Labels like "feminist" and "politico" (incredibly enough implying that feminism wasn't political) were flung around. It was like the old New York Radical Women polarities—but now I was on the feminist side. The majority of the collective appeared to feel that issues such as rape, abortion, sexuality, child care, and menopause were basi-cally insular and bourgeois when compared to those issues that were universal and radical, like GI rights. Or organizing the workers (house-wives were never considered bona-fide "workers" in the Left). For each token article the feminist caucus was able to push through in an edi-torial meeting, there were three or four on the NLF, the IRA, the FLN, or the BPP. There was an area of compromise, to be sure: we ran articles on how well women drove tractors in Cuba, threw grenades in Palestine, carried rifles in Vietnam, and, by implication, obeyed orders with dedi-cated socialistic consciousness. One eight-hour editorial "dialogue" en-sued when the feminist caucus insisted on printing a statement critical of Cuba for having held a Miss Havana Beauty Contest.

There was little space left for me to avoid facing The Awful Truth: that it was the politics of the Left, not solely the men who mouthed them, which were male supremacist. It was the politics, the analysis itself, which ignored or patronized more than half the human species. Because of that analysis, which had stopped short at its greatest chal-lenge, the Black Liberation Movement as well as the New Left was sexist—and doomed to perpetuate that oppression. And the student movement. And the GI and war-resister movements. And the emerging Native American movement, the Puerto Rican rights movement, the revolutionary governments of China, Cuba, North Vietnam, Algeria, North Korea—all, all had sacrificed women in their struggle to attain freedom for "man." It was not merely the practice, but the very poli-tics—which had been created by men—that was responsible. And that politics was as responsible for the continued suffering of women as the capitalist system—which had also been created by men for the freedom of a comparative few. The realization of these no longer avoidable ideas kept me in labor pains through all of that year. I was terrified of such thoughts. Then, three dramatic contractions broke through and deliv-ered me into an unequivocal feminist position.

One was a paper written by some Detroit feminists,[1] entitled The Fourth World Manifesto, *in which the authors talked about female cul-*

---

[1] Kathleen Barry, Barbara Burris, Terry Moon, and Joanne Parrent, among others. Reprinted in *Notes from the Third Year,* available from KNOW, Inc. (P.O. Box 86031, Pittsburgh, Penn. 15221).

ture and history, and in which they said "goodbye to all that" to the politics of the New Left, whether held by women or men. It was (and still is) a brave and historic statement.

The second was Shulamith Firestone's brilliant book The Dialectic of Sex: The Case for Feminist Revolution,[2] in which Firestone proved that both Marx and Freud were less than radical, and herself devised a lucid political analysis more far-reaching than either—more revolutionary, in fact, than any theory I had yet encountered. Today, Dialectic seems almost axiomatic to current feminist thought; it is a basic building block, and as such, one on which we have built. I even find myself disagreeing with parts of the book for not going far enough. But I could not have got Here from There without it, and it still stands for me as the classic articulation of what I could call the antithetical feminist position; I feel we are now in a new synthesis (which in turn will become a new thesis, of course), and so it goes. In 1970, however, Shulamith Firestone helped save my feminist soul, and I shall always be grateful.

The third and final ingredient in my conversion came about because my writing, the core of my existence, was being threatened. We were all (in the Left, in the Women's Movement, in the alternate culture) indulging each other at that time in an orgy of downward mobility and anti-intellectualism, accompanied, expectably, by a rejection of art. When I look back at such attitudes from my present perspective, they seem to indicate a guilt reflex carried to almost suicidal extremes combined with contempt for the real poor, for whose sake we were supposedly making these sacrifices. (The poor, the black, the working class, naturally, were thought of as anti-art dolts.)

Thus, when the Rat collective decided it was elitist for any member to sign her name to her work, I dutifully dropped my by-line (back to Anon.; do not pass Go). The articles in this section of Going Too Far were written during this period and some are here acknowledged for the first time as my own. When the collective, a few months later, criticized me for writing in a style which was apparently still identifiable to our readers ("You write too well" was the flattering accusation), I even tried to worsen my writing: I spelled America with three k's instead of one, as I had done previously in the Left; I dropped my g's in print; I peppered my articles with words like imperialism, running-dog-of-a-capitalist-swine, and other phrases which would have given George Eliot the vapours. But this still was not sufficient, and at one meeting it was suggested that I not write for the paper at all—but not quit, either (that would be a cop-out); I should stay and work on proof-reading, layout, and distribution—just not write. Appallingly enough, I even did

---

[2] Published by William Morrow, Inc., New York, 1970.

that, *wearing a fixed Maoist smile to cover my indignation—for about a month. Then something cracked open inside me, and it was all over.*

I went on a trip around the country to promote the publication of the anthology; I threw myself into the plans for Sisterhood is Powerful, Inc., into which all the royalties from the book were going in order to further women's projects; I met women in Detroit and Chicago and California and Boston and Cincinnati and Baltimore—and they were feminists. They were working on all those counter-revolutionary, middle-class issues like rape and child care and abortion and gynecological care (do only middle-class women have cervixes?), and they were working steadily, uninterrupted by guilt binges about men (oppressed men or unoppressed, black or white, GI or civilian). They were not all white women, either, not all young, not all middle-class-ashamed-of-their-origins, not all hip or heavy. They were coolly going about making a genuine revolution—and liking one another while doing it.

The explosions chain-reacting inside my skull were indescribable. I felt as if I had discovered a whole new continent: the authentic Women's Movement. When I returned to New York I told the Rat collective that I was leaving because the paper was not and at this rate never would be a paper for women. The other last few feminist-sympathizers were leaving, too, it turned out, and the parting was tearful but firm. In fact, it was more of a drift-away than a doorslam, which was fitting, since we were all women. A few months later, Rat ceased publication; during those months, three separate groups of Leftist women had taken over from each other in turn as the publishing collective, each one holier and more "correct" than the preceding.

Rat has become fiction in many recollections—especially those of women who never were in the core collective but who since claim to have been, by the hundreds. I've heard Rat referred to as a "radical-feminist newspaper" (meant, depending on the speaker, either pejoratively or complimentarily), and as a "women's voice of the Left" (also meant, depending on the speaker, as insult or praise). To me, Rat was neither, and should not be condemned or eulogized for other than what it was: a spirited, precedent-setting attempt to seize some power for women within the Left; to articulate the concerns of young, white, guilty, but idealistic women; to learn and teach each other the skills involved with putting out a newspaper; to reach out to one another; to work committedly together. Once Rat was seized, the New Left was never to be the same.

More important, none of us women would ever be the same. When I think of the Rat year, I remember anger and tremendous excitement and exhaustion and much laughter and not a little love. I only wish we had done what we talked of doing so many times: I only wish we had changed the paper's name.

GOODBYE
TO ALL THAT

"Goodbye to All That" was my contribution to the first issue of what came to be called "The Women's *Rat*," in January 1970. Beneath the by-line, I identified myself as a member of WITCH—in this case, "Women Inspired to Commit Herstory"; this was the debut of that word. (The coinage has literally changed history.) Since this women's seizure of a male-run newspaper was the first such action in the Left (though not by any means the last), it seemed the right moment to say those things which had been boiling inside me for some time. I knew that such a step would alter my own life, but I could never have foreseen the effect "Goodbye" was to have on so many other women. It apparently articulated the felt experience of most women in the Left and so became an instant classic. It was read aloud in struggle meetings, quoted, fought about, cried over, excerpted on posters and banners, used (individual lines and phrases) for slogans, and widely reprinted. The Leftist media almost always editorialized shockingly while reprinting: the tendency was to cut the critical reference to whatever group was strongest in the local area. (In Michigan, the denunciation of Sinclair disappeared; in Boston, ellipses replaced my attack on the Progressive Labor Party; in Berkeley, the Weatherman section was deleted.) This outrageous attempt at co-optation was ultimately overshadowed, however, by the more accurate reprinting of the article in most of the then existing feminist media. San Diego women named their newspaper after the article, and in the following months and years women making their own farewells to various male-dominated groupings (the Gay Liberation Front, the Catholic Church, certain Third World movement groups) would refer to their statements as "daughters" of "Goodbye to All That." Leftist men, as could have been expected, were furious, and the former *Rat* men tried unsuccessfully to re-seize the paper. This piece clearly had "gone too far." I received death threats from quite a few revolutionary brothers—a radicalizing experience, that. I had shut one door behind me forever, and when I looked back it had vanished; a solid wall stood in its place. I was free, then, to go forward, wherever that direction should take me.

Although "Goodbye" has been anthologized repeatedly, this will be the first time it appears in print complete with my own footnotes. I have written these clarifications specifically for the article's inclusion in this book, because (O, triumph of feminism!) most of the men and male-dominated groups named in the article—all of them so "heavy" and notorious at that time—have since oozed ignominiously into oblivion. Women reading the piece for the first time in anthologies both in the United States and abroad frequently write to ask me who in hell these men *were*. It is a heartening irony that their names seem to be relevant only as historical curiosities fortunate enough to have been at one point denounced by a feminist.

So, *Rat* has been liberated, for this week, at least. Next week? If the men return to reinstate the porny photos, the sexist comic strips, the "nude-chickie" covers (along with their patronizing rhetoric about being in favor of Women's Liberation)—if this happens, our alternatives are clear. *Rat* must be taken over permanently by women—or *Rat* must be destroyed.

Why *Rat*? What not EVO[1] or even the obvious new pornzines (Mafia-distributed alongside the human pornography of prostitution)? First, they'll get theirs—but it won't be a takeover, which is reserved for something at least *worth* taking over. Nor should they be censored. They should just be helped not to exist—by any means necessary. But *Rat*, which has always tried to be a really radical *cum* life-style paper— that's another matter. It's the liberal co-optative masks on the face of sexist hate and fear, worn by real nice guys we all know and like, right? We have met the enemy and he's our friend. And dangerous. "What the hell, let the chicks do an issue; maybe it'll satisfy 'em for a while, it's a good controversy, and it'll maybe sell papers"—runs an unoverheard conversation that I'm sure took place at some point last week.

And that's what I wanted to write about—the friends, brothers, lovers in the counterfeit male-dominated Left. The good guys who think they know what "Women's Lib," as they so chummily call it, is all about—and who then proceed to degrade and destroy women by almost everything they say and do: The cover on the last issue of *Rat* (front *and* back). The token "pussy power" or "clit militancy" articles. The snide descriptions of women staffers on the masthead. The little jokes, the personal ads, the smile, the snarl. No more, brothers. No more well-

---

[1] *East Village Other*, an "underground" newspaper celebrating the so-called hip culture—at the expense of women; no longer being published.

meaning ignorance, no more co-optation, no more assuming that this thing we're all fighting for is the same; one revolution under *man*, with liberty and justice for all. No more.

Let's run it on down. White males are most responsible for the destruction of human life and environment on the planet today. Yet who is controlling the supposed revolution to change all that? White males (yes, yes, even with their pasty fingers back in black and brown pies again). It just could make one a bit uneasy. It seems obvious that a legitimate revolution must be led by, *made* by those who have been most oppressed: black, brown, and white *women*—with men relating to that the best they can. A genuine Left doesn't consider anyone's suffering irrelevant or titillating; nor does it function as a microcosm of capitalist economy, with men competing for power and status at the top, and women doing all the work at the bottom (and functioning as objectified prizes or "coin" as well). Goodbye to all that.

Run it all the way down.

Goodbye to the male-dominated peace movement, where sweet old Uncle Dave[2] can say with impunity to a woman on the staff of *Liberation*, "The trouble with you is you're an aggressive woman."

Goodbye to the "straight" male-dominated Left: to PL,[3] who will allow that some workers are women, but won't see all women (say, housewives) as workers (blind as the System itself); to all the old Leftover parties who offer their "Women's Liberation caucuses" to us as if that were not a contradiction in terms; to the individual anti-leadership leaders who hand-pick certain women to be leaders and then relate only to them, either in the male Left *or* in Women's Liberation—bringing their hang-ups about power dominance and manipulation to everything they touch.

Goodbye to the Weather Vain,[4] with the Stanley Kowalski image and theory of free sexuality but practice of sex on demand for males. "Left Out!"—not Right On—to the Weather Sisters who (and they know better—*they know*) reject their own radical feminism for that last desperate grab at male approval that we all know so well, for claiming that the *machismo* style and the gratuitous violence is their own style by "free choice" and for believing that this is the way for a woman to make her revolution . . . all the while, oh my sister, not meeting my eyes because Weather*men* chose Manson[5] as their—and your—hero.

---

[2] David Dellinger, a leader in the male-run peace movement, subsequently divorced by Betty Peterson, his wife of many years.

[3] Progressive Labor (Party).

[4] Weathermen, or the Weather Bureau. A reference to their pre-fugitive attitudes, as sexist as their later ones.

[5] Convicted mass murderer and self-styled harem-keeper of "slaves."

(Honest, at least, since Manson is only the logical extreme of the normal American male's fantasy [whether he is Dick Nixon[6] or Mark Rudd[7]]: master of a harem, women to do all the shitwork, from raising babies and cooking and hustling to killing people on order.) Goodbye to all that shit that sets women apart from women; shit that covers the face of any Weatherwoman which is the face of any Manson Slave which is the face of Sharon Tate[8] which is the face of Mary Jo Kopechne[9] which is the face of Beulah Saunders[10] which is the face of me which is the face of Pat Nixon[11] which is the face of Pat Swinton.[12] *In the dark we are all the same*—and you better believe it: we're in the dark, baby. (Remember the old joke: Know what they call a black man with a Ph.D.? A nigger. Variation: Know what they call a Weatherwoman? A heavy cunt. Know what they call a hip revolutionary woman? A groovy cunt. Know what they call a radical militant feminist? A crazy cunt. Amerika is a land of free choice—take your pick of titles.) Left Out, my sister—don't you see? Goodbye to the illusion of strength when you run hand in hand with your oppressors; goodbye to the dream that being in the leadership collective will get you anything but gonorrhea.

Goodbye to RYM II, as well, and all the other RYMs[13]—not that the sisters there didn't pull a cool number by seizing control, but because they let the men back in after only *a day or so* of self-criticism on male chauvinism. (And goodbye to the inaccurate blanket use of that phrase, for that matter: male chauvinism is an *attitude*—male supremacy is the *objective reality, the fact*.) Goodbye to the Conspiracy,[14] who, when lunching with fellow sexist bastards[15] Norman Mailer[16] and Terry Southern[17] in a Bunny-type club in Chicago found Judge Hoffman[18] at the neighboring table—no surprise: *in the light they are all the same.*

Goodbye to Hip Culture and the so-called Sexual Revolution, which has functioned toward women's freedom as did the Reconstruction toward former slaves—reinstituted oppression by another name.

---

[6] Alleged used-car salesman.

[7] Used-revolution salesman.

[8] Victim (murdered) of Manson "Family."

[9] Victim (?) of Senator Edward Kennedy.

[10] Victim of the welfare system; organizer in welfare rights.

[11] Victim of alleged used-car salesmen.

[12] Victim of Leftist loyalties which led to her indictment in a bombing conspiracy, but saved from Rightist patriarchs by the sacrifice and support of feminists.

[13] Revolutionary Youth Movements (I, II, and III), spin-off groups from SDS (Students for Democratic Society).

[14] The Conspiracy Seven or the Chicago Seven. Male activists who were on trial for conspiracy in organizing demonstrations against the previous Democratic Convention.

Goodbye to the assumption that Hugh Romney[19] is safe in his "cultural revolution," safe enough to refer to "our women, who make all our clothes" without somebody not forgiving that. Goodbye to the arrogance of power indeed that lets Czar Stan Freeman of the Electric Circus[20] sleep without fear at night, or permits Tomi Ungerer[21] to walk unafraid in the street after executing the drawings for the Circus advertising campaign against women. Goodbye to the idea that Hugh Hefner[22] is groovy 'cause he lets Conspirators come to parties at the Mansion—goodbye to Hefner's dream of a ripe old age. Goodbye to Tuli and the Fugs[23] and all the boys in the front room—who always knew they hated the women they loved. Goodbye to the notion that good ol' Abbie[24] is any different from any other up-and-coming movie star who ditches the first wife and kids, good enough for the old days but awkward once you're Making It. Goodbye to his hypocritical double standard that reeks through the tattered charm. Goodbye to lovely pro-Women's Liberation Paul Krassner,[25] with all his astonished anger that women have lost their sense of humor "on this issue" and don't laugh any more at little funnies that degrade and hurt them; farewell to the memory of his "Instant Pussy" aerosol-can poster, to his column for *Cavalier*, to his dream of a Rape-In against legislators' wives, to his Scapegoats and Realist Nuns and cute anecdotes about the little daughter he sees as often as any proper divorced Scarsdale middle-aged (thirty-eight) father; goodbye forever to the notion that he is my brother who, like Paul, buys a prostitute for the night as a birthday gift for a male friend, or who, like Paul, reels off the names in alphabetical order of people in the Women's Movement he has fucked, reels off names in the best locker-room tradition—as proof that *he's* no sexist oppressor.

---

[15] An example (along with the phrase "son-of-a-bitch") of male-supremacist linguistics which can transform a word into a pejorative term in order to place the blame for sins of the son upon—who else—his mother. This had not been borne in upon me yet, in 1970.

[16] and [17] Two hack writers.

[18] The extremely conservative judge who presided over the trial of the Conspiracy Seven. Supposedly their adversary.

[19] A counter-culture "leader," dictator of the traveling commune so delicately named The Hog Farm.

[20] A New York discotheque of the period, capitalizing on sexism.

[21] A misogynistic cartoonist.

[22] Founder and owner of *Playboy* magazine. Enough said.

[23] A vulgar rock band of the period; specializing in sexist lyrics.

[24] Abbie Hoffman, a minor "nonleader" leader of hip culture at that time. Currently a fugitive from the FBI (after having been charged with selling hard drugs), and a self-proclaimed bigamist of wives #2 and #3.

[25] Editor of *The Realist* (a sexist paper of satire), and a used-humor salesman. Also the former son-in-law of Norman Mailer, cited earlier.

Let it all hang out. Let it seem bitchy, catty, dykey, frustrated, crazy, Solanasesque, nutty, frigid, ridiculous, bitter, embarrassing, man-hating, libelous, pure, unfair, envious, intuitive, low-down, stupid, petty, liberating. *We are the women that men have warned us about.*

And let's put one lie to rest for all time: the lie that men are oppressed, too, by sexism—the lie that there can be such a thing as "men's liberation groups." Oppression is something that one group of people commits against another group specifically because of a "threatening" characteristic shared by the latter group—skin color or sex or age, etc. The oppressors are indeed *fucked up* by being masters (racism hurts whites, sexual stereotypes are harmful to men) but those masters are not *oppressed*. Any master has the alternative of divesting himself of sexism or racism; the oppressed have no alternative—for they have no power—but to fight. In the long run, Women's Liberation will of course free men—but in the short run it's going to *cost* men a lot of privilege, which no one gives up willingly or easily. Sexism is *not* the fault of women—kill your fathers, not your mothers.

Run it down. Goodbye to a beautiful new ecology movement that could fight to save us all if it would stop tripping off women as earth-mother types or frontier chicks, if it would *right now* cede leadership to those who have *not* polluted the planet because that action implies power and women haven't had any power in about 5,000 years, cede leadership to those whose brains are as tough and clear as any man's but whose bodies are also unavoidably aware of the locked-in relationship between humans and their biosphere—the earth, the tides, the atmosphere, the moon. Ecology is no big *shtick* if you're a woman—it's always been there.

Goodbye to the complicity inherent in the *Berkeley Tribe*smen being part publishers of *Trashman* Comics; goodbye, for that matter, to the reasoning that finds whoremaster Trashman a fitting model, however comic-strip far out, for a revolutionary man—somehow related to the same Super-male reasoning that permits the first statement on Women's Liberation and male chauvinism that came out of the Black Panther Party to be made *by a man*, talkin' a whole lot 'bout how the sisters should speak up for themselves. Such ignorance and arrogance ill befits a revolutionary.

We know how racism is worked deep into the unconscious by our System—the same way sexism is, as it appears in the very name of The Young Lords.[26] What are you if you're a "*macho* woman"—a female Lord? Or, god forbid, a Young Lady? *Change* it, change it to the Young Gentry if you must, or never assume that the name itself is innocent of pain, of oppression.

---

[26] Puerto Rican radical group of the period.

Theory and practice—and the light-years between them. "Do it!" says Jerry Rubin[27] in *Rat's* last issue—but he doesn't or every *Rat* reader would have known the pictured face next to his article as well as they know his own much-photographed face: it was Nancy Kurshan, the power behind the clown.

Goodbye to the New Nation and Earth People's Park[28] for that matter, conceived by men, announced by men, led by men—doomed before its birth by the rotting seeds of male supremacy which are to be transplanted in fresh soil. Was it my brother who listed human beings among the *objects* which would be easily available after the Revolution: "Free grass, free food, free women, free acid, free clothes, etc."? Was it my brother who wrote "Fuck your women till they can't stand up" and said that groupies were liberated chicks 'cause they dug a tit-shake instead of a handshake? The epitome of female exclusionism—"men will make the Revolution—and make their chicks." Not my brother, no. Not my revolution. Not one breath of my support for the new counterculture Christ—John Sinclair.[29] Just one less to worry about for ten years. I do not choose my enemy for my brother.

Goodbye, goodbye. The hell with the simplistic notion that automatic freedom for women—or nonwhite peoples—will come about ZAP! with the advent of a socialist revolution. Bullshit. Two evils pre-date capitalism and have been clearly able to survive and post-date socialism: sexism and racism. Women were the first property when the Primary Contradiction occurred: when one-half of the human species decided to subjugate the other half, because it was "different," alien, the Other. From there it was an easy enough step to extend the Other to someone of different skin shade, different height or weight or language—or strength to resist. Goodbye to those simple-minded optimistic dreams of socialist equality all our good socialist brothers want us to believe. How liberal a politics that is! How much further we will have to go to create those profound changes that would give birth to a genderless society. *Profound*, Sister. Beyond what is male or female. Beyond standards we all adhere to now without daring to examine them as male-created, male-dominated, male-fucked-up, and in male self-interest. *Beyond all known standards*, especially those easily articulated revolutionary ones we all rhetorically invoke. Beyond, to a species with a new name, that would not dare define itself as Man.

I once said, "I'm a revolutionary, not just a woman," and knew my own lie even as I said the words. The pity of that statement's eagerness

---

[27] Still another "nonleader" leader of the hip Left. Currently into "bio-karma."

[28] New Nation and Earth People's Park: both of them so-called radical organizing projects which dissolved.

[29] Then leader of the "White Panther Party," jailed for ten years on a drug charge—but soon after, of course, released.

to be acceptable to those whose revolutionary zeal no one would question, i.e., any male supremacist in the counterleft. But to become a true revoluntionary one must first become one of the oppressed (not organize or educate or manipulate them, but become one of them)—or realize that you *are* one already. No woman wants that. Because that realization is humiliating, it hurts. It hurts to understand that at Woodstock[30] or Altamont[31] a woman could be declared uptight or a poor sport if she didn't want to be raped. It hurts to learn that the sisters still in male-Left captivity are putting down the crazy feminists to make themselves look okay and unthreatening to our mutual oppressors. It hurts to be pawns in those games. It hurts to try and change *each day of your life right now*—not in talk, not "in your head," and not only conveniently "out there" in the Third World (half of which is women) or the black and brown communities (half of which are women) but in your own home, kitchen, bed. No getting away, no matter how else you are oppressed, from the primary oppression of being female in a patriarchal world. It hurts to hear that the sisters in the Gay Liberation Front, too, have to struggle continually against the male chauvinism of their gay brothers.[32] It hurts that Jane Alpert[33] was cheered when rapping about imperialism, racism, the Third World, and All Those Safe Topics but hissed and booed by a Movement crowd of men who wanted none of it when she began to talk about Women's Liberation. The backlash is upon us.

They tell us the alternative is to hang in there and "struggle," to confront male domination in the counterleft, to fight beside or behind or beneath our brothers—to show 'em we're just as tough, just as revolushunerry, just as whatever-image-they-now-want-of-us-as-once-they-wanted-us-to-be-feminine-and-keep-the-home-fire-burning. They will bestow titular leadership on our grateful shoulders, whether it's being a token woman on the Movement Speakers Bureau Advisory Board, or being a Conspiracy groupie or one of the "respectable" chain-swinging Motor City Nine.[34] Sisters all, with only one real alternative: to seize our own power into our own hands, all women, separate and together, and make the Revolution the way it must be made—no priorities this time, no suffering group told to wait until after.

---

[30] and [31] Rock festivals attended by masses of people, where women and blacks were vulnerable to rape and murder.

[32] This, of course, was before most lesbian activists deserted the "Gay Movement" for the Women's Movement.

[33] A leading Leftist revolutionary woman, later a fugitive who, in an open letter from the underground ("Mother-Right—A New Feminist Theory," *Ms.*, August 1973), denounced male-style politics and embraced radical feminism.

[34] A male-approved "toughie" group of Leftist women who had contempt for feminist issues.

It is the job of revolutionary feminists to build an ever stronger independent Women's Liberation Movement, so that the sisters in counterleft captivity will have somewhere to turn, to use their power and rage and beauty and coolness in their own behalf for once, on their own terms, on their own issues, in their own style—whatever that may be. Not for us in Women's Liberation to hassle them and confront them the way their men do, nor to blame them—or ourselves—for what any of us are: an oppressed people, but a people raising our consciousness toward something that is the other side of anger, something bright and smooth and cool, like action unlike anything yet contemplated or carried out. It is for us to survive (something the white male radical has the luxury of never really worrying about, what with all his options), to talk, to plan, to be patient, to welcome new fugitives from the counterfeit Left with no arrogance but only humility and delight, to push—to strike.

There is something every woman wears around her neck on a thin chain of fear—an amulet of madness. For each of us, there exists somewhere a moment of insult so intense that she will reach up and rip the amulet off, even if the chain tears at the flesh of her neck. And the last protection from seeing the truth will be gone. Do you think, tugging furtively every day at the chain and going nicely insane as I am, that I can be concerned with the puerile squabbles of a counterfeit Left that laughs at my pain? Do you think such a concern is noticeable when set alongside the suffering of more than half the human species for the past 5,000 years[35]—due to a whim of the other half? No, no, no, goodbye to all that.

Women are Something Else. This time, we're going to kick out all the jams, and the boys will just have to hustle to keep up, or else drop out and openly join the power structure of which they are already the illegitimate sons. Any man who claims he is serious about wanting to divest himself of cock privilege should trip on this: all male leadership out of the Left is the only way; and it's going to happen, whether through men stepping down or through women seizing the helm. It's up to the "brothers"—after all, sexism is their concern, not ours; we're too busy getting ourselves together to have to deal with their bigotry. So they'll have to make up their own minds as to whether they will be divested of just cock privilege or—what the hell, why not say it, *say* it!— divested of cocks. How deep the fear of that loss must be, that it can be suppressed only by the building of empires and the waging of genocidal wars!

Goodbye, goodbye forever, counterfeit Left, counterleft, male-

---

[35] I have learned since that it has actually been ten to twelve thousand years since the rise of patriarchy.

dominated cracked-glass-mirror reflection of the Amerikan Nightmare. Women are the real Left. We are rising, powerful in our unclean bodies; bright glowing mad in our inferior brains; wild hair flying, wild eyes staring, wild voices keening; undaunted by blood we who hemorrhage every twenty-eight days; laughing at our own beauty we who have lost our sense of humor; mourning for all each precious one of us might have been in this one living time-place had she not been born a woman; stuffing fingers into our mouths to stop the screams of fear and hate and pity for men we have loved and love still; tears in our eyes and bitterness in our mouths for children we couldn't have, or couldn't *not* have, or didn't want, or didn't want *yet*, or wanted and had in this place and this time of horror. We are rising with a fury older and potentially greater than any force in history, and this time we will be free or no one will survive. *Power to all the people or to none.* All the way down, this time.

Free Kathleen Cleaver!
Free Anita Hoffman!
Free Bernardine Dohrn!
Free Donna Malone!
Free Ruth Ann Miller!
Free Leni Sinclair!
Free Jane Alpert!
Free Gumbo!
Free Bonnie Cohen!
Free Judy Lampe!

Free Kim Agnew!
Free Holly Krassner!
Free Lois Hart!
Free Alice Embree!
Free Nancy Kurshan!
Free Lynn Phillips!
Free Dinky Forman!
Free Sharon Krebs!
Free Iris Luciano!
Free Robin Morgan!

Free Valerie Solanas!

FREE OUR SISTERS!   FREE OURSELVES![36]

January 1970

---

[36] All of the women on this list were at that time captives of a male-supremacist Leftist man and/or of patriarchal Leftist political beliefs—with two exceptions: Kim Agnew, the publicly rebellious daughter of Spiro Agnew (used-cash salesman), and Valerie Solanas, then serving time on a conviction of having shot Andy Warhol (used-decadence salesman).

ON VIOLENCE
AND FEMINIST
BASIC TRAINING

I am including the following article in this section of *Going Too Far* because it was originally drafted for the Women's *Rat*, although it never appeared there, due to our plague of priorities. It went through several reconceptions and revisions and over a year later, in the spring of 1971, I finally presented it as a paper at the Radical Feminist Conference in Detroit. Yet the piece still bears the unmistakable influence of that year at the newspaper: the *tone* of *Rat* is present—Leftist style mixed uneasily with Feminist content, the whole thing whipped to a froth of urgency to avoid curdling at the boil. There is an aura of Playing War in this article, which at the time did seem preferable to Playing House, but which now strikes me as equally infantile and even more unsatisfying.

Still, we were not playing games. Agnew was calling for "preventive detention" camps; friends were going underground or being sent to prison for twenty-year terms in punishment for political actions. People one had known and worked with and demonstrated with were suddenly dead of gunshot wounds in the middle of their college quads or on the city sidewalk two blocks away. To dare focus energy on women's needs per se seemed at times to constitute a betrayal of humanity. Fortunately, such "betrayal" continues today, in 1977, where the magnificent women forging a peace movement in Northern Ireland are termed "traitors" by both Protestants and Catholics —for demanding an end to the massacre of their children.

Betrayal or no, I was unable to escape my own feminism; unable to deny that another woman could better teach me how to handle a rifle in one afternoon than all my patronizing Leftist brothers could in months. (Why? something in her manner? I couldn't understand; sympathy? patience? humor? *why?*) I was unable to overlook child-care demands as "bourgeois" now that I was a mother (even though I still treated the issue of child care peremptorily and guiltily, as I do in this paper).

No, we weren't playing games. The *Rat* year was the same one in which both Kenneth and I were fired from our jobs in publishing—he for refusing to remove a poster denouncing the My Lai atrocities from his office wall, and I for union organizing on the job. It was the year, too, that I first went to jail. "Bring the war home!" was one chant I remember, and it seemed that the war certainly came home to us in 1970.

I had been working at Grove Press as an editor for two and a half years when, in the spring of 1970, I and four other employees were summarily fired. The reason officially given was "reorganization needs," but the real motive for the firings, as later confirmed by Arbitrator Thomas A. Knowlton, appointed by the National Arbitration Association of the National Labor Relations Board, was punishment for the sin of trying to organize a union.[1] Grove Press had built a façade reputation as a Left-liberal, avant-garde publisher, but much of its output consisted of sexist paperbacks which objectified women. I had refused to work on these, restricting my editorial duties to the political books, but I could not ignore the unequal treatment of women employees (from editor to janitor) all around (and including) me.

Publishing, a white-collar business and the third largest industry in New York, was beginning to experience feminist stirrings. More than 80 percent of all publishing employees are women, and we are mostly at the bottom of the pyramid; men control the field.

There was talk of forming an industry-wide women's group in publishing, possibly an industry-wide vertical union. Meanwhile, organizing efforts were going on in a number of individual houses—the Grove Press firings (which amounted to more than seventy people by the end of what we dryly called The Purge) were broadcast as a clear warning to publishing employees elsewhere. In this, at least, Grove was avant-garde. It was also an exception in playing unwilling host to a seizure and barricade of the executive offices by myself and eight other feminists protesting the firings, the discrimination against women, the sexist publications. This action was the first such militant move taken in the current feminist wave. It was also the first time since the days of the suffrage fight that women were arrested in a purely feminist cause (Grove Press had us

---

[1] On August 4, 1970, in New York City, Arbitrator Knowlton sustained the contention that Grove Press had illegally discharged employees "solely for union activities," and ordered our reinstatement with full back pay. I could never go back, but the extra money came in handy; it was split between baby needs and *Rat* needs —it paid the pediatrician, and it paid the printer for two issues of the paper.

charged with criminal trespass and criminal mischief, a felony—
and we pulled down resisting-arrest charges in addition, by
demanding policewomen as our arresting officers, since we
refused to recognize male authority). It was the first time the
liberal realm of publishing had been attacked by women;
the first time feminists openly declared pornography as an
enemy; and the first time feminists proclaimed our sympathy
with women who were jailed as prostitutes, accurately naming
such women political prisoners.

In strategic terms, the action was a success. The punishment was comparatively light, the results rewardingly vengeful.
Not only the Women's Movement but much of the Left supported the feminist action. Boycotts of Grove Press books, both
by individuals and by radical bookstores, became commonplace. Carl Oglesby (a leading New Left theorist who had,
along with Kathy Boudin, James Forman, and other Grove
political writers, joined the support demonstrations for the
feminists) severed his publishing association with the house.
In a letter to the GP-owned magazine *Evergreen Review*, he
prophesied, in part:

*"You've squandered the only coin that's current among the people
you've tried to speak for . . . Nobody is going to pay the slightest
attention anymore to what you have to say . . . Maybe you have half
a year before the word gets around . . . of every three women you
meet, or maybe of every seven men, one will be thinking of ways to
deal with you for what you've lately done."*[2]

In personal terms, the action had a more complicated
effect, of course. I experienced the redundantly radicalizing
effects of losing my livelihood, seeing the liberal mask peel
from the faces of white-collar coworkers, being behind bars
while my nine-month-old baby was enduring a high-fever
reaction to his smallpox inoculation and, in general, feeling
the impotence of powerlessness. That frustration left me impatient with rhetoric and lustful for action and the means
wherewith *to* act, and it, more than anything else, influenced
the reworking of the following piece.

All this time later I find that I completely affirm what I
wrote about discipline, and about our need to learn how to
teach one another without the intervention of power games.
The subsequent years have created their own versions of feminist learning situations: institutes on political theory such as
Sagaris, feminist retreats, women-run self-defense dojos, and
even educational institutions like Womanschool in New York
City, providing courses in everything from garage mechanics to

---

[2] Oglesby's long resignation letter appeared in full in *Evergreen Review* No.
80, July 1970.

poetry—these are flourishing today. If the emphasis is less on militarism than proposed in my article, this is for a number of reasons. I would number among them the raised consciousness of the American public, in part due to the war and to Watergate, which in turn creates a (slightly) more responsive environment and permits of less extreme forms of protest. Perhaps the most important ingredient, though, is emerging still as the insistence of most women on finding a way to better the world with a minimum of violence. This is not expressed in a goody-goody-aren't-all-women-peaceable manner, but rather in a ferocious refusal to give in to old means and become the very enemy we claim to be fighting.

The entire question of violence is one the Women's Movement has engaged only indirectly, and I sometimes wonder if it isn't a question that preoccupies mostly those women who like myself came to feminism from the Left. In my more cynical moments I ruminate that the reason is simply because feminists spend all our violence on one another, which nicely settles the question of whether or not to employ any of it against the patriarchy. Yet the question runs deep, and remains unanswered. I find myself both envious and contemptuous of those for whom such questions seem simple.

Less than a month ago, in broad daylight one block from where I live, a man assaulted me on the street. Because I yelled bloody murder and there were people around, he ran. Had it been nighttime, he probably would have reacted differently, and then I would have been reminded again—by my own bloodpulse, by the surge of adrenaline along my limbs, by the gush of rage exploding into fury inside my brain and along my muscles and through my very nails and teeth, I would have been reminded that I do not reject defensive violence, that my reflexes recall their martial-arts training, that hatred must be released against the cause someway, somehow, or be turned in against the victim who has been forced to host that feeling.

Yet less than one week ago, the television screen glared at me with hours-old scenes of children lying dead in Londonderry streets, of women killed in Lebanon, of men slain in Soweto. On my streetcorner pavement, pale bloodstains remain one morning from a knife fight the night before. It's always defensive violence, isn't it? My son's schoolmates revive their pressure on him to play war games, which he tries to translate at least into playing Knights of Queen Guinevere (the Malory influence from poet parents) or Robin Hood (Marxism *cum* the English literary folk tradition) or even Followers of Wonder Woman versus the Bad Men. I watch him suffer the scorn of his peers, watch the message of death-as-diversion trickle into his games, watch his natural human longing for adventure be-

come corrupted by their already socialized male longing for
violence.
    And I want to smash their little war-mongering faces.
    So am I caught, trapped, cramped suddenly with horror
at my own rancor.
    Somebody tell me again this is simple.
    Damn, damn, damn.

W‎OMEN IN GENERAL, and the Women's Movement in particular,
have always had our strategic options shockingly limited by our lack of
certain tactical skills, especially those required for independent survival
and militant struggle. This is a condition common to all oppressed
people, and is not their/our fault. But it becomes our fault if we do
not act to change that condition. At a certain point it is contingent
upon the oppressed to seize knowledge and skill for themselves, in
order to free themselves. It is no longer sufficient to bewail our lack
of the very tools we will need in order to create a Feminist Revolution. We must begin, by hard work and commitment, to take ourselves
seriously.

This does not mean that every skill we acquire we must use.
Rather, it means that we begin to amass our own independent resources
of knowledge and effective practice so that we are prepared for any
situation. If we lack the skill altogether, that most certainly limits our
chances of using it—unless of course in the crunch we are willing to rely
on men who have those skills. Myself, I prefer to be prepared.

The idea behind the following proposal was born out of personal
frustration with my own ignorance and technical incompetence, as well
as political despair at seeing myself and many other women drop out
of training programs, such as karate, which require an intense and
lengthy commitment. For women with jobs outside of as well as in
the home, and/or children, plus political meetings, demonstrations,
etc., the discipline required for nightly karate class falters, particularly
given the atmospheric noninducement of a male-dominated dojo
(which is almost always the case). Lack of progress creates discouragement, laziness, apathy. This goes for other learning commitments, too.
So much of the dropout syndrome is attributable to a pathology of
oppression—the self-fulfilling prophecy of inferiority which is so well
taught by the powerful to the powerless as to make the latter group
collaborate in its own undoing, thus proving the rule in order to win
the approval of those who invented the rule. This is a kind of success-
in-failure, frequently the only type of success available to the oppressed.

It occurred to me that perhaps if a "crash plan" could pack into
a short time some basic facts and opportunity for practice, possibly

women who, like me, find it difficult to integrate long-term study into their daily lives could, as I could, somehow set aside time during the summer (vacation from job or whatever) to single-mindedly commit themselves for just that period—and consequently have the reward of seeing a few fast results, at least enough to carry us psychologically through follow-up at home the rest of the year. It's easier to keep up a skill once you're trained in the rudiments of it and the awesome mystique of it has been penetrated.

This is a proposal, then, for (possibly regional) Women's Skill Summer Sessions. These would be six-week-long sessions, held away from home, in a "summer camp" atmosphere, on land donated or rented. Child care could be provided nearby or even on the premises, although the latter presents problems requiring continually divided attention for the mothers. Between thirty and sixty women could attend one "term" and there could be three such terms or sessions a summer. It would not be impossible to keep expenses down so that each woman would have to pay only about sixty dollars for the entire six weeks. Food preparation and cleaning tasks would be rotating and all would participate, in addition to teaching and studying with and from each other. The attached list (meant only as a draft) shows proposed required skills as well as optional ones. The required concept is included at all because (1) The list is based on an informal survey of what many feminists (myself included) seem to feel is necessary for us all to know, and (2) It is embarrassingly true that we all carry tendencies which would tempt us to learn only what interests us rather than what is most needed—by us and others.

All areas would be taught by women. These would be women with a serious professional knowledge of what they were communicating, though not a "professional" stake in status. There would be no half-information passed on sloppily to others (a temptation surrendered to frequently among the oppressed in our dual hunger to learn and to feel important). Those women who would be sharing their skills also would be present in other classes to learn from someone else. This would go a long way toward breaking down any resentment toward authority-teacher roles. Everyone also would be living together collectively, in dormitories or houses or whatever could be arranged to further emphasize equality.

The structure of the whole session would have to be based on some form of self- and collective discipline, since people would be there with a serious investment of time and energy, and those who were not pulling their share of the work or study or teaching would be hurting the chances of others. If the purpose of the plan were stated clearly enough in advance, however, I believe that those women who actually became involved would be in earnest about using the time effectively.

I am *not* proposing a joyless cramming nightmare. To learn, and especially to learn from other women, to feel yourself grow skilled and strong—that's a very real pleasure. There also would be time for rap sessions and political cross-fertilization, but these would not constitute the purpose for the sessions, so such time would be of necessity limited. This proposal is not for a vacation, a retreat, or a conference, after all. It is for women who can see themselves getting up at 5:00 or 6:00 A.M. and going through an uncushioney day of solid work which would leave relatively little energy for conversation at its close. The discussion can come before, after, or even throughout the session, but not, for once, at the expense of taking practical steps to learn how to survive, fight, and win.

The primary purpose of the Skill Sessions would be to train sisters who in turn could go back home and share those skills with other women, extending the capacity and knowledge of the entire feminist movement. There is a great need for the survival and service skills to be used as well as taught in every community of women, and to be further developed locally. This is one way of saving women's lives, meeting their/our needs, providing genuine alternatives, and building strength.

It certainly has occurred to me that six weeks is a very short time for such a learning process (see the list of required and optional classes). But then I remembered what may strike some sisters as a dangerous analogy, and so I ask that this analogy be recognized only as a very limited one. Basic training in the army has in certain periods (during wartime) taken only six weeks, during which time they can take a raw recruit, a potbellied young American male, and turn him into a professional killer. This of course is not our aim, nor would their fascistic teaching methods even remotely serve as models for us. But the time factor is undeniably interesting, and encouraging, since we wouldn't have to waste any of our precious moments learning rank, procedure, how to salute whom, and other such idiocies. In fact, the only similarity would be hard, serious work compacted into a short period. But ours would be wholly voluntary, and a step toward freedom.

WOMEN'S SKILL SUMMER SESSIONS
(Six Weeks Basic Training)

CODES: R = *Required*
O = *Optional*

R   Orientation
R   Firearms *(How to use and care for rifles and handguns)*
R   Self-Defense *(street-fighting combination of judo, karate, akhito, tae kwan do, etc.)*

R   Motor Vehicles *(How to drive, understand, and repair basics in cars and trucks)*

R   Basic Emergency Medical Techniques *(including emergency surgery basics)*

R   Basic Plumbing *(sinks, toilets, etc.)*

R   Basic Carpentry

R   Basic Electrical Skills *(How to wire lamps, appliances, etc.)*

O   Tactical Electronics *(bugging and de-bugging; how to wire "other things")*

O   Basics in Ham Radio Communications

O   Basic Tactical Chemistry *(odors, poisons and antidotes, etc.)*

O   Paraprofessional Abortion Techniques *(D and C, suction, saline, Louenbach, other)*

R   Basic Bivouac and Survival Techniques *(wooded areas/urban areas)*

O   Morse Code and Semaphore Signals

O   Basic Cryptology

O   Basics in Photography, Videotape and/or Filming

O   Basic Conversational Spanish

O   Basic Printing Skills *(using a press, layout, typesetting)*

TWO COMMON CRITICISMS
AND TWO ATTEMPTED REBUTTALS

I HAVE SPOKEN of the proposal to quite a few women, and the majority have reacted favorably and expressed excited interest in creating and attending such a session. Those who have opposed the idea have done so usually on one of two premises, which I would like to rebut here, if only to clarify what I *don't* mean by this proposal—and also to clear the path for more complicated criticisms which I hope will manifest themselves. Each criticism and reply follows.

1) "It sounds like an army camp. Discipline, getting up at dawn, studying and working all day. It's an authoritarian-sounding, cold, un-sisterly, non-Women's-Movement, real male trip."

I would venture in reply that discipline is not a male prerogative. There certainly have been male ways of using discipline as a sadistic means to grasp and hold power, to whip others into line, to create patterns of submission and dominance. But a sense of structure, form, or cooperation that doesn't trample over others out of (an equally oppressive) pretended spontaneity—in fact, form which reflects our own radical feminist content—that kind of form is necessary to any people who are serious about seizing power in order to become free, to free others, and ultimately, to destroy the notion of power itself. We women have been capable of discipline for millennia—about our children, about not forgetting to take the roast out of the oven, about remembering to get to the laundromat before it closes, *ad infinitum*. What about putting it to use for once in our own behalf, for our own survival and struggle? Yes, we must create new ways—collective, collaborative, egalitarian disciplines, but to fear the word "discipline" itself is tantamount to accepting for women conditions that we oppose: dependency and powerlessness.

2) "The idea sounds good, but why the preparation for violence? Doesn't that make violence an inevitability? What do you want—a women's army? We should concentrate on survival and service skills. Violence is a male trip."

My answer is that violence is no more a solely male capability than is rage or anger, and it may turn out to *be* a survival or service skill. Men have used their rage in a murderous manner against women for centuries. Does that mean that we now have no right to our own healthy, revolutionary rage against *them?* On the contrary, feminists have affirmed that rage in us as the first step toward freeing ourselves. We may or may not need to use violence in our revolution. I myself do not believe that men as a class will cede their vast power for the mere asking. The "normal," everyday violence of that class directed against women is staggering (rape, wife-beating, institutionalized violence such as birth-control and abortion statutes and legal discrimination, not to speak of the psychic violence done to females from the birth moment on). What then can we expect in reprisal to our demanding better treatment, equality, power, freedom? Further, I believe that the "violence" of the oppressed is inherently a form of extended self-defense —that is, a desperate response to the older violence of the oppressor. (This is not meant as an attempt to escape blame or responsibility, but merely as recognition of a fact. It is not a chicken-or-egg business of which came first; clearly oppression predates revolution. Without the former there would be no need for the latter.)

Yes, I have thought about a feminist army, more than once. And yes, I feel stronger and more committed and even happier with every skill I learn to further defend myself and my sisters. *Competence feels good.* But that is, in a sense, beside the point. One wants to learn how to swim even if one doesn't plan a career as a deep-sea diver. Only when you have access to the tools can you make a fair choice between which ones you will want to use at any given time. If, then, we find that we are ever forced into using "violent" means to survive or fight, it is then contingent on us to avoid that very same violence-for-its-own-sake attitude that men are into (including Leftist men). We must be sneakier, wittier, and more efficient—as our foremothers were. The witches, the gypsies, the Amazons, the Turkish harem rebels were into no "male trips" but freedom. We have a long and militant, if buried, herstory of our own. But *we must know what we are doing*—know as many options as we can learn. We can no longer limit ourselves through ignorance. We must be able to choose.

This, then, would be the reason for the Summer Skill Sessions. There are other times and places where we can share other tools for change: poetry, music, child care, dance, rapping, on and on. But we have neglected certain tools too long. These skills are *only* tools; they have proven murderous or at least exclusive options in the hands of men; they could be liberating in the hands of women. Not all—perhaps even not many, at first—will want to attend the sessions. Many of those who do attend may never pick up any weapon of force again. Instead, they may return to their communities to do paraprofessional abortion work, or teach other sisters auto mechanics, or even just be better able to cope with leaks, wiring, first aid, etc., in their own lives, instead of being dependent on men for help or instruction. Still others may use what they have learned in more explosive ways.

The sessions themselves, like this initial proposal, would have to be open to ongoing criticism and revision. No one can imagine what forms they will ultimately take, or what our People—Women—will do in making use of those forms. I trust the buried rage and wisdom of those people, and I believe that if we begin to provide the skills, to each other and to other women, together we will all find that we know how to use them.

TEACH EACH OTHER TO TEACH EACH OTHER TO TEACH EACH OTHER.

June 1970–June 1971

A COUNTRY WEEKEND:
THREE PROSE POEMS

Rat, while it had become a women's paper, had never become a feminist one. The ongoing and intense struggles within the *Rat* collective always came down to a Marxist analysis (which in practice meant Women Should Wait Until After the Revolution), *versus* a feminist analysis. During the summer of 1970 these differences reached a crisis point, and the sense of sisterhood was so depleted that we all decided to go on a "retreat" together in an attempt to recapture some solidarity. One woman knew of a friend's house in the country which would be available, and the entire collective, including children, went up there for almost a week. Those days and nights were one long consciousness-raising session, and the results were most encouraging. Regrettably, upon our return to the city and the pressures of deadlines (not to speak of the pressures from men and their politics), much of the good feeling melted away again. It would have required more than emotional solidarity; it would have required a political understanding of the real imperative of feminism, to have transformed *Rat*. That transformation, sadly, never occurred.

At the end of five days, most of the women returned home, but six of us remained behind for the weekend, to be joined by the men with whom we were each involved, for a brief (we thought) vacation. The weekend was to turn out otherwise, however, with more struggle and still more consciousness-raising.

1

Twelve women in a circle, dancing to a recording of sister Aretha's version of "Respect"—and my body is eleven others and our one voice and the power of my own blood makes me blind to this century and we are all suddenly old, older than all the myths.

We *are* the myths. We are the Amazons, the Furies, the witches. We have never not been here, this exact sliver of time, this precise place.

There is something utterly familiar about us.

We have been ourselves before.

2

L.'s STORY of her little black baby girl being murdered by the hospital, taken out of the incubator too early because the parents couldn't pay for an extra day, taken out on purpose, even though the doctors knew it would suffocate the child eventually.

And my own baby playing on the grass meanwhile, in the sunshine: white male, sunburned and sunblond, strong, healthy, giggling at the clover-chain garland one of my sisters wove for him.

Dear god who I would hate if I believed in, what have they done to us, that my white male blond baby's tiny hands already are stained with the delicate blood of his little black sister!

How have they managed to make the *air* a commodity so that his small breaths deprive some little black girl's lungs? Why was the only ointment available for his special infant skin infection manufactured by the same petroleum-chemical company that also produces Napalm Baby Lotion for other babies, of a different shaded skin?

How can we learn to avenge our unborn and undead children, our children, our children, as well as ourselves?

3

So THE MEN came up to the country after most of the collective had left. We were stunned by the contrast. Even the most well-meaning brothers who are struggling with their own sexism still carry the arrogance of power and "leadership" crap in their brains and guts. Collectivity is a concept to them, not a reality. And they fucked things up within fifteen minutes after setting foot in the house and we (the six women who had stayed on) had a long confrontation session with them and while it was exhilarating to feel each other's support and shared consciousness, it was still a drag to have to go through it all again. And I had a spill-over confrontation with my man, and we went for a walk to try to heal it but couldn't.

So I went up to bed and he stayed downstairs reading underground papers. And I lay under the eaves trying to fall asleep, thinking the thoughts I've thought a hundred times before, about sisters, about the men we love and hate and are committed to and oppressed by. And then I heard B. and her man in the next room, talking softly.

I knew that she'd been going through the same pain, groping toward the same consciousness, as I had, and I thought for a minute that they were crying together on the other side of that wall. It was a few minutes before I realized that they weren't crying; they were making love. And I went through lightning-fast, acid-like changes.

Envy. They had battled and struggled and now at least were fucking and here I was in bed alone and my man downstairs alone and the taste of struggle still bitter in our mouths.

Guilt. I was being too hard on my man. I was driving him into a corner, demanding too much, too fast; not being grateful enough, understanding enough, gradual enough. It was my own fault that I did not have what B. had in the next room.

Contempt. I was right—and B. was too "easy." It was she who wasn't really committed, really struggling. She who was ready to risk, for a moment of compromised closeness, her human freedom.

Fear. At my own readiness to be divided from that sister, from any sister—and fear at the specter of more permanent aloneness; fear at risking everything, anything, including the familiarity of my own oppression.

Desire. If he would only come upstairs and lie down beside me and it could be beautiful and tender and fiery and perfect and totally devoid of memories and roles and mechanics.

Despair. Because even if he were to appear at that very moment and we were to go through all the motions, it would not be beautiful and perfect, but rather a charade of what we both wished desperately it might be.

Relief. Horrifying relief, at realizing I was glad to be alone, glad not to have to go through that charade, not to have to settle for any-thing less than what I needed and desired and deserved. Relief at being able to turn over and go to sleep, unmolested, alone, and free in my bed.

Embarrassment. Omigod, what had I been doing, anyway, listen-ing in on people fucking? It just isn't done, by my mother's standards or even by our own hip, radical ones. Am I turning into some sort of a sickie? The certainty that I would (1) never be able to tell B. about the experience, let alone (2) share all those feelings in the context of the awkward situation with other sisters. Which I *have* done, a sign that I'm beginning to really trust that sisterhood.

And then, just as I dozed toward an exhausted sleep, one last-minute flash of something unexpected, sharp.

Anguish. Because my man and I had been out in a country meadow earlier that night, lying silent under a mandala of stars we never even glimpse in the city, breathing warm air heavy with the smell of earth and honeysuckle and wild roses, watching the summer moon tip the buttercups all silver and feeling the dew settle on our hair. And we had not spoken. Had not touched. Because his confusion and my pain grew between us in that meadow, and because I could no longer "make it right," reach over as I have done a thousand times before and say it didn't matter.

We don't get out into the country and lie in a night-summer meadow much—hardly ever. We live in a poisoned-air city and are justly paranoid and tight and tired and rushed and fighting the System and we may be dead soon. And it was my *right*, goddammit, to have had my moment in that meadow, just the way it could have been in some other world, society, culture, dream. Because I'm only here once and I'll die and never, never have that moment. Because I can't settle for anything less, any more. Because I may never be the free, laughing, brain-awake, sex-alive, whole woman I'm struggling to be, and I may never live with the true brother I'm struggling to love still—but unless I go further and further, all the way, and throw every risk to the winds in my commitment to that struggle, unless I settle less and less for nothing other than the total ecstasy of freedom, then I am dead. Not in a superficial way, like being killed, but in the more profound way: dead, like that part of myself I left behind in that redneck country farmer's summer meadow, where I lie on wet grass forever, not understanding, and waiting for a love that will not happen.

June 1970

A BRIEF ELEGY
FOR FOUR WOMEN

The details for the following article were taken from the *New York Times* and the *New York Post*. It was no small task for the "feminist caucus" at *Rat* to convince the rest of the collective that a short article on the massacre of some secretaries had a place in the paper. But the piece was printed, and seemed to change some minds both within the collective and among our readers.

The type of everyday atrocity mentioned in the "Elegy" still goes on, of course. Each hour women are brutalized, beaten, and terrorized—as well as raped and murdered—and the patriarchy still conveniently refuses to see such crimes as "political" (even as the lynching of blacks in the South and, yes, North was "political"). But now *women* view such acts with a new consciousness, and have begun to mobilize against them.

PATRICIA CHROMICK, *22 years old*
SANDRA L. PETERS, *24 years old*
MARY ANN REINSCHE, *27 years old*
LINDA D. WILLIS, *21 years old*

LAST WEEK, Joseph White, a twenty-five-year-old administrative analyst in the State Employment Insurance Offices in Albany, New York, killed four women with a pump-action shotgun.

He had taken a sick leave from his job and had come in to pick up his first paycheck, which was not ready for him. Becoming enraged at the bureaucratic foul-up, he went on a rampage against the women in the office, and finally shot himself.

It was not a case of indiscriminate murder. White was in fact discriminating enough to pass up all the men he saw in between his killings of women. When one male bureaucrat tried to question him, White ran past him—until he found another woman to kill.

White had been screwed by his employer. So his natural response was to take out his rage on the people he had power over—women, all of whom were themselves powerless to live a decent life or even die a meaningful death. They were all four workers in the secretarial pool.

No matter where they are on the status ladder, men can always feel better as long as they can oppress women. White was a man who himself was oppressed, as a worker and a victim of bureaucracy, but his hatred detoured the real enemy—the System and his employer-job-whole-life-misery—and exploded instead against the convenient lightning rods: women.

Every day newspapers carry stories of atrocities committed against women: murder, rape, beatings, mutilations. Such news is presented as being either titillating or irrelevant. To us it is intensely political.

Sexual crimes are political assassinations, and at the rising rate and ferocity with which they are being committed, they approach attempted genocide of a people on the basis of sex and gender.

Only one thing can protect us. Women must defend our lives and bodies and minds against male violence, by any means necessary. We must learn and practice self- and sister-defense on all levels: physical, mental, emotional. We must learn to understand weapons. We are doing this already, but not fast enough, hard enough, seriously enough. *Too many sisters who would be willing to die defending a radical brother would on the other hand find it difficult, if not impossible, even to relate to the daily suffering of any woman in a secretarial pool.*

Such a shameful attitude must stop. We can afford no more arrogant dismissals of secretaries, housewives, file clerks, nurses, etc. No more snobbish, vicious statements like "But she's so *straight*. But that's so *bourgeois*. But they're not *hip*. But that one reminds me of my *mother*."

One of the four sisters who was murdered in Albany lay dying in a room where she had lived a daily death, in the midst of gray typewriters and gray metal file cabinets and gray chrome desks. Littered around her were squares of white paper to be typed and then filed—some "unfortunately" ruined now, because they were stained with her blood. She kept whimpering, "Please, please somebody help me. Somebody help."

Remember The Albany Four, sisters. Never forget. . . .

October 1970

A DAY IN THE LIFE (OF A WOMAN)

Given *Rat's* emphasis on covering the melodramatic actions that seemed endemic to the Left (those ejaculatory tactics again), it was vital that at least now and then there be some articles in the paper representing the commonplace, hackle-raising, undramatic forms the oppression of women often takes. This piece, "A Day in the Life (of a Woman)," while hardly purporting to represent all women, was an attempt to insinuate those realities into the frenzied rhetoric about male-defined radical issues. The reference deploring "NOW-type women" stemmed from my leftover Leftism, which had me trapped into playing more-radical-than-thou games. I have since discovered that the overall membership of the National Organization for Women is, across the country, dedicated and admirable. If I still find myself in political disagreement with some of NOW's positions I have learned, at the peril of my own feminist consciousness, not to sneer stupidly at the entire organization. The reference deploring the Socialist Workers Party and its offshoot the Young Socialists Alliance, however, still stands. I confess that the women enmeshed therein evoke my pity for the utter irrelevance of all their hard work—and the men therein evoke my loathing, to this very day. I *have* changed, on the other hand, in that I no longer refer, as I do in this piece, to men I dislike as "bastards." Epithets such as "pusillanimous troglodyte," or even simply, "creep," seem more to the point. I have also changed in that I no longer try to hide the sex of my child, euphemistically referring to him as "it."

I'M A WHITE WOMAN in my late twenties, married, and with a small child just over a year old. I guess I've been a feminist for some time and also am struggling continually with the issues of class and race. Last week I had a "day in the life" of a woman, a day which certainly intensified the very contradictions we struggle with *every* day.

I had brought the baby to the opening of a new sort of "people's park" on the Lower East Side, where we live. The community had taken an old junk-filled lot and turned it into a playground and park. In the afternoon, it was great: free food was being cooked outdoors, steel bands were playing, women and children laughing and talking in Spanish and English.

The men arrived toward nightfall. Wham. Sexual overtones. *Machismo* everywhere. And I was called a racist for asking an older kid not to swing his honest-to-god pickaxe around in the sandbox near the toddlers—until a Puerto Rican sister (also a mother) came to the rescue and made the kid put the axe away—*and* made the adult male "organizer" who had screamed at me back down fast, himself. Whew. I got depressed.

But I was lucky enough to have a pleasant evening to look forward to: my husband would be taking care of the baby, and I was going to an Open House at the Women's Center. I decided to treat myself to the pure luxury of first having dinner out, alone, with a good book. What heaven.

I had forgotten that women do *not* dine out alone in New York on a Saturday night. But I was swiftly reminded, by being made to feel like a misfit, and/or a whore. Twice the waiter asked me when my dinner partner would join me (although he *was* gracious enough to permit me seating—two other restaurants, neither very fancy, had turned me away at the door for being unescorted). Twice I told him I was alone. By the time my food arrived, the joy of a quiet dinner by myself had deteriorated into despondency: I was obviously so awful no one wanted to share food with me. Then they turned the lights way down and lit candles for a romantic Saturday evening atmosphere—and I almost went blind trying to read my book. Enough, I thought. Off to my sisters at the Center; that will be a lift, at least.

I hadn't reckoned on entering in the middle of a confrontation between some NOW-type women and some Young Socialist Alliance–Socialist Workers Party types. Gawd. Only one thing could unite them: a shared disgust for those crazy feminists who seemed to hate men and mistrust hierarchical organizations. So much for the Women's Center. I split in the middle of a playwright's lecture on how painful it was to sell out to Broadway but how her life had been saved by the Socialist Workers Party. I hit the street and started to walk downtown.

One block away, I was stopped by two young women (neither could have been more than sixteen years old) who were both *very* high. One seemed drunk as well as stoned, and was positively reeling. They actually identified themselves as "groupies," and wanted to know if I knew how much it would cost to get into a nearby discotheque. I said I didn't know but told them that they could go up to the Women's

Center for free, where there would shortly be dancing and music as well as beer, soda, and coffee.

We were standing there rapping, and might all have returned to the Center, but for two bastards who cruised by in a convertible, came on to us, and managed to pick up the kids. One girl said to me, "We'll rip 'em off for admission to the disco," and shrugged sadly when I suggested that women are the ones who ultimately pay. The other girl was too far out of it to care. I couldn't stop them.

Alone again, I resumed my walk, trying, at least, to enjoy the night air. After being hassled three times in the next block (once quite menacingly), I decided I couldn't hack it, daren't wait for a bus, was too far from the uninvitingly deserted subway in any event—and I hailed a cab. Emergency-gloom-splurge.

Settled in. Safe at last.

But the driver had seen my Women's Liberation button. Oops. All the way home he proceeded to tell me how abortion was okay for them nigger and spic broads who breed so much, but no good for nice white girls like me. Soon I was shouting at him, then screaming for him to stop the cab and let me out. He blithely ignored my orders— and my basic consumer-rights. Finally, at the end of the ride, he told me that if we women really pushed "this liberation thing," men like him were going to start killing us, literally. "You talk about 'male violence'— you ain't seen nothin' yet. These rapes and beatings are going to soar up, baby. You can't tell me I'm not a king in my own home and get away with it." Besides, he informed me, he was a union man. Refraining from asking him whether his union had been organized for the express purpose of maiming women or whether that was a fringe benefit, I contented myself with sputtering that I was studying karate, as many other women were, and that we'd take a few of him and his friends with us if we had to go. I also didn't tip him. Which was less a gesture of courage than a cowardly bow to reality, since after paying the damned fare I had no more money.

Anyway, home. All I could do was run for the baby and clutch its warm good little body, waking it up of course, then crying over it and rocking it until it fell asleep again.

I know this must somehow be relevant to other women's struggles. All day long I had been properly, correctly, revolutionarily aware of the "contradictions": race *versus* feminism at the park; social rituals *versus* feminism at the restaurants; sexual economics (and *sub*culture social rituals) *versus* feminism with the two women on the street; and finally class *versus* feminism with the taxicab driver.

Being correctly aware didn't help—because the other people weren't. And how do we fight *for* ourselves without all the other oppressed assuming we are fighting *against* them? Or must we educate them and fend off blows at the same instant? What do we do with *our* pain, so busy feeling guilty about everyone else's? Are all those other issues golden apples flung in the path of Atalanta's race, to divert her?

We *must* find a way. Because, to be honest, this day, this evening "out on the town" was one of the *better* ones, in my experience.

How long, oh sisters, how long?

October 1970

PART FOUR

Radical
Feminism

PART IV:
INTRODUCTORY NOTE

January of 1971 saw the beginning of multiple processes of change so rapid, simultaneous, and many-dimensioned as I never could have conceived until I found myself living them.

There were the political realizations, chief among these the glimmering comprehension of radical feminism. So it wasn't merely a way of approaching socialist revolution; it wasn't, in fact, a wing or arm or toe of the Left—or Right—or any other male-defined, male-controlled group. It was something quite Else, something in itself, a whole new politics, an entirely different and astoundingly radical way of perceiving society, sentient matter, life itself, the universe. It was a philosophy. It was immense. It was also most decidedly a real, autonomous Movement, this feminism, with all the strengths that implied. And with all the evils, too—the familiar internecine squabbles.

This section of essays reflects many of the realizations of that period. We were developing our own political theory, exploring our own terms, as I do in "On Women As a Colonized People." We were beginning to articulate anger we had not even dared acknowledge before, to fight back, to make the connections—as in the article on rape and pornography. We were growing up—as individuals, feminists, as a movement in fact. True, we indulged ourselves, as perhaps every political group inevitably does, in attacking each other instead of our adversaries (see the piece on lesbianism and feminism, for example); it was safer and it felt deliciously self-righteous. But most of us were also seriously committed to a Feminist Movement which could transform our culture; and this meant study and respect for intelligence—as in the trends expressed in this section's piece on women's studies. We were spreading— ourselves, our consciousness—all over the globe; becoming a truly international movement, as the essay on the Three Marias demonstrates. And we were at the same time doing what no other political mass movement had dared: we were continuing to explore the personal—because for us this was political. We were reaching out to trust each other as women in new ways, which I try to express in "A New Fable of the Burning Time."

The early seventies will always seem "filmic" to me—like a montage of thought, emotion, action. In a sense, I could date my commitment to radical feminism from my attendance, in late spring of 1971, at the Radical Feminist Conference in Detroit, organized by the same women who had written the Fourth World Manifesto (see pages 118 and 131). It was an exciting weekend—and one in which I discovered that, even if a large room is crammed strictly with radical feminists (no Trotskyites, Weathervanes, or the like) there is still sufficient disagreement within the fold to boggle the mind: Is marriage "incorrect"? Is any relationship with a man impossible at this time in history? Possible, hell—is it worth it? What about children? What about male children? Is lesbianism (1) an alternative, (2) a political choice, (3) a personal proclivity; (4) a vanguard position, (5) an escapist trend, (6) none of the above, or (7) all of the above? What about our ageism and older women? How can white feminists concretely support the growing feminism among minority women? What forms of organization and structure are unsalvageably hierarchical and male—but which alternate structures are so anarchical they lead to chaos? What about leadership? Do we need it / can we find it / how do we use it / what in fact is it / who do we believe / do we believe anyone but ourselves / what about tactical crises and the need for experienced people / what about the follower mentality / how can we redefine responsibility and accountability?

Yet this was only the beginning. There continued to be pressures from within and without, from all sides—the women of the male Left and, on the other hand, those women active in the civil-rights front of feminism (who were sometimes termed reformists). We were in danger of repeating what had happened in the suffrage days, where there were also, so to speak, three parts to the movement: the reformists, who wanted to settle for the vote, thinking that that eventually would win freedom for women in all areas—they were feminist but not radical. There were the social crusaders, who did superb work in exposing the brutality in the asylums and hospitals and factories but who shrank from having women as their priority—they were radical but not feminist. And there were real radical feminists—like Elizabeth Cady Stanton—whose challenging thought was finally ignored, ground down in the friction between the other two groups. That friction and, ironically, its reverse, a kind of bonding of the two across radical feminism, goes on to this day and requires the vigilance of radical feminists. Perhaps the peculiar bonding occurs because the women's-rights-oriented feminists respond guiltily to the radical women's accusation of their being "privileged" and "reformist." They feel they must become radical, and that being radical must mean Marx. Somewhere along the way, radical feminism *gets missed. And it's a pity (and most irritating) to think of women sitting around in study groups reading Lenin and Mao for political direction when they might be reading Stanton, Anthony, Pankhurst, Mott, Willard, and Fuller (not to mention Eliot, Austen, Sand, Brontë, Rossetti, Barrett, and Stowe, etc. etc.!).*

There are few creatures more zealous than the convert. I, in 1971 a new refugee from male politics, seized the torch and lofted it high for my sisters still standing where I had lagged ten seconds earlier. And we learned from each other.

This was the year of that Radical Feminist Conference. It was also the year of the founding of Sisterhood is Powerful, Inc., or, as it came to be called informally throughout the Women's Movement, "The Sisterhood Fund," which I established to receive all the royalties from the anthology and "recycle" those monies into feminist projects. It was the first such feminist institution, and in the four years of its existence, it set a proud precedent. The year 1971 was also when I attempted initiating a Feminist Studies Program at an experimental college in Florida— an experience described in "The Proper Study of Womankind" on p. 189. Most of all, 1971 was my first year as a feminist "outside agitator."

This condition had been brought about by the appearance of Sisterhood is Powerful, *which had been published in the fall of 1970. Soon afterward I faced a pile of requests from women for me to lecture, organize, advise, and agitate around the country. I recalled with a sense of irony how desperate we had been both in WITCH and at Rat to reach "those women out there"—and now the book actually had done it. However much willful dullards might accuse literature of being hopelessly elitist, even plain old-fashioned by McLuhan's standards, those first books from the new feminist wave certainly did have their effect. (If this relevation aroused the temporarily imprisoned persona of myself as an artist, though, I dismissed the yearning—and the lesson.) The Movement needed money, the colleges were willing to pay it, groups needed benefit speakers. Women needed help, advice, support, and sometimes just classic outside agitation in the best Susan B. Anthony tradition. I packed my bag.*

The montage gets positively blurry at that point. The years 1971 through 1975 shift and merge and then freeze in a series of stills: The spontaneous circle-dance of hundreds of women in a gymnasium in Michigan after a speech; The physical eviction of a particularly obnoxious heckler from a seminar in New Mexico—all six-feet-football of him hefted daintily out the door by five petite women; Forty-degree-below-zero dawn in Saskatchewan, Canada—sitting up and talking with women all night (as usual) before my 7:00 A.M. plane on to another town, another college, another feminist community; The closing circle of jocks on the Pennsylvania campus, drunk and in a hazing mood, each one of about twenty men carrying lit torches, each one crying, "Burn the witch!"; The growing presence of minority women in audiences and at women's centers and feminist gatherings; The growing presence of working-class women, of housewives and community women; The face of the sixty-year-old woman who stood up at the rap session after a speech and, crying softly, said she realized that she'd been raped every night for thirty-five years; The bomb threats in auditoriums before or during lectures; The menacing letters and phone calls; The radical feminist nuns in a far-west state who were doing secret abortion referrals; The nascent rage everywhere budding into energy and organization and determination, the faces the voices the meetings and partings and indelible encounters where consciousness meets consciousness and the connections are electric . . .

In time I would come to grouse about the traveling, which indeed was exhausting, and which wreaked havoc with my personal life and my writing. Yet I know that I would trade those years for nothing—for I might have become an embittered organizer twitching at her laurels, had I not been forced out into the world where women were fighting to stay alive and love and live and give birth to themselves and each other.

That discovered vision—and the personal cost—rang out clearly from the poems in Monster, *my first collection, which was published in 1972. Kenneth's third book of poems,* Color Photos of the Atrocities,[1] *published the next spring, contained poems from his side of the struggle —the two volumes argued and quoted and reflected one another like facing pages of the same document: the record of a woman and a man who loved each other, trying to change their lives. Which we were in fact doing: both of us trying to survive by free-lance editing, me gone for approximately one week out of every month and whirling in harried political activity when I was in town—what with the sudden emergency actions like seizures of buildings, demonstrations, rallies—and the protracted projects as well, like the New York Women's Center, or the Women's Law Center. Our child, cared for at this point well more than half the time by his father, was growing golden and toddly and of necessity (in such a household) precociously and loudly verbal. Meanwhile, words like patriarchy, gynarchy, and matriarchy entered my vocabulary together with the realization of how vast the implications of feminism were. And this realization, strangely enough, seemed to bring me even closer to my beloved, exasperating, guilt-provoking family. I remember reading somewhere, in one of the mythographic analyses of the ancient gynocratic societies, that the model for all relationships was originally the love between mother and child—not as we know it today in its*

---

[1] *Color Photos of the Atrocities: Poems* by Kenneth Pitchford, Atlantic-Little, Brown and Company, Boston, 1973.

patriarchally corrupted form, where women sometimes misuse power over children because child-rearing is the one area in which we are allowed power at all. The model, rather, of that relationship in a pristine state of mutual love and sensuality, interdependence (the swollen breast needing the infant's relieving hunger); vigilance and sensitivity to unspoken need; true nurturance. I remember realizing with a shock that to live in such a culture would mean that I could feel about every single thing—male and female, child and adult, human and animal and plant— the way I feel about Blake. And I was suddenly cramped with the pain of an intense longing I knew was realer than all our rhetoric, for this represented the loss and the desire that lay beneath that loss.

This was authentic, and other women felt it, too. Of such stuff are made changes in world consciousness—sometimes called revolutions.

ON WOMEN AS A COLONIZED PEOPLE

This short essay was written at the request of sisters in the Women's Health Movement as the introduction to a self-health handbook, *Circle One*, published by Colorado women.[1] Although the piece was written in 1974, I had been making the analogy between women and other colonized peoples for a number of years in lectures, as it was borne in upon me that the oppression of women was more pervasive (and evasive) than I had thought. One could compare sexism with the issues of class and race and even caste, and still be left with an alienation more fundamental. Such comparisons are invidious in terms of human suffering—no scale dare weigh that, and no analysis, political or otherwise, had better "compare and contrast" that—although precisely such more-oppressed-than-thou approaches are attempted all the time by patriarchal politicians of the Left *and* Right. I was among those feminists who were, rather, searching for a means of *articulating* sexism—a handle, a lever, a way of translating into generally understood and accepted terms of political philosophy "what it was we people wanted." Hence the analogies—which were always dangerous, since the terms themselves had been coined and analyzed, the conditions themselves had been formed and at times even reformed *by men and by patriarchy*.

The search continues. We not only define and redefine but create entirely new terms to interpret—and change—our condition as women. When I first proposed that we view women as a colonized people, the suggestion was met with incredulity, even from other feminists. But what was "going too far" yesterday inevitably becomes something already assumed, even taken for granted, tomorrow. So has the theory of women's colonization been assimilated into feminist thought. And so we go on further, from there.

---

[1] *Circle One—A Woman's Beginning Guide to Self Health and Sexuality*, Campbell and Ziegler, eds., P.O. Box 7211, Colorado Springs, Colorado 80933.

As a radical feminist, I make an analogy between women and colonized peoples, a parallel which works well—inevitably, even—if one dares to examine it carefully, overcoming a sense of shock or our women's curse of guilt.

Frantz Fanon and Albert Memmi, as sexist as other men but considerable authorities on the process of colonization and its effects, wrote of certain basic characteristics by which that process could always be identified. Primary among these were the following: The oppressed are robbed of their culture, history, pride, and roots—all most concretely expressed in the conquest of their *land* itself. They are forced (by a system of punishment and reward) to adopt the oppressor's standards, values, and identification. In due course, they become alienated from their own values, their own land—which is of course being mined by the oppressor for its natural resources. They are euphemistically permitted (forced) to work the land, but since they do not benefit from or have power over what it produces, they come to feel oppressed by *it*. Thus, the alienation from their own territory serves to mystify that territory, and the enforced identification with their colonizing masters provokes eventual contempt both for themselves and their land. It follows, of course, that the first goal of a colonized people is to *reclaim their own land*.

Women are a colonized people. Our history, values, and *cross-cultural culture* have been taken from us—a gynocidal attempt manifest most arrestingly in the patriarchy's seizure of our basic and precious "land": our own bodies.

Our bodies have been taken from us, mined for their natural resources (sex and children), and deliberately mystified. Five thousand years of Judeo-Christian tradition, virulent in its misogyny, have helped enforce the attitude that women are "unclean." Androcentric medical science, like other professional industries in the service of the patriarchal colonizer, has researched better and more efficient means of *mining* our natural resources, with (literally) bloody little concern for the true health, comfort, nurturance, or even survival of those resources.[2] This should hardly surprise us; our ignorance about our own primary terrain—our bodies—is in the self-interest of the patriarchy.

We must begin, as women, to reclaim our land, and the most concrete place to begin is with our own flesh. Self-and-sister-education is a first step, since all that fostered ignorance and self-contempt dis-

---

[2] Adrienne Rich has assembled chilling documentation about this subject, with particular emphasis on medical industrialization of childbirth, in her important work *Of Woman Born, Motherhood as Experience and Institution*, Norton, New York, 1976.

solve before the intellectual and emotional knowledge that our women's bodies are constructed with great beauty, craft, cleanliness, yes, holiness. Identification with the colonizer's standards melts before the revelations dawning on a woman who clasps a speculum in one hand and a mirror in the other. She is demystifying her own body for herself, and she will never again be quite so alienated from it.

From education we gain higher expectations, and from there we move through anger and into the will for self-determination, to seizing power over our own lives, to reclaiming the products of our labor (our own sexual definition, and our own children), and, ultimately, to transforming the quality of life itself in society, as a whole—into something new, compassionate, and truly sane.

This is why, as radical feminists, we believe that the Women's Revolution is potentially the most sensible hope for change in history. And this is why the speculum may well be mightier than the sword.

Spring 1974

THEORY AND PRACTICE: PORNOGRAPHY AND RAPE

The following article is based on what to my horror got termed in hard-boiled organizer's jargon "The Rape Rap." I must have communicated some version of it hundreds of times, with a ripening anger as women came forward with their own experiences of rape and I realized how far-reaching and quintessentially patriarchal the crime was. There was a time when rape and pornography were embarrassing issues even in the Women's Movement: such things were deplorable, to be sure, but they had to be deplored with a sophisticated snicker—not with outspoken fury. Today, there are Rape Crisis Centers in major cities all over the nation, and feminist Rape Prevention Brigades. Many metropolitan police departments have special anti-rape squads run by women officers and new rape-reporting procedures devised by women; and self-defense classes for women are no longer seen as passing strange. When *Against Our Will*, Susan Brownmiller's comprehensive book on the subject from a feminist perspective, was published, it immediately became a best-seller, which it well deserved, and which also indicated that the general public's awareness of rape as a political issue has been greatly heightened. Feminist sorties against the attendant issue—pornography—are still somewhat more awkwardly conducted, but women are every day becoming less concerned with being graceful and more bent on being free.

THERE IS PERHAPS no subject relevant to women so deliberately distorted as that of rape. This is because rape is the perfected act of male sexuality in a patriarchal culture—it is the ultimate metaphor for domination, violence, subjugation, and possession.[1]

But the most insidious aspect of rape is the psychological fiction that accompanies it—with which all women are besieged until, for survival's sake, we even pretend to believe that what we *know* is a lie. The fiction has many versions. We can look at a few representative examples.

There is the Pity the Poor Rapist approach. This version tells us that we must be sorry for our attacker. He is sick, he cannot help himself, he needs help.

He decidely does need help (if he can be apprehended), but his victim needs it more—and first. She is not even supposed to defend herself, for fear of being unwomanly. I find it educative that a woman who, for instance, notices her child being molested by a dirty old (or young) man on the playground, and who shampoos the man with a brick—she is considered a proper mother, "the tigress defending her cubs." Yet should the same man molest *her*, she ought to, in society's view, welcome him and admit that she relishes being pawed, or if she must, plead winningly with him to stop. It is acceptable to defend one's child but not oneself because it is considered the epitome of selfishness for the female to place her own concerns first. We are supposed to wipe the noses of all humanity before we dare think about ourselves. Well, we must learn to mother those *selves*, and defend them at least as valiantly as we do our children.

The Spontaneity Lie is an offshoot of Pity the Poor Rapist. It informs us that he was just an average guy walking along the street (the lamb), who was positively seized with the urge to attack a woman. Sudden lust. In combating the spontaneity approach, one should remember that more than half of all rapes occur in breaking-and-entering situations—which do require, one would think, a modicum of premeditation.

There is always the basic Every Woman Loves a Rapist / All Women Want to Be Raped / Good Girls Never Get Raped / It's Always the Woman's Fault cliché. This is frequently carried to ludicrous extremes. Thus, if she wears slacks, that's obviously meant as a challenge; if a skirt, it's an incitement. If she glowers as she strides down the street it's meant as an attention-getter; if she looks pleasant it's a come-on. *Et cetera, ad nauseam, ad infinitum.* And besides, what was she doing out walking all alone by herself anyway at eleven o'clock in broad daylight? Doesn't she know her place?

---

[1] This does *not* mean that men in another cultural context would necessarily be the same, or that all men have acceded to the male sexual standards in this culture. Biological-determination theories will remain treacherous until we have enough feminist scientists to right the current imbalance and bias, and to create genuinely value-free research.

Knowing our place is the message of rape—as it was for blacks the message of lynchings. Neither is an act of spontaneity or sexuality—they are both acts of political terrorism, designed consciously *and* unconsciously to keep an entire people in its place by continual reminders. For that matter, the attitudes of racism and sexism are twined together in the knot of rape in such a way as to constitute *the* symbolic expression of the worst in our culture.[2] These "reminders" are perpetrated on victims selected sometimes at random, sometimes with particular reason. So we have the senseless rape murders of children and of seventy-year-old women—whom *no* one can salaciously claim were enticing the rapist— and we also have the deliberate "lesson-rapes" that feminist students have been prey to on their campuses for the past four years—acts based on the theory that all these frustrated feminists need is a good rape to show 'em the light.

Thus the woman is rarely unknown to her attacker, nor need the rapist be a stranger to his victim—although goddess help her deal with the more-than-usual scorn of the police if she reports rape by a former jealous boyfriend, or an ex-husband, or her faculty advisor or boss or psychiatrist. Many policemen already delight in asking the victim sadistic and illegal questions such as, Did you enjoy it? Consequently, any admission on her part, whether elicited or volunteered, that the rapist was actually an acquaintance seems to invite open season on *her* morals.

But radical feminists see the issue of rape as even more pervasive than these examples. For instance, I would define rape not only as the violation taking place in the dark alley or after breaking into and entering a woman's home. *I claim that rape exists any time sexual intercourse occurs when it has not been initiated by the woman, out of her own genuine affection and desire.* This last qualifier is important, because we are familiar with the cigarette commercial of the "Liberated Woman," she who is the nonexistent product of the so-called sexual revolution: a Madison Avenue–spawned male fantasy of what the liberated woman should be—a glamorous lady slavering with lust for his paunchy body. We also know that many women, in responding to this new pressure to be "liberated initiators" have done so *not* out of their own desire but for the same old reasons—fear of losing the guy, fear of being a prude, fear of hurting his fragile feelings, *fear.* So it is vital to emphasize that when we say she must be the initiator (in *tone* if not in actuality) we mean because *she* wants to be. Anything short of that is, in a radical feminist definition, rape. Because *the pressure is there* and it need not be a knife-blade against the throat; it's in his body language,

---

2 Susan Brownmiller has since demonstrated this point in depth, with courage and clarity, in her book *Against Our Will: Men, Women and Rape,* Simon & Schuster, New York, 1975.

his threat of sulking, his clenched or trembling hands, his self-deprecating humor or angry put-down or silent self-pity at being rejected. How many millions of times have women had sex "willingly" with men they didn't want to have sex with? Even men they loved? How many times have women wished just to sleep instead or read or watch the Late Show? It must be clear that, under this definition, most of the decently married bedrooms across America are settings for nightly rape.

This normal, corn-fed kind of rape is less shocking if it can be realized and admitted that the act of rape is merely the expression of the standard, "healthy," even encouraged male fantasy in patriarchal culture—that of aggressive sex. And the articulation of that fantasy into a billion-dollar industry is pornography.

Civil libertarians recoil from linking the issues of rape and pornography, dredging out their yellowing statistics from the Scandinavian countries which appear to show that acts of rape decline where pornography is more easily procured. This actually ought to prove the connection. I am not suggesting that censorship should rule the day here—I abhor censorship in any form (although there was a time when I felt it was a justifiable means to an end—which is always the devil's argument behind thought control, isn't it?). I'm aware, too, that a phallocentric culture is more likely to begin its censorship purges with books on pelvic self-examination for women or books containing lyrical paeans to lesbianism than with *See Him Tear and Kill Her* or similar Spillanesque titles. Nor do I place much trust in a male-run judiciary, and I am less than reassured by the character of those who would pretend to judge what is fit for the public to read or view. On the contrary, I feel that censorship often boils down to some male judges sitting up on their benches, getting to read a lot of dirty books with one hand. This hardly appears to me to be the solution. Some feminists have suggested that a Cabinet-level woman in charge of Women's Affairs (in itself a controversial idea) might take pornography regulation in her portfolio. Others hearken back to the idea of community control. Both approaches give me unease, the first because of the unlikeliness that a Cabinet-level woman appointee these days would have genuine feminist consciousness, or, if she did, have the power and autonomy from the administration to act upon it; the second because communities can be as ignorant and totalitarian in censorship as individual tyrants. A lot of education would have to precede community-controlled regulation to win that proposal my paranoid support. Certainly this is one problem to which simple solutions are just nonexistent, rhetoric to the contrary.

But women seem to be moving on the issue with a different strategy, one that circumvents censorship and instead is aimed at hurting the purveyors themselves, at making the business less lucrative by making the clients less comfortable. In one Southern town, women planned their action with considerable wit; they took up positions on their local porn strip and politely photographed each man as he entered or left the bookstores and movie houses. They used a very obvious camera—the large, newspaper-photographer type—sometimes chasing the man for a block as he fled in chagrin. One group of women who used this tactic deliberately worked with cameras that had no film—scaring and embarrassing the men was their aim. Another group, however, did use film, and developed the shots. They then made up Wanted Posters of the men which they plastered all over town—to the acute humiliation of the porn-purchasers, some of whom turned out to be influential and upstanding citizens of the community. In Seattle, women's anti-pornography squads have stink-bombed smut bookstores—and the local papers were filled with approving letters to the editors. In New York, three porn movie houses have been fire-bombed.

The massive porn industry grinds on, of course. In a replay of the liberated-woman shill, we are now being sold so-called female-oriented pornography, as if our sexuality were as imitative of patriarchal man's as *Playgirl* is of *Playboy*. It must be frustrating to the pushers of such tacky trash to realize that for most women *Wuthering Heights* is still a *real* turn-on, or that there are quite a few of us who remained loyal to Ashley Wilkes (especially as portrayed by Leslie Howard) and never were fooled by that gross Rhett Butler. Yet pornography today is becoming chic—serious movie houses which usually run art films are now cashing in on so-called art-porn. The Mick Jagger/sadism fad, the popularity of transvestite entertainers, and the resurgence of "Camp" all seem to me part of an unmistakable backlash against what feminists have been demanding. It is no coincidence that FBI statistics indicate the incidence of rape *increased 93 percent* in the 1960's. When people refuse to stay in their place, the message must be repeated in a louder tone.[3]

And what is this doing to us? We are somewhat educated now as to the effects of rape on women, but we know much less about the effects of pornography. Some obvious trends can be noted: the market

---

[3] The *New York Post* of October 1, 1975, carried a story about a nationwide investigation into "snuff films" or "slashers"—pornographic movies which culminate in the actual murder and dismemberment of the actress. These movies, shot for the most part in South America, appear to be circulating, according to the *Post* story, on the "pornography-connoisseur circuit" where the "select clientele" can afford fifteen hundred dollars for a collection of eight reels. Four months after the *Post* story, a porn movie called *Snuff* opened at a first-run movie theater on New York's Broadway. Advertised as "the bloodiest thing ever filmed" *this* print was priced to make it available to Everyman. As usual, the message is clear through the medium.

for go-go girls, nude models, and pornofilm "actresses," which in turn affects women's employment (why be a secretary when you can make more money taking off your clothes?); the overlapping boundaries of the porn and prostitution industries; the erosion of the virgin/whore stereotypes to a new "all women are really whores" attitude, thus erasing the last vestige of (even corrupted) respect for women; the promotion of infidelity and betrayal as a swinging alternative to committed relationships. But how to chart the pressure sensed by women from their boyfriends or husbands to perform sexually in ever more objectified and objectifying fashion as urged by porn movies and magazines? How to connect the rise of articles in journals aimed at educated, liberal audiences—articles extolling the virtues of anal intercourse, "fist-fucking," and other "kinky freedoms"?[4]

But how far-reaching is the effect, how individual, how universal? Individual in terms of the specific humiliation felt by the woman whose husband hides *Penthouse* or some harder-core version of it in the bathroom and then forces himself on her at night—or on other women when she fends him off—and then blames her for her frigidity and his inconstancy? Individual and universal enough to explain the recent horrifying rise in the rate of marital violence? [See Del Martin's definitive book *Battered Wives*, Glide Publications, San Francisco, 1976.] Universal enough to have influenced all of twentieth-century theology? Yet this has happened, through the work of that intellectual giant, the Christian theologian Paul Tillich—he who is revealed to us with such compassionate but uncompromising honesty by his widow in her brilliant, controversial book *From Time to Time* (Stein and Day, New York, 1973). After his death, Hannah Tillich tells us, she "unlocked the drawers. All the girls' photos fell out, letters and poems, passionate appeal and disgust." There was the pornographic letter hidden under his blotter; the knowledge of his favorite fantasy of naked women, crucified, being whipped; the discovery of all the affairs, the mistresses, the sexual secretaries, the one-night stands, the abuse of the worshipful female students who had sat at his feet, his "houris . . . tinkling their chains." She writes: "I was tempted to place between the sacred pages of his highly esteemed lifework these obscene signs of the real life that he had transformed into the gold of abstraction—King Midas of the spirit." Instead, Hannah Tillich dared write a book about herself, alchemizing her own integrity out of "the piece of bleeding, tortured womanhood" she says she had become.

So we can admit that pornography is sexist propaganda, no more

---

[4] Surely the currently (1976) popular Punk Image of the half-gangster, half-fifties-high-school-dropout male is related to these themes, an image described in the *Village Voice* as bringing back "masculine chic."

and no less. (There is no comparison here with genuine erotic art—such as *The Tale of Genji* by Lady Shikibu Murasaki, 978–c. 1031 A.D., the great Japanese novelist of the Heian period.)

Pornography is the theory, and rape the practice. And what a practice. The violation of an individual woman is *the* metaphor for man's forcing himself on whole nations (rape as the crux of war), on nonhuman creatures (rape as the lust behind hunting and related carnage), and on the planet itself (reflected even in our language— carving up "virgin territory," with strip mining often referred to as a "rape of the land"). Elaine Morgan, in her book *The Descent of Woman* (Stein and Day, New York, 1972), posits that rape was the initial crime, not murder, as the Bible would have it. She builds an interesting scientific argument for her theory. In *The Mothers* (1927; Grosset and Dunlap Universal Library Edition, 1963), Robert Briffault puts forward much the same hypothesis for an evolutionary "fall" from the comparable grace of the animal realm; his evidence is anthropological and mytho-historic. In more than one book, Claude Lévi-Strauss has pursued his complex theory of how men use women as the verbs by which they communicate with one another (they themselves are the nouns, of course), rape being the means for communicating defeat to the men of a conquered tribe, so overpowered that they cannot even defend "their" women from the victors. That theory, too, seems relevant here. The woman may serve as a vehicle for the rapist expressing his rage against a world which gives him pain—because he is poor, or oppressed, or mad, or simply human. Then what of *her*? We have waded in the swamp of compassion for him long enough. It is past time we stopped him.

The conflict is escalating now, because we won't cast our glances down any more to avoid seeing the degrading signs and marquees. We won't shuffle past the vulgarity of the sidewalk verbal hassler, who is *not* harmless but who is broadcasting the rapist's theory and who is backed up by *the threat of capacity to carry out the practice* itself. We will no longer be guilty about being victims of ghastly violations on our spirits and bodies merely because we are female. Whatever its age and origin, the propaganda and act which transform that most intimate, vulnerable, and tender of physical exchanges into one of conquest and humiliation is surely the worst example patriarchy has to offer women of the way it truly regards us.

1974

LESBIANISM AND FEMINISM: SYNONYMS OR CONTRADICTIONS?

This essay, as the opening passages make clear, was written as a speech in a departure from my usual practice of speaking extemporaneously or from notes. It was delivered as the keynote address at the West Coast Lesbian Feminist Conference in Los Angeles in 1973. The division in the Feminist Movement between lesbian women on the one hand and heterosexual or bisexual women on the other had been growing and intensifying for some time, and had reached a peak that year. I knew there was really only one honorable place to engage that issue, to speak the truths I felt needed utterance. It would *not* be in the overground media; it had to be at that very conference. I admit, though, that the thought of expressing such intricate yet severe ideas aloud in an atmosphere which contained the crowds, infights, and festivities of a political convention combined with a tangle of correct lines as might have befitted a shag rug—this did alarm me somewhat.

It was everything I had hoped for—and feared. Fifteen hundred women convening on the campus of UCLA, mostly white, mostly young, mostly furious, and in a celebratory mood. They came from as far away as Florida, Massachusetts, Canada, and even France because, although the conference was strictly speaking a regional event, word had got round that it was to be in actuality The Big One. This meant that everyone with a political line to put forward, a feminist project, magazine, pendant, or sweatshirt to sell, *had* to be there. Also anyone who was dying to see a long-lost lover, friend, relative, rival, or political enemy was revving up for the dramatic moment. Caucuses caucused all over Los Angeles, thinking up bad names to call other caucuses. Hip, garish, old L.A. itself even was a bit rocked—and women walking arm in arm were hassled and threatened more than usual. A mysterious murder with religious overtones (a cross carved on the body) had occurred in the L.A.

homosexual community two days before the conference and fanatics called "Jesus freaks" were leafleting everywhere against the "Sodomite Invasion." The conference organizers apparently had not slept for days and were speeding so fast on the requisite pills that they positively glowed from behind sunken eyepits. Finding accommodations, parking space, child care, workshop and entertainment and caucusing and plenary areas, and scheduling and rescheduling events over three days for almost two thousand militant women obviously had them so proud and so bone-tired that body and spirit would barely hold together until Monday evening.

Friday night was reserved for arrival and registration, with some get-acquainted entertainment by lesbian-feminist performers. (Women musicians and singers had been arriving all day in gasping VW panel trucks gravid with amps.) Yet all hell broke loose that very first night, caused by the gate-crashing presence of a male transvestite who insisted that he was (1) an invited participant, (2) really a woman, and (3) at heart a lesbian. (It is, one must grant, an ingenious new male approach for trying to seduce women.) The conference promptly split—over this man. More than half the women there Friday evening demanded he be forced to leave an all-woman conference; others, into the "brotherhood of Camp"—whatever that meant—defended him as their "sister." Some women left the conference for good, and returned to their home states in disgust. The situation was exacerbated when he insisted on performing during the entertainment. He apparently wished to embark on a nightclub career and thought this was a fine place to begin, what with both controversy and press at hand. But the gen-yoo-ine-real-women-lesbian entertainers present were not amused when they were asked to cede their place on the program to this man in drag. By the time I arrived, this was *the* issue of the conference—the one around which all hostilities and divisions magnetized. It was incredible that so many strong, angry women should be divided by one smug male in granny glasses and an earth-mother gown (he was easily identifiable, at least—he was the only person there wearing a skirt).

I sat up half the night revising my speech so as to include the issue, trying to relate it to the points I was already endeavoring to raise, attempting to show how male "style" could be a destroyer from within.

The next day was unforgettable. All that power and rage vibrating in surroundings of Frisbee-throwing sleepy students on their orange-grove-tacky campus of UCLA. There was no auditorium available big enough to seat such a crowd, so the keynote address had been moved outdoors, with the podium positioned halfway up a long flight of broad steps, facing a lawn where people could sit and listen. When I saw this, my heart sank. I remember exchanging glances with Margaret Sloan; both she and I knew the tactical disadvantages, which ranged from mere discomfort and annoyance (planes roaring overhead, sirens yowling on nearby streets) to more serious trouble (there was now no way of restricting the audience to women—men could wander on and off the quad as they pleased, to chant, heckle, threaten, or aim whatever other disturbances they chose at the speaker *and* the audience). In addition, the scene was surrounded by several low buildings on whose roofs men were already gathering—in groups, yet. The police were nowhere to be seen (they were less than welcome), but neither were there any other formal security arrangements at the conference, although about fifteen good women and true voluntarily positioned themselves near the podium, and Margaret stood close, putting on her mean-militant scowl for the occasion. I recall feeling strangely unreal, as if the whole scene were a dream, or a play—the action already "wound up tight like a spring," needing only to uncoil into tragedy.

We began. I can't remember how far into the speech I had got, although others have told me it was about halfway through—when it happened. Intent on the drama unfolding before me in the audience's concentration on my controversial words, I hardly noticed when some women squatting on the steps right in front of the podium leaped to their feet, looking not at me but behind me. Then everything was a blur of movement and people shouting and I remember whirling around, except it seemed as if my body spun in slow motion. And I saw him. He was standing at the top of the steps, a tall, exceedingly thin young man with a beard and long dark hair, wearing the soiled white robes of a Jesus freak. In one hand he carried a sign dooming the women before him to eternal hell, and in the other, the sun catching glints of it as it flashed in and out of the folds of his gown, the knife.

Slowly, oh how slowly everyone moved, as if through stroboscopic light. He danced toward me so slowly, although his skirt flew backwards with the speed of his rush down the steps. *The Angel of Death*, I thought, my own gaze locked onto his demented eyes filled with woman-hatred and woman-fear.

What have I done to you, my son, that you should hate me so?

You have given me life. You made me live and I cannot bear it.

Is life so terrible then, my son, my son?

It is terrible because somewhere I have lost you and lost the way. You gave me life. Your fault, your fault.

I stood motionless for an eternity while he moved toward

me, his disgust of me and of the women on the lawn spilling tears down that gaunt face.

He was only three steps away, they said, when they stopped him. Women. Women moving up the steps from all sides, convening on that tall frame like the Bacchae on Pentheus. I heard later that Kate Millett probably saved his life, throwing the cloak of her pacifism over the scene long enough for him to escape with only two or three Erinnyes in pursuit. Somehow, I remember asking people not to panic but to return to their places. Somehow, everyone did. Somehow, the keynote speech was continued, and finished.

The rest of the day piled jolt upon jolt into what I could only term an emotional overload. There were women, that day and the next, who refused to leave my side. There were women I'd never met or spoken with or seen before who came up out of nowhere and thrust armloads of flowers at me; one gave me a little silver ring, one a sketch she had done. There were other women who threatened to beat me up—for not having championed their transvestite "sister," I gathered, or for having refused to urge lesbian feminists to seek salvation in the Young Socialists Alliance. There were tidal waves of intense love and equally intense hatred, neither of which was really meant for *me* but which was aimed, instead, at the woman who had ventured certain political thoughts against a current tide—and (most of all) who had almost died before their eyes.

Well. We know the mystique of martyrdom. There were those who attacked or defended the content of the address for no political reason but for solely emotional ones. I couldn't decide which was worse—being detested or adored. I did know that being understood was preferable to both.

I also knew, every moment of that weekend and for the necessary "recuperation" days which followed, that without the fortuitous revelation previous to my flight to L.A., I could not have survived. For it was the morning of that flight that the Rochester, N.Y., women had taken me to visit Susan B. Anthony's house, and it was on that plane I had written to Blake the letter which begins on page 55 of this book.

V ERY DEAR SISTERS:

It seems important to begin by affirming who, how, and why, we are. We all know the male mass media stereotype of the Women's Movement: "If you've seen one Women's Libber, you've seen 'em all— they each have two heads, a pair of horns, and are fire-spouting, man-hating, neurotic, crazy, frigid, castrating-bitch, aggressive, lesbian, broom-riding witches." So I want to start by saying that this shocking stereotype is absolutely *true*. The days of women politely asking for a crumb of human dignity are over. Most men say, "But you've become so *hostile*," to which one good retort is a quote from a nineteenth-century feminist who said, "First men put us in chains, and then, when we writhe in agony, they deplore our not behaving prettily."[1] Well, enough of that. We *are* the women that men have warned us about.

That settled, I want to talk about a number of difficult and dangerous themes relating to what others have variously called "The Lesbian-Straight Split," "Lesbian Separatism from Straight Women," and even "The Lesbian-Feminist Split." This is the first speech, talk, what-have-you, that I have ever written down and then *read*—and it may be the last. I have done so because the content can so easily be misunderstood or willfully distorted, because misquoting is a common occurrence, because the risks I will take today are too vital for me to chance such misrepresentation.

Before I go any further, I feel it is also necessary to deal with who, how, and why *I* am here. As far back as a month ago, I began hearing a few rumbles of criticism about my "keynoting" this conference—all from predictable people, and none, of course, expressed directly to my face. "Is she or isn't she?" was their main thrust. "Know anyone who's been to bed with her lately? Well, if we can't *prove* she's a lesbian, then what right has she to address a lesbian-feminist conference?" Now, I am hardly devastated by such charges, having been straight-baited before. So. It is credential time once again.

I am a woman. I am a feminist, a radical feminist, yea, a militant feminist. I am a witch. I identify as a lesbian because I love the People of Women and certain individual women with my life's blood. Yes, I live with a man—as does my sister Kate Millett. Yes, I am a mother— as is my sister Del Martin. The man is a faggot-effeminist,[2] and we are together the biological as well as the nurturant parents of our child. This confuses a lot of people—it not infrequently confuses us. But there it is. Most of all, "I am a monster—and I am proud."[3]

Now all of the above credentials qualify me, I feel, to speak from

---

[1] Actually, the quote is from Olive Chancellor, a nineteenth-century feminist *character* in *The Bostonians*, Henry James' superb novel on the fight for women's suffrage. I was still a closet Jamesian at this point, and too cowardly to acknowledge (particularly before such an audience) that this pithily perfect riposte came from the brain of a male, even if he was one fortunate enough to have been Alice James' brother, wise enough to have comprehended the female condition, and genius enough to have conveyed it exquisitely in book after book wherein live some of the greatest female characters in all of fiction.

[2] A self-descriptive term evolved by those radical homosexual men who, after helping to found the Gay Liberation Front, broke with it because of its oppression of women and effeminate men. See footnote 9, below; see also, footnote on p. 235.

[3] From the title poem in *Monster*.

concrete experience on: Feminism, Lesbianism, Motherhood, "Gay Male Movements" *versus* Faggot-Effeminist consciousness about women, Tactics for the Women's Revolution, and a Vision of the Female Cosmos. I am an expert with the scars to prove it, having been, in my time, not only straight-baited, but also dyke-baited, red-baited, violence-baited, mother-baited, and artist-baited. As you can see, the above credentials further qualify me for being an excellent target, available not only to the male rulers but also to any women just dying to practice—even on a sister.

But, finally, to the subject. In order to talk intelligently about the so-called "Split," it is necessary to recap history a little. In the early days of the current Women's Movement, many of us were a bit schizoid. The very first consciousness-raising session I ever went to, for example, gave me the warning. We were talking about sexuality, and I described myself as a bisexual (this was even before the birth of the first Gay Liberation Front, and long before bisexual became a naughty or cop-out word—besides, it did seem an accurate way of describing my situation). Every woman in the room moved, almost imperceptibly, an inch or so away from me. Wow, I thought. It was not the last time I was to have such an articulate reaction.

Later, with the creation of GLF, a few of us Jewish-mother types spent a lot of time running back and forth between the two movements, telling the straight women that the lesbians weren't ogres and telling the lesbians that the straight women weren't creeps. Simultaneously, the intense misogyny coming against lesbians from gay men drove many women out of the "gay movement" and into the Women's Movement. There was a brief and glorious sisterhood-glazed honeymoon period among all women in our Movement. Then, those contradictions began. For example, a personal one: I had announced my lesbian identification in the *New York Times* (which is a fairly public place, after all) in 1968, before the first GLF had been founded. Then, in 1970, one group of Radicalesbians in New York said to me, "Don't you dare call yourself a lesbian—you live with a man and you have a child." Now, while I might (defensively) argue the low-consciousness logic of this, since statistically most lesbians are married to men and have children, I had nonetheless learned one important thing from all my previous years in the Left: *guilt.* So all my knee-jerk reflexes went into action, and I obeyed. Six months later, another group of Radicalesbians confronted me. "We notice you've stopped calling yourself a lesbian," they said. "What's the matter—you gone back in the closet? You afraid?" Meanwhile, the monosexual straight women were still inching away from my presence. Wow, I thought, repeatedly.

The lines began to be drawn, thick, heavy. Friedan trained her cannon on "the Lesbian Menace." (In a show of consistent terror and hatred of lesbians, and indeed of women, one might say, she only recently announced last March [1973] in the *New York Times* that the lesbians and radical feminists in the Movement were CIA infiltrators. We met her attack with a firm *political* counter-attack in the press, never descending to a level of personal vilification or giving the media the cat-fight which they were trying to foment.) In 1970, backlash began, starting in NOW[4] and infecting radical feminist groups as well. The bigotry was intense and wore many faces: outright hatred of and revulsion at lesbian women; "experimentation"—using a lesbian for an interesting experiment and then dumping her afterward; curiosity about the freaks; dismissal of another woman's particular pain if it did not fall within the "common" experience, and many other examples.

Meanwhile, lesbians, reeling from the hatred expressed by the gay male movement and the fear expressed by the Women's Liberation Movement, began to organize separately. Of course, a great many lesbians had been in the Women's Movement since its beginning—a great many had, in fact, begun it. These included some women who were active in Daughters of Bilitis[5] under other names, not only to keep jobs and homes and custody of their children, but also so as not to "embarrass" NOW, which they had built. In addition, a great many formerly heterosexual or asexual women were declaring themselves lesbians, as they found the support to "come out" of their kitchens and communes as well as their closets. Some women *were* pressured, not necessarily, although certainly sometimes, by lesbians. The pressure came mostly from confusion, contradictions, pulls in different directions, paths which each might have led to a united feminism but which the Man exploited into warring stands; he was aided, of course, by the internecine hostility of any oppressed people—tearing at each other is painful, but it is after all safer than tearing at the real enemy. Oh, people *did* struggle sincerely, hour upon hour of struggle to understand and relate—but the flaw still widened to a crack and then to a split, created by our collective false consciousness. We are now teetering on the brink of an abyss, but one very different from what we have been led to expect.

At present, there are supposedly two factions. On one side, those labeled heterosexual, bisexual, asexual, and celibate women. On the other, those labeled lesbians. Not that the latter group is monolithic—far from it, although monosexual straight women can, in their fear, try to hide their bigotry behind such a belief. No, there are some lesbians who work politically with gay men; some work politically with straight

---

[4] National Organization for Women.
[5] A civil-rights-for-lesbians group begun in the fifties, which became a national organization loosely built of autonomous chapters.

men; some work politically with other lesbians; some work politically only with *certain* other lesbians (age, race, class distinctions); some work politically with *all* feminists (lesbians, heterosexuals, etc.); and some, of course, don't work politically at all. As Laurel has pointed out in an incisive and witty article in *Amazon Quarterly*, there are sub-sub-sub-divisions, between gay women, lesbians, lesbian-feminists, dykes, dyke-feminists, dyke-separatists, "old" dykes, butch dykes, bar dykes, and killer dykes. In New York, there were divisions between Political Lesbians and Real Lesbians and Nouveau Lesbians. Hera help a woman who is unaware of these fine political distinctions and who wanders into a meeting for the first time, thinking she maybe has a right to be there because she likes women.[6]

Still, the same energy which created *The Ladder*[7] almost twenty years ago is now evident in the dynamism of *The Lesbian Tide*, the dedication to the fine points of struggle and contradiction in *Ain't I A Woman?*, in the analytical attempts of *The Furies*, and in the aesthetic excellence and serious political probings of the new *Amazon Quarterly*, to name only a few such publications.[8] That energy, contorted into hiding and working under false pretenses for so long, has exploded in the beautiful and organized anger of groups like Lesbian Mothers Union (begun in San Francisco and now spreading across the country), to defend and protect the rights of the lesbian and her children, and, by extension, to stand as guardian for all women who, the moment we embrace our own rage, strength, and politics, face the danger of having our children seized from us physically by the patriarchy which daily attempts to kidnap their minds and souls. The energetic development of this consciousness, so tied in with ancient mother-right, is, I think, of profound importance to lesbian mothers, all mothers, indeed, all women —it is one of the basic building blocks in our creation of a Feminist Revolution. And again, that energy, in the radical lesbian-feminist presses. That woman-loving-woman energy, freed into open expression and in fact into totally new forms of relationship *by the existence of the Feminist Movement*, has exploded in marches and demonstrations

---

[6] The definition of "lesbian" itself came to depend on the strictness of one's interpretation. There were various rigid souls whose requirements were stern enough to be confused with the rules for contestants in the Miss America Pageant. For example, as the feminist newspaper *Her Self* reported in May of 1976, the pageant has added a new clause to its constitution stipulating that a contestant must not be and never have been pregnant. This was tacked onto a rule stating that she must be single and never have been married or had her marriage annulled. Nor may she ever have had an abortion. One might well assume that the pageant directors have borrowed their standards from certain lesbian-separatist purists.

[7] A pioneer magazine on lesbian rights and culture, edited by Gene Damon.

[8] *The Lesbian Tide* is, at this writing, still publishing. All the rest are, sadly, defunct.

and dances and films and theater groups and crisis centers and so on and on—a whole affirmative new world within the world of women.

And yet.

A funny thing happened to me on the way to the Feminist Revolution: both Betty Friedan and Rita Mae Brown condemned me for being a "man-hater." Both *Ms.* magazine and *The Furies* began to call for political alliances with men, *The Furies* at one point implying that lesbians should band together with gay *and* straight males (preferably working-class) in a coalition against the enemy: straight women. Indeed, in one by now infamous statement, Rita Mae declared that lesbians were the only women capable of really loving men. Now of course this did come as a shock to many a lesbian who was obviously under the misguided impression that one had become a lesbian because she in fact loved *women*, and was indifferent-to-enraged on the subject of men. But now that the "correct line" had fallen from heaven, one was supposed penitently to dismiss such counter-revolutionary attitudes, learning to look at them *and* other women who still clung to them with contempt. One was also supposed to place issues such as the Vietnam War, political coalition with men, warmed-over Marxian class analyses, life-style differences, and other such un-lavender herrings in the path, in order to divide and polarize women. While doing all this, one was further supposed to hoist the new banner of the vanguard. (You know, the vanguard—Lenin leading the schlemiels.)

Before we get into vanguarditis, we have to backtrack a little, take some Dramamine for our nausea, and talk about men—and male influence, and male attempts to destroy the united Women's Movement. This is such an old subject that it bores and depresses me once more to have to wade through it. I feel that "man-hating" is an honorable and viable *political* act, that the oppressed have a right to class-hatred against the *class* that is oppressing them. And although there are exceptions (as in everything), i.e., men who are trying to be traitors to their own male class, most men cheerfully affirm their deadly class privileges and power. And I *hate* that *class*. I wrote my "Goodbye to All That" to the male Left in 1970—and thought I was done with it. Del Martin wrote her now classic article "If That's All There Is" as a farewell to the male gay movement soon after—and said it all again. We were both touchingly naïve if we thought that sufficient.

Because there is now upon us yet another massive wave of male interference, and it is coming, this time, from *both* gay men *and* their straight brothers. Boys will be boys, the old saying goes—and boys *will* indulge in that little thing called male bonding—and all boys in a patriarchal culture have more options and power than do any women.

Gay men first, since they were the ones we all thought were incipient allies with women, because of their own oppression under sexism. I won't go into the facts or the manners of the male-dominated Gay Liberation Movement, since Del did all that superbly and since most women have left the "Gay Movement" a long time ago. But I will, for the sake of those sisters still locked into indentured servitude there, run through a few more recent examples of the "new changing high consciousness about male supremacy" among gay organizations and gay male heavies. Are we to forgive and forget the Gay Activist Alliance dances only a few months ago (with, as usual, a token 10 percent attendance by women), at which New York GAA showed stag movies of nude men raping nude women? Are we to forgive and forget the remark of one male gay leader, who told Susan Silverwoman, a feminist active for years in the Women's Movement and a founder of New York GLF, that she could not represent GLF at a press conference because she saw herself too much as a woman, as a feminist? Are we to forgive the editors of the gay male issue of *Motive* magazine for deliberately setting women against women, deliberately attempting to exacerbate what they see as the "Lesbian-Straight Split," deliberately attempting to divide and conquer? Are we to forgive the following:

> Once, when I was telling one of you *Motive* editors about the estimated nine million Wicce (witches) who were burned to death during the Middle Ages—something that appeared to be news to you—you paused for a moment, and then asked me, "But how many of those nine million women were actually lesbians?" For a moment, I missed your meaning completely as a variety of sick jokes raced through my mind: How many of the six million Jews were Zionists; how many of the napalmed Indochinese babies could be said to have lived outside the nuclear family?
>
> Then it hit me: you had actually expressed a particle of your intense hatred for *all* women by asking how many of the nine million were lesbians, *so that you would know how many of these victims to mourn, because* YOU DIDN'T OBJECT TO WHAT WAS DONE TO THE OTHER WOMEN! This is as close as I have ever heard a man come to saying in so many words that he didn't object to men torturing and incinerating millions of women (provided only that they met his standards of burnability).

—this is a quote from the second issue of *Double-F, A Magazine of Effeminism,*[9] in which even the faggot-effeminist *males* proclaim *their* Declaration of Independence from Gay Liberation and all other male ideologies.

Or are we, out of the compassion in which we have been posi-

---

[9] Winter/Spring 1973, published by Templar Press, P.O. Box 98, FDR Station, N.Y., N.Y. 10022.

tively forced to *drown* as women, are we yet again going to defend the male supremacist, yes obscenity of male tranvestitism? How many of us will try to explain away—or permit into our organizations, even—men who deliberately *re*emphasize gender roles, and who parody female oppression and suffering as "Camp"? Maybe it seems that we, in our "liberated" combat boots and jeans, aren't being mocked. No? Then is it "merely" our mothers, and *their* mothers, who had no other choice, who wore hobbling dresses and torture stiletto heels to survive, to keep jobs, or to keep husbands because *they* themselves could *get* no jobs? No, I will not call a male "she"; thirty-two years of suffering in this androcentric society, and of surviving, have earned me the title "woman"; one walk down the street by a male transvestite, five minutes of his being hassled (which *he* may enjoy), and then he dares, he *dares* to think he understands our pain? No, in our mothers' names and in our own, we must not call him sister. *We know what's at work when whites wear blackface; the same thing is at work when men wear drag.*

Last night, at this conference's *first* session, women let a man divide us, pit woman against woman and, in the process, exploit the entire Lesbian Conference to become the center of attention and boost his opportunistic career.

The same man who four years ago tried to pressure a San Francisco lesbian into letting him rape her; the same man who single-handedly divided and almost destroyed the San Francisco Daughters of Bilitis Chapter; the same man who, when personally begged by women *not* to attend this conference, replied that if he were kept out he would bring federal suit against these women on the charges of "discrimination and criminal conspiracy to discriminate"—this is the same man some women defended last night.

Kate Millett pled for peace. What about the women who had a right to a peaceful conference for *women*, Kate, with no past *or* present male here? A true pacifist should be consistent, and preferably on the side of her own people.

The organizers of the conference pled ignorance: that they didn't realize the issue would be "divisive" of women when they *invited* him! Yet they *knew* his San Francisco history. And it is too late for such ignorance. The same fine sisters who have for months worked day and night to create and organize this event, have—in one stroke, inviting this man—*directly* insulted their San Francisco sisters he previously tried to destroy, and indirectly insulted every woman here. I'm afraid they owe us a public apology on the grounds of divisiveness alone.

My point is that if even *one* woman last night felt that he should go, that should have been sufficient. Where The Man is concerned, we must not be separate fingers but one fist.

If transvestite or transsexual males are oppressed, then let them band together and organize against that oppression, instead of leeching off women who have spent entire lives *as women* in women's bodies.

And I will not name this man who claims to be a feminist and then threatens women with federal criminal charges; I will not give him the publicity he and his straight male theatrical manager are so greedy for, at our expense. But I charge him as an opportunist, an infiltrator, and a destroyer—with the mentality of a rapist. And you women at this conference know who he is. Now. You can let him into your workshops—or you can *deal* with him.

And what of the straight men, the rulers, the rapists, the right-on radicals? What of the men of the Socialist Workers Party, for example, who a short two years ago refused membership to all homosexual people on the grounds that homosexuality was a decadent sickness, an evil of capitalism, a perversion that must be rooted out in all "correct socialist thinking"—who now, upon opportunistically seeing a large movement out there with a lot of bodies to organize like pawns into their purposes, speedily change their official line (but not their central-committee attitude on homosexuality), and send "their" women out to teach these poor sheep some real politics? Are we to forgive, forget, ignore? Or struggle endlessly through precious energy-robbing hours with these women, because they *are* after all *women*, even if they're collaborating with a politics and a party based on straight white male rule? We must save our struggle for elsewhere. But it hurts—*because* they are women.

And this is the tragedy. That the straight men, the gay men, the transvestite men, the male *politics*, the male styles, the male attitudes toward sexuality are being arrayed once more against us, and they are, in fact, making new headway this time, using women as their standard-bearers.

Every woman here knows in her gut the vast differences between her sexuality and that of any patriarchally trained male's—gay or straight. That has, in fact, always been a source of *pride* to the lesbian community, even in its greatest suffering. That the emphasis on genital sexuality, objectification, promiscuity, emotional noninvolvement, and coarse invulnerability, was the *male style*, and that we, as women, placed greater trust in love, sensuality, humor, tenderness, commitment. Then what but male style is happening when we accept the male transvestite who chooses to wear women's dresses and makeup, but sneer at the female who is still forced to wear them for survival? What is happening when "Street Fighting Woman," a New York *all-woman* bar band, dresses in black leather and motorcycle chains, and sings and plays a lot of Rolling Stones, including a racist, sexist song like "Brown Sugar" by that high priest of sadistic cock-rock, Mick Jagger. What is happening when, in a Midwest city with a strong lesbian-feminist community, men raped a woman in the university dormitory, and murdered her by the repeated ramming of a broom handle into her vagina until she died of massive internal hemorrhage—and the lesbian activists there can't "relate" to taking any political action pertaining to the crime because, according to one of them, there was no evidence that the victim was a lesbian? But the same community can, at a women's dance less than a week later, proudly play Jagger's recorded voice singing "Midnight Rambler"—a song which glorifies the Boston Strangler.

What has happened when women, in escaping the patriarchally enforced role of noxious femininity, adopt instead the patriarch's *own* style, to get drunk and swaggering just like one of the boys, to write of tits and ass as if a sister were no more than a collection of chicken parts, to spit at the lifetime commitment of other lesbian couples, and refer to them contemptuously as "monogs"? For the record, the anti-monogamy line originated with men, Leftist men, Weathermen in particular, in order to guilt-trip the women of their "alternative culture" into being more available victims for a dominance-based gang-rape sexuality. And from where but the male Left, male "hip" culture have we been infected with the obsession to anti-intellectualism and downward mobility? Genuinely poor people see no romanticism in their poverty; those really forced into illiteracy hardly glorify their condition. The oppressed want *out* of that condition—and it is contemptuous of real people's pain to parasitically imitate it, and hypocritical to play the more-oppressed-than-thou game instead of ordering our lives so as to try and meet our basic and just needs, so that we can get on with the more important but often forgotten business of making a Feminist Revolution.

What *about* the life-style cop-out? The one invented by two straight white young males, Jerry Rubin and Abbie Hoffman, for the benefit of other unoppressed straight white young males? What about the elite isolation, the incestuous preoccupation with one's own clique or group or commune, one's own bar/dancing/tripping, which led one lesbian to announce that the revolution has already been won, that she isn't compelled, like the rest of us, to live in a man's world any more? As Jeanne Cordova has written in *The Lesbian Tide*, "An example of these politics is Jill Johnston's calling for tribes of women capable of sustaining themselves independent of the male species. How very beautiful! Truth, justice, and the womanly way! How very unreal." And Cordova is right in pointing out that this is the "personal solution" error—the deadly trap into which so many heterosexual women have fallen. It should be obvious how painfully much everyone wants even a little happiness, peace, joy, in her life—and should have that right. But to remain convinced that your own personal mirage is a real oasis while a sandstorm is rising in the desert is both selfish *and* suicidal. There is a war going on, sisters. Women are being killed. And the rapist doesn't wait to ask whether his victim is heterosexual or lesbian.

But the epidemic of male style among women doesn't stop there. No, it is driving its *reformist* wedge through our ranks as well: women breaking their backs working for McGovern (only to have him laugh in their faces[10]); women in the lesbian community especially breaking their backs to elect almost invariably *male* gay legislators, or lobbying to pass bills which will, in actuality, primarily profit *men*.[11] Myself, I have never been able to get excited over tokenism, whether it was Margaret Chase Smith in the Senate or Bernardine Dohrn in the Weather Underground, let alone a few women to give GAA a good front (which women, by the way, are finally getting wise to, and leaving), or to serve as periodic "good niggers" for the cheap porn reportage of the *Advocate*, *Gay, Gay Sunshine*, and the like.

Susan Silverwoman has written a courageous paper called "Finding Allies: The Lesbian Dilemma." In it she writes: "Men have traditionally maintained power over women by keeping us separated. Gay men capitalized on the split between feminists and lesbians by suggesting and insisting that we [lesbians] were somehow better, basically different from straight women . . . Gay men preferred to think of us not as women, but as female gay men." She goes on to say that "it is imperative that we identify with the total feminist issue . . . if we continue to define straight women as the enemy, rather than sisters . . . we rob from ourselves a movement which must be part of ourselves. We are choosing false allies when we align politically with gay men who can never understand the female experience and who, as men, have a great deal of privilege to lose by a complete liberation of women. Whether or not straight feminists come out, as potential lesbians they are far more likely to understand our experience."

Language itself is one powerful barometer of influence. More and more women use "lesbian" proudly in self-description, calling on the history of that word, dating from an age and an island where women were great artists and political figures. Why do *any* of us still use "gay" to describe ourselves at all—that trivializing, male-invented, and male-defining term? If we are serious about our politics, then we must be responsible about the ways in which we communicate them to others,

---

[10] In the process of winning the presidential nomination at the 1972 Democratic National Convention, candidate George McGovern jettisoned certain feminist issues, including stands on sexual and reproductive freedom, and withdrew support for women involved in the credentials challenge of the South Carolina delegation.

[11] Proposed "gay" legislation often emphasizes areas of great concern mainly to homosexual males: cruising, transvestitism, sado-masochistic practices, and even sodomy when defined as an act requiring the presence of a penis.

creating new language when necessary to express new concepts. But the sloppy thinking and lazy rhetoric of the straight and gay male movements pollutes our speech, and when Jill Johnston in one column claims Betty Friedan as a lesbian and then, a few months later, after Friedan's attack in the *New York Times*, calls Friedan a man—I, for one, get confused. And angry. Because the soggy sentimentality of the first statement and the rank stupidity of the second *mean nothing politically*. The point is, very regrettably, that Friedan *is* a woman. And can stand as one of many examples of the insidious and devastating effect of male *politics*.

There *is* a war going on. And people get damaged in a war, badly damaged. Our casualties are rising. To say that any woman has escaped —or can escape—damage in this day on this planet is to march, self-satisfied, under the flags of smug false consciousness. And get gunned down anyway for one's pains.

Personally, I detest "vanguarditis." I never liked it in the Left, and I find it especially distasteful weaseling its way into the Women's Movement. I think that if anything like a "vanguard" exists at all, it continually shifts and changes from group to group within a movement, depending on the specific strategies and contradictions that arise at given times, and on which groups are best equipped and placed to meet and deal with them—when and if called for by the movement as a *whole*. The responsibility of a vanguard, by the way, is to speak from, for, and to *all* of the people who gave it birth. "Lesbian Nation" cannot be the feminist solution, much less a vanguard, when it ignores these facts. And it won't do to blame the straight women who wouldn't cooperate—after all, it is the *vanguard's* responsibility as leadership to hear messages in the silence or even hostility of *all* its people, and to reply creatively, no matter how lengthy or painful that dialogue is. A willingness to do this—and to *act* on those messages—is what *makes* the vanguard the vanguard.

I don't like more-radical-than-thou games any better than more-oppressed-than-thou games. I don't like credentials games, intimidation-between-women games, or "you are who you sleep with" games. I don't like people being judged by their class background, their sexual preference, their race, choice of religion, marital status, motherhood or rejection of it, or any other vicious standard of categorization. I hate such judgments in the male power system, and I hate them in the Women's Movement. If there must be judgments at all, let them be not on where a woman is coming *from*, but on what she is moving *toward*; let them be based on her seriousness, her level of risk, her commitment, her endurance.

And by those standards, yes, there could be a lesbian vanguard. I think it would be women like Barbara Grier and Phyllis Lyon and Del

Martin and Sten Russell, and others like them who, at the height of the fifties' McCarthyism, stood up and formed a lesbian-civil-rights movement, and whose courage and staying power are ignored by the vulgar minds of certain younger women, newly lesbian from two months or two years back, who presume to dismiss such brave women as "oldies" or "life-style straights" or, again, "hopeless monogs."

There is a new smell of fear in the Women's Movement. It is in the air when groups calling themselves killer-dyke-separatists trash lesbian-feminists who work with that anathema, straight women—trash these lesbian-feminists as "pawns, dupes, and suckers-up to the enemy." It is in the air when Peggy Allegro writes in *Amazon Quarterly* that "at a certain point, flags can begin to dominate people. For instance, women are oppressed by the flag of the freak feminist dyke. There are all kinds of rules, shoulds and shouldn'ts, in this community, that result because of the image's power. We must beware the tendency to merely impose a new hierarchy . . . a new ideal ego image to persecute people." It is in the air when ultra-egalitarianism usurps organic collectivity, or when one woman is genuinely scared to confront another about the latter's use of "chick" to describe her lover. It was in the air when I trembled to wrench the Stones record from a phonograph at a women's dance, and when I was accused of being uptight, puritanical, draggy, and of course a hung-up man-hating "straight" *for doing that.* The words are familiar, but the voices used to be male. And the smell of fear was in my gut, writing this talk, and is in my nostrils now, risking the saying of these things, taking a crazy leap of faith that our own shared and potentially ecstatic womanhood will bind us across all criticism—and that a lot more feminists in the lesbian movement will come out of their closets today.

Because polarization does exist. Already. And when I first thought about this talk, I wanted to call for unity. But I cannot. I am struck dumb before the dead body of a broomhandle-raped and murdered woman, and anyway, my voice wouldn't dent the rape-sound of the Rolling Stones. So instead, my purpose in this talk here today is to call for further polarization, but on different grounds.

Not the Lesbian-Straight Split, nor the Lesbian-Feminist Split, but the Feminist-*versus*-Collaborator Split.

The war outside, between women and male power, is getting murderous; they are trying to kill us, literally, spiritually, infiltratively. It is time, past time, we drew new lines and knew which women were serious, which women were really committed to loving women (whether that included sexual credentials or not), and, on the other side, which women thought feminism meant pure fun, or a chance to bring back a body count to their male Trot party leaders, or those who saw the Feminist Revolution as any particular life-style, correct class line, pacifist-change-your-head-love-daisy-chain, or easy lay. We know that the personal is political. But if the political is *solely* personal, then those of us at the barricades will be in big trouble. And if a woman isn't there when the crunch comes—and it is coming—then I for one won't give a damn whether she is at home in bed with a woman, a man, or her own wise fingers. If she's in bed at all at that moment, others of us are in our coffins. I'd appreciate the polarization now instead of then.

I am talking about the rise of attempted gynocide. I am talking about survival. As one lesbian-feminist with a knack for coining aphorisms has said, "Lesbianism is in danger of being co-opted by lesbians." Lesbians are a minority. Women are a majority. And since it is awfully hard to be a lesbian without being a woman first, the choice seems pretty clear to me.

There are a lot of women involved in that war out there, most of them not even active in the Women's Movement yet. They include the hundreds of thousands of housewives who created and sustained the meat boycott in the most formidable show of women's strength in recent years. They are mostly heterosexuals, but there are asexual and celibate women out there, too, who are tired of being told that they are sick. Because this society has said that everybody should fuck a lot, and too many people in the Women's Movement have echoed, "Yeah, fuck with women or even with men, but for god's sake *fuck* or you're *really* perverted." And there are also genuine functioning bisexuals out there. I'm not referring to people who have used the word as a coward's way to avoid dealing honestly with homosexuality, or to avoid commitment. We all know *that* ploy. I agree with Kate [Millett] when she says that she believes that "all people are inherently bisexual"—and I also know that to fight a system one must dare to identify with the *most* vulnerable aspect of one's oppression—and women are put in prison for being lesbian, not bisexual or heterosexual per se. So that is why I have identified myself as I have—in the *Times* in 1968 and here today, although the Man will probably want to get me for hating men before he gets me for loving women.

We have enough trouble on our hands. Isn't it way past time that we stopped *settling* for blaming each other, stopped blaming heterosexual women and middle-class women and married women and lesbian women and white women and *any* women for the structure of sexism, racism, classism, and ageism, that no woman is to blame for, because we have none of us had the power to create those structures? They are patriarchal creations, not ours. And if we are collaborating with *any* of them for *any* reason, we must begin to stop. The time is short, and the self-indulgence is getting dangerous. We must stop settling for anything less than we deserve.

All women have a right to each other as women. All women have a right to our sense of ourselves as a People. All women have a right to live with and make love with *whom we choose when we choose.* We have a right to bear and/or raise children if we choose, and *not* to if we don't. We have a right to freedom and yes, power. Power to change our entire species into something that might for the first time approach being human. We have a right, each of us, to a Great Love.

And this is the final risk I will take here today. By the right to a great love I don't mean romanticism in the Hollywood sense, and I don't mean a cheap joke or cynical satire. *I mean a great love*—a committed, secure, nurturing, sensual, aesthetic, revolutionary, holy, ecstatic love. That need, that *right*, is at the heart of our revolution. It is in the heart of the woman stereotyped by others as being a butch bar dyke who cruises for a cute piece, however much she herself might laugh at the lesbian couple who have lived together for decades. It is in their hearts, too. It is in the heart of the woman who jet-sets from one desperate heterosexual affair to another. It is in the heart of a woman who wants to find—or stay with—a man she can love and be loved by in what she has a right to demand are nonoppressive ways. It is in the heart of every woman here today, if we dare admit it to ourselves and recognize it in each other, and in all women. It is each her right. Let no one, female or male, of whatever sexual or political choice, dare deny that, for to deny it is to *settle*. To deny it is to speak with the words of the real enemy.

If we can open ourselves *to* ourselves and each other, as women, only then can we begin to fight for and create, in fact reclaim, not "Lesbian Nation" or "Amazon Nation"—let alone some false state of equality—but a real Feminist Revolution, a proud gynocratic *world* that runs on the power of women. Not in the male sense of power, but in the sense of a power plant—producing energy. And to each, that longing for, that right to, a great love filled in reality, for all women, and children and men and animals and trees and water and all life, an exquisite diversity in unity. That world breathed and exulted on this planet some twelve thousand years ago, before the patriarchy arose to crush it.

If we risk this task then, our pride, our history, our culture, our past, our future, all vibrate before us. Let those who will dare, begin.

In the spirit of that task, I want to end this talk in a strange and new, although time-out-of-mind-ancient, manner. Earlier, I "came out" in this talk as a Witch, and I did not mean that as a solely political affiliation. I affirm the past and the present spirit of the Wicce (the Anglo-Saxon word for witch, or wise woman), affirm it not only in the smoke of our nine million martyrs, but also in the thread of *real* womanpower and *real* Goddess-worship dating back beyond Crete to the dawn of our lives. In the ruling male culture, they have degraded our ritual by beginning conferences and conventions with a black-coated male, sometimes in full priestly drag, nasally droning his stultifying pronouncements to the assemblage. Let us reclaim our own for ourselves, then, and in that process, also extend an embrace to those lesbians who, because they go to church, are held in disrepute by counter-culture lesbians. And to those women of *whatever* sexual identification who kneel in novenas or murmur in quiet moments to, oh irony, a male god for alleviation of the agony caused by male supremacy.

The short passage I am about to read is from "The Charge of the Goddess," still used reverently in living Wiccean Covens, usually spoken by the High Priestess at the initiation of a new member. I ask that each woman join hands with those next to her.

I ask your respect for the oldest faith known to human beings, and for the ecstatic vision of freedom that lies hidden in each of your own precious, miraculous brains.

> Listen to the words of the Great Mother. She says:
> "Whenever ye have need of anything, once in the month, and better it be when the moon is full, then shall ye assemble in some secret place . . . to these I will teach things that are yet unknown. And ye shall be free from all slavery . . . Keep pure your highest ideal; strive ever toward it. Let naught stop you nor turn you aside . . . Mine is the cup of the wine of life and the cauldron of Cerridwen . . . I am the Mother of all living, and my love is poured out upon the Earth . . . I am the beauty of the Green Earth, and the White Moon among the stars, and the Mystery of the Waters, and the desire in the heart of woman . . . Before my face, let thine innermost divine self be enfolded in the raptures of the Infinite . . . Know the Mystery, that if that which thou seekest thou findest not within thee, thou wilt never find it without thee . . . For behold, I have been with thee from the beginning. And I await you now."

Dear Sisters,
As We in the Craft say, Blessed Be.

April 1973

THE PROPER STUDY OF WOMANKIND: ON WOMEN'S STUDIES

One month after the Lesbian Feminist Conference took place in Los Angeles, I returned to California to speak at the Western Women's Studies Conference in Sacramento, an address on which the following article is based. This conference, too, belied its regional title, and welcomed women from all over the country. It too was beset with destructive confrontation-for-confrontation's-sake and also with authentic and fruitful struggle. An example of the former was the approach taken by a small "cadre" of women who had resolutely driven up from Southern California to announce to the conference that women should drop out of school and go organize the factories. This eminent morsel of nonlogic was offered, of course, by women who themselves held down teaching jobs in a women's-studies program started by feminists (who were later forced out by these same women); no fools they, this cadre knew but refused to admit that the "vanguard worker" on the assembly line usually wants nothing so much as to drop out of the factory and go to school. I have never been able to comprehend a train of thought which purports to make a revolution by urging those revolutionaries who have a modicum of education, mobility, or power not to use such tools but rather, out of guilt, to join the downtrodden masses who are themselves too damned weary and bitter and beaten to make that same revolution.

An example of constructive dialogue, on the other hand, was the serious communication that went on in small groups for the duration of the conference and continued for some time afterward, the open discussions established between black, Chicana, Asian, and white feminists, and the uncompromising intellectual integrity of women like Joan Hoff Wilson and Kathleen Barry, who refused to permit the conference to dwindle into an exchange of rhetoric but who insisted instead on an exchange of ideas.

The proliferation of women's-studies courses, programs, even entire schools is to me one of the most encouraging developments in the Feminist Movement to date. If during my years in the Left and my years as a Marxist-oriented "Women's Liberationist" I was forced to become ashamed of being an intellectual and an artist, the blame surely must be shared at least three ways: by myself, for ever being cowardly or defensive about what I knew to be important and *worth* defending; by what had passed itself off as the American intellectual and artistic "community"—in reality a hypocritical establishment which had permitted itself to become ineffectual and cynical; and by the dogmatic pressure of hard-line politicos themselves. Between those who will take no side and those who insist there *is* no side but their own there must be people of courage who persist in exploration. If a political movement is unconcerned with or suspicious of gaining knowledge, *or* conversely is naïve about the bias which those in power will have layered *over* that knowledge, *or* is lazy about stripping away those layers and seeking the truth—then such a movement ultimately condemns itself to the obscene and deliberate ignorance of, say, the Nazi scientists' position "on race," or the propagandistic rigidity with which the Soviet Union once adopted Lamarck's theory of evolution via the inheritance of acquired characteristics.

U.N. statistics note that of the eight hundred million illiterates alive today, five hundred million are women. While there are women alive who still are not permitted to learn to read, education is for us not only a right but a rallying cry.

We are sowing the seeds of new knowledge. The renaissance which will flower from the release of such energy—the energy of focused intelligence—is only now beginning, and the fruit will ripen for decades to come.

I WANT TO START by our congratulating each other: the sisters all assembled here at the West Coast Women's Studies Conference, and especially the sisters who organized it. (You can't be in the Women's Movement for very long without knowing that to organize a conference of any sort is an exercise either in heroism or masochism or both.)

Yet this conference takes place not in a vacuum but in an authentic historical context. The history of women in education is, I think, important as a foundation for Women's Studies. I am afraid relatively few people know that Susan B. Anthony (about whom too little is popularly known anyway), devoted her last energies to the cause of women's education. She lived in Rochester, New York, for most of her life, and when she was quite old and ill, she took on the battle of the admission of women to the university there. Between bouts of pneumonia and exhaustion, she lobbied and organized, even putting up her life's savings of two thousand dollars to guarantee the program. She died a matter of weeks after victory was assured. Women university students were her pallbearers.

The first women's schools and colleges were originally feminist institutions, of course, because we were not permitted into male colleges. The tragedy of these places, such as the Seven Sisters, is that what was originally a feminist concept has been turned around in some cases into a training school for corporate wives. One fine women's college, for example, had a token course not too long ago called "Women in Literature" which I naïvely had thought referred to a course on women writers. Wrong. This was a course on women *characters* in the novels of *male* writers and it was taught by a man who thought that the greatest twentieth-century literary artist was Norman Mailer.

Up Against It

The obstacles we face are basic, even to including issues such as the *hiring* of female faculty and the *admission* of female students in many places (and not only in areas of Women's Studies). Salary differentials and tenure discrimination and, in general, attitudes hostile to experimentation are still common. You rarely find women in positions of power: department heads, top administrative posts, the jobs which control content and define style. You do find administration *use* of unthreatening "good ladies" to teach their women's-studies programs or their token courses—they find a woman who can be depended on as safe or "unpolitical"; they take her out of one department and suddenly, *shazam*, she becomes the official resident feminist, even if she herself is mystified by or indifferent to the Feminist Movement. (As Gloria Steinem has perceptively—and wryly—observed, we are triumphantly galloping toward tokenism.)

Then there are the obstacles from within, at least regarding feminist consciousness. These are so often understandable if pathetic defenses against seeing a cruel truth. In a campus context, for instance, there are the professional women who sometimes have fallen into the trap of being "exceptional women" (that's the "pull yourself up by your own G-string" line, which blames others in one's own group for a mutual oppression). The student women can tend to claim, "Well, *we're* not oppressed; we're outside parental control for the first time in our lives and we're not yet up against marriage or kids or the job market. We have all this comparative freedom." This freedom—in the middle of educational tracking and dorm rules and dress codes and campus rape and having to type their boyfriends' term papers.[1] The staff women at a college are not surprisingly scared of losing their jobs. Then there is the fourth part of the women's community, probably the most invisible faction on any campus, and often, for shame, ignored even by the Women's Movement: the faculty wives—the women who are just not considered or who are considered only as appendages to their husbands. And *their* obvious defense is "We are happy because if we say we are not happy, our world will fall apart."

All these areas, it is true, have been tremoring with the feminist earthquake; professional women forming caucuses in their national academic associations, student women organizing, and staff women organizing, and faculty wives, too, forming consciousness-raising groups.

But the really important thing is that they *begin to unite*. Unfortunately this happens less often than it should. What usually does happen is: The faculty women will approach the student women and say, "Will you sign this petition on hiring and firing?" The student women will reply, "Six months ago we had a demonstration to get a child-care center on this campus, and you didn't support us in that because you said demonstrating was unladylike. So now we are not going to help you on *your* petition." So we are divided—and conquered. And the administration relaxes while we squabble. So are wedges driven between women, usually from the two expectable sources, the male Right and the male Left.

Cannon to the Right of Us

Pressure from the Right is familiar to everybody, but I want to read from a *New York Times* clipping dated November 1972 with this headline: "Colleges Scored on Hiring of Women, U.S. Aid Sees Backlash by Male Faculty Members." Briefly: "The federal government's program to enforce equal hiring and promotional opportunities for women and minorities on college faculties is losing ground to a growing rhetorical backlash from male faculty members and administrators, the

---

[1] Not that this last ceases at graduation. In fact, such typing is often broadly translated into unacknowledged coauthorship, or even into doing the entire job "for him." One of many such examples is provided by Aurelia Plath, the mother of Sylvia and herself a fascinating woman; in *Letters Home* (Harper & Row, New York, 1975, p. 12), Mrs. Plath writes movingly of having done all the reading and note-taking for her husband's book, then having written the first draft, and at last having put the manuscript into "final form" for the printer. At some point in this process Otto Plath revised a bit and inserted a few notes—including adding his name on the title page as sole author, a regrettably not uncommon practice. Yet another instance of appropriation of the wife's writing by the husband (in this case, F. Scott Fitzgerald) was explored by Nancy Milford in her absorbing book *Zelda: A Biography* (Harper & Row, New York, 1970).

director of the office for civil rights said here today." This was at a national conference on affirmative action sponsored by Syracuse University. They came right out and said it.

Pressure from the Right in more informal ways? Well, there's the whole funding argument: the same school which has limitless funding available to support the jock mentality on any campus—from a new basketball hoop to a new football field—cannot come up with even two hundred dollars for a small child-care center, let alone fund a women's-studies program. They're too poor. And there is always pressure in the form of veiled or open threats of firing (or, in the case of students, suspension or expulsion), or of outright killing the program if you already happen to have one. There is also plain old pedantry and dullness, and of course the manipulation tactic. A beautiful example of this is what happened at an Ivy League coed college which claimed to have a really stunning women's-studies program—sixteen courses. It turned out that only three of those courses were for credit. The rest of them were all volunteer-taught by women who knew there was a need for women's studies, and volunteer-*attended* by women who wanted to learn. Women got no credit for it as students, no salary for it as teachers, yet administration representatives would go to women's-studies conferences and brag that they had a program of sixteen courses!

In any list of fundamental obstacles, we daren't forget the academic-*versus*-the-political approach. You know, are we going to be academic, objective, and *scholarly* about this, or are we in some way going to relate this program to—godforbid—*feminism?* (As if these approaches were mutually exclusive.) This administration line always interests me: *who determines* whether something is academic or political? I find it ironic that the very people who have that power happen to be the men or the sons of the men who buried our history in the first place, and now will judge what we shall or shall not be permitted to learn about it. The point is that *there is no approach which is not political.* The so-called objective, apolitical, or nonpartisan stand is itself a political stand. There are no innocent bystanders any longer.

It's odd how feminism changes you—I no longer believe in coeducation, at least not for the present. I do believe, obviously, that there should be no schools which are closed to women. But I do think that there should be schools which are closed to *men*.[2] I confess that my

---

[2] Women students at Sarah Lawrence have been quite vocal in their regret at their own vote to make the school coed. Less than a year after males were admitted (and they were a distinct minority), the women found themselves being edged out of leadership positions in the student councils and being subtly overlooked in classes by teachers who favored the men students. Old stereotypes reasserted themselves as the men (trained to compete and to rule from birth) challenged the numerical strength of the women with simple aggressiveness. Conversely trained

own anti-coeducational position discomfits me: it's as if I found myself in agreement with John Birchers, and it's unnerving. But I came to this position at New College and so must digress for a moment and explain.

It was the first time I ever "taught." I was asked by the women students at New College, a small experimental college in Sarasota, Florida, to come down and start a feminist-studies program. New College prided itself on being more radical and hip than Antioch or Goddard. I was to be the Student Chair, which was pleasant, because although I had faculty status, I was answerable only to the students.

It was at New College I discovered the sexist hypocrisy of academia first-hand. Orientation week was jovially nicknamed Rape Week. The school expressed Marcuse's theory of repressive tolerance with the most exquisite clarity. Everybody was completely cooled out on grass in their coeducational dorms. There was no *backup* for the women, of course. When the women got pregnant, there was no abortion referral. There wasn't even contraception counseling available on campus, only "sexual liberation" and a lot of fake freedom. And of course this had so effectively defused the students that they sat glassy-eyed and passive through courses with titles like "An Analysis of Radical Action."

The first thing the college did was to renege on our agreement that I was to teach only women. After much growling on both sides, a compromise was worked out: the radical-feminism course would be for women only, but I would permit male students into the women's-history course. This did annoy me for all the obvious reasons but especially because I had wanted to use an experimental form. I hadn't wanted to stand up there and lecture, I had wanted my classes to be collective explorations. In the all-women's class we *were* able to do that. In the mixed group, however, I had to control the situation more tightly.

I decided that there had to be some way at least to selectively lower male participation. It was a large class, about fifty people, and approximately half men. I announced in the first meeting with students that I would not grade women in either class, because I didn't see how women could fail in the subject of themselves. I also said I hadn't yet made up my mind whether to fail all the men automatically or to grade them on individual merit. This had the dramatic effect of driving fifteen men out of the mixed class that day. They had thought it was

---

(also since birth), the women found themselves distracted from their own intellectual climate and low-key, relatively noncompetitive style. They speak now of missing that peace, that freedom to exchange ideas in their own atmosphere, and the easy camaraderie they had felt among themselves. There is so little space in the patriarchy for women to be friends, let alone intellectual colleagues sharing a mutual sense of adventure, that we ought at least to preserve those few female educational communities we have left.

going to be an easy credit, poor dears. Then I announced that there were no formal course requirements for any women, and no required papers. I said I thought it would be helpful to the whole Women's Movement if people *wanted* to do papers, because we needed research, theory, personal testimony, whatever the women students wanted to write. (To my delight, every woman in both courses voluntarily wrote a paper.) On the other hand, I announced that a sixty-page paper was required from each man. In addition, it was required that the men set up and run, under women's leadership, a child-care center. This further winnowing left us with four men. That rather surprised all of us; I thought they must be insane or actually serious, and we knew we'd soon see. In fact, three of the four did turn out to be serious, which is a pretty high ratio out of twenty-six men.

The real test, however, came a few weeks later. The administration had been harassing us all along: no department would Xerox anything we needed copied, the bookstore happened not to carry any of the books I had requested three months earlier. Finally, the administration announced that the feminist-studies program was over and that there would be no budget allotment to bring in other feminist speakers from around the country, as we had agreed. The women students and I had a long talk about this, and to shorten the saga, we seized the president's office for five days and nights. And won a number of points— not all, but some.[3]

This experience gave me a small insight into what women face in an academic community. Previously, I'm afraid that I'd thought of academia as relatively safe. But the infighting alone, the politics *between* departments, was frightening. We started a faculty wives' consciousness-raising group, for example, and that was the most difficult experience of all because the women were terrified about talking. It might get back to John, who was Mary's husband over here, that Phil, who was Grace's husband, was really going for his job. I suddenly understood about fear in an "intellectual community." Nor were things helped by the administration, which was not overly fond of me, since following the seizure nobody related to them any longer as warm-hearted papas. So they called me an outside agitator (which I definitely was and which role I affirm, I might add). They threatened to have me up on charges of what I refer to as "moral turpentine," since evidently I was corrupting the minds of youth. All this taught me a new-found respect for feminists who are trying to survive, let alone function, in an academic community.

---

[3] New College closed a few years later, due partly to the public-relations damage the feminist seizure wreaked on the school's radical image. "Change or die" was one of our rallying cries. Many institutions chose the latter course.

Cannon to the Left of Us

Of course not all the obstacles are thrown up by administrations, i.e., the Right. There *is* also the Left. This is rather a problem to me because I get bored talking about the Left. I spent seven years in it. I spent two or three years trying to get out of it. Since then I have been healthy and happy in the Feminist Movement, but certain ugly heads keep getting reared. We endure recurring waves, tiring and irrelevant as they are, of Marxism or of Trotskyism—or of the holy class analysis. Since many people talk *around* this and it's always accusation and counter-accusation, I am going to try and talk some theory. About why I feel that the class analysis is inapplicable at best and destructive at worst to the developing of a revolutionary feminist movement.

I will give only one of many examples. Capitalism is based on a marketplace economy; that is, wages paid for labor (exploited). Most women in this country work as housewives, on the average of a 99.6 hour work-week. For this there is no pay, no remuneration, no honor, no dignity, no respect, nothing. Neither the capitalist society *nor* the Marxist analysis considers housewives workers. What in fact the work of housewifery *is* in a "class analysis" is *invisible labor*. It is labor at the bottom of the pyramid, on which the total edifice rests. Invisible labor that exists without any pay has another name: feudalism, or slave labor. We know that were every housewife in this country paid a wage commensurate to her work, we would have a bloodless revolution overnight—the economy could not support it, the economy would fall. I find it alarming that a class analysis overlooks or ignores that area where the great mass of women (of *people*, numerically) work, just as I find it unfortunate when our own language picks up on it as in references to "working women." I think that we really ought to try to refer to women who work *at home* and/or women who work *outside the home*. Of course, many women do both. But housewives *are* working women.[4]

Our Own Approach

I agree with Joan Hoff Wilson's position that we must not look to other revolutions as models. Because we are not Cuba, we are not Al-

---

[4]In 1898 the feminist writer Charlotte Perkins Gilman suggested that housewives be paid salaries. Lately this proposal has been taken up and dusted off as a possible feminist demand. Among the women who have explored "home economics" in this sense are the Canadian Margaret Benston, the British sociologist Ann Oakley, feminist theorists Betsy Warrior and Lisa Leghorn, Helena Lopata, and Elizabeth Windschuttle. Recently there are even Marxist exponents of wages-for-housework, notably Juliet Mitchell, Mariarosa dalla Costa, and Selma James.

geria, we are not China, and we are not *men*, which should suffice. *The point is that we as feminists must search for ourselves, and for the connectives between women. It is the Man who looks for the differences.* Until and unless each oppressed group begins to have as its priority looking for the things it has in common, the strong points, the similarities, it is lost.

We must be careful not to contract contagious patriarchal thought. Sometimes it wears the face of pedantry; sometimes it masquerades as anti-intellectualism. The "anti-articulate line," for example: you should not be able to phrase anything in words over one syllable. My response is that a serious revolutionary would no more wield ineffective language than she would carry a clogged gun. Because language is a weapon like anything else, and I for one want us to use it as best and movingly and efficiently as we can. I want us to seize that tool like any other. I want to have everything, in fact: feminist colleges, feminist universities, a feminist world.

In the meantime, though, I must admit that mere survival is a priority. So let's examine the temporary solution—the women's-studies program. I shall share with you my fantasy of the ideal program, if we all keep in mind that settling for less than everything is absurd—and eventually unnecessary.

I know, as I'm sure you do, most of the arguments for and against a program's being interdisciplinary or autonomous; obviously the approach taken would depend largely on the school, the support for such a program, and other local "tactical" elements. Personally, I favor the autonomous program, where the university gets to write the funding check and thereafter is permitted to maintain a respectful silence. My ideal program would be run collectively by that aforementioned coalition of women: student/faculty/staff/faculty wife. Other features would include:

—a "floating credit": I don't think that's an official academic phrase, but by it I mean that any woman could take a course for credit and then apply it anywhere she wished, to another school or program.

—a minor, a major, *and* a graduate-studies program.

—courses in every discipline, all taught by women.

—an emphasis on history because, politically, if we do not know our own past we are, cliché or not, doomed to repeat it. (History not only to cover the suffrage struggles, of course, but also to explore the ancient gynocratic societies, tying in with anthropological and archeological studies in these areas.)

—self-defense *for credit*; this is *not* an extracurricular activity, as most schools today regard it. For women, it is a basic survival need.

—classes in legal rights and consumer rights.

—paramedical and midwifery training, in addition to pre-med courses.

—free child-care facilities controlled by the people (adults *and* children) who use them, but funded by the university.

—a generous athletic budget, emphasizing noncompetitive sports.

—a strong emphasis on outreach—to grammar schools, high schools, adult education, and community women—to keep the program from becoming an incestuous campus-based clique.

—new and exploratory disciplines: mythography, medical ethics, etc.

—new approaches to old disciplines: I, for one, want to know less who won which battle as the boys played war games, and more about women's history; not only about which remarkable women entered the male history as exceptions but about the women who were never permitted entrance at all or only invisibly. And what about the *trends* made invisible? For example, when was the tampon invented and what effect, socially, did it have on women? When did the pressure begin, in modern times, for women to start shaving legs and armpits? Was it with the invention of the modern razor blade; was it with the marketing of silk stockings? What did that *mean* in a socioeconomic context? I think this is part of history. I think we must transform the subjects we study as well as be willing to be transformed by them. There must be an emphasis on the hard *and* soft sciences. We need to know about inovulation, or as men call it, cloning. We need to know about the technology. You cannot rant about seizing power and then turn around and say all education is bourgeois.

There are people at this conference who came with the admitted purpose of "turning women off" to women's studies. Why? Why are women the only oppressed group who should be ashamed of going to school? You don't hear the black community saying that it's bourgeois to go to school. On the contrary. The black community wants *open admission* to get those educational tools. Yes, it's odious to have to go to the Man for them, but we must take them and use them in a new way. Not to move up the ladder: to destroy the ladder. *That* is the revolutionary approach.

Meanwhile, back to the harsh realities of ivory-tower academia. Survival measures for women currently struggling day by day in a co-educational institution might include some of the following demands:

—a grievance board to deal with complaints about the sexist comments made in class by male instructors, the emotional and/or physical rape of women students, the offensive material on the reading list, the contempt with which feminist papers are met by so many male professors.

—a lesbian counselor chosen by the lesbian feminists on the campus; this, in addition to a heterosexual feminist counselor. No male counselor should presume to counsel women, whatever their sexual proclivities.

—an emphasis on the issues of rape and abortion; abortion referral and contraception available *on* the campus, as well as childbirth and post-partum care and advice;

—maternity *and* paternity leave—he should be home dealing with the baby, too, if he's around. And he should *be* around if she wants him around and *not* if she doesn't.

The demands could go on and on. Women's work is truly never done. But there are many ways and means. Study the curricula, organizing suggestions, and advice in the literature from the Feminist Press and KNOW, Inc., in Pittsburgh. The work they have done in creating the Clearing House for Women's Studies and the *Women's Studies Newsletter* is invaluable. Read the journals coming out on this whole new area. In addition, read the *Penn Women's Studies Planners Pamphlet.*[5] (This began as a summer project required of Penn women by the university. The women felt that as long as it was an obligatory task they would do a really comprehensive study to be of service to other women elsewhere. I highly recommend it for its wit as well as its expert counsel.) Investigate the plans for a National Women's Studies Association.[6]

One more hint about winning. There is something that all of the following have in common: New College, Florida; University of Kansas at Lawrence; Boston State College; American University; Penn at Philadelphia campus; Berkeley; University of New Mexico at Albuquerque; Harvard; Barnard College. Within the past two years feminists on these campuses, after going all the proper routes and channels, have become fed up and have seized property. And I offer this to you in case, at some point, everything else fails. I say it obliquely so as to avoid getting in trouble again for crossing another state line to incite another you-know-what.

In this vein, the last thing that I would leave you with is a quote from Emmeline Pankhurst, who is part of our herstory. Emmeline Pankhurst, if anybody here doesn't know, was a British suffragist. In fact, she was a militant and therefore a suffragette, as they were called in Britain. She and two of her daughters, Christabel and Sylvia (unlikely names for feminist terrorists), formed the WSPU—the Women's Social

---

[5] *Penn Women's Studies Planners Pamphlet,* 3601 Locust Walk, Philadelphia, Pa., 1974.

[6] The founding conference of this association took place on January 13–16, 1977, at the University of San Francisco.

and Political Union—after some sixty years of women having asked politely for the vote in the British Empire and having got nowhere. The WSPU moved from setting fires in all the mailboxes in London to trashing the National Gallery, to throwing bags of flour at the king when he rode in open procession, to writing "Freedom for Women" in acid on the royal golf links, to riots, to burning down two pre-Reformation cathedrals in the north of England, and finally to fire-bombing the prime minister's summer home. Women were jailed, women died, in that struggle. Pankhurst herself invented the prison hunger strike, and I must say that she didn't do it in the genteel way for which male radicals are now famous, taking tea and milk and other liquids. None of that for Emmeline. When she was on a strike in jail it meant that she did not eat, she did not drink, she did not sleep, she did not sit down.

This particular quote comes from a period when she was already in her sixties and had been jailed again on charges of conspiracy; she immediately entered into her strike. For three days she had not eaten or drunk or slept or sat down. She had simply walked back and forth in her cell until finally the British Empire couldn't stand it any longer, and they let her go. That night she came out and addressed a women's rally saying, in part, the following, which I quote from her auto-biography:[7]

> From henceforward the women who agree with me will say, "We disregard your laws, gentlemen, we set the liberty and the dignity and the welfare of women above all such considerations, and we shall continue this war, as we have done in the past; and what sacrifice of property, or what injury to property accrues will not be our fault. It will be the fault of that Government who admit the justice of our demands, but refuses to concede them . . ." I called upon the women of the meeting to join me in this new militancy, and I reminded them anew that the women who are fighting in the Suffragette army had a great mission, the greatest mission the world has ever known—the freeing of one-half the human race, and through that freedom the saving of the other half. I said to them: "Be militant each in your own way. Those of you who can express your militancy by going to the House of Commons and refusing to leave with-out satisfaction, as we did in the early days—do so [a classic sit-in—R.M.]. Those of you who can express militancy by facing party mobs at Cabinet Ministers' meetings, when you remind them of their falseness to principle—do so. Those of you who can express your militancy by joining us in our anti-Government

[7] My Own Story, Emmeline Pankhurst, Eveleigh Nash, London, 1914, pp. 265–66.

by-election policy—do so. Those of you who can break windows —break them. Those of you who can still further attack the secret idol of property, so as to make the Government realise that property is as greatly endangered by women's suffrage as it was by the Chartists of old—do so. And my last word is to the Government: I incite this meeting to rebellion."

May 1973

INTERNATIONAL FEMINISM: A CALL FOR SUPPORT OF THE THREE MARIAS

James Baldwin once commented that to be black and conscious in America was to be in a continual state of rage. I would paraphrase him: to be female and conscious anywhere on this planet is to be in a continual state of rage. Since early 1970 I had been one of a number of American feminists who were in touch with like-minded women organizing all over the globe. Synchronicity, word-of-mouth, books smuggled into countries where the fascist, capitalist, socialist, Protestant, Catholic, Jewish, Moslem, Hindu, or atheist male governments did not smile upon such literature—these were the ways our ideas were shared. But 1973 and 1974 saw the first truly united international feminist action, focusing on the arrest of three Portuguese feminist writers, as the accompanying article describes. It was written for and delivered as the introduction to a Broadway evening in support of the Three Marias, a presentation of their work dramatized and directed by Gilda Grillo, and produced by Lois Sasson. Women were responsible for the acting, the music, the slide projections, the total ambiance. It was a beautifully executed and moving event (and I shall never forget, as long as I live, the rehearsal encounters between that arch-conservative male supremacist, the Broadway stagehand, and our female technicians!).

Soon thereafter, a revolution toppled the Portuguese regime which had been entrenched for so many decades. In time, the Marias were found not guilty of the crimes charged, although Maria Isabel Barreño has made it clear since that the ultimate verdict was brought about not by the revolutionary coup, but by international feminist pressure on the Portuguese governments, old *and* new. This analysis seemed borne out when, only weeks after the glorious revolution had taken place, women marching in the first open feminist demonstration Lisbon had ever seen were set upon, stoned, beaten, and forcibly dispersed by a mob of "revolutionary" men who had fought for freedom for all, but who thought that demands for contraception, abortion, economic and emotional and legal autonomy, and spiritual freedom (in a Latin Catholic country) were—you guessed it—going *too* far.

I WANT TO WELCOME YOU to this evening of dramatic readings from the forbidden texts of the Three Marias of Portugal. As part of the international feminist protest action attendant on the case—which I will explain more fully in a moment—this one-time performance has been put together by women, including, of course, the three actresses who will read from the texts and the feminist musicians who will accompany that reading.

Some background on why we are here seems in order, for although the whole world appears to know about the censoring of Solzhenitsyn, shockingly but not surprisingly few people are aware of, or concerned about, the repression of the work of three *women*.

In April of 1972, a book entitled *New Portuguese Letters* was published in Portugal. Its authors were: Maria Isabel Barreño (who previously had written two novels about the problems of being female in a patriarchal world), Maria Teresa Horta (who has written nine books of poetry and one novel—and who has been persecuted by censorship before, regarding one of her books of poetry), and Maria Velho Da Costa (who also has written a book of short stories and a novel). All three women work. All three women have children. All three women are feminists. All three women are published writers. And all three women are therefore regarded as dangerous to the patriarchal state of Portugal.

Their collectively written book explores themes such as the loneliness and isolation of women, the exploitation of our sexuality and the denial of our own fulfillment as whole human beings. It speaks of the suffering caused by rape, prison, sadistic abortions; it explores our political and economic condition; it talks of religion and the cloister, of adultery and madness and suicide. It is not a timid work—it is a strong and womanly book.[1]

Two-thirds of all copies in the first printing sold out within a few days of the publication. By May 1 of that same year the remaining one-third had been seized by the Portuguese political police. One month later to the day, the Portuguese Committee of Censorship requested that the authors be sued. This was quite a departure, since the seizure

---

[1] I regret to say that when the book was published in the United States, the English translation seemed to me somewhat less inspiring than the selections done by Gilda Grillo and Louise Bernikow for this evening's performance.

of books is frequent in Portugal but suits are rare. Seven or eight years ago there were two government suits over literary works, but the defendants were not required to pay bail. The Three Marias, however, were arrested, and bail was subsequently set at approximately six hundred dollars for each women. The actual charge accuses the authors of having committed "an outrage to public morals and good customs."

Meanwhile the book is being sold—but only in a clandestine manner. The publisher himself, using the seizure as a reason for his action, paid the authors only one-third of what had been promised them in their contracts—thus each of the three has received only a little more than one hundred dollars for her work.

In May of 1973, a copy of *New Portuguese Letters* reached some feminists in Paris, almost by accident. These sisters took the issue to the world feminist community, with the result that there have been protest demonstrations before Portuguese embassies and consulates in major cities all over the world, including large and militant demonstrations in London, Paris, and New York. Feminists have readied a statement presenting the case to the Human Rights Commission of the United Nations. Portuguese intellectuals have signed petitions demanding that the charge be lifted. These and other activities germinated by the international feminist community have functioned so far as what could be called "holding actions"—the Portuguese government has responded to the pressure by delaying sentencing of the Three Marias, hoping, no doubt, that we would all go away and the case would become yesterday's news, in which circumstance the three women could be sent to prison for a minimum of six months to two years on the charge of "outrage to the public morality" alone. One of the three, Maria Teresa Horta, is tubercular. We do not know if she has medical care. But we do know that it is vital to continue pressure on the government, by demonstrations, by information about and press coverage of the case, and by events such as this one tonight. This Thursday, January 31, 1974, is the date set for the final sentencing of the Three Marias in Lisbon.

Those are the simple facts of the case, the superficial facts, one might say. Because the issues at stake here go much deeper than a mere recitation of those facts may imply.

It would be possible, for example, to see the case merely as another in a deplorable series of repressive acts against artists by governments all over the world, each in their turn. It might be especially tempting for some to come away with an analysis that pointed an accusing finger at the reactionary politics of the Portuguese government, that same government which has on its hands the blood of Angola. Yet both such interpretations, while valid in part, stop short of the issue itself—the heart of the matter.

Because the Three Marias are not solely artists—they are *women* artists. And they are not solely free-speaking persons living under a reactionary political regime—they are free-speaking *women* living under a reactionary political regime. They are feminist artists writing passionately on the condition of women. And their persecutors, coincidentally, are all men.

So we must look at these three women in their and our historical context—which is larger and older than Portugal and 1974. Radical feminists have said for some time now that until the issue of the oppression of women is dealt with, all revolutions will continue to be coups d'état by men, that feminism with all its reverberations is, in fact, the central issue facing the human species today. One could use the metaphor of a tree—the Tree of Ignorance, if you will— and note that for a long time progressive peoples have been hacking away at various evils represented by its branches: one branch, war; one branch, racism; one, ecological disaster; one, greed; one, competition; one, repression of the young and callousness toward the old, etc. Well, the word radical does imply "going to the root" after all, and if one wishes to do that and not merely hack away at branches that continually grow back then one must eventually deal with the oldest oppression on the face of the earth, the primary contradiction which entails the subjugation of half the species by the other half. One must deal with the largest oppressed group on the planet—the majority of humans not only in the United States but in the world. One must deal with women— and with sexism, male supremacy, and what de Beauvoir called the initial "alienizing act"—for once *women* could be viewed as "the Other" then it was a simple, inevitable, and tragic process to see more "Others" —people of a different height or weight or skin color or language or age. So the Tree of Ignorance has grown.

We as feminists have begun to un-recognize those male-defined and patriarchally imposed false barriers. National boundaries, for one. Women didn't create them; it has been a big boys' game to carve out the earth and claim "this country is mine, that yours"—and it is absurd. Which is why there is a growing international feminist community, from Melbourne to Montana, from Senegal to Switzerland, from mainland China to Cherbourg. And which is why we are here tonight, one part of that whole.

The Three Marias stand in a long and honorable tradition of women—women artists in this case—who have been repressed, persecuted, prosecuted, or killed, overtly or covertly, for daring to speak our truths. This process is how the history of women, like that of other oppressed peoples, has been hidden, and how we have been robbed of our culture. It isn't new, but it *is* necessary—how else can the oppressor continue to ask his tedious question "But then where are your great women _____?" Fill in the blank. First the evidence must be destroyed or at least distorted; only then may the inquiry be put.

So it was with Anne Hutchinson, who dared speak out against the theology of her day in Puritan New England, who was silenced, ostracized, exiled. So it was with George Sand, who was ridiculed and reviled, and her contemporary George Eliot—both great writers forced to use male pen names to be published—both considered female aberrants, and treated accordingly by the male literary establishments of their time. Male pen names—the enforced masquerading as men in order to be taken seriously as artists at all—were also used of necessity by the genius Brontë sisters, one of whom, Emily, was in effect killed by the world's attitude toward her work. The other, Charlotte, literally vomited to death during pregnancy. So it was with Elizabeth Barrett (let's begin using the name she wrote under, shall we, even if it was her father's; we needn't compound the indignity any more by adding her husband's for identification): Elizabeth Barrett, who was an articulate feminist and radical writer and a poet whose effect on Emily Dickinson was the one influence that later writer acknowledged; Elizabeth Barrett, who read Mary Wollstonecraft when she was fourteen—and whose work has been so trivialized by male literary historians that her image is now one of the stereotyped "poetess" reclining in lavender and lace on her sofa, writing love poems to her more famous husband. Made more famous by whom, we might ask.

So it has been all along. So it was with Akhmatova, who saw the suffering of Russian women, wrote of it, and then saw the grim prison-wall reply of Russian men. So it was with Anna Wickham, dead of despair by her own hand, a hand that had written about the female condition. So it was with Virginia Woolf, for whom the writing of these truths became too much to endure—another suicide. Or with Charlotte Mew, driven by patriarchal literary indifference to suicide. *Another* suicide. I call it murder, you see. As I call the deaths of great women artists such as Bessie Smith and Billie Holiday—poets both—murder. As I call the death of Sylvia Plath, revered and reviled and analyzed over and over in the desperate attempt to defuse that electric voice— I call it murder.

And these are only a few such examples. Most of the above wrote in English. And most even squeaked through to the extent that we know they existed. There have been other such women, singing their genius onto the page (when they were allowed to learn how to read and write, that is) or singing it onto the empty air, in every language humans are capable of. What of the lost ones—the creators who died never having been permitted to solidify their art in something lasting at all? Is that censorship? What of those who did create art but were refused publication or gallery showings or performance of their work—because they were women and to give them such credence even if (or especially if) they deserved it would be to "outrage public morals"? What of those who scribbled their insights and visions on diary leaves, letters, recipe books, in between housework and child care and husband-nurturing? What are the names of these silenced ones? Who can compute the loss to human society of their voices, their knowledge, their creative passion?

The censor has used differing means. He has quite a repertoire. The repression has ranged from blatant (death, exile, imprisonment) to subtle (male pen names, ridicule, distortion). But such categorization and comparison seem obscene when suffering is the end result. What *are* "public morals and good customs"? Does patriarchally defined public morality include the rationalization of everything from Vietnam to Watergate, from pollution of life-sustaining natural resources to the colonization and murder of the Angolans? And what are "good customs"? Rape? Enforced sterilization or enforced child-bearing? "Proper" sexual conduct for women—as defined by men? Economic deprivation, educational discrimination, emotional repression, psychological channeling, artistic censorship, political invisibility, spiritual suffocation? "Good customs" all—for women. Honored traditions all—originated by men.

Today, such morality and such customs are being challenged, not only by individual women of courage and genius forced to fight alone, without support, accompanied only by their despair. Today we speak in all languages. We see past the patriarchal barriers of age, race, class, economic distinction, and national boundaries. We will not be ignored. We will not be patronized. We will not accept the institutions which have tried to destroy us, whether the institution be one of a certain type of sexuality, or a certain mode of motherhood, or a certain standard of literary excellence which either corrupts us or indulges us, when it notices us at all.

Today Maria Isabel Barreño, Maria Teresa Horta, and Maria Velho Da Costa are not alone. They are three specific voices singing in a great and varied chorus which is determined, whatever its differences, to speak the unspeakable, to create our song even out of our singing, to approach the universe within and without us on terms which have never been conceived, let alone allowed.

Join us. You have fingers—write or wire or telephone the Portuguese Embassy, the Portuguese Consulate, the Portuguese Mission to the United Nations, the Portuguese Airlines and other businesses in this city. You have feet—visit these places, picket them, pressure them. You have tongues—speak of these three women, tell their/our story. Tell of their bravery, their risk. Tell of the extra punishment inherent in long prison sentences for women who must think about their children on the outside. You have minds—act.

Most of all, open yourselves to what you as women are feeling, to what you as men are being told—more clearly now than at any other time in history. The survival of sentient life on this planet depends upon it.

Nor will we be stopped this time. There are too many of us. Furthermore, if speaking out was made impossible for us before, silence is impossible now.

Listen, then, to the inexhaustible, uncontainable words of the Three Marias. Different voices speak them, but they sing for all of us.

January 1974

A NEW FABLE OF
THE BURNING TIME

As the sixties ceded to the seventies and the Vietnam War ended, what had been called the New Left in America was directionless and dying—and those who remained in it frequently blamed the demise on the Feminist Movement. How ironic—that the vision originally expressed so stirringly in the early SDS "Port Huron Statement"[1] should have degenerated into the cock-rock culture celebrated at the Woodstock rapes and the Altamont murder; into the jargon and one-upman(sic)ship of a central-committee mentality. How tragic that the uniquely American character-mixture of impatience and pride and violence should have put its indelible mark on a movement which was supposedly antipathetic to it. The failure was due to "the patriarchy within," not to the Feminist Movement. It is decidedly true, though, that as women in the Left (and Right and Center, for that matter) began to see a similarity in all those groups—patriarchal structure and content, one might call it—as such women began to move out on our own and create a stronger, more independent, and more universal movement of our own, those "divorced" groups undeniably were left high and dry without their basic labor force of secretaries and cooks and speechwriters and Panther-Breakfast-program fixers (at 4:00 A.M.) and mimeograph-machine churners. The New Left, like the Old (and every other direction including north, south, up and down), ran on womanpower. And womanpower was now beginning to be recycled toward women.

But the vision died hard and bitterly, and blame was fixed unfairly wherever it could be smeared. The early 1970's have seen a mini-McCarthyism among radicals (and I don't mean Eugene McCarthy—I mean The Other One). Suspicion, accusation and counter-accusation seemed to feed like birds of prey on the carrion of the sixties. Watergate had made the most fantastic paranoia seemed perfectly rational, and panic,

---

[1] See Kirkpatrick Sale's book, *SDS*, Random House, New York, 1973.

that most contagious of superficial emotions, seized many good women in its grasp.

The last article in this section, my little "New Fable," while written in loving friendship and with a particular relationship in mind, was also an attempt to comment on that panic, to shake us into a better mood about one another, and to remind us, possibly, of the concrete and continuing danger we claimed to be fighting (instead of each other).

Humor can be a weapon of extraordinary power. For years we feminists have been accused of having lost our sense of humor because we no longer chuckle good-naturedly at dumb-blonde stories, farmer's-daughter jokes, and other examples of boyish wit. More recently, though, our own style has been surfacing, and it has all the marks of classic "oppressed" humor; it is sharp, rich, acrid, sourly perceptive, and sometimes self-deprecating, like the humor of the black street-rap, the Yiddish curse, the Irish yarn. It is a sign of health that we are ready now to display our creation to the world. Much great humor is born of pain; not surprisingly does one speak of "laughing till we cried." For those who would use that pain to probe their way to freedom, another skill must be learned, that of crying till we laugh.

O NCE UPON A TIME, there lived a witch. Her closest friend in all the village was a peasant woman who, alone among the others, knew she was a witch. They had good times together, and they helped each other out.

But it was quite important that no one else around discern their friendship, in case, you see, the witch should be discovered and her friend, by their association, implicated. They both were very careful.

But then, the witch was also lonely, for although it wasn't known she was a witch, it was suspected. She wasn't . . . "popular." Now and then, when the townsfolk paid her any mind, she found she talked with pride about her friend.

Horrified later, she would blurt out her error to the peasant woman, and together they would try to estimate the danger. Never in this talking of betrayal did they speak except in jest of how the peasant woman held within *her* hands a possible betrayal of the witch greater than any error the latter could commit. Nor did this strike them as peculiar.

One day, the townsfolk noticed that the peasant woman had a cat who always followed her. They gossiped that she kept strange hours, and she could read and write. They came and took her, for to burn her as a witch.

Someone remembered that the other woman (the real witch) once had claimed to be this witch's friend—but they dismissed the notion that the other crazy ever could have *had* a friend, even a witch, and let her go.

One version of this story ends that when the priest came in the morning to fetch the prisoner to the stake, he found both women—their stone-stiff hands clutching their ribs, and pools of salt tears gathered in the creases of their rigor-mortis grins.

"Dead," he gasped, "of laughter! They have eluded us," he droned. The people marveled.

The other version goes that they both disappeared on one or the other's broom, and still circle the moon on dark nights, like two amused Sonja Henies coasting the sky.

There are three morals to this story—fragments of a conversation overheard one night by village idiots who could comprehend no meaning in these words:

Whisper One:

> *All your betrayals of me, my dear,*
> *are somehow payments against what we both fear*
> *and never speak of: mine.*

Whisper Two:

> *Friendship is mutual blackmail*
> *elevated to the level of love.*

Whisper Three:

> *We may as well trust each other.*
> *They're going to try to burn us, anyway.*

1974

PART FIVE

Beyond the
	Seventh Veil:
	Recent
		Writings

PART V:
INTRODUCTORY NOTE

Five years of traveling, lecturing, and giving poetry readings taught me much about my country and my movement, and not a little about myself. For one thing, I learned that the unavoidable course required by nature—entropy—and the inescapable process entailed in any serious politics or aesthetics—growth—are inseparable, congruent, and diametrically opposed. Which is a sobering realization.

At the first, it was not only the physical, emotional, and intellectual "high" communicated by women which gave me such intense pleasure. It was also admittedly the glamor of travel, an activity which I had done to death in my theatrical working-childhood, but one which the intervening years had glossed over with nostalgic romance. All those airplanes! All that toy food served with toy-sized plastic knives and forks by competent human-size flight attendants who were treated by most passengers as toy women! All those podiums and phallic lavalier microphones! All those motels and hotels and all that room service! All those local communes hostessed by feminists! All those receptions at which one was in turn lionized, criticized, deified, and crucified.

Except that, after a year of such questionable exoticisms, life began to appear a deadly round of airports echoing flight announcements, of deserted terminals at 11:00 P.M. or 6:00 A.M., of Holiday Inns and Ramada Inns and Travelodges and local motels, these last also often used by Big Men On Campus to celebrate their successful campaign against some other young woman who was finally "going too far," whose emotions they were callously manipulating and whose reputation they were light-heartedly corroding. Life became never being able to sit at my desk for more than three days at a time without having to pack again. Life became long-distance phone calls with my husband and child, calls squeezed in after the afternoon guest-seminar and before the evening lecture, while I hunched over a room-service sandwich in my motel room and nursed a container of rapidly cooling tea for my ever-present cold. Life was trying to pack one small bag for a February trip which would span Canada and Arizona; life was revising old poems and trying to draft new ones on seat-back tray-tables in every airborne vehicle from a 747 to a two-seater helicopter; it was a chronic stiff neck from dozing off in trains and buses and waiting rooms and ladies' rooms and backstage green rooms.

Life was also learning that the at-first temptingly homey stay at the local feminist commune was to be avoided, if possible, and without giving offense, since, with a few rare and memorable exceptions, it usually meant some or all of the following: (1) Being kept awake through the night for the "intimate, exclusive lecture"—the unstated but equivalent price of room and board (after which the local sisters went to bed and their bleary guest lurched off to the airport for another round of same); (2) Being fed some gaggingly healthy gummy brown rice with a puddle of soy sauce thereon and a limp cabbage leaf thereunder, this repast suitably accompanied either by surprisingly abundant cans of beer (which I happen not to drink) or more likely by teensy cups of lukewarm tea which had the color of herbal shampoo but, I am certain, less flavor; (3) Feeling compelled to insist on washing up after dinner, because after all one did not wish to appear like a horrible New-York-type-star-leader who let other women wait on her forgodsake, and consequently doing dishes for ten people after having lectured and before the all-night private pump-her-for-information rap; (4) Finding that if one were permitted, reluctantly, a few hours of sleep, this relaxation was supposed to take place in a sleeping bag on the floor. To complain and be a rotten sport was out of the question. To reject these sisters, hurt the feelings of women who were, after all, genuinely and flatteringly hungry for whatever one had to share with them, women who really were trying to treat their guest as best they knew how—this rejection was also unthinkable. One grinned, talked, rasped cheerfully hoarse, sucked cough drops until one's tongue glistened chartreuse, washed chopsticks, actually learned to enjoy it all—and tried to sleep on the plane.

Later, to be sure, one rediscovered the miraculous luxury of privacy at hotels, except that such accommodations were rarely paid for by the school, and were cumulatively costly. In time, too, they began to appear hallucinatingly identical. The smell of plastic philodendrons in certain motel lobbies, particularly at dawn, when one is waiting half comatose for the town's sole taxi, operated by the town's sole surly taxi driver, to convey one to the single-runway airport which lacks even a coffee machine—that gangrenous fake green smell shall hover in my nostrils, I think, at my dying, especially if I have led a wicked life. As will return, in my worst nightmares, the apparition of those iridescently orange cabbage roses with which it seemed most of the motel-room walls were papered, the design carried through coyly in the bedspread fabric. Since the boreal air conditioner rarely could be turned off and an extra blanket was nowhere to be found, the luckless inhabitant would appropriate the bedspread as additional covering—only to find, once tucked in, that its matching pattern made her feel as if she had become subsumed into the wall and was now peeping out through a rip in the paper.

There was in addition the educational experience of being a woman traveling alone. This subject requires a book in itself, which I yet may write, if I can quell the retching sensation that rises in my throat when I think of reliving those experiences in order to write at length about them: the hotel elevator at 2:00 A.M. filled with potbellied, boozy, balding, cigar-chomping conventioneers—and me, replete with feminist buttons, returning from a late C-R session. There was the veritable parade of discharged soldiers flying the last lap home from Vietnam, to be met by wives, mothers, and girlfriends all unaware of how earlier, on the plane, their loyally awaited man had maneuvered the seat next to a single woman and then, despite discouragement, had launched into bragging about his exploits, sexual and military, in "Nam." But there was also an unexpectedly quick trust and friendliness among the traveling women strangers, particularly where children were involved; oh, the whole vocabularies exchanged in a simple offer to hold her baby while the mother wipes the takeoff throw-up from the front of his three-year-old sister!

I learned, too, that our current system of campaigning by public officials is not only as gross a ritual as I'd always thought, but an appallingly dangerous tradition as well, and least of all from the threat most articulated: assassination. Rather, the danger lies in one's seeing too many faces, shaking too many hands, facing too many audiences, answering too many of the same questions, repeating too often what may once have been sincerely meant statements but which are reduced inevitably to platitudes. The danger is in watching complexities "of necessity" simplified (not enough time, not enough space, not enough attention), then oversimplified, then debased into the very kind of nonthought one fancied one was opposing. The degree of cynicism in this Gresham's law school is horribly unavoidable, as is the exhaustion, the spiritual embitterment, the emotional megalomania (since one tries to use this meaningless aimed-at-the-celebrity "love" to fill that life's personal loneliness), and the self-disgust at having let oneself be trapped in such a squirrel cage. Whoever has gone this round is unfit, for at least five years after, to hold public office. By that time some sense of the individual and of reality may have returned. (I hasten to add that I saw, met, spoke to and at and with only a fraction of what our so-called political leaders—those who wield power over our daily lives—face.) This process is a vile, corruptive one. It slackens the spirit and evokes contempt for the very people on whose behalf one is purportedly acting;

they begin to appear as a faceless and manipulating mass. And one begins to feel like an equally faceless and manipulable demagogue.

I ought to have feared this hypocrisy, ought to have recognized or rather remembered it from the almost twenty years of my life spent in the theater. But there is honor, at least, in that profession—one's very job is to appear to be something other than who and what one really is; one's skill, in fact, is bent toward that end. This is hardly comparable to the political candidate (or radical organizer) who claims to be her own self but learns not to expose authentic aspects of that self for fear of losing the attention or affection of the constituency. Because in our society the political message does depend to a lamentable degree on who delivers it, and how.[1] The actor's pretense is a translucent art, and is therefore decent. The politician's pretense is an opaque charade, a deliberate deception.

There were times when my own life seemed to curve back on itself and mockingly return me to the same progression of stages, cameras, and mikes I had fought so hard to escape as an adolescent. What child's talent my family once had seen fit to exploit became an adult's skill which my cause now saw fit to conscript. Plus ça change . . . , I would mutter, in my crabbier moments. Yet the responsibility for one's life choice ultimately is one's own—that is, after sexism, racism, and the other cage-bars of existence have set the boundaries within which that choice can be made, although sometimes it can be made bravely enough to bend the bars, or render them irrelevant.

During this siege of disillusion, I learned that the forging of a public face, seemingly so necessary for the political activist (whether a senatorial candidate or an outside agitator) and perhaps even useful to the interpretive artist, can be quite destructive to the creative artist. How can it be otherwise, when one's replies perforce become shortened, self-protective, and superficial in a question-and-answer session: it is neither the time nor place to be particularly confidential (although I found myself trying, and in consequence often sustained internal emotional bleeding). Yet the real answers, and more importantly the questions themselves, self-asked, are the stuff of the artist, in whose context the time and place are unimportant, and for whom length, self-exposure, and depth are all assumed prerequisites, givens. I chose this latter course a long time ago, and in 1975 I renewed that vow, never again to be quite so successfully diverted from these "orders."

---

[1] Ronald Reagan's hybrid character, for example, is no coincidence. He is the logical apparition conjured up by a public taught to trust the worth of celebrity and mistrust the work of cerebration. (Thespian Nation, indeed.) It's not his fault that he is no more qualified to be called a public servant than he was to be called an actor.

But then that year saw the mid-decade shift in so many different ways. The war, that pustulating sore in the soul of America, had ended. Vietnam "fell" to those who lived there—the Vietnamese. The first piece of writing in this section, "Letter from a War," speaks to the trauma of that trauma's close. The seventies were, because of or despite this episode, turning on an inward-directed course: self-discovery, self-analysis, an approximation if not a return to the psychological world view so popular in the fifties. It is as if external political action must appear for the moment less necessary or possible or too frightening or exhausting—then people will reencounter the personal. But the motivation is too often retreat instead of risk, and sometimes it's just too late—one has lost the whole world and not gained one's soul, since the internal political action (and knowledge) has been repressed into nonexistence, even at the expense of that external politics for whose urgent sake it was supposedly sacrificed in the first place. What a pity, and how senseless, anyway, is this dichotomy! It sends so many straight from the street demonstration to the dropout farm, from the rhetoric of the central committee (or of the Nixon White House) to the jargon of the latest guru (or of new-found fundamentalist Christianity). This is change?

Is it merely pride, then, which makes me feel that the Women's Movement has weathered such a shift admirably well? And is that because we are founded on a belief that the personal is political, the insistence on a breakdown of patriarchal distinctions, neat categories, and linear thought? I hope so. I do notice that women seem bent on learning as much as possible about ourselves, each other, children, men, the world—and that most of us are no more willing to sacrifice internal psychological truths than we are to genuflect before the shrine of The One Truth According to Saint Freud. The essays on sado-masochistic fantasies and on paranoia in this section of Going Too Far describe a continuing attempt on my part to synchronize that same interior landscape with exterior "reality" and thus discover a synthesis which can teach us something about each, and about the third thing they constitute, anew, together.

The mid-seventies saw yet another major development in the Women's Movement, the birth of what we might call women's culture. This trend, in tone as celebratory and in cost as excruciating as labor contractions, is explored in the last essays of this section, for it is as a feminist and an artist that I rejoice in the embrace of art and politics—and it is as an artist and a feminist that I am unnerved at the betimes lewd quality of that embrace.

W. B. Yeats wrote, "All things can tempt me from this craft of verse," as he schizophrenically endured one magnetic pull toward his art and another toward his vision of a transformed Ireland. There

*must be, for the artist who refuses to hide in the ivory tower or to serve
as a door-mat propagandist, some wholly new approach, some synthesis,
some rejection of these narrow extremes. Can the feminist artist create
this space? Is she uniquely in a position to do so, since as a woman it has
been more difficult for her all along—to be an artist, to be political, to
be? Can her life-act of rebellion contain in itself the disparate forms
of rebellion as well as clues to their harmony? Time and herstory will
tell us. A terrible duty is born. But the last section of this book of
personal documents is a reaching toward that goal. It contains writings
which have not been published before, which were conceived away
from (and sometimes in reaction against) the podium, and written
behind all the rhetoric.*

*I could tremble, if I let myself, that the reader who has generously
accompanied me this far might feel betrayed by or at least unprepared
for some of the pieces in this last section. It is even possible, though
less likely, that a rare reader in an excess of misinterpretation might
suspect that I have finally made good a warning in one of my poems:
"And I will speak . . . more and more in crazy gibberish you cannot
understand . . . " That this is neither my intention nor my hope will be
clear to those who comprehend the imperative of going beyond the
confessional style to the analytical, beyond the philosophical to the
poetic, beyond the aesthetic to the ecstatic. Or, to put it more plainly,
these last essays are merely about the manner in which feminism can
be defined as daring to constitute that forbidden junction of those three
subjects all well-brought-up members of Western civilization were told
never to discuss in polite company: sex, politics, and religion. Women
face the difficulty of inventing the gesture through which we grasp our
reality and thereby simultaneously invent ourselves. It is a life-and-death
dance, and in this sense we are truly a new kind of movement. I have
tried, in the later pieces in this section, to refuse a certain self-indulgent
vulnerability in myself the refuge of mere confession without attempted
conclusions. If my gestures in this endeavor appear unfamiliar or awkward, I am genuinely sorry—which is hardly meant as an apology but
rather as an expression of real sorrow that we have been kept from
making such gestures, or recognizing them, for so long. The dance is,
after all, that progression of movements from gravity toward grace, in
the midst of which, and almost by chance, the dancer finds herself dis-
carding one veil of superfluous skin after another. That she is offered
great rewards for this act—entire realms of material power and even
the dedication of human sacrifice—is a consideration beneath contempt.
Likewise, the certainty that she will be called upon to pay for this act
with her own life is an eventuality unworthy of diverting her attention.*

*Entropy and growth. At this writing I have turned thirty-five
years old. Certain ground beneath my feet, certain corridors of my*

psychic life, are so familiar I can move along them unconsciously, not even groping or feeling my way: My writing, the primary rock, the reason for tolerating this glorious, senseless existence at all; Kenneth, his writing, his capacity for change, all his deaths and his resurrections; Blake, growing older and more aware every day of the unutterable beauty and unspeakable cruelty of living and loving with consciousness; a few— very few—beloved friends; certain works of art—the Bach B Minor Mass *and* Lear, Middlemarch *and* The Women at Point Sur *and* The Trial; *the challenge of Anne Bradstreet and Albert Camus and Christina Rossetti and Andrew Marvell and Mary Cassatt and Maurice Ravel and Emily Brontë; the examples of Elizabeth Tudor, of George Sand, Saint Teresa, Nina Simone, Emmeline Pankhurst, Martha Graham, Hetshapsut, and Louise Labé. So much more, so many more.*

If one further surprisingly obvious discovery lay in wait for me beneath the cynicism encountered in these past few years, it surely is my own capacity for a peculiar, arrogant humility. Arrogant because it is based on a new-found pride in what I have done, where I have come from and where I go, what I am and even more what I am becoming. And humble because, despite the intentionally ironic title of this book, it is simply not possible to go far enough. *I am continually reminded of this, even while I reach to steady myself from a dizziness at the vast space imperceptibly traveled. It is that space ultimately which counts, not the distance one thinks one has covered. It is that space across which one never dares sufficiently go too far, but across which, if one is fortunate, one might perhaps venture a few faltering steps.*

LETTER FROM A WAR

The following letter, like those in Part I of this book, was written with no eye to publication. It was a spontaneous outpouring in the middle of a spring night, penned from a small town in Midwest America to another woman in a similar small town. The recipient of the letter, Jane Alpert, was—and still is, at the writing of this prefatory note—in prison, serving a term for militant anti-war actions during the sixties. She had been a fugitive from the law for four years, during which time she courageously declared her "conversion" to radical feminism in an open letter from the underground. In 1974 she surfaced, prepared to serve a prison term in order to function openly in the service of her feminist politics and freely as the writer she wished to become. We had been friends years earlier, at *Rat*, before her period of fugitivity; it seemed that we had gone through so many similar changes in our very different ways.

The reference in this letter to "Sam" pertains to Samuel Melville, Jane's lover, who in 1969 was arrested on the same charge as she, sentenced, and killed in the Attica prison uprising, in 1971. The reference to Kenneth's being muzzled for his political beliefs was meant as an indictment against those who found his newer work too threatening to publish—as it dealt with a man's struggle to transform himself through love, to comprehend and rise to what feminism asked of him. The mention of Ti-Grace Atkinson's "denunciation" of Alpert refers to the former's attempt to cast a cloud over Jane's motives for surrender. The Left had been foreseeably unenchanted with Jane's criticism of it, and with her dedication to feminist politics—but the Feminist Movement was strong in its defense and support of a woman whose honor was unquestionable and whose commitment to feminism was obvious. At one point, Atkinson, apparently isolated from feminist consciousness, declared in effect that women should be led by Weathermen and acknowledge a total identification with the men at Attica—or else be drummed out of the human race. This was meant as a special cut to Jane, who had lost Sam at Attica, but who had nevertheless some years later drawn the courage from her new-found feminist consciousness to analyze their relationship in retro-spect. She found it virulently sexist—and she said so publicly.

The other minor characters are Leftist activists Jane and I had known in the past—Rosa and Tricia and "Chowder," this last my version of the rather soupy pseudonym used by one pathetically anti-feminist woman. I fear that all three women could be counted on to reflect the feelings expressed by the young man at a Boston rally toward the war's end who, it was reported to me, exhorted the crowd not to "drift away from the Left" but to "carry *the nostalgia we all feel for the war that brought us together* further into *other organizing opportuni-ties.*" The italics are mine but the sentiments, seriously, were his. As for Tom Hayden and Jane Fonda, the former anti-war crusaders are at this writing campaigning for the jobs of U.S. Senator and U.S. Senator's wife, respectively.

This letter is in a sense out of context, in that Jane has been a presence in many of my poems—and there are other letters between us. But those are for another book, at another time. I include this one letter now because in it, without par-ticularly intending to do so, I summarized for myself most truly what the grief of Vietnam has meant to me as a woman, and what that grief—which had so indelibly scarred the sixties and which was now ostensibly over—would continue and con-tinue and continue to mean, to a woman.

> *Travelodge*
> *Galesburg, Illinois*
> *29 April 1975*

D EAR JANE:

You see from the stationery where I am, just back a little while ago from a seminar-then-faculty-dinner-then-poetry-reading-then-rap-session-then-drink-with-faculty-wives.

And while undressing and unpacking I turned on the little black-and-white television set, to encounter a night-long special broadcast on the surrender of Saigon and the NLF entry into the city. *It is over now,* Harry Reasoner reports. *Over now,* he says.

And all the expectable films are shown—the old ones, like shards of horror fossilized on film: that soldier setting fire to a thatched hut with his Zippo lighter; that pistol going off against the temple of the plaid-shirted young Viet Cong, full-face into the camera as his skull fragments; the cadaver heads of aged grandmothers bent over baby bodies; the bare-breasted corpses of young women sprawled by roadsides; the children, the children—numb-faced, lost forever, peddling chocolate or cocaine or themselves in the streets.

And the new films, also expectable: the triumphant grins worn by soldiers riding tanks into Saigon; the frantic clawing hordes of terrified South Vietnamese trying to follow their former U.S. employers out, clogging the airstrips, hanging on plane wings, swarming around helicopters; the bar-girls welcoming a new set of conquerors with the same smiles, empty eyes above set lips; the children filmed in emergency orphan camps, already being taught to sing new songs that convey the message of a new political education—the children, waving a different flag now, but in the same uniform rhythm.

And I'm sitting on the bed in this tacky little room with a dingy mustard-colored rug and fluorescent bulbs overhead and a freight train chugging by somewhere off in the Illinois countryside around this small college town, and I'm tired from having flown and spoken and read and talked with women for hours and I'm thinking of you and I'm weeping like a fool.

The newscasters speak at length about guilt, national guilt—how we as a nation *must* feel it, or how we must *not* feel it, what lessons are to be learned from the 500,000 American soldiers dead or crippled (their torn bodies now being displayed across the flickering screen). I feel no guilt. For once I feel as guiltless as I am powerless. It is not guilt that makes me sob ridiculously, my voice loud and ludicrous in an empty room. Oh, and I know well the lesson they could learn—if they would.

No, I weep for us, dear Jane, for this tragedy which at once so disfigured and transfigured our lives that I write this from my portable prison of required survival, to you in your fixed prison of required endurance. Because we were changed forever by the decade they now calmly analyze. We came out of it, we cried out our protest and committed our actions and risked our lives and sanities and sacred honor *and then continued*, daring, even further. In a way, we, as women, are alone escaped to tell.

I'm weeping at the cost, I know. The bloody cost, the bloody pain, always and forever. I'm weeping for Sam, tonight, I know. I'm weeping for the fatuous celebration going on at this moment in the Hayden-Fonda house or in Chowder's apartment. I'm weeping for the baby-lifted orphans abducted into a nation of Disney and Christian names. I'm weeping for the bar-girls and their race-mixed children, unwanted by America *and* Vietnam; for the peasants who *still* have no voice in their own destiny; for the blinded amputee GI who spits out bitterly, "We should've stayed and atom-bombed 'em"; for the cadre women busing into the South, to take charge of child-camps and to organize the governmental bureaucracies with brisk secretarial precision. I'm weeping because our own struggle is so infinitely complex and enormous in its scope that you and I will never live to enter *our* metaphorical Saigon in triumph—which is too petty a goal for desiring, anyway. I'm weeping because the very air in this stuffy room rings with the screams, moans, pleas, gasps, and silences of a billion intricate miseries and needs and deaths. I'm weeping because earlier this evening a middle-aged faculty wife broke down in my arms and cried out her desire to learn to love freedom as much as she loved her husband and children, at least enough so that she could wrestle *with* them to achieve it *together* with them.

I'm weeping because Rosa or Tricia or any of their friends would seriously think you and I are indifferent to what is happening tonight; because they see no link between that Galesburg housewife and these television films; because they don't understand how much more we understand. For I cannot celebrate simplistically when I am mourning. I cannot rejoice to see one rigid regime replace another, however much I once devoutly wished for this. I cannot feel relief when I know that nothing, really, has changed, nothing really is over—merely in faulty translation. I cannot even ignore all these familiar films, turn off the set, force myself to sleep so that I can teach an 8:00 A.M. class and then catch a plane. Because I am grieving.

The class is on "The History of Women." I wonder what exists in the universe that would not come under that heading. Or should we merely retitle it "Suffering and Endurance 101"? As we balance rice sacks on one hip and a baby on the other, dodging shells in a city gone mad? As we plan a Wiccean Beltane Sabbat ritual in the teeth of a culture which worships despair? As we dare write poems with the ink of our blood? As we mourn men we have loved or love—one killed for his politics, and one slowly, mercilessly muzzled for *his* politics? As we answer letters to prison from women we've never seen, or read poems aloud to women we'll never see again—a fragile but real thread of communication spun throughout what can appear even to oneself as dutiful or, worse, hypocritical gestures? As we pen desperate midnight letters from Galesburg, Illinois, to Muncy, Pennsylvania?

"We are Attica," rants Ti-Grace in her denunciation of you—choosing an all-male conclave for her identification. Poor soul, that she cannot realize you and I know better than that. *For we are Vietnam.*

And Auschwitz. And Cologne. And Hiroshima. And Como—where one thousand witches were burnt in a single day. And Harlem. And Galesburg. And China. And South Africa. And Williamsport. And the open seas where the great whales are slaughtered, spuming red geysers. And the dying forests, where the eggs we lay in our birds' nests have thin pesticide-rotted shells. We are this whole agonized weeping grieving heaving anguished furious mad-with-pain planet crying out against the insupportable burden we have borne for so long.

Revolution, triumph, winning—too small, too minuscule, such

words. We must rediscover the older, larger words: life, creativity, love. And, simply, *change*. Somehow.

You are much with me tonight, in this vulgar little room, in the immensity of this vision, where we are both weeping together, as if the tears of women could save a world.

My love,
Robin

THE POLITICS OF SADO-MASOCHISTIC FANTASIES

The apocryphal story goes like this: At one of the earliest conferences of this feminist wave, during the late 1960's, a curious
confrontation-and-avoidance maneuver was executed in the
workshop on sexuality. About eighty women were gathered
together in the room, and the discussion had been open, supportive, warm, and truly consciousness-raising. During a lull,
one woman ventured in a quavering voice, "I wonder, uh,
could we maybe discuss—I mean, it's odd, as feminists, I know,
but, uh . . . well, I, um, sometimes have these sexual fantasies
which are kind of, uh, masochistic—and . . . I, well, wondered
if anyone else here had that experience. Uh . . . maybe they
could just raise their hands if they did, or . . . maybe we could
figure out what it meant, uh, I mean . . ." She trailed off. A
thundering hush ensued. Then, slowly, every woman in the
room, one by one, raised her hand. This pantomine, performed
in complete silence, was followed by yet another more pro-
longed stillness, which in turn was broken by some hearty
comment on an unrelated subject. Everyone's relief was palpable. The subject of fantasies—particularly *such* fantasies—was
dropped, and rarely has been picked up again in the Women's
Movement until now.

There are, to be sure, various books recently published on
the fantasy lives of women. These books range from the pseudo-
scientific to the soft-core-porn in their approach. Here we can
encounter the virulently anti-feminist thought of such Freudians
as Marie Robinson, whose book *The Power of Sexual Surrender*
is to women what a tome called *Why You Know You Love It
on the Plantation* would be to blacks or one titled *How to Be
Happy in Line to the Showers* would be to Jews. Here too we
may gag at that fake sexual-liberation approach so popular
with men in the sixties—with its parallel implication that if you
are "turned off" by something (*anything*) or someone (*anyone*)
you are a hung-up prude. These books usually are non-written

by a person claiming to be female who bears a name which consists of one supposedly titillating initial. The double-whammy of Marie Robinson and "J" (not to mention "O") has spun more than one woman into vertigo. In sum, the new crop of books on female fantasies seem to be lecturing us that (1) all women are masochistic anyway, ergo it's in your nature so don't fight it and if that makes you somehow uncomfortable it shouldn't, or, (2) "anything goes" and if you don't like it you should. Do you sense in this a rather consistent message of Whatever It Is, It's Your Fault, Lady? Ah.

The point is that salacious descriptions of made-for-the-market fantasies, or patronizing psychiatric analyses of the same, or hip pressure to get with it and "be groovy" are not, any of them, helpful approaches to the woman who wishes to *understand* her condition, her feelings, her desires (or who simply cherishes her own sense of good taste). *Feminism is about precisely such understanding*, and this can be gained only through slow and hazardous work *by* ourselves, the ultimate experts *on* ourselves—aided perhaps by that rare leap of consciousness that can make the connections through myth, art, revelation.

The following essay is an attempt to begin such work on this interestingly ignored subject. Because of its content and the requirements of personal honesty in writing about it, this is possibly the article included here which could tempt me to fear the greatest embarrassment, despite my having already dealt with the subject matter more than once in my poetry. But then psychology, sexuality, dreams—these are more at home in a work of art than in a work of political analysis; what is nude in a poem seems so naked in prose. Again, the feminist imperative is to surmount the barrier between those forms; hence, my adopted device of the parable.

One can still sense the forbidden quality of the topic in the careful omission of it from most discussion in the Women's Movement. This is doubtless because despite the, I have learned, widespread shared occurrence of such fantasies among feminists, we all wince at what appears to be the inconsistency: "What? A feminist, a fighter for women's rights and power—a *feminist* having fantasies of being dominated, humiliated, forced into submission? Intolerable." I can hear the male voices even now, finding in our search for understanding merely a confirmation of their worst stereotype: "I *knew* all these feminists needed was a good rape. Women need to be struck regularly, like gongs. All women love the cave-man approach, no matter what they pretend." This was one predictable if sickening reaction to such a line as "Every woman adores a Fascist"—despite the very point that Plath was making. Irony's ultimate irony may lie in its capacity for making itself invisible.

One should not care about the reactions of such willfully brutal and clodpated persons, of course. Yet the certainty that they wait like spectators in the arena drooling over their ices and settling down on their cushions *is* unsettling for those who, no matter how well trained for the encounter, emerge to confront and wrestle with newly uncaged beasts. Most absurd of all is the notion that one is engaged in such an encounter for—oh hilarious thought—their entertainment. But too much consideration already has been given to such an audience. It is time they were forgotten. The spark glowing like an impatient insight in the eye of the wild adversary throws everything else into shadow. It is here that one must begin.

I: THE BACKGROUND

I BEGAN WORK on this subject—sado-masochistic fantasies—before I knew such a name for it. I was less than ten years old, but intelligent, curious, and self-respectful enough to be irritated by feeling a vague sexual stimulation at the thought of someone dominating me. I do know that by the time I was thirteen or so, I was consciously trying to combat such thoughts—not because I thought them "perverted" (yet) but because it perplexed me that what *worked* in fantasy was so different from reality. I knew already that when, in real life, anyone had power over me (as all adults do over all children) I liked it not at all; I also knew that if anyone laid a punishing hand on me (exceedingly rare in my family) I hated their guts and found it utterly *un*exciting. So what in hell was this fantasy stuff I was getting off on? I had an active masturbation life as a child and a fittingly wide repertoire of fantasies to go along with it—but the set and costume changes all revolved around the same plot. By early adolescence, then, I set myself the task of trying to understand this. Naturally, I had no way of knowing that I was not alone in both my tendency and my search for an understanding of it. It would be many years before I would have an inkling that this experience was shared at all—let alone so widely, and even among my feminist peers.

I can't recall the exact chronology of my theories, but I do know that during my teenage years I read widely on the subject and at one point or another came up with various explanations, some of my own making, others personal versions patched together from ostensibly expert theories—each time hoping that *this* one would be the magic key which would liberate me from these damned fantasies.

One theory explained it all as Longing for the Absent Father-Figure; that is, I yearned for his nonexistent attention and care. Since fatherly attention and care most often expressed itself as authority and discipline (classic patriarchal role), it must follow that I longed psycho-sexually for such discipline—i.e., for the father.

Another theory was that the entire theme was simply one of Flesh-Loathing—fantasy punishment linked of necessity to flesh-enjoyment. Another was *Self*-Loathing; I must hate myself to wish such release via humiliation.[1]

There was the Sexual Guilt Theory: "I'm afraid of sex and must be relieved of responsibility for sexual enjoyment by the projected force-ful figure who rapes." There was of course the Helene Deutsch-Marie Robinson theory: "It's in my nature, it's natural to all women to be sexual and emotional masochists—we love pain."

There was the Physical Reality Theory, based largely on my read-ing of Karen Horney's work. Horney, grappling with the subject as an early feminist psychiatrist, rejected the Freudian notion that female sexuality perforce was masochistic, although she did note that women were socially pressured to act passively, and she suggested that various objective realities might bolster this conditioning—factors such as wom-en's being generally of less weight, height, and physical strength than most men, and of women's vulnerability to greater bodily changes (sometimes painful ones): menarche, defloration, childbirth, and meno-pause. Horney posited, too, that masochistic fantasies in women could be tied in with feelings of repressed rage and guilt about the mother—a reverse projection in which a daughter fantasizes violence done to her-self rather than to that archetypal female figure with which she so iden-tifies and about which she is so passionately ambivalent. This theory, touching as it does on the emotional and sexual cathexis between mother and daughter, has held my interest for a long time, and its influence can be spotted in quite a few of my poems, including "Matrilineal Descent" in *Monster*[2] and "The Network of the Imaginary Mother" in *Lady of the Beasts*.[3]

There was even the Self-Indulgent Theory, also known as the

---

[1] A variation on this is the hypothesis of Signe Hammer as put forth in "The Rape Fantasies of Women: Up from Disrepute" (*Village Voice*, April 5, 1976). Ms. Hammer, in an intelligent but too-brief essay, posits that "Our basic rape fantasy reflects our anxiety about asserting ourselves in *all* areas—in work, sex, and relationships" (italics mine). This is a refreshing advance beyond the Freudian-influenced strictly sexual interpretation. It also provokes the startling thought that assertive women in general and feminists in particular might be especially prey to such culturally implanted self-punishing devices. Molly Haskell, in an essay in *Ms.* (November 1976) analyzes rape fantasies as they have been exploited and distorted by the film industry, and reaches an interesting set of conclusions directly related to Signe Hammer's theory.

[2] *Monster*, p. 33.

[3] *Lady of the Beasts* (Random House, New York, 1976), p. 61. First pub-lished in *American Poetry Review*, Vol. 5, No. 4, 1976.

Will-Power Approach: "This whole thing is ridiculous and overanalyzed; if I wish these fantasies to cease then I simply must stop having them *and* dissecting them."

Each of the above hypotheses was far more intricate than I have space or concern for here. But the difficulty was that none seemed satisfactory, none rang true, and none, in terms of exorcising the fantasies *or* making me feel comfortable with them—*worked*.

In my late adolescence and early twenties I got even more sophisticated about the fantasies. For one thing I began to write about them. "The Improvisers," a long poem written in 1962,[4] was the first time I had dared, in print, to deal with the subject so graphically. During this period I encountered the work of Frantz Fanon, the black Algerian psychiatrist and revolutionary who was among the first to place certain aspects of the psyche in a political context. His studies of psychoses in colonized peoples, his theory of an evoked and required identification with the colonizer, his charting of this process—all this work seemed to open up a whole new approach to analyzing my fantasies. It was necessary to "translate," of course. Fanon's unflinching consciousness positively cringed when it came to the subject of women. But women develop the skill of such translation (for Algerian, read female—because the author assuredly will not extend his insights in your direction) and I was already fairly accomplished at reading my invisible self into the "mankinds" of everyone from Confucius to Sartre. From this translation emerged a number of absorbing questions. Were masochistic fantasies in women, then, a sexual "psychosis" evoked and required by the patriarchal system? Was this a response—in a deliberate code of "madness"—to oppression? Was it then capable of transformation through varying the characters, i.e., the symbols of political power and powerlessness?

I began to recast my fantasies, to play at an intentional reorganization of them. At first I did the obvious: I tried to reverse the roles of dominant and submissive—I would be the master and the faceless male figure the slave (or: teacher/student, parent/child, sultan/favorite, rapist/victim, etc.).[5] No flicker of interest there, despite repeated at-

---

[4] In *Monster*, p. 3. First published by *The Sewanee Review* in 1965.

[5] It is more direct to simplify all the plots into a verbal shorthand for which we may use the words "dominance" and "submission." If this disappoints some readers I am sorry, but they must look elsewhere for their pleasure. The silly—or gory—details are of little consequence here, because even if there is a differing of intensity in the various fantasies (I learned that mine were quite tame compared to the branding irons of other imaginations) *the quality, the message, the politics are identical*. It is generally more useful to focus on the *connectives* among oppressed peoples, and leave emphasizing the differences to the oppressor. He does it so well, anyway.

tempts to will such a response. I felt stymied. Then I thought of lifting the scene whole-cloth into the area of homosexuality, which hitherto had played only a small part in my fantasy life; it was a piquant condiment for now and then, but not a staple, like bread. Aha. Here, with an all-woman cast, the reversal (myself as dominant character) worked! Startling. So it was considered by my subconscious permissible to dominate another woman but not a man! Did this mean that an all-female context provided me with an organic freedom of possibility, a lessening of general inhibition? That would be a positive gain. Or did it mean that basically I had contempt for my own people, that I saw women in effect as submissive inferiors, and could project myself as such onto another woman but never onto a man? A debasing insight, that.

I tried playing the submissive role in the all-woman fantasy. Sometimes it "took," more often not. Hmmm. I tried absenting myself entirely, reforging the scenario into one with myself as voyeur. In this approach the following were most effective, in declining order: Male-dominant/female-submissive; All-male cast, both roles; All-female cast, both roles; Female-dominant/male-submissive. Omigod, I thought. A certain pattern is beginning to emerge.

At this point I remember I was so disheartened at what I thought was the inevitable core motivation (a deep-lodged feeling of justified inferiority to men) that I retreated into the Will-Power Approach and refused to let myself fantasize any more. This precipitously reduced my capacity for orgasm, which was, I decided, even more depressing, and as I feared myself approaching a near-frigid state, I "capitulated," feeling like an alcoholic gone back on the bottle.

It wasn't until a few years ago, in my early thirties, that I attempted yet another analysis in this (pathetic? amusing? brave?) life experiment. Exorcism be damned. If the fantasy-theme seemed enjoyable to me, I was not about to punish myself with guilt for that pleasure. But I did still want to feel comfortable with it, and most of all to *understand* it.

The gradually rediscovered areas of women's history, the increasingly reexamined (and newly validated) theories on matriarchal origin, and the reconsideration of the power (and reality) of myth began to come together for me, to pattern themselves into a possible explanation of what these fantasies meant, in their political metaphor, for myself and other women. This explanation is offered here because for me it works, makes sense, feels right as no other theory has, and because it consequently has helped me to *understand* something (which may be the only real freedom available to sentient life after all). I hope it may be of some use to other women who, like me, have agonized over their own desire—never even knowing what that desire meant, or how it was deserving of their pride.

II: THE TERMS

To CONSTRUCT a political analysis of the occurrence, let alone the frequency, of sado-masochistic fantasies among women we must venture to use the tools offered us by mytho-history. By mytho-history I mean that area of serious scholarship explored, for example, by Robert Graves in *The Greek Myths* and *The White Goddess*, and by Joseph Campbell in *The Masks of God*, as well as by Murray, Frazer, Jung, Lévi-Strauss, Bachofen, Briffault, Harrison, and other key anthropologists, mythographers, and historians. This necessitates leaving behind us a rigid adherence to what is claimed as historical fact; it requires an admission that what is fact one day may be discovered the next to have been bias, and what had been considered myth may actually have been fact (depending on who writes the books and runs the academies; male-dominated scholarship, we now realize, just as white-dominated scholarship, has not been as value-free as one would have wished). A mytho-historical approach requires of us at one and the same time a suspension of disbelief *and* a dedication to truth—or else it would descend into sloppy thinking and sentimentality. It frees us to discover what we may discover, without preconceived assumptions or denials or even ideals—but then we must *admit* what we discover. (This is one definition of a *real* "scientific method.") Last, a mytho-historical approach necessitates a sensitivity to metaphor. By that I mean a willingness to decipher the code of myth—which may, for example, have cast the thawing of the Ice Age into the biblical story of the Flood, which may have translated the building of the pyramids into the Tower of Babel, and which certainly anthropomorphized (and does, to this day) mystical ideas, emotions, and concepts into "gods."

It has been said, and I think correctly, that myth is the very "stuff" of poetry. It may also be the very stuff of pre-history, of that time for which we have no written record except a few cave paintings of abiding splendor, certain circular configurations of stones, some burial ornaments resonant with possibilities of interpretation, and that other record—shared, verbally bequeathed and embroidered and elaborated on, created and preserved by what Jung called the "collective unconscious"—that encoded record of events and their effects on humankind and the planet itself: myth. What was yesterday's magic is today's science. It seems as likely that what was seen through a glass darkly yesterday as myth forms the basis for what tomorrow will be understood as history.

Some caveats are necessary before we approach the parable of sado-masochism in women. The first is that I am examining *fantasies* on the theme. This is where my own experience has lain, and it is this subject which I have discussed at length with other women. I know next to nothing about "real-life" acts of sado-masochistic sexuality. I have never sought such situations or participated in them, and what knowledge I have of them is vague and second-hand. It may be that an extension of the theory advanced here (about the fantasies themselves) would be applicable to the real acts. I honestly don't know, nor have I given that possibility much attention. Actually, it seems irrelevant to me, since I know that I myself (and most of the women with whom I share the penchant for such fantasies) would never seek their reality. In fact, if forced to encounter that reality, we would be turned *off* sexually by it. Our disgust would be genuine, and we would all probably fight like hell to free ourselves from real pain and real degradation. Ah, but the fantasy which one controls oneself, in the safety and privacy of one's own brain and body! *That* is another matter, and that is my concern here. Should others wish to attempt relating my theory to sado-masochistic practice itself, they are welcome. The results might be interesting. For me however, and for this essay, the world of such actual practice and that of the fantasy are totally separate.

It should further be stated that I am not exploring what I might call *emotional* sado-masochistic tendencies. I mean by this the disposition of some women to become involved in relationships which are masochistic in a broad sense of the word—where the partner may never seem to dominate her and may never touch her except lovingly, but is nevertheless emotionally sadistic. As one woman put it, "Masochistic fantasies don't turn me on erotically, but I certainly have got myself into masochistic relationships!" Such relationships, while peripherally related to the theory offered here, are still as tangential to our present concerns as are physical sado-masochistic sexual practices. The emotional quotient is definitely present in our construct—but as an erotic ingredient, not as a separated psychic expression.

It is also necessary to explain why the parable is couched solely in heterosexual terms. I believe that, moving from the obvious to the less obvious, (1) sexism is at heart an issue between women and men, (2) heterosexuality is numerically the largest and culturally the most influential form of sexual expression in patriarchal culture, (3) this last requires of "sexual minorities" (by enforced laws or by equally enforced social pressure) an imitation of the modes of the reigning sexuality (i.e., "husband-wife" sex roles among some homosexual couples). In other words, through no fault of its own, the homosexual subculture often finds itself mirroring the dominant culture (patriarchally heterosexual), with the very standards which oppressed that homosexual subculture in the first place now being adopted by it. (See "On Women As a Colonized People," p. 160.)

Thus, the occurrence of sado-masochistic fantasies and/or behavior among lesbians, and the far more prevalent occurrence of both fantasies and practice among faggots,[6] are, to me, a function of the enforced identification of the homosexual with heterosexual roles in a patriarchal culture.[7] It is therefore those roles which we must examine. It is to the nexus we must return, to the battle *between* the sexes. For no woman today can escape living in a patriarchal world, whatever her sexuality, just as no man can escape the responsibility of his power and privilege, whatever *his* sexuality. Sexism is, after all, the *attitude* which describes the *fact* of male supremacy, and until we engage the subject at that level and therefore between the female and the male, we are avoiding the real issue.[8]

Last, I should explain why I am here examining the politics of sado-masochistic fantasies only when the woman experiences them. Surely men have such fantasies, too—what of them? Do they fit in with the analysis offered here, or would a pat reversal of this analysis suffice for them? Hardly. My replies to these questions would have to

---

[6] I do not use this term pejoratively, but rather in accordance with the express wish of most radical anti-sexist homosexual males. By calling *themselves* "faggots," they affirm those homosexual males persecuted in the Middle Ages: "When a woman was to be burned as a witch, men accused of homosexuality were bound and mixed with the bundles of kindling (faggots) at the feet of the witch, and set on fire 'to kindle a flame foul enough for a witch to burn in.' So the enemy has always seen that strong women and gentle men are a real threat to masculine domination." This quote is from *Double-F, A Magazine of Effeminism.* See footnotes on *Double-F* in "Lesbianism and Feminism," above.

[7] Ironically, during 1976, and with the sudden intensity of a fad, sado-masochistic *practice* erupted as a political issue in lesbian-feminist circles. Articles in the so-called mixed-gay media, as well as in women's newspapers such as *Big Mama Rag, Hera,* and *Off Our Backs* extolled or condemned these practices, yet repeatedly failed to probe for an *analysis,* taking sides, instead, on whether such acts were (1) politically correct, (2) inherently classist or racist, and (3) permissible for lesbians but not for anybody else. No one seemed particularly concerned with the implications of radical-chic in this new issue, or with its echoes of the current Decadent Camp fashion, the Punk Image, the Mick Jagger message, and other such related themes already mentioned in "Theory and Practice: Pornography and Rape." Further, no one seemed to question whether this controversy was linked to a recent reidentification with male homosexuals (among whom such practice was more openly affirmed by a larger number for a longer time)—a possible by-product of the new "bonding" within the "gay community," a way of gaining male approval from many homosexual "brothers." In other words, no one appeared to wonder whether this S-M proliferation was a lesbian copy of a faggot imitation of patriarchal backlash against feminism.

[8] When I speak of "patriarchal heterosexuality" I mean just that—the current institution of heterosexuality *as defined in our androcentric culture.* I see no reason to assume that heterosexuality under other conditions, in which women had free choice and self-determining power, would be oppressive. On the contrary, I believe it could become Edenically joyous again.

include the following: I am concerned primarily with women (if we are not for ourselves, who is for us?) and consequently have focused my study *on* women.[9] This was made at once more organic and more imperative by my own experiential—and female—reality. But there is another, and more objective, reason for the female emphasis.

Sado-masochistic fantasies are themselves symbols for realities of dominance and submission, which are in *them*selves metaphors for power and powerlessness. In patriarchy men have power. In patriarchy women are powerless. These are facts. It is also a fact, though perhaps a less evident one, that he who has power can do what he likes, *including playing at powerlessness* in a manner never available to the powerless. For him it can be an experiment, a game, a fad, a fake (or even genuine) attempt to divest himself of his power, or a mere kicky new experience. It can be whatever he likes or imagines it to be, because it is his *choice*, by nature temporary and dismissible the instant it no longer amuses him. That men should sometimes fantasize themselves as masochists therefore strikes me as ironic but not surprising (perhaps it is merely a novel break from the real-life sadism patriarchy both requires and permits of them).

Some politically co-optive men even have claimed their masochistic identification is "woman-identification" and that it is meant as evidence of sympathy with feminism—which shows how abysmal is their understanding of women *and* feminism. But that any men should *wish* to experience what they *think* women experience—this is old news, as old as Pentheus' curiosity (and as rooted, I think, in envy). Men who see themselves as relatedly masochistic, "femme," feminine, etc., obviously are insulting the female (in person and in principle). If they grovel to a male master they are mimicking (for *fun*) an experience all women in patriarchy are in some way or other forced to endure in *reality*. If they cower before a female "dominatrix," they are superficially reversing, and therefore trivializing, real women's real oppression. The one act literally makes fun of the pain of our reality by ignoring our powerlessness; the other act mocks the reality of our pain by denying our powerlessness. Both are vicious, expectable, and for the purposes of our investigation, irrelevant.

---

[9] I refer the reader to Gertrude Lenzer's essay "On Masochism" and to Julia Sherman's "Commentary" in reply, in *Signs: Journal of Women and Culture in Society*, Vol. I, Nos. 2 and 4, respectively. Lenzer has written an interesting paper connecting male masochism with the German sensibility between the wars; Sherman, in her reply, questions Lenzer's emphasis (like so much of the psychiatric literature) on masochism in *men* when the culture generally considers masochism female. Sherman points out that Kinsey's statistics show males to be more masochistic than females, yet notes that the term itself has come to be generalized and more "naturally" applied to women for, we might well gather, reasons more political than scientific.

But the context does bear repeating: In patriarchy men have power. In patriarchy women are powerless. It is from this viewpoint, this *fact*, that we can start to imagine how we got here, to understand why, and thereafter to invent the way out for all of us. For we are our species; its story is our story, your individual life-story, and mine.

III: THE PARABLE

Ontogeny Recapitulates Philogeny
Progeny Recapitulates History

ONCE THE FREEDOM and power of Woman knew no shame. All acts of sexuality were inseparable from those of sensuality, and all these were within her definition and command.

This I remember. My cells remember this.

Man, driven by a sexuality seemingly more exterior to himself,[10] thought he could not understand Woman's *integrity* of sex, emotion, control, power, freedom, sensuality, shamelessness; he thought that perhaps he could not understand Woman's sexuality at all. He became afraid and impatient to learn.

What if she is wrong about me? What if I am not as she is?

For millennia (*one entire lifetime*), Woman has been saying, "Understand me. Learn me. Know me." This last she means in all senses, including that profound pun in the biblical use of "know." She has sought her consort, her challenge. This is the original quest of Atalanta, of Hippolyta, of Clorinda—for the Man who is capable of acute sensitivity to her desire and vast tenderness for her need, but also capable of strength equal to her own.

The possibility of their naked minds and bodies engaging one another—a joyous competition which must include any assumption of defeat as (1) temporary and (2) utterly lacking in humiliation; of any triumph as, obversely, impermanent and meaningless. The taking and giving of turns.

Man has tried to impersonate such a consort, challenge, equal. He has feared his inability to succeed. He has feared as well the possibility of his succeeding, because this contains a potential power equal to that of Woman. He fears having such power. He fears not having such power.

Yet this is the balance she has been searching for. It is the

---

[10] This concept was perfected in its expression by D. H. Lawrence's "character" John Thomas in *Lady Chatterly's Lover*—the penis as a separate self with "a will and a mind of its own."

balance he seems unable, deeply, to conceive. It is too terrifying. But the appearance of it, this he can manage. Will this suffice her? He attempts to fabricate it.

Thus is born: the rakish smile, the arched eyebrow and narrow-eyed intense stare, the attitude which bluffs, "I know what you really think/feel/desire, my dear" (or, depending on the class and delivery, "I know what you are/want, baby"). This is soon followed by—and notice the shift—"I know you *better than* you know yourself."

Woman, after centuries (*years of one human life*) of trying to reveal to Man or obtain from him the authentic response, begins to settle for even the pretense, finding it, in lack of what she truly wishes, somewhat stimulating—though merely as a synthetic approximation. She resigns herself almost humorously, to indulge him, to grant him a respite from effort. *But she never mistakes it for the real thing and is therefore not (yet) degraded by it.* Furthermore, she assumes it to be a temporary solution. Consequently, even at this stage, the tragedy could be averted, innocence retained, and the game gracefully played out.

But Man does forget (or deliberately blurs or ignores) that the pretense is not the reality, that it is merely a game. Because he forgets this, he therefore *does* see it as degrading to Woman. *This* was what she meant by the complement, the equal partner? How shallow of her! Such judgment after such mis-memory begins to be in Man's self-interest. He sees this both in confusion and in clarity. In confusion, he thinks it the best way to win her interest ("being sexy"). In clarity, he understands that this is a way to relate to her without ceding—in fact while gaining—a new-found power, one she did not intend him to have. That is, he can still claim to be trying to satisfy her requirement (the pretense) but can afford to be lazy about the intricate difficulty of her real demand.

Woman notices this change and chafes against it, beginning to learn fear in this either-way-you-lose dynamic: she can give up all hope of Man's really "knowing" her, hope of finding her consort, of being able to rest her burdens without it being seen as weakness, of encountering her complementary equal; but this ceding of hope would clearly be a real defeat. Or she can acquiesce to his pretense *as* the real and concede *that* as the best excitement available. This is surely another defeat. She begins to feel something alien to her. She begins to feel degraded.

This was not necessary . . .

Man has three choices in reaction to this, each of which mirrors three phases in history, as well as what we might characterize as three types of men:

1. He notices the shift in Woman (as she begins to learn how to feel degraded) and finds that he gets heightened pleasure from her

realization of her degradation. We can represent this choice as early, vengeful patriarchal revolution in an historical sense, and we can recognize it as the quintessential sadist in an individual sense.

2. He doesn't even notice the shift, so immersed is he by now in his own version of reality. We can characterize this phase as middle patriarchy consolidating itself and reigning in confidence. In the individual it appears as the "normal" masculinist male whose dullard mentality has cleverly developed the nonresponse (silence and passive-aggression) into a loudly articulated technique.

3. He secretly begins to despair that Woman, after eons (*decades of her life, decades*) of striving to teach him the real thing, is now giving up and settling him, dooming him, into his own pretense, with no hope from her of transcending it. He misses the excitement of the battle, but misses even more the loss of hope. This tendency might characterize the man in struggle, although it may be optimistic to expand that into a symbol of late, dissolving (?) patriarchy. It would be more reasonable, perhaps, to say that the approximations of the present period (effeminism and other sincerely supportive male replies to feminism, few as they are) *presage* such a reality—an actual surfacing of already subconscious tendencies in men.

But now Woman *is* degraded—in her view of herself, and in her view of his view of her.

How can he think I would settle for this?

To survive this realization, she must convince herself first of its irrelevance and then even of its inevitability, and construct an effective pleasure out of that very situation. This is the only way she can retain any pride. She even feels an echo of some ancient, almost forgotten, freedom, power, and creativity in the way she has instinctively known how to divert her pain into pleasure.

I remember this. My cells remember this . . .

All along, Man has not known her, not understood any of her real unshameful free unsullied desires. Now that he has corrupted his own attempts to fulfill them, he must castigate her for accepting such a cheapened solution as that which he offers. This *he* begins to enjoy, but even more important, to *mean*. He has forgotten that there ever was a game.

He glimpses that only she holds the key which can unlock them both from these postures. Yet all of his energies are bent on convincing her that, while she indeed holds the key, she has no power to use it.

Because she may be wrong. Because I may not be as she is. Because I may not be capable . . .

This construct, of remembering and refeeling her own power but being unable to act on it, drives Woman literally mad with longing. *The one connective route along which she actually can exercise her power now is to demand degradation from Man.* She is certain that this at least will be a "successful" exercise of that power.

Thus her ultimate shame contains within it some pure act risked in disguise of her ultimate power. She celebrates this gift with orgasm.

Simultaneously, his ultimate triumph contains within it some dread act attempted in disguise of his ultimate defeat. He mourns this loss with orgasm.

He has not yet learned an old lesson she has tried to teach him for ages.

She has learned a new lesson, and will find in it an ingenious strengthening, enabling herself to continue trying to teach him the ancient game she has never really forgotten.

In her refusal to release him into his own destruction she exercises over him that power of which he has been afraid from the beginning. His sole power exists in not seeing this.

This I remember.

What if she is wrong?

Years. Decades. Eons. History.

PARANOIA:
THE PARADIGM
AND THE PARABLE

A twofold initiation was central to the mysteries the sixties and the early seventies taught me. During that time I discovered the reality of my own suffering as a woman, and I began to comprehend how that suffering was related to, by, and in, the historic world. This process one could call Feminism. Further, I discovered my own reaction to that reality and how *that* was related to, by, and in the world. This revelation one might call Paranoia.

Many of us are familiar with the poster which shows a drawing of a haggard but still vigilant face beneath which the legend reads, "Even paranoids have real enemies." Just so. And how to differentiate? Can madness be "political"? Fanon, the Algerian revolutionist-psychiatrist, devoted more than one book to the subject, observing that "What is madness to the mother country is sanity to the colony—and the reverse." (As women, we must translate again: *father* country is simply more accurate—*men* run patriarchy.) Later, purportedly radical psychiatrists (R. D. Laing, David Cooper, and Thomas Szasz, among others), began to analyze madness anew from these psycho-political perspectives. Szasz, for example, has questioned which was objectively more insane: the so-called witch hysteria of mass hallucinations which swept parts of Europe during the Middle Ages, or the "sane" response of church and state—mass persecution, torture, imprisonment, and burning? Szasz, who cannot see witchcraft in its religio-political dimensions, does note that the word "hysteria" is itself a misogynistic one, from the Greek ὑστέρα or *hystera* meaning *the womb*; incredibly, this suggests not much more to the good doctor, who emerges with his sexist blinders intact, seeing no further connections.

Other, more drastically experimental psychiatrists have carried their political analysis to an extreme, almost to an adoration of madness as the only sane state in existence. At first this appears refreshingly intelligent, but a closer examination of the practice which follows this theory is less salutary. It can give madness a quality of radical chic, and create the inverse effect of another correct line similar to that of "sexual liberation." This last, you recall, was: "If you don't screw everyone in sight, you're hung up." The sanity version goes: "If you don't hallucinate continually, you're crazy." (Or: This is the way the world ends—not with a Laing, with a Cooper.)

But the person paralyzed in the grip of a negative schizophrenic hallucination (whether drug-induced or other) or reeling through the baroque architecture of a paranoid perception has seen madness not as a liberating state but rather one from which to be liberated with all due possible speed and by any means necessary. Such means include any help available, even those unimaginative, metallic, authoritarian doctors whose medical and psychiatric Big Business is justly feared and detested. And it is usually, and tragically, they who are available, since the industry of mental health is not coincidentally under their control. Real alternatives to this cartel are only beginning to function; feminist therapy, as an example, is in the process of defining itself.[1] For the moment, then, one's choice lies between the devil and the deep blue he. There is the pompous ass who aims to "normalize" his (sic) patient—to make the housewife more content with her namelessness, to bring the homosexual to an aversion of her or his own sexuality, to patronize the child, to cool out the adolescent, to tranquilize the rebel, to induce drug comas in the bothersome elderly—and to write books and papers, appear on talk shows, and keep his own malpractice rates low. The other choice lies with the self-styled radical shrink, who is also usually male (surprise!); he sports a dirty ponytail instead of a bald fringe, speaks in language that unwittingly parodies himself as a Jules Feiffer character, and chuckles at his patient disapprovingly if she confesses to a bad trip. "You didn't let yourself go," he lectures her, one of his hairy hands gumming its way up her thigh as he oozles. *Is* it greediness to feel that such choices are insufficient?

I discovered my own "madness" during the sixties, via

---

[1] There are of course quite a few practicing women psychiatrists and therapists. There are even a handful of honest-to-goddess *feminist* women in such practice. But the number and availability of these feminist professionals (in the best sense of the word professional) is still so small as to constitute, for the average woman in the United States, a utopian alternative. For the average woman across the globe this alternative is nonexistent. And, as Dr. Phyllis Chesler so memorably demonstrated in *Women and Madness* (Doubleday, New York, 1972), the problem is one of frightening magnitude. Patriarchy literally makes us mad.

hallucinogenic soft drugs such as acid (LSD), mescaline, and peyote, as well as the stand-by of my generation—grass. I never took hard drugs, both from great fear of them and even greater respect for my own body. Nor did I ever take drugs lightly. They were, for me, tickets to a psychic and religious space. Of the multitudinous experiences I encountered during this period, while tripping and sober (silly word) I've written else-where,[2] and without doubt shall do so again. Many of these experiences were ecstatic, lyrical, hilarious, peaceful, and wholly good. Quite frankly, though, I have had just as ecstatic, lyrical, etc. experiences with no drug inducing them—unless one con-siders a country dawn or childbirth or Elizabethan lute music or an act of love-making drugs. So more from a sense of, I hope, investigation than from a preoccupation with the grim, I include here some writings on the negative side of that experi-ence. For it was without question hallucinogenic drugs which first introduced me to the real state of paranoia. I don't mean paranoia as a cocktail-party phrase, or in a clinical sense, or in any other loose parlance. I mean paranoia as a system of perception in which everything in the entire universe seems intricately—and horribly—enclosed.

The following piece is about that system. The first part is based on a series of notes I rapidly made while "in" the state itself (a writer is a writer is a writer after all). These notes expanded, as an exorcise-exercise over subsequent months, especially as I compared experiences with other women and found that for many of us, the Stoned Sixties were less than groovy. Many men, for instance, simply substituted drugs for alcohol and proceeded to use this substance the way their square fathers had: to pressure and seduce (read: rape) women. If the women freaked out about this, you guessed it—we were hung up. For every woman who has recognized the religious and philosophical ecstasy shyly articulated in poems of mine like "Revolucinations" or "Credo," *five* women have apparently identified with the "bad trip" revolving around sex and power-lessness depicted in my longer poem "War Games." It was a not-uncommon experience, and the misuse of drugs by men against women for sexual purposes continues, viciously, to this day.

I set the task for myself of, as I saw it, "wooing" my madness and putting it to use. Awful as it was and loath as I am ever to return to it, I nevertheless would not have missed it for anything—and I somehow had the sense to know that at the time, even when I desperately wanted Out. I was fortunate;

---

[2] Among my poems that refer to these experiences are: "War Games," "Credo," "Freaks," "Revolucinations," and "Nightfoals"—all in *Monster*, and "The Beggar Woman" in *Lady of the Beasts*.

when I refer to my "madness" (and I shall now drop the coy quotation marks), I'm referring always to temporary states (drug-induced or spontaneous) never longer than twelve hours and often of only a moment's duration, never more frequent than perhaps fifty times in all, over a period of almost ten years. These states occurred in the company of loving family or friends (even if I didn't see them that way at the time), and I was never tranquilized (other than vitamin C or a Valium, self-requested, at home; never hospitalized or institutionalized). Very fortunate, much more so than others of my generation. "She calls this her madness?" you sneer? *'Tis not so deep as a well, nor so wide as a church door, but 'tis enough, 'twill serve.*

Wooing and using it, yes. *Understanding* it, again. Surely no artist would ignore it, or fail to try and document such colors, shapes, constructs—such a hypnotically alien cosmos. Surely no radical could dismiss the buried messages therein. Not I, at any rate. I refused to be ashamed of my hallucinatory journeys, even after they ceased being chemically induced (these "ticketless trips" were, in fact, the most vivid and fascinating of all). And while I found Laing and gang rather sophomoric, I also tried to remain on guard against the tempting cliché of the Mad Artist (Van Gogh, Smart, Schumann, Poe, Woolf, Sexton, and Plath, here we come). Yet I still intended to find out for myself as much as I could what these archeological digs in my own brain were unearthing. I could not have foreseen or said that any usefulness to feminists would lie in this search—although clearly none of the boys, from Fanon to Szasz to Laing to Cooper were much help, since none had seriously considered what Marxists so touchingly termed The Woman Problem. On the contrary, their male-supremacist assumptions were obnoxiously omnipresent. None of them appeared particularly interested in a political analysis of *female* paranoia. I—permanently a female and at least temporarily a paranoid—cared.

If, consequently, the political explorations made in the first part of this essay are consciousness-raising to other women, I am grateful. I must confess though that they were done not for this reason, but rather to discover for myself, my own personal Everywoman, *what my pain meant.* For me, the access to that discovery lay through the page; this essay is part of the result.

The Paradigm is a charting, a translation, of the state of paranoia itself. This is the section based on jottings made during the experience. I've never read or heard anything like it, including anyone else's version of paranoia—yet when I've shared this version with others I have been met with an unsettlingly intense recognition, as if I had encountered another traveler who had also once happened on that rarely frequented tourist spot known only to a few of us. The political probing of the Paradigm, as I have said, came later, evolving slowly but with at least as much startling impact as the discovery of the state itself.

The Parable is an account of a dream I had during my courtship of these states, although I was under no chemical's influence while dreaming it. The dream-parable does use imagery from a movie which had been influential on both Kenneth and me, and I include a poem of his to further demonstrate the connection. Relating dreams can be the dreariest of genres, but I think it worth hazarding when the dream works solidly on the mytho-poetic level one demands of one's waking creations, and when it resonates on a political level as well. Furthermore, if the Paradigm is an explanation of the experience and the political analysis is a meditation on the Paradigm, then the Parable is a confirmation of the political analysis. The dream is therefore essentially the metaphor for the experience itself.

The point to keep in mind is that this is real. One does not *believe* in the hallucinations—one *knows*. Even as the culture which created the reasons for such horror is real. As the insights are real. As the symbolism of dreams is real, as it can make the heart pound and the skin sweat and the muscles jerk. As the choice facing every woman who has ever loved a man in the patriarchal world is agonizingly, frighteningly, recurringly *real*.

I: THE PARADIGM

THE FEAR OF FEAR—that is the only valid terror. Surely a wise mind allows itself that one cautionary alarm.

But to admit even one fear is to admit the possibility of them all— to admit the potential for hostility, enmity, in everyone, everything, an expanding universe of They and Them against me.

Once "within" the mature flowering of the paranoid state this reasonless fear is so encompassing that it *must* be explained. Yet all explanations reduce to two alternatives, each with a subdivision; only two possibilities from which to choose:

1

    A)   I'm perfectly sane. (This is reassuring.)

    B)   In which case, since I fear Them, they truly must be out to destroy me. (This is terrifying.)

           1A + 1B = I'm not mad; They are evil.

2

    A) "They" don't exist, or if they do, they are not malicious or malignant. They are indifferent—or even possibly loving. (This is reassuring.)

    B) In which case, to have believed so strongly in possible harm from them—I must be paranoid, mad, actually insane. (This is terrifying.)

    2A + 2B = They're not evil; I am mad.

These states (1 and 2) alternate in one's consciousness, each having a subdivision of reassurance and terror. It is between these subdivisions that the tension is stretched, and between the states themselves that the balance of continuity is maintained, for the subdivisions trigger each other off to begin the cycle of alternation again. Thus one has the choice of being sane at the expense of others (1), or mad at the expense of oneself (2). Is the first state an expression of a supreme sadism, the second a comparable expression of an ultimate masochism? Or is the first a demonstration of individual self-determination, the second a demonstration of collective co-influence? Or is the first state mere selfishness, the second pure altruism?

.   .   .

Inevitably, when one is thoroughly "in" state 1, the other state does not exist; it cannot. The reverse is true. There is *no coexistence* in consciousness of the two states, only a ceding of place, one to the other, in turn. Indeed, when "in" one state, the captive seeks the reassurance of the other as a means of escape from the panic of the present state— only to find that the flight entails encountering "those evils that we know not of" as much or more than it does reaching a momentary breathing space. The rodent in Kafka's trenchant story "The Burrow."

.   .   .

It's revealing that the linkage of subdivision 1A with subdivision 2A equals what could be called "health."

    1A) I'm perfectly sane. (Reassuring)

    2A) They don't exist or, if they do, are indifferent or beneficent. (Reassuring)

    1A + 2A = "Health"
               (in the sense of relief and happiness).

Furthermore, the linkage of 1B with 2B also equals "health" (a normal response to a threatening situation *is* fear).

1B)   They truly are out to destroy me. (Terrifying)

2B)   I believe in possible harm from them. (Terrifying)

1B + 2B = "Health"
(in the sense of self-preservation).

Unfortunately, those subdivisions do not cross-relate this way in the process described here. If they did, we would have no problem.

Interesting too, that one cannot cross-link 1A with 2B, or 1B with 2A—because that would be a linkage of direct opposites which would then each cancel the other out. Such a strategy is very Buddhist, but regrettably it does not appear available to the captive paranoid:

1A)   I'm perfectly sane.

2B)   I'm mad to believe in harm from Them.

1A + 2B = Self-cancellation.

1B)   They are out to destroy me.

2A)   They don't exist, or are indifferent or beneficent.

1B + 2A = Other-cancellation.

However, in *reverse* order, 2A and 1B *can* relate:

2A)   They don't exist, or are indifferent or beneficent. (Reassuring)

1B)   They want me to think just that, to be reassured, drop my guard, be vulnerable again. (Terrifying)

And 2B and 1A can relate in a parallel reversed order:

2B)   I'm paranoid, mad, insane. (Terrifying)

1A)   To even recognize my madness, let alone fear it, I must be sane. (Reassuring)

This combination of subdivisions seems at first to break up the components more clearly. We get a less alloyed essence here: 2A and 1B combine to create a state of *pure* paranoia, unadulterated by *thoughts about* madness. But 2B and 1A seem to describe pure health, self-contained, even self-preoccupied, uncontaminated with threatening thoughts about "Them." At least this is relative health, in that 1A *accepts* 2B (just as, above, 1B takes 2A into consideration), and *by so doing seems to break the cycle.*

Is such a cross-linkage of subdivisions the solution, then? In an obvious way, of course: one walks that line between health and madness all the time. Everyone does this, in fact, but only the intelligent realize it. Yet it hardly seems right that the only way to stay relatively sane is to live in terror of one's madness. A peculiar sanity, that. The pat answer would be that one must stay *aware* of it, but not fear it—a smug, non-experiential logic. Go tell it to Kafka.

. . .

Duality-thinking might posit: either we accept something (love, life, etc. would come under this "Yes" heading), or reject it (fear, hatred, war, the concept of "the Other," etc.). Yin and Yang, simplistically put. And of course it is their interdependence, their unity, that creates harmony. This is a generally accepted definition of health, and of synthesis, as well.

The I/They dichotomy (or even the more universally practiced Us/Them so basic to most politics) is not necessary, of course. "Inner and outer are the same," teaches the *Tao Te Ching*. The wise soul combines all differences in her Nirvanic *in*difference.

But how in bloody hell do you combine them when they've splintered off into two separate factions at total war with each other? By standing apart and trying to make peace between them? Or by entering into one, even arbitrarily chosen, so fully that the other is obliterated or rediscovered within its opposite? And can one force that choice? Force oneself toward health (or madness)? Force oneself toward caring (or indifference)? Unlikely, such a storming of heaven. (As unlikely as passively drifting there?)

Let us return to the possibility of standing apart objectively. This course appears reasonable, yet it is precisely the course that enthralled in the first place. One *does* have to take sides eventually, or at the very least allow a side to take one. Still, there must be a more honorable way to go about doing this.

The paralysis of indecision is no answer. It is a stand in itself, and not one of the indifference it pretends to, but of fright and passivity. On the other hand, the blind choice (a stand, any stand, gimme a stand) is less a brave act than a brutal one. Of course the notion that any choice is *not* blind is illusion. Besides, to choose at all is to exclude every other possible choice, thus denying the possibility of choosing.

Are we then reduced to talking about greed, merely wanting to have it all at once? No, I think we are really talking about freedom in philosophical and psychological terms, which we can perhaps clarify by placing the argument under a political grid.

. . .

By freedom, I mean a reaching past all known or imagined conditions: freedom from the state of being oppressed, freedom from the state of accommodation to oppression, and freedom as well even from the state of rebellion against oppression. Each of these states has its relative frame of mind, political position, resultant emotion, and consequential act.

Thus, *the state of being oppressed* encompasses madness as the normal frame of mind, reaction as the normal political position, suffering as the resultant emotion, and fear informing all consequential acts.

The state of accommodation to oppression encompasses indifference as the normal frame of mind, nonalignment as the normal political position, numbness as the prevailing emotion, and guilt coloring all acts of consequence.

The state of rebellion against oppression encompasses a frame of mind enraged with sanity, and a political position stripped radical by deduction; the emotions are consumed by hostility and by an equally intense longing for a purgative of that hostility. The consequential acts are determined and sustained by that longing.

Naturally it is possible to travel back and forth between these states. Although the borders are fixed, each of us is equipped with passports honored by all three territories. In fact, it is even conceivable—and sometimes mandatory—that we are capable of occupying overlapping states in imperceptibly quick-shifting moments, actually the same moment. One may act, feel, think, and be at different stages of action, emotion, thought, and existence in all three categories. Perhaps it is possible that this compulsory virtuosity is the minimum condition of our current consciousness.

But to be free from *all* these states—the mere contemplation of such a freedom as actual, as imaginable beyond all existing forms, is so metaphysically dizzying, so all but incomprehensible that we discover a trap. What would we *do* with ourselves? The awe of a real if uncharted freedom is greater than the known terrors of our old existence.

Is this why revolutions have always settled for winning?

. . .

The oppressed have been forced to fear what is not there (the superiority of the oppressor) and even to be ashamed of this fear as the sign of inferiority. The radical must *choose* to fear what is not there, embracing the very insight of which she had been frightened in her former totally oppressed state, affirming it as the badge of a new-found vigilance, thus transforming fear into paranoia. (The liberal is generally preoccupied only with what *seems* to be there—a narrow definition of reality which the liberal defends with a fierce lukewarmth.) But the victor who merely renames the former palace the Citadel of the People while moving into the throne room—here at last is the creature who has discovered what *is* there, and so has been destroyed for all rational purposes as one who could define it. Freedom has been eluded once again, this time triumphantly.

Still. There's almost nothing I'm not afraid of. So if I am this afraid, it must be that I have within me, inevitably, a courage specific to this moment, one which has been waiting all my life to be used just here, precisely now, a courage I am bravely resistant to encountering, much less embodying—*if* I am this afraid.

Why assume such a resource, however hidden?

Why not? Either I have discovered it because it exists or it exists because I have invented it. In any case, it now exists.

.   .   .

The point is to *change the terms,* to alter totally the landscape on which the battle is waged, to reject the failure of a past reluctance to use any weapons and reject as well the success of a past dependence on traditional weapons—and to do this with *no* certainty, no assumption of "correctness." To approach what could be called a metaphysical feminism. To be meta-midwives?

.   .   .

Multiplicity is a word with positive connotations.

It is strange that duplicity is a word with negative connotations.

It is strange that no word at all exists for a multifaceted uniplicity.

Yet if we each were multifacetedly uniplicitous we might even combine to transform nefarious duplicity into multiplicitude.

.   .   .

The Paradigm again, this time in terms of the personal anguish inherent in female-male relationships struggling to grow in patriarchal soil. It is clear that the woman has a most unsavory choice. She can believe either that she is justified in her demands and that he, in his refusal to meet them, is out to break and destroy her; or she can believe that he really does love her and would change if only her demands weren't so thoroughly unfair (in fact, crazy). Most women spend their life ricocheting between these polarities of equally chilling conviction, although the second is probably the most common of the two, given its emphasis on guilt and inner-directed violence. Early glimmerings of a simplex feminist consciousness make possible the first conviction, which may appear less painful than the second, until she comprehends that it reveals the destruction of part of her capacity to love: a high price, too high for most women so far, even if they do realize that at present it is almost always a price paid with false currency from a treasury long ago emptied.

For centuries men have criticized women for this curious tic of wanting to love and be loved, for valuing this rather sentimental condition as one of True Emotion (up there on the level of Brotherhood, Ambition, Patriotism, Duty, and Other Adult Feelings as defined by men). The early phase of the current Feminist Movement saw women reacting against this patriarchal contempt with an answering flood of emotion, especially love, toward each other (so long denied us) and toward men (in that we demanded, *from* love, that they struggle to change). Naturally this flood did not accomplish an instantaneous breaking of the dam of resistance which had after all taken ten thousand years to build. Gradually it abated, dwindling to a trickle. Disappointed and impatient, some women began speaking about love in an eerily familiar tone of contempt. Numerous "corrective lines" ran out like cracks from this subtle parching at the heart. Women's oldest adversary, guilt, rose like a desert sandstorm, called up this time by other women:

You have no right to be concerned with the struggle of love; it is a bourgeois concern and people are starving. You have no right to want to love, or be loved—are the workers concerned with such sentimental questions? (The answer is Yes, but some new socialists ignore this.) You have no right to waste time struggling in love with a man; the only serious feminist is a lesbian. You have no right to struggle in love with your lesbian lover; that is bourgeois monogamy. You have no right to love your children; you are only oppressing them and they are only oppressing you. You have no right to love your friends; that is elitism. You have no right to love yourself; that is individualism. You have no right to love your work; that is privilege. You have no right to love art; that is decadence. You have no right to love nature; that is romanticism. You have no right to love the past; that is nostalgia. You have no right to love the future; that is utopianism. You have no right to loverhood, wifehood, motherhood, selfhood—because all these hoods have in the past covered the faces of institutions we now see as oppressive.

I have exaggerated the above correct-line formulae deliberately. Some (most?) may seem blatant cases of throwing out various babies with or without the bath water—a type of nonthought surely no one could advance seriously. Not so. From sufficient confusion just such nonthought can come, and frequently has, as in one notorious correct line which only a few decades ago conceived of transforming real babies into real soap, in which case throwing the baby out with the bath water appeared to the correct-liners as both sensible and sanitary.

So we reject force adopted out of correctness, since such an adoptive parent is only an excuse. But what of the original parent, who gave her infant Force up for adoption because she felt incapable of raising it? Her name is Suffering, and she is unconcerned with expedience. She has chosen to be mad rather than to define *any* Other as evil (The Paradigm, state 2). Perhaps she is saintly, but then women have been saints for millennia, and it has not brought us grace. So we can mourn with her, for her, as for our own past. But still we must leave her choiceless martyrdom, as well, behind us.

.   .   .

So. A good political movement could aim to imitate not the sand of a desert, but the sand of a beach:

—which sifts through the fingers of anyone who would grab it in a fist, thus eluding possession;

—which adapts itself with pillowing accommodation to any who would rest on it, including the shells of once-living creatures, thus risking the appearance of compassionate shapelessness, so confident is it of its own shape;

—which irresistibly wears down stone into sand, grain by grain, adding to itself;

—and which clings with ineradicable tenacity to any who have even remotely encountered or been touched by it.

But the sand of a beach, not a Sahara. For it must permit of dunes but also the stubbed growth of prickly evergreens; it must fathom erosion but welcome children building castles.

.   .   .

We must boil the paradigm down to its essence:

> 1
>
> A) I'm sane.
> B) They are out to destroy me.
>
> $1A + 1B =$ I'm not mad; They are evil.
>
> Thus, $1 =$ Their malignancy protects me from my madness.
>
> 2
>
> A) They don't exist, or are indifferent or beneficent.
> B) Then I must be insane.
>
> $2A + 2B =$ They're not evil; I am mad.
>
> Thus, $2 =$ My madness protects me from their malignancy.

So we can restate the Paradigm more succinctly:

My madness protects me from their malignancy.
Their malignancy protects me from my madness.

From which would you rather be protected? And is it not some-how an overarchingly beneficent structure which provides such a care-fully architectured protection? Or is it an encompassingly maleficent structure which can devise torture in such an airtight system?

. . .

A stepping outside that circle, then. Or rather a plunge to the center of it, the heart of a mandala where the vertiginous distractions fade.
No maps can be obtained for this place.

. . .

She has moved from loving him at her own expense to loving herself at his expense. This is no solution, since she loves him still, he has not changed *enough*, or rather he has, but she has changed more, and she is weary of such expenses. What have correct lines then to do with her, as she hangs out her wash in Kansas, slides shut the file drawer in Sacramento, loads the station wagon in the Tennessee supermarket park-ing lot, shifts her feet on the welfare line, freaks out on acid, or sits at my typewriter?

More: she has moved from *loving* (anyone—woman, man, child, the universe) at her own expense, to loving herself at anyone else's expense—only to find that she detests herself for having done so. No grace here, merely hopelessness, although it takes a certain courage to admit it. Is this perhaps the reason some feminists who wrestled with theory (as opposed to sophomoric correct lines) in the sixties went quietly mad with despair in the seventies?

. . .

The paradigm is that of Semiramis and the Petitioner, of Lear and the Fool. The paradigm is of Ariadne and Theseus, of Alcestis and Admētus, of Kore and Dis. The paradigm is in the mind of Antigone—who will settle for nothing if she cannot have everything. The paradigm is interknotted. Nor can it be sawed apart, in the style of patriarchy, with Alexander's sword. No, it must be unraveled stealthily by night in the style of Penelope, while for the near future we all pretend it still exists by day.

The female has ever been the one who spins, who weaves, who cuts the thread. She is the Norn, the Fate, the Spider. Now, like Saint Teresa's silkworm, we must even spin our own freedom, out of no one—and no one's expense, not even that—but ourselves.

For if paranoia is the dread of seeing the undying horror behind each face, all the while being driven endlessly to expose face after face after face—then grace is the ecstasy of seeing the immortal joy behind

each face, while possessing the exhaustionless energy required to uncover face after face after face.

This would be the revolumination that passeth nonunderstanding.

II: THE PARABLE

THE PARABLE, while an actual dream, clearly borrowed and transformed
one of its central images from a first-class "horror film" entitled *The
Island of Lost Souls*. The movie was made in 1932 and it starred the
incomparable Charles Laughton. It made an indelible impression on both
K. and me when we first happened across it, and we still seek out the
film every time it returns or is rerun on television. I don't know if the
religious metaphor of the movie staggers everyone as it does us, but
I do know that this influence made itself felt not only in my dream-
parable but in a poem of K.'s which so closely speaks to the paradigm
and the parable both that I reprint it here, with his permission.

TO THE MAD DOCTOR
by Kenneth Pitchford

(In the film *The Island of Lost Souls*, a doctor
tries to recapitulate evolution by performing
gruelling operations on living animals to raise
them step by step to the human level.)

"You made us in the House of Pain,"
shouts one of your wretched parodies,
now that these unbeasted creatures verge on riot,
no longer servile to their master
—an accusation salted by our almost human tears,
and then one last rising up
to tear apart our island, exploding
into the solar sea your slaves and you.

Made deaf to all of our complaints,
you made us in the House of Pain.
Yet you yourself, to all but the naive,
are only the boiling of matter and energy
endlessly up, hurled outward
into galaxy, sun, and planet.
One cinder more or less cannot put out your eyes
in the billions of embers you have made.

Us? Compassion for such creatures?
No, for unlike that mad scientist, Charles Laughton,
you made us in the House of Pain
without even blinking back through such misguided

good intentions at your handiwork,
gone subtly awry in ways you hadn't planned.
But plan itself is the last naivete
to credit to the forces that summoned us.

In the instant between this galaxy's decision
to fling the largesse of its stars away
and its inevitable extinction,
you made us in the House of Pain
for what? To mythologize you on the walls
of caves, temples, and cathedrals?
To slaughter each other in momentous disagreements
about what garments to portray you in?

The tools for drawing you have changed.
Theology, logic, intuition, all give way
to microscope and telescope. Indifferent destroyer,
I call your boiling zeal the accident by which
you made us in the House of Pain,
that accident the great cause of our punishment
—unless other forces we cannot see compel you.
If so, forgive my "the."

House, city, world have never held
anyone in whom those forces
written on the sky churned more at peace
here than there. We've mostly simpered and killed
and blanched the faces from other people's children.
You made us in the House of Pain
to give and take that harm, to want and hunger,
to shudder servile in that house.

Of other ways to live, women
speak every century or so.
And, yes, your configurations have a beauty
if seen abstractly. Yet how many civilizations
wiser than ours wink out in the sudden nova
quaking outward through Orion's belt?
You made us in the House of Pain;
what beyond that is still worth speaking of?

Pain has its patterns, its complexities
worth studying for the perfection of their form.
But to be born almost as stupid as your beasts,
less wise than perishing systems in some cinder
embittering our view?—unless any total knowing
or unknowing as we bubbled up through cell and tissue
is the one mercy you denied us when
you made us in the House of Pain.

It would do one well to keep in mind this poem, its subtle form, and its speaker, as if they constituted the threads of a guide-line, while entering the labyrinth of the parable.

.　　　.　　　.

K. and I are honored visitors being given a tour through the grounds of a famous "model" asylum. There are beautiful buildings, spacious lawns. The inmates live in the cottage system—no wards, dormitories, fences, straitjackets. The tour is conducted by the Director, an attractive if slightly pretentious man, silver-haired, kindly, his Claude Rains manner a bit disquieting. He is accompanied by the Assistant Director, a middle-aged woman of nondescript appearance (naturally) in a dark dress. His manner is leisurely, hers efficient, yet both are pleasant enough. We four pass by a stone building somewhat out of character with the other structures on the grounds; it is all on one level, but stretches out squatly for a good city-block's worth. I linger to squint at the barely decipherable legend carved above the main lintel. The words, cut deep into the stone, have been worn away by the elements or by some hand deliberately trying to rub them down, but to no avail, although they are much fainter than their carver intended them to be. The Director, the Assistant Director, and K., a bit ahead of me on the geranium-bordered path, drift back to stand near me while I slowly read aloud the words:
"The House The People Fear."

There is a short silence before the woman attempts to bustle us on to the next display. But I have grown curious to tour the stone building, and despite the dissuasive attempts of our hosts and the reluctance of K., I become adamant. I am the one who insists. We four enter the building together and proceed through various rooms, all of them appearing to be outer offices of some sort, equipped with desks, chairs, filing cabinets, bulletin boards, and other gray standard office furniture, brightened here and there by a rhododendron on someone's desk, a saved birthday card pinned to someone's bulletin board, a framed print on a regulation wall. There is clearly nothing to see here, in these unpeopled offices. The Assistant Director explains that no one, of course, works on a holiday such as this one. K. and I nod in understanding.

We come to a door which, when opened, reveals a vast laboratory, all chrome and white enamel and glass, scrupulously clean and, like the offices, completely empty. A peculiar odor, like ether mixed with gasoline and honey, seems to emanate from the laboratory. It sickens me, and I announce that I have seen enough of this building; the hosts were right, after all, there is really nothing to see here today. We begin to retrace our steps when K. suddenly stops, and declares that *he* now would like to tour the lab, having come this far. After all, what a pity to miss seeing the latest in lab techniques and instrumentation. Apprehensive, I waver at leaving without him, but then am convinced by the courteousness of the Director and his Assistant. They invite me to walk freely around the grounds while I wait for the three of them to complete their inspection of the stone building. There are no planned tours here, they smile, no censored sights, so I am at liberty to wander as I wish. They will join me shortly out on the wide lawn which looks like a college campus quad, grassy expanses marked out by gravel paths which cross and counter-cross from all points of the grounds. I am tempted to wander about by myself so I agree, and leave them to continue their tour.

Out on the path, in the sunshine, any anxieties I felt earlier seem absurd. I saunter toward the middle of the quad, passing people walking in groups of twos and threes. They reply to my smile with smiles, to my nod with a gracious bend of their heads, but they don't answer any of my verbal greetings. This seems odd, although under the influence of the hot sun and the fragrance of fresh-cut grass, I lazily dismiss such behavior as their shyness toward strangers. I find a pleasant spot in the center of the lawn, take off my jacket so as to enjoy the air's warmth, and sit down to wait for K. and our hosts, my gaze sweeping across the serenity of the grounds, the distant cottages picturesquely built from logs, with thatched roofs and geraniums in the window boxes, the thick circle of trees and hedges far out at the edge of the grounds, protecting all within from the curiosity or censure of any without. My eye comes to rest on a huge woodpile off to my left a ways, almost at the limit of the tree circle. Someone has been chopping firewood valiantly in great quantities for the coming chill—a cozy task, since every cottage has its own wood-burning fireplace in the common living room which the "residents" share, each having her or his own private room upstairs, six to a cottage. Whoever had cut all that wood so energetically had flung down the axe at last, in exhaustion no doubt, where it remained, handle at right angles to the chopping-block root in which its blade was thrust. A bit careless, I think uneasily, leaving an axe around all these lunatics, and immediately chide myself for having less progressive attitudes than the Director himself, who always referred to the inmates as residents and who was renowned for his radical solutions to modern madness. Pre-occupied with my own bigotry, I am surprised to notice a young woman—a girl, really—standing to one side of the woodpile. Has she been there all along, or has she only just come up?

Certainly her appearance is sufficiently nymph-like to make credible her manifestation from thin air. She seems between the ages of twelve and sixteen. Her slender body is whimsically dressed in some kind of ankle-length puff-petticoated organdy gown. The light skirt, which gives itself to every invitation of the breeze, billows prettily as she stoops low by the woodpile for a second, then bounces upright and runs with unconscious grace toward where I sit. As she draws nearer, I can make out the delicate face, the onyx eyes, the long blond braids which swing in rhythm to her step. She is smiling at me. She really is a charming sight.

I smile back, and she plumps down in a whoosh of petticoats beside me, her descent to the grass one motion consistent with her fleetness of a moment earlier. We laugh together. I seem to recognize her but cannot tell from where. Surely she looks too intelligent to be a resident, yet her costume *is* rather precious. Perhaps the child of a resident, here visiting? But my doubts about her sanity are quickly dispelled when, after looking intensely into my eyes for a moment, she ceases smiling, nods once, decisively, as if to herself, and places a frail hand on my arm.

"Be alert," she says. "It will be as you suspect, not as they re-assure you. Remember that. And you will need this."

From the folds of her dress she produces the axe which, to my horror, she swiftly places in my hand. I can do little else but stare stupidly at the axe, then at her, then at the axe again, my mouth open-ing and closing on questions it cannot frame. Nor do I have the time to let anything sink in, because the girl, looking past me, winces in alarm and says in a rapid, hoarse whisper, "Quick! They're coming! Hide it, quickly, so, under your jacket. Speak casually of me. My poor friend, when you have need, I can be found in the third cottage from the left, there, with the white shutters. Take care. Trust no one. Goodbye."

Then she is on her feet, light as a butterfly. She spins around once as if in a mad little dance, curtsies, smiles a big smile, and darts off in her flying gait toward the cottage she has pointed out.

Before I can recover, the Director, his Assistant, and K. come up. I feel the need to give them some explanation of the child I know they've seen.

"The most charming little girl was just here, Director. She sang a nursery rhyme for me, danced a bit, and fluttered off. But what about you?" I throw out, in my haste to change the subject, "Did you finish touring the building?"

The Director and his associate stare after the girl, but K. sinks down on the grass with me. He seems strangely exhausted. He explains that they had gone on, yes, and seen all the laboratories which were, after all, just laboratories, and he is now very tired and wants merely to rest for a while on the grass. He has a terrific headache, he says, and lays his head in my lap. I carefully move my jacket with its frightful contents to one side to make room for him.

The Director apologizes for having tired us out in his desire to be thorough, to give his visitors "the complete picture." He has other pressing duties now, and has to leave us, but the Assistant Director is highly capable of guiding us through the remainder of our visit. We say goodbye to him, and give him our thanks for his candor and hospitality. He leaves us. The Assistant Director remains, however, and seeing that K. still seems to be pained with his headache, she offers him two aspirin. I grow suddenly stiff with suspicion, although of what I cannot tell. But the anxiety is so strong that I find the excuse of asking her to get some water to go with the pills, although K. seems perfectly willing to swallow them dry. She, too, leaves us, and I try to speak of my suspicions to K., who hears little, woozy as he is. I taste the pills—they are indeed plain aspirin, and I feel like a fool. The atmosphere of the loony bin must be contagious, I think, and when the woman returns with the paper cup of water, I permit K. to swallow the aspirin and lie down again.

He falls precipitously into a deep sleep. Seeing my alarm, the Assistant Director sends for the Director. Together, they help him stagger to his feet, one of them supporting him on each side. The Director tells me that they will take him where he can lie down in comfort and sleep until his exhaustion wears off. He will be quite all right, they assure me. Would I care to accompany them?

But all at once I know that they will do—already have done—something ghastly to K. It somehow has been accomplished by his having toured the laboratory and repeatedly inhaled the strange odor there. Yet the substance is so subtle that it merely wearied him, and was then fully activated by the plain aspirin I myself acquiesced to his taking. One thing I know. I can be of no help to him while I am in their clutches. I break from them, freezing just long enough to see their gazes fix on what I have dropped in my haste: my jacket, bunched up on the grass—and lying beside it, only half hidden, the axe. Over the unconscious, lolling head of my lover, the Director and his Assistant flash me a look of unmasked challenge. I turn and begin running.

I know I have very little time. I race across the quad to the white-shuttered cottage, glancing back only once to see the Director and the Assistant Director dragging K. off between them.

My little friend is waiting at the door of the cottage, and she hurries me upstairs to her room. She seems to know all that has taken place out on the lawn without my having told her. She refuses me her name, but tells me hurriedly that the model asylum is one massive torture chamber to "recondition" rebels and misfits, and that she and a few others in her cottage are part of a small but effective underground resistance which has been operating for some time. They have arranged my escape; a taxicab with a male member of the underground posing as its driver is waiting now at the gate just some yards from the cottage —she can lead me there. I can be gone before any pursuit is possible.

I counter with refusals and questions. I cannot leave without K. And how do we get him free? What about her and the others in her house? Surely I have been seen entering here. Now she and others of the resistance will be endangered.

She dismisses all my concerns while throwing a dark cape over my shoulders, rearranging my hair, and bustling me toward the stairs. She tells me that the Director has for some time suspected her and this house—the underground is not afraid, and I can be of more help to them outside, rallying help and telling the truth about the so-called model institution. Rescuing K. is hopeless, she says. He belongs to them now, the aspirin-activated chemical having changed him utterly, as I somehow feared.

She rushes me downstairs and toward the back door of the cottage, but I refuse to go. I tell her it is impossible to leave without K., that I *can* undo whatever effects they have wrought on him, that I must and will, that she does not know him as I do. We quarrel, frantic in our urgency. Then, all at once, we hear shouts and cries from in front of the cottage. I rush to the window, to see advancing there across the broad lawn about twenty men—the Director, the rest in the white coats and trousers of hospital attendants, and K., in front like a leader. The girl tugs frantically at my arm, but I pull away. K. is coming, I must wait for him, together we will find our way out of this nightmare. She says he is changed forever, but I will not, cannot believe her. At last she leaves me, fleeing herself, though whether out back or upstairs I don't know.

The men now stand before the heavy wood door of the cottage. K. knocks and calls my name. Paralyzed with fear and indecision, I make no answer. The attendants begin growling at K. to let them handle this; they've had experience, they know how to deal with me. But he seems to refuse, and I hear his quiet voice saying, "She will open the door for me."

I feel I must trust him or die. I open the door.

The attendants make as if to rush me, but he restrains them at the threshold, merely standing there. Perhaps nothing can be done unless I myself invite him in. But I am riveted by the change in K.'s face, his manner, his whole appearance.

He seems older, statelier, more distinguished somehow. His hair is shaped in a suave cut and touched silver at the temples. His blue suit seems darker, better cut, and he is wearing, of all things, a matching vest. It is a look totally unlike him, although this person is clearly K. But the flavor is that of a politician, a judge, or even, yes, the Director himself. Yet it is K. who stands before me. But without his own soul.

My whole body hurls itself against the door, and I almost manage to force it shut again, taking the men by surprise. But then their combined force pushing back outbalances mine, and I am flung back into the room. K. enters, and the attendants crowd in behind him. He smiles at me. He is carrying the axe.

I am alone now in this log-cabin living room, among these chintz-covered chairs and this corduroy sofa, before this fieldstone fireplace, alone with these men and my lover.

"We are about to play a game," K. announces.

One of the white-coated men brings in a bushel of wood chips, each about the size of a silver dollar. He picks up one chip and throws it into the air, out toward where I am standing. K. hurls the axe at the chip, hitting it midair, near my head. An attendant retrieves the axe and another chip is hurled. I learn to spin and dodge and wheel and run about the room, between the furniture, like a mouse from a cat, twenty cats. The axe, of course, is never hurled at me, only at the wood chip—which is always thrown deliberately a few inches from my body. I know I am ridiculous in my terror, my movements panicked, contorted, slapstick—I know this myself, even before the attendants and K. begin laughing uproariously at me. I am too busy running about, scurrying in my humiliation, to know if I am sobbing or panting. I know that I alone am not laughing.

Then there is a split-second chance: one attendant has been slow at retrieving the axe. It lies at my feet, and it is in my hand before he can slide across the floor for it. I stand like a hunted animal at bay, breathing hard, the axe handle smooth in my sweating fist. The men fall silent. K. steps forward. "Give me the axe, my dear," he says calmly.

"Send them away," I hiss.

"Come. Give me the axe. You'll hurt someone. You don't want to hurt anyone."

"*First. Send. Them. Away!*"

At a look from him they all leave, although I know they are waiting just outside the closed front door. I have no plan now: only, perhaps, to talk with K., to get him alone and pull him back to himself, then to think together how we can leave this place . . .

But when he turns back to me he is changed again. The mask is gone from his face, which now wears its own dear familiar expression. And he seems dazed, lost. He staggers to a chair.

"How did I get here?" he murmurs. "What . . . how . . . what happened?"

So immense is my relief at his return to himself, even in confusion, that I rush to his side, forgetting everything else, dropping the axe at his feet, embracing him, laughing wildly at his blessed confusion, his needing me, his unmurderous clear blue eyes now filling with tears in recognition of me. He doubles over onto his knees, crying, as he begins to remember what has happened. But I am desperate now only to get us both free, and I run to the back door to look for any sign of the taxi driver. Off beyond the trees, I can see the taxi waiting, the driver in his seat, our deliverer. I turn back to tell K. the glad news.

He is standing in the middle of the room, changed again, the axe in his hand.

Whether the previous moment was genuine or a trick, this is unmistakably real now, and I know that it is a fight to the death. He comes to me, unsmiling, robot-like, swinging the axe. I whirl and run, dodging the furniture again, awkwardly eluding him as I try to think. I call his name. I call my love to him. He pursues, relentless, swinging the axe. He backs me up against one long wall, aims the axe at my forehead, and throws. But he has miscalculated, and it lands just beside my ear, embedded deep in the wood. He lurches closer, but I slip out of his grasp, and across the room, to what I have just now noticed hanging above the mantle—a rusty antique sword. I wrench it down and advance on him. He is still struggling to pull the axe out of the wall. But before he can manage this, I whisper his name. He wheels, that blank alien hatred in his eyes melting like snow into his own confused and loving blue. I watch the change. I watch it.

And I stab the sword deep into his body.

He slumps to the ground, crying for me. He does not know who he is, where he is. He asks, "What have I done that you should kill me?" And in time to each of my dry sobs, I stab him again and again and again, feeling muscle and gut and bone-shard and gristle shudder up through the blade, through my own arm, shock upon shock in waves to my brain. He is changing back to himself again, matching my rhythm, leaning up to meet my blows, gasping even, "Yes, my dearest, you must, you must kill me or you will never be safe. For love, for pity, oh destroy me so that I will never live having destroyed you. Take that too on yourself, this one last time, oh my love."

At last he lies still, his eyes open, conscious, his beloved face wet with tears and spattered blood. The sword is poised above his heart, but I cannot send it home.

"Save us both," he rasps. "*Strike!*" But I drop the sword and kneel beside him, leaning over that dear body, crying and kissing him. Then suddenly the young girl is back, with the taxi driver this time, and they are urging me to go while there is still a chance. I tell them that K. has been grievously wounded, by me, and that he must be rushed to a hospital or he will die. I *must* take him with me. They refuse, but I overcome their intransigence with my furious determination, and together we all carry K.'s barely alive body out to the cab. My young friend, she of the braids and frighteningly cool self-possession, embraces me and disappears. I am settled in the back seat, K.

lying across my lap, my clothes wet with his blood. It is a pietà of murderess and victim. The driver guns the motor and we are off.

For an endless space of time we speed, through countryside and city outskirts, through evening and then night, pursued at first by cars from the asylum, later, alone, having at last eluded them.

But K. is dying in my arms—the old K., my own lover and husband and friend, he who has always known and loved me best. Oh dear god, he is really dying. He is delirious, talking of poems we wrote and read aloud to each other once, of chess games we played until three in the morning, of love-making under our rain-drenched bedroom eaves. Once in a while he regains coherence and begs forgiveness for having been so changed against his will.

"No blame, no blame," I weep to him, begging his forgiveness, in turn, for my death blows. Yet he understands even that, pleading with me to put him out of the car now, before we reach the city, in case his presence should bring suspicion on me. I tell him that we'll be safe in the city, that he must go to the hospital. No, no, he moans in desperation. He says I don't understand. That the asylum reaches far beyond its own hedges. That the city too will destroy me when it learns what I have done. That he, dead or alive, must not be found with me. That I should go where the underground driver knows there is safety.

But I am past listening now, knowing only that I hold what is most dear to me, that it is ebbing away each second, staining my fingers with the loss of love. Nothing matters, nothing is real, but this. The driver leans back and adds his urgings to K.'s. But I am deaf to them both. Nothing again will ever part me from my loving what I have a right to love. Nothing can break the pure pity of this moment, where we cling to one another, casualties each of the other and of what had lain in wait for us all along, live sacrifices bleeding out our love above relentless wheels.

"I love you, I have always loved you, my darling. I always will," I murmur over and over. And he replies with the same words, blood bubbling from his mouth at every breath. Two children saying their prayers against the night.

Then the lights outside the taxi are city-street bright, and we are pulling up to the emergency entrance of a large hospital, the driver nervously cursing to himself at being in this situation. And the attendants rush out, white-coated, efficient, with a stretcher. K. is placed upon it, and I prepare to leave the taxi and follow where they wheel him. But as I step from the cab, more attendants close round me.

They were right then, after all. The asylum reaches out into the world. It is becoming the world. But it doesn't matter, if I can save my love; if I can be near him, even if he is dying, stay with him, he whom I risked killing rather than let live without his soul.

Then the earth's crust opens before my feet.

For K., as he is wheeled away on the stretcher, leans up and props himself casually on one elbow, smiling at me through the alien face, self-confident, unhurt, vindicated, saved. He is not ill, not dying, not even wounded.

Is this the Parable of Paranoia? Or the Parable of Love?

ART AND FEMINISM: A ONE-ACT WHIMSICAL AMUSEMENT ON ALL THAT MATTERS

The following feminist "entertainment" emerged from a collage of writings jotted in fits and starts over a long period. At times these notes were motivated by the thrill of realizing a feminist culture was coming into being. At other times they were motivated by anger—at censorship (see "International Feminism: A Call for Support of the Three Marias" p. 202), or at ignorance, or at dogmatism. Yet how much more often I have reveled in the proliferation of women creating art. In poetry alone, even a partial list of names chosen almost at random hints at the diversity: Alice Walker, Joan Larkin, Kathleen Fraser, Dolores Prida, Honor Moore, Michelle Wallace, Louise Bernikow, Yvonne, Marge Piercy, Marilyn Hacker, Audre Lorde, Margaret Atwood, Susan Griffin, Fran Winant, Alta, Leah Fritz, Ntozake Shange, Dianne Di Prima, June Jordan—the words of these women and many others have exploded across the consciousness of an American reading public composed largely, though not exclusively, of women. Still others, like Eve Merriam, Josephine Miles, Ruth Pitter, Adrienne Rich, Muriel Rukeyser, Louise Bogan, Elizabeth Bishop, Carolyn Kizer, Elizabeth Jennings, Laura Riding, and of course the silver-tongued ghosts of Plath and Sexton—these are the "womandarins," the more established poets. Of differing generations and consciousnesses, nonetheless these are the women who were carving in English the pain of being female even before they themselves could actually name that pain; whittlers, as it were, of their own transformation shining back at them in the runes of their feminist poet daughters.

This feminist renaissance, not content with its creative artists, has also produced feminist scholars who are researching and reclaiming older forms of women's art. I am indebted for the references in this "Amusement" on the background of quilting to Patricia Mainardi (herself a painter), whose comprehensive study "Quilts: The Great American Art," first appeared in *Feminist Art Journal*, Winter, 1973, and to Carol Edelson, whose article "Quilting: A History," was published by *Ms.* in December 1973. The continuing research done by Rachel Maines and her colleagues at the new and feminist Center for the History of American Needlework (5660 Beacon Street, Pittsburgh, Pennsylvania 15217) will doubtless prove, in time, that Penelope was a perfectionist artist who unwove her tapestry at night merely to revise; the suitors, and Odysseus for that matter, had nothing to do with it. I want to express publicly the grateful excitement I have felt upon reading *Feminist Art Journal*—the interviews with women who are poets, painters, sculptors, and composers; the eye-opening retrospectives on medieval women artists; the analyses of women architects, and film-makers. I am grateful, too, to Meg Bogin for her book *The Women Troubadours* (Paddington Press Ltd., New York, 1976), recently published and already a basic resource which inspired part of the following piece.

Nor does my gratitude restrict itself to new feminists, for without the voices of those who sang earlier, we could not exist. I think of so many women whose different insights have been of incalculable worth: I think of Susan Sontag—the intellectual integrity of her prose; and of Mary McCarthy, whose genius for fiction encompassed a dazzling feminist sensibility—this, decades ago, and alone. I thank them. I think of Dorothy L. Sayers, who in a thoughtful book called *The Mind of the Maker* (1941; Living Age Editions, Meridian Books, New York, 1960) posed the privileges and griefs of the artist in such a way as to impress me deeply; her terms were of her background and her time—Christian and patriarchal—but her perceptions were her own, and so organically feminist, radical, and daring as to be ours. I thank her, too.

I even must thank, on this occasion, those who have irritated me into the gall of various statements hazarded in this "Amusement." I mean certain dear sisters who have sent me terribly sincere and sincerely terrible "political" poemlets. I mean that feminist (who claimed to be an art student, yet) who inspired in me a giddy consternation when I heard her pronounce Daphnis and Chloe "Daphne and Chloe, those great lesbian lovers." (I waited for her to acknowledge Hero and Leander as her gay brothers, but clearly she'd never heard the names.) I'm grateful to the woman who organized a conference workshop entitled "Poetry as Yoga Practice"—thus making me realize how bad things really were. (A kind soul, surely she meant well, but would she, I wonder, have called a workshop "Brain Surgery as Yoga Practice"? "Thermonuclear Dynamics as Yoga Practice"? Even "Learning French the Berlitz Way as Yoga Practice"? I think not—yet the art, craft, and *science* of poetry is at least as exacting as any of the above—and merits as much courtesy, if not respect.)

I thank those who were honestly surprised at my answer to their question about influences on my work: the Metaphysical Poets of the seventeenth century, especially Donne and Marvell; and Pitchford and Raine and Jeffers and Wylie and Crane and Mew and Yeats and Plath and so many others the list could go on for hours. In prose: Kafka and Faulkner and Eliot and the Brontës, Austen and Hawthorne and Cather and James and Olsen, to be admittedly eclectic. In theater: the Elizabethans and Jacobeans, and Shaw, Sophocles, Anouilh; Sartre, too, and Bagnold and Hellman. And Brecht. And Williams. And all such lists are ludicrous.

My listeners were thunderstruck. I had cited some men. In certain feminist circles it is not yet fathomed (for understandable if maddening reasons) that there has been a peculiar synchronicity even in some male artists (fine ones, that is), a symbiosis between art and real understanding of *all* human beings. Henry James' female characters are more profoundly feminist, to me, than Isadora Wing. Furthermore, I'm afraid that if I am forced to choose between Donne's complex braiding of respectful misogyny and uxoriousness on the one hand and some new volume called *Riding the Red Rag to Amazon Nation* on the other, I shall not be un-Donne. If, in our expectable nationalist phase, we feminists forget that the most sublime art is mercilessly sexless, raceless, and ageless, then we shall be in danger of losing sight of our own eventual goals—and what is perhaps even worse, we shall never produce great artists, or we will destroy those we do produce.

Successful revolutions are as well known as their recently overthrown previous regimes for treating two groups in particular with especial vengeance: revolutionaries and artists. On a bad day I can look at the Feminist Movement and see some alarmingly familiar tendencies, despite all my self-assurances, that *we* shall do this differently. (Another way of saying "It can't happen here"?) Artists, a feisty lot, have generally responded to suspicion from others with a manner defiantly calculated to provoke such suspicion all on its own. We do get shot, of course. We also get the last word, albeit one uttered posthumously.

Can women artists and feminist revolutionaries change all this? Tune in next century, if there is one. If you find on your futuristic tele-screen klutzy statues in town plazas memorializing conveniently massacred feminist artists whose works are no longer available, you'll know that nothing much has changed.

On good days, I know you won't find this nightmare, though. On good days, I know that god, whether or not she's a feminist, is at least an artist.

THE AMUSEMENT

Cast of Characters:
  (*in order of appearance*)

THE POET

> *The Nine Muses:*

URANIA, the Muse of Cosmic Science
THALIA, the Muse of Comedy and the Pastoral
EUTERPE, the Muse of Lyric Song
POLYMNIA, the Muse of Sacred Song
TERPSICHORE, the Muse of Dance
ERATO, the Muse of Love Poetry
CLIO, the Muse of History
CALLIOPE, the Muse of Epic Poetry
MELPOMENE, the Muse of Tragedy

THE POET

The Time: The Present

The Place: Rafters above THE POET's desk

(*As the Curtain of our consciousness rises, we see* THE POET *sitting at her desk. She is hunched over her typewriter, and something about the curve of her shoulders bespeaks a certain weariness, yet she peers, squinting, at the ceiling, and her expression is one of apprehension. Above her, assembled in various postures and perches,* THE NINE MUSES *float, cushioned on their own portable ectoplasm. With the exceptions of* MELPOMENE *and* POLYMNIA, THE MUSES *are all chattering animatedly at once*)

URANIA (*raising her voice to be heard above the amiable din*) Sisters, Sisters! Please, can we have some order? There is a most important subject under discussion at tonight's meeting. We have a full agenda, and we really must begin. (THE MUSES *settle down*) Thank you so much for your cooperation. (*Then, a bit sternly, to* THALIA, *who continues whispering to* TERPSICHORE) I said THANK YOU FOR YOUR COOPERATION. (THALIA *accepts the rebuke and is silenced*) Now. Let us start, as ever, with The Toast.

(THE MUSES *all float to a standing position and raise brimming goblets which are suddenly manifest in their hands.* POLYMNIA *leads them in their ritual, which they chant with great dignity*)

ALL THE MUSES (*in unison*)   To The Mothers from whence we, Creatrices of all creativity, have been created. To the Old Ones who began us all. To Melete, She who is Meditation. To Mneme, She who is Remembrance. To Aoide, She who is Song. To the Three, who became the Nine, who became the soul of the world.

(THE POET *shudders with awe. Something ancient and chilling is so palpable in the room that she pulls her shawl tighter about her shoulders*)

URANIA   Let us begin our meeting, then. The central concern tonight—

THALIA (*interrupting*)   I apologize for the interruption, Urania, but I must lodge two teensy protests. First, garrets. Can we never find a more comfortable meeting place than a garret? (CLIO *opens her mouth to reply, but* THALIA *burbles on*) I know, I *know*, darling Clio. I realize the situation of most artists on this particular barbarous planet. Didn't my own beloved Mozart starve to death here? Didn't my gem Dorothy Parker have to survive by writing Hollywood screenplays here? But when are we going to *do* something about this situation?

URANIA   Thalia, this is a subject for another whole meeting. Please—

THALIA   And then there's this abominable wine. (*She holds her goblet at arm's length, eyeing it with contempt*) It isn't that I'm a hedonist, you know, but there *was* a time when we could get a decent ambrosia for our meetings. *This* stuff isn't a fitting refreshment for us; there's no ecstasy in it. It merely gets us tiddly—and you all know Melpomene when she gets tiddly: Ms. Morbid herself. I mean, with all due affection, Melpie—

EUTERPE   Thalia dear, Melpomene does *not* become morbid. As for you, though, you are permanently in a tiddly state, you irrepressible wag. Oh, Thalia, do *try* to be kind. And quiet.

THALIA   Very well, quiet perhaps. (*She smiles at* EUTERPE) For you, Euterpe. But kindness I can't promise. That is too often a form of hypocrisy, which isn't in my nature. I'm a country girl at heart.

POLYMNIA   Sisters. (*There is a solemn quality in her bearing which seems to command everyone's attention*) I suggest to you that, loving banter aside, we have a sacred duty to perform here. The issue we are to examine could be called "Art and Feminism" or "Female Culture" or perhaps "Women and Art" or a thousand other such titles. Indeed, the title is less significant than the urgent need for our concern; this subject is of vital importance to our children below, in particular our precious Daughters.

TERPSICHORE   Well, then, let's do begin. What shall our form be tonight? Shall we go around the room in personal testimony, or have a Chair, or shall we do free-floating space? I prefer the last; I think we do it so well.

ERATO   Oh, I agree. After all, we're not doing C-R in a strict sense this meeting, so we needn't hew to personal testimony. Terpsichore's right. Besides, free-floating *feels* so good.

(*There is a chorus of approving comment for use of the free-floating form of discussion.* CLIO *interrupts, waving a cautious finger*)

CLIO   I would remind you all that our past experience with free-floating discussion, while at times most fruitful, has not been without difficulty. Certain of us tend to dominate the conversation. Terpsichore, on the other hand, says very little (although her gestures are of course so eloquent), Polymnia retires almost completely into meditation, and Melpomene sits quietly in some dormer cranny and weeps without uttering a sob. This *has* happened, you know.

URANIA   A valid point, Clio. Perhaps we should have a firmer structure. I think a Chair would be an excellent idea—

THALIA   *I* don't. Sorry to be a bucolic bother, but it's almost always either Chair or Testimony, Testimony or Chair, and I get bored. Are we the Muses or not? De we create creativity or not? Also, we always wind up with either Urania or Clio as the Chair. I'm too naughty, Euterpe's too gentle, Polymnia too contemplative, Terpsichore too nonverbal, Erato too excitable, Calliope too long-winded, and Melpomene too severe. So it's Clio or Urania. Poor things, they've both been Chairs so often we could upholster them and have a matched pair—Louis Quatorze, I think.

(*There is a clamor to be heard from every voice, including that of* TERPSICHORE. *But it is* EUTERPE *who manages to gain the floor—or, rather, the ether*)

EUTERPE   Sister, Sisters. Surely we can compromise. Do let us have a free-floating discussion, but let those of us who babble on (*everyone looks at* THALIA, *who is not in the least disconcerted*) restrain our verbosity, while others of us who tend toward less active participation strive to be more, well, *present*. Surely we can manage that, can we not?

(EUTERPE *is so winning in her earnestness and grace that* THE MUSES *subside into agreement. Good will appears to prevail*)

CALLIOPE   I see only one last objection to this choice of form. Remember, Sisters, why we are in this particular garret. (THE MUSES *exchange glances*) Yes. And as soon we open her ears, that Daughter will find herself seized with our thoughts and our presences. If we choose free-form discussion, will she be able to grasp us at such a speed? Can her mind dance with light?

MELPOMENE   No. (*She has not spoken before, and now we notice that the other Muses regard* MELPOMENE *with a grave respect, all except* THALIA, *who, oddly, gazes at her tall sister with love born of a sense of intimacy*) She will hear only our echoes, read only our footprints. But we will be no clearer to her should we take a million different forms. It is no matter. In her striving to understand what grasps her she will grasp us. That is all she can hope for. It is sufficient.

(*The Nine are silent. Then, a glance and a nod passes from one to the other, until exchanged by all. The communication ends at* POLYMNIA, *who then rises, leans down toward* THE POET, *and lightly claps her hands once.* THE POET *rubs her eyes and runs her fingers jaggedly through her hair in a suddenly nervous gesture. Then she gulps a mouthful from a coffee cup on her desk, grabs a fresh sheet of paper, inserts it in her typewriter, sits up straight in her chair, and takes a deep breath. It is as if she is listening to an internal voice*)

POLYMNIA Let us begin.

(*As* CALLIOPE *begins to speak,* THE POET *starts typing. She continues this activity soundlessly but without cease throughout the dialogue, except where indicated*)

CALLIOPE The question is raised as to female culture. Has there always been one? Is one possible only now? Surely the Muses have always been female—and feminist, too, to the degree this foolish planet would recognize that—but how much of ourselves have we been able to communicate to our children? Is there a feminist culture, a feminist approach to art? There are those who answer flatly that there is not.

THALIA They are called men.

CALLIOPE Thalia, please. That is not necessarily true. Besides, we mustn't get diverted from our subject. There are those who say that there *is* such a special approach, but some of them seem to trivialize it, defining it solely in terms of uterine shapes, or eternally self-justifying confessions, or the numbing overuse of such words as *menstruation, struggle, labia, consciousness, teardrop,* and *liberation.*

EUTERPE Dear me.

CALLIOPE But there are also those, so far almost entirely women, who feel committed to the creation of what might become a feminist culture. Even some of these children lack the realization of how real that woman's culture already has been, for eons. So when they are asked the basis for their commitment, they fall silent with their faith alone. The question goes, "How can you speak of female culture when in fact culture differs from group to ethnic group? You cannot think, for example, that the culture of a white woman in, say, North America, is the same as the culture of a black woman, even in the same continent, country, city—can you?" The answer at first is "No. They are not the same."

MELPOMENE Different. Separate. Isolate. Not the same.

CLIO The answer is deeper, and older, and simpler. They are separately sprung from one root. Look, Sisters, at a single example. Let us try to find a meaningful difference between this quilt (*a patchwork quilt of mandalic beauty materializes across* CLIO'S *lap*) and this bowl (*a clay bowl shaped in perfect balance and painted in hues of startling intensity appears, similarly, in* CLIO'S *cupped hands*). Let us, for the sake of argument, restrict ourselves to that North American continent—although precisely the same point could be made about any two or ten or thousand cultures on the planet Earth. That point is this:

Quilting, in North America, began as a frontier necessity. As the years passed, it became less of a necessity and more of a leisure occupation—needlework. We could characterize this, at least from the (by patriarchal date-reckoning) (THALIA *sniffs in derision*) nineteenth century on, as a part of white middle-class women's culture.

Now let us move backward in time to that age when this continent of which we speak was cared for by its native peoples. Let us examine the handiwork, especially the pottery, of those Native American peoples. Today such pottery is displayed in the museums of those who conquered and destroyed the creators of the work, and in these displays it is labeled "Native American art and culture."

Yet it was the women who invented pottery; the women are still the great artist-potters in Native American societies. In some Native American nations it is *tabu* for men to throw pots at all; only the women may create from clay.

So, my sisters. Is that women's culture or Native American culture? I say it is women's culture, women's art. Predominantly. I say this because of the *connective* between the purportedly middle-class quilt and the ostensibly primitive pottery. (CLIO *lifts a corner of the quilt in one hand, and the bowl in the other, as if finding a balance in their weight*) Both combine *beauty and use*. The patriarchal overculture has usually dismissed anything which was both beautiful *and* useful as a "craft." Yet our Daughters, restricted to materials that were perforce useful, invented the techniques to make them articles of loveliness.

URANIA More than loveliness—*meaning*. They invented the techniques to universalize these materials into art. And this, while weaving a means to keep the children warm in bed. And this, while molding a means to carry food for nourishment.

MELPOMENE And these, while the weaver of the quilt was raped and murdered by the brother of the potter, and while the potter was raped and massacred by the husband of the weaver. This quilt. This bowl.

CLIO So say I, then, that there has been from time before time something which can be called a female culture. Let those who will deny it!

THALIA Don't exercise yourself, they will. But many of those same unfortunate souls deny the existence of art itself, all art, any art. If I must overhear one more combat-boot-brained young woman asking if all art isn't "inherently bourgeois," I shall find myself fleeing to the Establishment—and you know how I feel about *it*. All I would encounter there would be self-indulgent ignoramuses who regard art as A Good Investment or The Met Opening or who are too busy jockeying for the newest award or biggest foundation grant to divine my presence.

CALLIOPE   Come come, Thalia, none of us have visited such people since the days of Tiberius. You know that. We could march before them as in armies, wave on cresting wave of us, artist and artisan alike— they would not recognize us for who we are. We could descend openly as Muses—massive, magnificent, mellifluous—and they—

THALIA   —would patronize us with their attitudes but not with their alms? Ah yes, Calliope. But before you spin more images to demonstrate how all unknowing these reactionaries are, look to the revolutionaries, and defend art, too, against the slings and arrows of *this* audience.

EUTERPE   How much more painful to confront those who claim to be devoted to new forms, to change!

THALIA   This is the hook that gets us every time. And then they bark, "Bourgeois!" and exile their best hopes.

CLIO   Surely the concept that culture is irrelevant to radical change is itself born of a sexist, classist, racist, and elitist attitude (all the venalities of which they accuse culture).

THALIA (*jumping up and down with partisan glee*)   Oh, I *say*, Clio! Go to it! *What* an imitation! I never thought you had it in you. Why, you're marvelous.

CLIO (*drawing herself up in stately fashion*)   I am not trying to impress you with my mimetic talents, Thalia. I am merely trying to point out how breathtakingly stupid is the notion that art is "bourgeois" because, ostensibly, the poor don't like or understand it. How does this attitude account for the Italian immigrant who, no matter how penniless, somehow managed to possess a musical instrument or a phonograph and some cherished recordings of opera?

CALLIOPE   And what about enghettoed Jews who died of starvation rather than sell their books?

POLYMNIA   Where does the black slave fit into this theory, the slave who forged the soul of American music, who would not be silent, who swallowed pain, alchemized it in the forge of the throat, and spit it out again as sung glory?

URANIA   Yes, you are right. I too have been repelled by this idea that the poor somehow are dullards who hate art. The thought itself is middle class and middle-brow and . . . middling. And *why*?

CLIO   It is that same white middle-class liberal guilt we saw so much of in the decade called the sixties.

ERATO   Or is it something more? Is it a virulent resentment that, despite the Marxist formulae about alienated labor as the rule under capital-ism, the artist alone has managed to perform *un*alienated labor everywhere, at all times, and under all systems? As if it were an act of love?

POLYMNIA   Or an act of prayer.

EUTERPE   You mean it could be envy, then? At the artist for being the intrepid exception? Ah, I see . . .

MELPOMENE   . . . the intrepid exception who pays with her life, and who could even, if given a chance, prove the rule better than the formulae —since a real revolution could make artists of everyone. Or is *that* the fear?

EUTERPE   Everyone an artist. How exquisite.

THALIA   A bit excessive, I'd say.

EUTERPE   No, no, Thalia, think back. They've come within visionary distance of it a few times. Remember the Middle Ages? Chartres? The anonymous collective united shared chorused expression of aesthetic love? Think of the troubadours, the jongleurs, the tapestry weavers working together on one loom—

MELPOMENE   They were burned for being who they were. There were millions of common artists, for once. And then there were millions of torches who screamed in the night. And then there was silence again. (*At this last* THE POET, *who has been steadily taking everything down and who has broken rhythm only once or twice to insert a new sheet in her typewriter or to gesture frantically at the air as if her own thoughts were coming too fast and thick to be got down on paper*—THE POET, *at this last comment of* MELPOMENE's, *buries her face in her hands and utters one long rasping groan of despair.* THE MUSES *above her exchange pitying looks.* POLYMNIA *reaches out a hand as if to stroke* THE POET's *hair, but does not touch her.* TERPSICHORE *is rocking slowly from front to back, as if she were keening for her dead.* THALIA *has moved lightly from her place to sit next to* MELPOMENE; THALIA *draws* MELPOMENE's *head down to her breast.* MELPOMENE *submits to this embrace in grateful silence*)

CLIO   If we mourn, we will be given over to mourning.

EUTERPE   (*softly*)   Can not one of us speak something which will bring us back to gladness? We must celebrate our living as well as our dead.

URANIA   Yes, my dear sister. And we have work before us. Erato?

ERATO   I—cannot speak yet. That age Melpomene spoke of was my own. The Age of Courtly Love, it has been called. My Daughters bore it, ruled it, wrote, sang, strung, wove, painted it, and perished for it. No, I—cannot speak yet, not of other things.

THALIA   (*after a pause, almost glumly*)   It certainly makes you long for the good old days when Euphrosyne and Aglaia were still tripping about, doesn't it? (*She sighs and scuffs her toe*) All this mythomorphosizing into new versions gets me down sometimes. I'm the only Grace left.

URANIA   (*appealing for help in reviving the discussion*)   Calliope?

CALLIOPE (*slowly rousing herself to the task*)   Yes. Yes, I hear. Celebrate the present and future as well as the past. (*She clears her throat and adopts a brisk tone*) But for celebration we must look to what is being produced. And for this we need create new standards for a new age, for these new artists, for these Daughters who would give birth to a new culture. (THE MUSES *begin to return from their grief, resuming their old positions, drying their eyes, and once again giving their attention to the conversation. At this* THE POET, *too, blows her nose, sighs deeply, and settles back to her work*) Authentic art is not born of chaos, but of an order all unto itself. (CALLIOPE, *seeing the effect her speech is having on her Sisters, smiles, pleased with herself, and exchanges a proud look with* URANIA.) How do our Daughters develop new standards—their own—for artistic excellence? Because some criteria *are* necessary; art in a very real sense is not democratic.

URANIA   The Daughters are of course suspicious of standards because of the way the Sons have used them.

THALIA   To say the least.

EUTERPE   But ought that mean that the Daughters refuse any standards at all? I think not. It is merely that in their flight from the old oppressive restrictions they have preferred formlessness to any structure. One can sympathize with that, surely.

CALLIOPE   To a point, yes. But art *is* structure. The form is to the aesthetic as matter is to energy—without it there is no life.

EUTERPE   Agreed. I also chafe at ignorance, especially in the Daughters. Yet I rejoice at the number of women who are writing poems, more than I can ever remember. Even formless, aimless, artless poems. They have the longing, I rejoice at that.

THALIA   Then you do your own Daughters a disservice, Euterpe. Please. Don't misunderstand me. I too rejoice at this catharsis, expression, exorcism, release. But it is one thing to rejoice because so many women are at last putting their feelings on paper. It is quite another thing to consider this *writing*.

CALLIOPE   For once I find myself in agreement with Thalia. Women have the right to this expression, and it is wondrous that feminism has exploded a space in which that right may finally be exercised. Art, however, requires something more.

THALIA   Also there is just so much catharsis one can take without being put in mind of laxatives or reduced to quoting Nietzsche on the creativity of the artist: "One does not get over a passion by representing it; rather, it is over *when* one is able to represent it."

CLIO (*dryly*)   Nietzsche seems an unsavory example to raise in any political context, don't you think, Thalia?

THALIA   *Touché*, Clio. But it's hard for me to pass up a good quote when I inspire one.

CALLIOPE For myself, I confess that I am becoming impatient with Daughters who appear to feel that any set of words blatted out on a page with the right-hand margins unjustified is a poem. Do you think that I am becoming a crochety old grump?

EUTERPE No, you are an admirable old grump, Calliope. You're right, of course. "Having a lot to express" is all very well, but if one is indifferent to color and line then one should refrain from making that expression on canvas, and if one is indifferent to language, to the richness of vowels and the wit of consonants, indifferent to rhythm and echo and music and rhyme and simile and metaphor, then one had best refrain from making that expression on the page. Or *do* so, by all means, but have the civility not to call it art.

ERATO *Brava*, Euterpe! "And where love's form is, love is; love *is* form."

CLIO Chapman said that.

THALIA A man, tsk-tsk.

ERATO Indeed, Thalia. And why, pray, should *I* pass up a good quote when *I* inspire one?

THALIA (*throwing up her hands in a gesture of surrender*) *Touché* again! (*She is laughing wickedly*) I see I'm actually infecting you all with wit.

MELPOMENE (*with a nod toward* THE POET, *who has just ceased typing and begun twisting her hands nervously*) She sometimes refuses to tell these harsh truths to her people. For fear. Of hurting them, of their hating her as the messenger of such news. As if the kindest lie were owed any but one's adversary. This fear is her gravest sin against her people. If she loves them she owes them some truth, and the most severe judgments of art are the best and most enduring form of that truth, for her.

TERPSICHORE She will unlearn her fear in time, and move on her truth.

MELPOMENE Truth needs no time, and art has none to give. Her people waste themselves on trivialities. She knows this; she must speak.
(THE POET *has become increasingly agitated during the above speeches; she has left her desk and begun pacing back and forth, wringing her hands*)

CALLIOPE She must do more. She must inspire them to develop excellence.

URANIA More. To redefine excellence so that it means not excelling over someone else but excelling and exceeding the *self*, so that the Daughters compete each with the best in *herself*, bettering herself and the Work thereby.

CLIO They will not understand for a long time. She will have reason to fear.

POLYMNIA She must pass beyond the fear, into devotion.

ERATO Into love.

MELPOMENE She will need love and devotion indeed when at last she ceases to fear. For then she will have most cause.

(*A sudden calm seems to steal over* THE POET, *as if the exhortatory statements of the Muses above her have woven a cloak of peace which now enfolds her. She seems to stand taller and move with confidence, as someone resigned to a fate. She walks quietly to her desk, seats herself, and, smiling faintly, returns to work*)

THALIA (*deliberately breaking the tension*)   Well, I shall steel her courage and entertainingly demonstrate to you, dear Sisters, how great is the need for those aforementioned standards. I happen to have with me (*she extends an empty hand into the air and a sheaf of papers appears in it*) a few wee exercises in parody which I could not resist after leafing through certain feminist publications which the Daughters, in their well-meaning but sometimes soporiferous manner had produced. Ahem—

CALLIOPE   Must we?

THALIA   Indeed you must! (*In mock pain*) I burned with a hard, gem-like flame when I wrote them. (*Impatiently*) Is it true, then, that Muses have lost their sense of humor?

ALL (*with assorted moans*)   Very well then, Thalia. Have done. All right, get it over with. Go ahead, then.

THALIA (*delighted*)   Well. You'll miss the spelling and visual jokes, but it can't be helped. This one is an exercise on the current "Heavy" Radical Woman poem which-must-touch-all-the-correct-bases. It has alternate titles (THALIA *reads all the following in dramatic fashion*):

"How Now Frau Mao"
or
"The Bilge My Sisters Won't All Burble with Me"
Wimminlovers we
burn my tongue in yr lap
here in the streets of Hanoi oy o O labia
O Ho O Ho Chi Minh
who saw them bomb the dykes
O melting oreo cookie in the jeans
I hate my square old mother O but Ho
is my dear uncle   angle   ankle lick my ankle
she u   u she O she u
inkling of chlorine   chorine   water
Drown she said and I bid, I bid
two posters at the wimmincenter auction
            (*of those great wimmin Evelyn Waugh*
                and that Maria Rilke)
in exchange for one NLF flag I sooed
into the crotch of my womon's wombone's pants
for you are who you creep with
and Susan Sexe she tells it like it his
O Ho u she i ho Ho to t—
to touch ano—

to touch anoth—   another—
to touch another wo—
to touch another wommon's
wommon's wombon's woman's
little
red
book.

(THE MUSES *valiantly are trying to sit in prim and judgmental postures and to refuse* THALIA *the sight of their genuine amusement. Small, revealing smiles prickle at the corner of their mouths.* CLIO, *however, is simply unable to resist correcting an historical inaccuracy*)

CLIO   I just want to say that "dear old Uncle Ho" put all the lesbians he knew of in dear old jail.

THALIA   O Ho. As if we didn't know.

ERATO   Which reminds me. (*She has a twinkle in her eye*) If male artists always claimed to woo us and have us as their mistresses, whatever must they think goes on between the woman artist and her Muse? (THE MUSES *all giggle, except for* POLYMNIA *and* MELPOMENE)

MELPOMENE   They never understand that every artist, female or male, is ultimately alone with the self. An onanist, if you insist.

POLYMNIA   Not quite, dearest Melpomene. Alone, rather, with what is eternal *in* the self. That is quite different, you know, and *that* is what they do not understand.

THALIA   Pish-tosh. What they don't understand would fill the Library at Alexandria and did. They probably refuse to visualize The Poet and *her* Muse (*the giggles again, lovely and wicked*) and so translate *us* into great hairy jockish hulks—*voilà!* The solution: male muses!

CALLIOPE   (*wrinkling her delicate nose*)   I may die. (*Then, noticing:*) Oh look, Terpsichore's rolled herself into a ball!
(*They give themselves over to unashamed laughter, while* THALIA *seizes the opportunity for another dramatic delivery*)

THALIA   Girls, girls, do settle down, I'm not finished. There are a few more short examples which I must share with you so that you'll be Up On Current Trends. This next one is my version of the Real Woman Poet's work; if the first example I read could be found in the center-fold of something that might be called *Sappho Gurley Flynn Speaks* then this one would be lodged in the pages of a prestigious journal with a name like *The Duluth Poetry Forum of America.* Now you must remember, Sisters, that the Real Woman Poet is abstract on self-protective purpose. Look not for concrete images herein. And yet, show pity: our parodied author has imitated masculinist poetry and dutifully gone to literary cocktail parties for decades. She is at last Accepted. Now, hoist by her own Petrarch, she kicks lovingly at other women, will not publish in anthologies of women's poetry (because she's "not a woman poet, but a poet"), yet runs the feminist fashion through her subject mill, you bet. I call this one:

"The Ontological Anatomy of Areopagitica Assessed"

or, simply,

"Poem"

To make
    & unmake
   ourselves & each   other
    makes for a making
    of others & selves
      unmade & unselfish
  but selflessly making
     a selfmade made self.

  & if I am angry
    & if I am guilty
my needs & my anger
     are guiltless & grouchy
   and if I am thoughtless
  la plume de ma tante
     your thoughts for the making
of my self, my guilt, needs, & anger are made.
To believe   )   *is to alter*   *Once more into*
the bleach, split ends,
humming upon a peak in Darien.

EUTERPE (*doubled over and holding her stomach*)   I can hardly breathe, but I can't tell whether it's from laughter or from pain.

THALIA (*barreling on while she has them enthralled*)   Both, dear, both. But take comfort. Here's one for you, Erato. It's my humble version of the New Raunchy Women's Lib Poet who thinks Mailer, Miller, and no doubt even Mahler are just *wonderful* guys and who has created the new sex-and-food genre:

"Brussel Sprouts and Balls"

Ooooo honey your balls are just like
brussel sprouts and you
know how I love them all adribbling Promise
margarine and just a
      smidgen
       dollop
       of
        fresh
        pepper
  I adore to grate myself.

ERATO (*Opening her eyes wide and taking a deep breath*)   I. Can. Tell. You. Euterpe. For. Certain. It's. Pain. (*Then she explodes in laughter, the contagion running through the rest of the helpless Muses.*

Tears course down their cheeks and they strive in vain to recover their solemnity)

TERPSICHORE (*gasping*) Thalia, you're a ham. Incurable.

EUTERPE (*wiping her eyes*) I do think, Thalia, that you might try to be a bit more charitable. Look, you've made our Poet exceedingly uncomfortable.

THALIA Only a false love lies, Euterpe. You know that. My love for the Daughters would carve away their laziness with the sharp blade of humor. And as for *her* (THALIA *peers down at* THE POET, *who is indeed looking discomfited, albeit amused*), *she* isn't uncomfortable *enough*. If she were secretly chortling at my little efforts before, perhaps she'll laugh out loud at my last offering. It is my Big Cheese poem—a rallying cry to all women to take to their noses, put their barricades to the wheel, stand fast at the shoulder, and raise high the grindstone. It is too long for recital here (or anywhere) but I shall read you a sample fragment. The poem is called:

"Muenster"

Listen.
I said listen.
LISTEN, *DAMMIT!*

Ah, sister.
There they are, around us, all
the biggest cheeses:
cheddar, parmesan, romano,
see?—there's cream, and cream-with-chive
and oh dear goddess there's the big
oppressor stinky cheeses: gorgonzola,
stilton, roquefort, danish blue, and liederkranz:
my sisters, hear me

we are marching
        they will crumb before us
we are winning
        they will melt before us
sisters listen hear me say it;
let us say it openly, without shame, and together.

I
    am
        a muenster.
I am
        a muenster.
I am a muenster.

And I am loud.

(THALIA *finishes with a flourish of melodrama, and* THE MUSES, *despite themselves, applaud her heartily. The feeling of shamefaced good will has even extended itself to* THE POET, *who, chagrined and chastened, has ceased smirking at others, laughed openly at herself, and once again settled down to record the meeting—or what she can manage to catch of it*)

MELPOMENE   I know you better than most, Thalia, and I love you for what you dare see and sing. I too have watched the Daughters hunger for their own culture, for too many centuries. Now that that hunger can be fed, I worry in a different way. I know it is a voracious hunger; they are at present so starved as to be indiscriminate. They can make themselves ill by gorging and then turn away from such fare entirely, nauseated at the thought of art and culture when they have glutted themselves on whatever was offered them. And in the meanwhile, what of the cooks, the artists? When faced with famished people does one fuss over correcting the seasonings? The temptation —and the pressure—*not* to is considerable. Yet one must, even if this means watching other cooks offer unbalanced menus and bad nutrition to be gulped down eagerly by those whom one would rather see fed well, sustained. One must wait and create nothing less than the best one is capable of—and those standards rise like a further challenge from within onself, never from the crowd.

EUTERPE   To reevaluate everything! What an enormous task lies before the Daughters! I wonder, for instance, what would a wholly new feminist humor be? What do you think, Thalia?

THALIA   I am evolving through them, as are you, Euterpe. I cannot tell yet. But I do know that laughter itself has almost always necessitated a retreat into the self. If I wish to laugh at something in X's situation I must separate myself from it (objectify it) and then I may see the humor. If I empathize, much less give myself to a spiritual exercise into her reality, I lose all sense of humor.

ERATO   Is laughter then born of alienation?

THALIA   Some might say it is born of worse—hostility and aggression. But I believe there is another possibility, a laughter born of recognition, of surprised similarity, of identification. A defenseless laughter, lovely, loving, and new. (THALIA *turns to* MELPOMENE *and addresses her with a humility we have never seen in the brash* THALIA) Yet all of these would still comprise the laughter of humor; not, of course, of joy. (THALIA's *eyes fill with tears and her smile is like a beacon through their dazzle*) Joy has nothing to do with alienation and is quite beyond such a tepid emotion as empathy. Joy is born actually of a sense of tragedy, and the laughter that rings from joy knows that nothing funny exists.

(MELPOMENE *has risen to her feet and moved slowly toward* THALIA *during the above speech. Now she throws back her head, the dark veil of her hair streaming out behind her, and from her bared throat issues a soundless laughter so terrible that all* THE MUSES *but one cover their ears to escape it, and avert their gaze from her face. Only*

THALIA, *rapt at the sight of her sister glistening through thalian tears, leans closer to listen. Below,* THE POET *shudders again, and darts a glance over her shoulder; then, her known world seems for an interminable second to splinter into a vast space as if her skull had just burst through a narrow corridor into light such as she had never dreamt. The spheres sing at her with the familiar buzz of a cat's purr and everything seems arriving and departing at once, coming too near and going too far and* THE POET *suddenly flings up her arms and stares above her at her own dark garret rafters and she sees them,* she can see them, *for one moment in her brief eternity they show themselves to her as clearly as her own handprint: Tragedy and Comedy, identical twins, laughing and weeping each in the other's arms.*

THE POET, *stunned, falls to the floor, unconscious.* TERPSICHORE *floats down to her and, while softly speaking to* THE POET *and her own Muse Sisters, raises* THE POET, *slowly awakens her, and moves her gradually and gracefully back to her desk*)

TERPSICHORE My Daughter Martha Graham has spoken of the divine fallacy, by which she says she means that which is eternal, the continuation of the spirit. She notes that although the Brontës lived in the "period of the pointed foot," they kept up their relationship with death. The divine fallacy means the joyous error, as well; that which fools call ugly, un-pretty art. I think of the Native American blanket into which the woman maker deliberately weaves a conscious mistake, to let the soul out. The result would otherwise be static, dead. "The one thing perfection lacks is the struggle to achieve it. This is perfection's thirst for consciousness." Blake must have meant this when he wrote "Energy is eternal delight." Movement, not stasis. The reach, not the grasping.

POLYMNIA Is this not the quality all governments fear in the artist? The Central Committee has always tried to bully the artist, and the Board of Directors has always tried to buy her. The former attempt is simply naïve: the artist is involved in what to her (or him) is an effort to tell some portion of a difficult truth, to relate some detail of an intricate vision—and this will never jibe with any party line. The latter approach, while cleverer because it attacks self-preservation, is also co-opted ultimately by its own co-optation: in buying and selling the artist, the Board cannot stop some fragment of the artist's message getting through, however encoded, and this too is disseminated, creating in turn and in time the genuine "market" for the authentic "product"—to use the Board's terms.

CALLIOPE Either way, as long as there exists a human spirit, there will be artists blessedly doomed to express it—despite the campaigns of all governments to order and categorize even, or especially, that part of it which cannot be expressed.

CLIO Marx himself knew this, you know, and unlike so many of his followers, he respected it. In "The Writer's Profession," he wrote: "The writer in no way regards his (*sic*) works as a *means*. They are ends in themselves; so little are they a means for him and others that, when necessary, he sacrifices his existence to theirs and, like the preacher of religion, takes as his principle: Obey God more than men . . ." I refer you, Sisters, to *Literature and Art: Selections from Their Writings*, by Marx and Engels, International Publishers, New York, 1947, page 63.

URANIA Clio dear, no one finds the thoroughness of your scholarship more laudable than I, but sometimes I fear you overdo.

EUTERPE I want to return to something we spoke of earlier, in passing. Objectification. It's such a scorned word among the Daughters who are feminists—and for excellent reasons which we all now know. But in the context of art? I wonder. I wonder if there are not some moments when the political and artistic sensibilities do not *at heart* antagonize. I say at heart because we know and already have spoken of the superficial way in which patriarchal thought has divided the two, to the detriment of both. I have a particular reason for this concern.

URANIA I think all art is in some way intense objectification. To attempt distilling the "reality" of something into art is to set it apart, study it from all possible angles with what Keats called negative capability, make it one's own (or part of one's own) vision—

POLYMNIA —or become part of *its* vision—

URANIA —yes indeed, and to scrap some segments of it and totally invent others, all this in the process of molding the vehicle to give reality a new reality which simply did not exist before. There is no being faithful to some appearance of truth that others claim to see, only to the truth the artist cannot avoid seeing.

CLIO This should not mean, by the way, that the artist is therefore given license to trample over the sensibilities of others—although patriarchy has deliberately misread it this way, at least in the cases of Gauguin, Beethoven, legions of others, mostly men.

EUTERPE So we are agreed then that to insist art represent reality is absurd. To insist that art *not* represent reality is equally ridiculous: both attitudes muzzle and thus destroy art.

THALIA And think of what they do to reality.

ERATO Real relationships, occurrences, emotions—these are hardly ignoble for being real; that is their beauty and their power. But they are still only the pegs on which the poem hangs, the triggers that fire the play, the skeletons which must be clothed with the novel's flesh. They are grains of sand in which the artist cannot help but see the universe entire.

URANIA This is why the artist usually assumes that the (sometimes willful, sometimes all unconscious) distortions in her depiction of any real relationship are at least as valid as any other view of it—including the other person's or even some third "objective" view. Now if that is classic objectification and a political sin, then art has just been purged from the revolution.

CALLIOPE   Wait. Perhaps it *is* objectification, and art alone has a right to it, since art alone does it with no motive to impress or oppress, but only with an intent to hazard being *subjective* about something (therefore *objectifying* it) in order to break open a new view of it.

CLIO   Being subjective always runs this risk. Men have said to feminists, to our own Poet below, "When you talk about men as a class you objectify *me*." Thus, at one move, they deny their own initiating act of self- *and* other-objectification, and deny her her self-defense—the validity of her *subjectivity* (only one validity among many, I grant, but one not to be denied).

TERPSICHORE   Mostly, I think, the artist objectifies herself, himself. The process from life into the page or canvas or song or mime or block of marble implies *a standing back from it,* a critical viewing of it—

ERATO   —and at the same moment an involuntary love for it that drives forth the act of creation and recreation.

THALIA   Emotion *anticipated* in tranquillity?

POLYMNIA   It's possible, my dear. Our Poet down there "objectifies" herself in her poems. And then she sometimes discovers that the portrayal in the poem is more honest than she could have admitted to her realistic self. How many times she has written the prophetic poem she could not herself fully comprehend at the time of its writing!

CALLIOPE   Clearly the "stuff" of any relationship, any insight, any shard of intellect or emotion, *any*thing, is material for the Work. Nothing is beyond use. This is an earned right, though, hard-won by those who take art in dead earnest—*and* who are trying to reject patriarchal license to be gratuitously cruel. No one, in any event, will be able to get it all "in." What a touching thought that would be.

CLIO   In most cases what will be "in" won't have any presence in the actual world at all. But the art will then teach reality what it *should* contain.

EUTERPE   You make it sound as if that were the job of art.

URANIA   The purpose of the lilies of the field?
(*There is gentle, knowing laughter aripple among* THE MUSES *at* URANIA's *question. It is an old subject, a family joke*)

CLIO   Ah, dear Daughter Poet! If you and your sister rhetoricians of the feminist movement could manage to objectify the patriarchy with half the relentless accuracy of the artist facing her subject matter; if you could manage to objectify one another with half the love that moves the artist as she objectifies her content; if you could create your alternatives with half her discipline—

POLYMNIA   —that would be grace.

CLIO —*that* would be a revolution.

CALLIOPE Before grace or revolution, there must be song. Before song there must be remembrance, before remembrance meditation. Melete. Mneme. Aoide. The Daughters are learning. They think back. They are remembering, reclaiming their own. From Hrovtsvitha's medieval mystery plays to Sor Juana's lyrics. From the frescoes of dancing priestesses on the sunken island of Thera to the metal cubbyholes of Nevelson. From the troubadour verses of the Countess of Dia to the chiseled fury of the young Lena Horne. They are beginning to remember. They are beginning to connect.

MELPOMENE Many remain forgotten, disowned, misunderstood, misclaimed.

EUTERPE (*bursting out with it*) One of my dearest ones is still disowned and I cannot think why!

URANIA Euterpe, darling gentle Euterpe, how unlike you! What is it? Which of your dearest? Who can you mean?

EUTERPE (*trying to become calm again but babbling*) It's pained me for so long. I mean Elizabeth Barrett, who is unregarded and unread by our feminist Daughters. I reread her work the space before yester-space, and that of my other Daughter Emily Dickinson. And Sisters, I must admit to you that I was shocked. The scandal aside, Rebecca Patterson's theory and that of J. E. Walsh does bear itself out: Emily did repeatedly plagiarize Elizabeth. Or perhaps not plagiarize because it's hard to know for certain whether Emily wanted those poems published or kept hidden, as exercises, perhaps, but *copy* she did—whole phrases, lines, and images galore.

THALIA Euterpe, do go slower, you sound like me. What theory? Rebecca who? And J. E. what?

CLIO (*ever ready with the footnote*) J. E. Walsh, *The Hidden Life of Emily Dickinson*, Simon & Schuster, New York, 1971. Rebecca Patterson, "Elizabeth Browning and Emily Dickinson": article in *Educational Leader*, July 1956. Also, Ms. Patterson's book, *The Riddle of Emily Dickinson*, Houghton Mifflin, New York, 1951.

EUTERPE (*controlled, but still angry*) The ethics of the rather overwhelming "influence" Emily claimed from Elizabeth aside, I find myself curious about the resurgent interest expressed by feminists for Emily, concurrent with resurgent contempt for Elizabeth. Why, *why*, I wonder?

ERATO Perhaps because Emily never married and Elizabeth did (and in a great and literary love affair, no less)? Perhaps because Elizabeth bore a child (a son, no less)?

TERPSICHORE Really, Erato, I fail to see the connection. I mean not between the husband and the son, but the connection between *them* and her literary reputation among feminists.

THALIA Darling Terps, how innocent you are. This is *politics*. Isn't this what you meant earlier, Euterpe? About art and politics being antagonists? Erato is wondering whether Elizabeth is held in disregard in feminist circles as a symptom of that antithetical feminism which rebels against all imaginable "traditional" roles—even when chosen freely and acted upon creatively.

CLIO   It is an antithetical feminism which, in a sense, *would* like women to become as men.

TERPSICHORE (*with an evocative shiver*)   Ohhh. How distasteful.

EUTERPE   It infuriates me that the male literary establishment has for a century snickered at Elizabeth (and to some extent at her Robert, too, as "the henpecked Browning"); this cabal has buried her best work, sniped at her political activities, and granted her fame only on the basis of her love poems to him (a "proper" subject for a woman)—which happen to be superb love poems, I might add. And now the Feminist Movement perpetuates this very image. Oh! What do they know of Elizabeth's book-length verse novel, *Aurora Leigh*, which Ruskin said was the "greatest poem in the English language"? It was *Aurora Leigh* which the Daughter Susan B. Anthony carried with her like a bible on her lonely tours of campaigning for women's suffrage. Yet by her feminist sisters today Elizabeth is forgotten. Not so Emily, despite the regrettable fact that Emily did not borrow Elizabeth's feminist consciousness along with her metaphors—

URANIA   Euterpe, don't you think you're being a shade unfair?

EUTERPE   If I am, it's time someone was, on this subject. No, Urania, don't reproach me. Emily's feminist sensibilities *are* at best uneven. It's hardly that I begrudge Emily her place as a major American poet; she is my own cherished Daughter and I love her—and frankly, certain work of hers stuns as no other can. But I do think it a fair question to have our Scribe down there challenge her sisters with: Why are feminists rushing to claim Emily and still ignoring Elizabeth? Because they wish to imitate the male literary mandarins? Look to it, I say.

THALIA   I have another theory, actually. I think it's the fault of that inane play *The Barretts of Wimpole Street*. It's been adapted into movie versions and late-show television reissuings and so has leaked its odious, inaccurate, and sexist bias into the popular imagination.

MELPOMENE   There is a simpler explanation yet. Few read Barrett any longer, except in valentine editions of excerpts from her sonnets. Many of the Daughters are lazy. They condemn in ignorance.

CLIO   Our Poet must urge her sisters on this issue.

ERATO   Our Poet needs no urging to do so, Sisters. She feels for Barrett that sympathy sprung from identification—she is a poet, married to another poet. And she is a feminist. Her griefs and joys are not so different from Elizabeth's.

MELPOMENE   I know her thoughts. She and her love have a bitter joke: they say the world requires of them that they play out the story of

A Star Is Born or *The Red Shoes*—two minor films of undeniable poignancy. In both films, both members of each couple are artists; in one, the husband kills himself so as not to be an impediment to his wife's career; in the other, the wife leaps to her death rather than obstruct her husband's art. Our Poet and *her* poet have this bitter joke: they say the world requires of them that they play out one or the other of these stories; they say the world has made it clear to them it will not yet accept them both.

ERATO   They are still trying. They love each other and their own work and each other's work. Is that not something?

CLIO   I also know her thoughts. She thinks of Clara Schumann and of Robert. She thinks of Sand and Chopin. She thinks of Virginia Woolf and of her Leonard. She thinks of Mary Ann Evans and of George Henry Lewes. She knows their thoughts.

THALIA   And I know hers. Our Poet and Our Poet's poet shared another joke when he was offered wealth and honor to divorce her and then write his *Memoirs of Life with a Feminist*. He turned the offer down. Our Poet and her poet share this joke beneath their garret eaves.

CALLIOPE   I also know her thoughts. I read the letter *K* among her thoughts. She notices the letter is for Kenneth, and for Kafka, and for Kafka's *K.*, and for the old word *kneccht*—to know, to understand, and to connect. I see this Daughter tread the journey of the little girl in Andersen's great tale "The Snow Queen," Little Gerda who walked barefoot on ice across half of the world to claim her Little Kay, who was the victim of a glassy sliver in his heart which made it difficult for him to love. Wise Hans, our Son who wrote for children what adults should not forget. Little Gerda found her Little Kay and saved him into love. This too is feminism. I also know her thoughts.

EUTERPE   I also know her thoughts. Listen to them. They spill over. "I affirm all of my transformations." "We will be torn from one another and ourselves." "Blessed Be, it is he I have chosen." "Nothing is not enough." "What have they done to us?" "Scorian lips can wear a dolphin smile." "These are my people." "Weaving for the weave's sake." "I know now they can never save me." "I am come into my power." "Beholding this, my one desire."

URANIA   Our Daughter Poet is in no danger from which her own art cannot save her. Our Scribe merits no more attention from us for the present.

POLYMNIA   All of the Daughters are in no danger so grave their own discovered art cannot save them.

URANIA   They must discover that art then, speak that word, utter themselves. They have the holy gift of language, to be no longer abused. Language! When will revolutions learn to revere its power, not merely employ it? And if feminism is the first real revolution worthy of the name, then where are the signs that the Daughters love words, cherish language, and will take responsibility for it?

THALIA   Well, I don't think the epidemic misuse of "chauvinism" was a particularly auspicious beginning, myself.

CLIO   "*Insects. Vermin. Pigs.*" Once the Nazis, more recently American New Leftists, and now some feminists have used the words to describe human beings. The aim of such language, conscious or not, is to dehumanize one's enemies, the more easily to conceive of eradicating them.

THALIA   Not to mention the indignity done to the animals whose names and sacred honors are so abominably misused!

CALLIOPE   Could Hitler have "exterminated" so many *persons* had he not first linguistically transformed them into vermin? How, in this, is he different from the Symbionese Liberation Army, which called this country's rulers "insects"? How different from those who call women chicks, foxes, birds, or cows? When, too, will people learn that even those they abhor are also human, that the human capacity stretches from miracle to murder and that it *is* human—no more and no less . . . except perhaps where it reaches through exact and honest language—then it is holy.

CLIO   Nor is it any excuse to babble that Hitler's sin was to call a *powerless* people insects and vermin, while radicals today, after all, use such appellations about the powerful (who "deserve" it). Such a recollection of history is based on amnesia. Hitler saw the Jews, quite contrarily, as extremely powerful—as that old familiar international conspiracy which was bleeding the brave Aryan races financially dry, as the scourge of the little people, the masses, the grass roots. Language, Language! How easy they seem to find it, even the Daughters, to give in to that desire to unrecognize the human as un-human, to forget who and what and why they are killing what they wish to kill.

URANIA   And how inevitable that, if they have not even any species-loyalty left, they should treat other creatures, other living matter, with still more contemptuous cruelty than they reserve for their own kind?

MELPOMENE   The Daughters know this better than anyone else at present. It is their burden. They have only begun to utter this burden aloud.

POLYMNIA   Let it be sung, this new word. For the word is miraculous. Not for nothing have all patriarchal religions realized this, locked the word into silence and then murdered any who tried to speak it aloud. The origins of poetry were religious and ecstatic. Poets were one with seers, the bard and the pytheness singing with a single voice. Think, Sisters. Think, Daughters: The power of spiritual frenzy is sufficiently threatening all unto itself, but think of the danger to every enforced system of order should such a mystery again be *reunited with intelligent expression*—and wake and stretch and move and come alive in a form that is intricate and beautiful, even as it was of old.

There are worlds not even we can understand until they have been spoken. Not until we—any of us—recognize that we have said precisely what we mean do we know what we meant, after all.

EUTERPE   The dawn is trickling in at the window, Sisters. Castalia calls.

TERPSICHORE   Oh! We must fly. And we're not *finished.*

THALIA   We never are, you know. It's typical of us. But it's kept us going for a thousand thousand thousand years.

EUTERPE   I'm glad we helped The Poet a little.

THALIA   More likely drove her frothy.

CALLIOPE   *I'm* glad we lodged some thoughts with her that might just help the Daughters.

THALIA   More likely make them commit her somewhere for being frothy.

URANIA   There *was* more business to conduct. We'll have to take it up next time, I guess. Whether to open the group, for instance. Dogmata still wants awfully to join—

(*During this,* THE MUSES *are gathering up their veils, flutes, quills, harps, and other signs of office, and making ready to depart*)

ERATO   (*snarling sweetly*)   I don't want to sound unloving, but if Dogmata comes, I go. The next thing, she'll bring in Jargonē. Why don't they start their own group?

EUTERPE   (*patiently*)   Because, like everyone else, they want to be in the *original* Muses. You know how it is. I think we should consciousness-raise on it.

THALIA   Euterpe darling, you think we should consciousness-raise on everything. You thought we should consciousness-raise while Marsyas was being flayed, Arachne transanimated, and Orpheus torn limb from limb. I get dizzy from going "around the room" for fifty centuries.

(*Chattering and teasing, the Muses slowly fade to translucency, then transparency, then invisibility.* MELPOMENE *alone remains, standing, transparent, still watching* THE POET. *That human creature has typed her last key and now sits staring at the brightening window square. Finally she reaches out and turns off her desk light. As she does so, another* POET *stumbles in sleepily, in a bathrobe, rubbing his eyes. She senses his presence and smiles*)

THE POET   I've had a good night's work.

(THALIA *glimmers again faintly, glances over at the two poets, and grins. She takes* MELPOMENE *by the hand and tugs gently. They fade out together. And the Curtain of our consciousness*

FALLS.)

METAPHYSICAL FEMINISM

"This possibility: That you are God, and God is You."
—Christine de Pisane, feminist poet
and philosopher, c. 1364–1431

I: APOLOGIA

Let us step off the edge.

"The basic demands"—they are never basic enough. Nor are we, yet, really demanding them. Which is not to say that they don't exist, cannot be insisted upon, fought for, won. It's just that they cannot be defined.

We can recognize some of them, the most obvious ones: equality before the law, equal pay for equal work, the right to political representation, to education, decent jobs and credit, self-determination over our own bodies—which means access to safe contraception and abortion and the right of sexual preference, satisfactory and affordable child-care facilities which are controlled by the people (including children) who use them, freedom to walk down the street without fear of verbal and/or physical rape. Yet the *basic* demands include everything—an unpolluted planet, the end of all wars and the elimination of money; reverence for the very young and very old, indifference to pigmentation, height, or weight; no more poverty, ignorance, starvation, despair . . . the list is endless. And utterly insufficient. We must go beyond what we sense (I am assuming that we already are beyond what we *know*), and test our perceptions of reality. We must admit the entire cosmos as the ground on which such a search takes place. We must recognize the dissolution of the illusion of linear form. Yet we must go beyond, in effect, at the same time that we embrace the past, and act openly in the present. (Simultaneously to demand equal pay for equal work while questioning what is *meant* by "pay" and what is *meant* by "work." But to demand *and* question *at the same time*.)

How much this needs repeating: I fear being misunderstood, as if I were recommending a withdrawal from political action to some ivory tower of abstract thought. Such simplification has happened before, and the burnt witch fears the fire. Again and again "mass" thinking stops (or is carefully halted) at the patriarchal Either/Or border, and thus never attempts the third possibility, which is no destination in itself but a direction leading toward still further approaches. The third, the synthesis. That *earned state* of transition from thesis through antithesis. The dialectic. How dangerous to overlook it in others, and how exasperating to have it overlooked in oneself—to have one's synthetical position on a given issue praised or denounced by thetical or antithetical minds as their own (or each other's) position!

Some feminists are disturbed by dialectical terms because Marx used them in his time, although the concepts behind those terms long pre-date Marx; they were used by Socrates, adapted advantageously by Firestone, and can still be helpful as tools with which to analyze the feminist process. For example:

The Left views feminism as bourgeois, pacifist, and conservative. The Right views feminism as proletarian, violent, and rebellious. Individual feminists, when accused of any of these traits by whichever side their sympathies tend toward, can fall into the trap of denying and explaining: No, we're really good radicals; No, we're really respectable citizens. We can forget that the names are actually euphemisms for how both sides *really* perceive us—shrill, divisive, and threatening. True perceptions, for once.

Furthermore, the Left is accurate in seeing conservative tendencies among feminists; childbearing and rearing are still so far the responsibility of women, and this responsibility is most easily borne in conditions of stability, where the quantities and qualities are known and the territory familiar. If we thus appear bourgeois in our values it is hardly because we have so much to lose, but because what we do have we cherish with a fierceness that betrays us oftimes into pacifism, particularly since the little we have is usually our children—which generals of red, white, and black armies feel no compunction about drafting, raping, and murdering.

The Right is also correct in seeing feminism as the epitome of revolution. Indeed, of every NO uttered by an oppressed group to its rulers, there is none more earthshaking than the NO women as a people begin to say to men—across cultural, racial, national boundaries. We *are* proletarian, the essential proletariat, one might well argue, since we constitute not only the largest exploited group but have endured the model oppression for all other forms, and for the longest time. And our capacity for violence runs deep, surfacing mostly in defense of our children, but nonetheless possible on behalf of ourselves, if challenged beyond toleration.

So we can see that both the Right and the Left are quite accurate in their analyses. We *are* what both of them say we are—but most important, we are something *more*, some third perception, an entirety and integrity which is greater than the sum of any parts they can understand, greater than we ourselves have yet recognized.

This failure of recognition is due in part to our reluctance to examine the dialectical process in our own movement and our own selves. We have been impatient for simple solutions, a yearning which has afflicted all political groups most of the time. But if we do not understand the process, to paraphrase, we are doomed to repeat it (and have). We could, for example, track an individual on a typical dialectical course, remembering that an entire movement can go the same route, step by step:

Let us say that one may begin by pleading for equality, which seems a logical, fair, and eminently attainable goal (*thesis*). When the reactions to this plea are not requitedly logical or fair, and when the goal appears less and less attainable, one takes refuge in justifiable anger. This leads to a desire for vengeance, and for power (no longer power *equal to* but power *over*). This in turn often expresses itself as separatism, which is a cleverly self-deluding name for collaboration with one's rulers in their enforcement of one's own enghettoed state. ("Who wants to be in your old clubhouse anyway! We want *out!*"— which is where the overlords have intended one to be and where, in fact, one has been all along.) To demand such a self-imposed ghetto is the sole power and source of pride available (see "The Politics of Sado-Masochistic Fantasies," p. 239). Thus one denies being anything at all like one's oppressors, all the while mirroring more precisely that very image (*antithesis*). But the ghetto still feels like a ghetto and in time other realizations are borne in upon one, such as the fact that one's own people, while oppressed, are also human—and possess the capacity for misuse of power as much as any other group. Indeed, the same old grievances—not all attributable to the oppressor—are evident *within* the separatist ghetto. One becomes more interested in some entirely new definition of power, in exploring how it might be used differently, diversified. At the same time one begins to be less fire-and-brimstone condemnatory of imperfections in oneself and others (at no parallel loss of standards, incidentally), and gains a new respect for the individuality of persons and the composition of relationships. One begins to reject that arbitrary categorizing process which makes of each person a grass root (ready for mowing?). One even begins to be able to acknowledge change on the part of those who have power, *when* the change is real. This would constitute a *synthesis*; it is fragile, fraught with dangers *of which one is aware*, trepidatious, complex, and unclear—but worth it.

So, one articulates this emerging synthetical position (in an experimental whisper) to one's movement—and is promptly slammed. "Theticians" applaud one's return to a rational position and "Antitheticians" denounce one accordingly as a lapsed heretic. Or "Theticians" close ranks suspiciously against this untrustable seeker while "Antitheticians" smile wisely to one another that *they* know one is being temporarily pragmatic and tactically manipulative. Or vice versa. Sometimes Either *and* Or unite long enough to accuse one of variance in the ranks, narrowing vision, desertion of the cause, and that old stand-by indictment, liberalism (*omigod*). Still others might glimpse what one really is implying; they are the ones who rush to declaim that one is, this time, really going too far. One binds up the wounds and proceeds, because every synthesis is only a new thesis, and the process must begin again.

At this point, then, I am tempted to make a personal plea (knowing that it may do no good whatsoever and knowing, too, that I make it for the last time). A "Goodbye to All That," saying farewell this time to simplification and intolerance, no matter the source? Perhaps. Like many other women (and even a few men), I've suffered my sea changes through art, motherhood, monosexuality, bisexuality, the Left, violence, etc. Some of us have gone at least enough rounds on the spiral, the dialectical turn of the screw, to earn the assumption that we just might be approaching a problem from a complex vantage point and not a Zinjanthropian one. I say *earned* and I mean that. If, for instance, two artists criticize the way political movements use (or misuse) art, but only one of those two artists has risked difficult years of life-endangering activism in a revolutionary cause, then these two do not criticize, in my opinion, with quite the same right. One has paid her dues and the other hasn't. Which is another way of saying that criticism which doesn't spring from commitment (and love?) is not criticism but judgment, arrogant and aloof. Its insights may even be valuable, but they certainly should be regarded with healthy skepticism.

In certain areas I have earned my synthetical position. It has cost me dearly, and continues to do so whenever I see it being reduced backward to a thesis or antithesis. Nor are my halting attempts on any given subject to be envied, let alone lauded, denounced, or imitated. If recognized at all, they might be seen as steps in the journey of a woman whose peculiar private grief includes having found herself, as an artist, seized by her time and typecast into a political figure (this in a patriarchal culture, don't forget, where Either/Or presides).

Thoughts are living things, their movement an active process. To try freezing them so as to make them immortal is to miscomprehend totally their native deathless quality. To settle for two-fold thought when the third possibility shimmers just beyond is to lock oneself forever in the dual system of the paranoid's tennis court, with oneself as the ball. Such a settlement also is to successfully avoid any ongoing and dismaying confrontation with what freedom might really mean.

If we are to develop meta-midwifery then, and deliver ourselves and all life into new forms of freedom free even from the terror of freedom, we enter the realm of what I call metaphysical feminism.

II: THE METAPHYSICAL POETS

THE USUAL DICTIONARY definition of metaphysics or metaphysical will include such descriptions as: "a division of philosophy which includes ontology and cosmology . . . of or relating to what is conceived as transcendent, supersensible, or transcendental"—*Webster's III*; and "Of or pertaining to ultimate reality or basic knowledge, beyond or above the laws of the physical; transcendental"—*Funk & Wagnalls Standard College Dictionary*. *Webster's* further defines "metaphysical truth" as "the truth of ultimate reality as partly or wholly transcendent of perceived actuality and experiences."

Here I must alert the reader to some of the ways in which I do *not* intend to explore metaphysical concepts. I am not using the word in the Aristotelian sense, nor indeed in any traditional sense of strict philosophical terminology. Metaphysical feminism may or may not "work" on those levels; I welcome sisters better trained in such disciplines than I to pursue that subject.[1] I am a poet and so have drawn on the traditions of my own discipline for the feminist purpose: I am using the word "metaphysical" as it pertains to "the metaphysical poets." Again, it must be made clear that I am not discussing poetry written *on* metaphysical subjects (such as that of Lucretius, Dante, Blake, Christina Rossetti). Rather, I am referring to the work of those writers whom Dr. Samuel Johnson (of whom more later) termed "metaphysical"—as they have subsequently come to be called generally in English studies:

---

[1] Dr. Mary Daly, both as a friend and a feminist philosopher, has been a cherished influence on me in general, but she is not to be held responsible in the slightest for the ideas I present here. In a different instance, no relationship, either of influence or idea, intentional or inadvertent, exists between Ti-Grace Atkinson's pejorative phrase "metaphysical cannibalism" and my construct, metaphysical feminism. (Although the first words in both cases are identical, the second words reflect the difference in our entire approach and emphasis.) I do not claim to be one of Ms. Atkinson's sources of inspiration, nor is she one of mine.

various poets in seventeenth-century England, most notably John Donne, but including others, primarily Marvell, Crashaw, and Herbert. The work of this group, and of Donne in particular has, I think, special relevance for our exploration into the beginnings of metaphysical feminism.

It should be noted, too, that I do not refer to this approach as a philosophical one (although it is), because for too many people the word "philosophy" is a signal that the issues have now been moved to some illusory higher ground—which means that we are safe from discussing who will take out the garbage, and happily are no longer threatened with anything so mundane as being arrested. Our seventeenth-century poetic template and our own nascent metaphysical feminism do not permit of such self-deluding twaddle. We are always reminded of the real world. "No metaphor . . . too high, none too low, too triviall."[2] Contrarily, I do not refer to this approach as a pragmatic one (although it is), because for too many people the phrase "practical politics" is tantamount to (1) a caucus meeting, (2) a telephone booth (where the payoff takes place), or (3) a "militant riot." Again, these excuses are inadmissible to the metaphysical knowledge that the means and goals must justify each other—and that *every gesture is capable of grace.*

.   .   .

Definitions

Of metaphysical poetry, *Webster's III* says, "highly intellectualized poetry marked by bold and ingenious conceits, incongruous imagery, complexity and subtlety of thought, frequent use of paradox, and often by deliberate harshness or rigidity of expression." But there are better definitions, both for our own purposes and in general.

In his wise and beautifully written introductory essay to *Metaphysical Lyrics and Poetry of the Seventeenth Century*,[3] H. J. C. Grierson points out that Donne, the "great master" of the metaphysical poets, "is metaphysical not only in virtue of his scholasticism, but by his deep reflective interest in the experiences of which his poetry is the expression, the new psychological curiosity with which he writes of love and religion." Grierson goes on to define the work of The Metaphysicals as containing "above all the peculiar *blend of passion and thought, feeling*

---

[2] John Donne, "Sermon Preached to the King at White-Hall, the first Sunday in Lent (February, 1626/7)," in *The Sermons of John Donne*, selected and introduced by Theodore Gill, Living Age Books, published by Meridian Books, Inc., New York, 1958.

[3] Selected and edited, with an essay, by Herbert J. C. Grierson, Oxford at the Clarendon Press, 1921.

and ratiocination, which is their greatest achievement. Passionate thinking is always apt to become metaphysical, probing and investigating
the experience from which it takes its rise" (italics mine). Still another
distinguishing characteristic would be "the double motive, the desire
to startle and the desire to approximate poetic to direct, unconven-
tional, colloquial speech." (As Coleridge would later note, rather devas-
tatingly: "The style of the 'metaphysicals' is the reverse of that which
distinguished too many of our recent versifiers; the one conveying the
most fantastic thoughts in the most correct language, the other in
the most fantastic language conveying the most trivial thoughts.")

In his "Elegie upon the Death of Donne" Thomas Carew,[4] another seventeenth-century poet, lists six specific wrongs in poetry which
Donne redressed and four positive virtues that he attained. Even
greatly reduced (and prosified) by space requirements here, the two
lists read like a composite of model requirements which every poet
(and revolutionary) should strive to emulate. Very briefly, the *wrongs*
redressed are (1) the pedantic, (2) servile imitation due to laziness,
(3) licentious theft from ancient and foreign models, (4) "the subtle
cheat of slie exchanges," (5) "the jugling feat of two-edg'd words," and
(6) wrongs done "by ours" to other cultural and linguistic traditions.
The *virtues* are: (1) rich fancy, (2) bold expression, (3) mastery of
language, and (4) originality. Certainly Donne's originality has been
the subject of much analysis, and it is true that "if we except Donne's
Holy Sonnets (although even here, their directness is dramatically different from the Elizabethans) and the heroic couplets of his *Satires*
and *Elegies,* nearly every other poem is cast in a form of his own
devising."[5]

T. S. Eliot's key essay "The Metaphysical Poets"[6] is greatly
indebted to the pioneer work in this field done by Dr. Helen Gardner,
yet is itself so rich in perceptions relevant to our political adaptation
of the sensibility of these poets that I am at a loss as to which of his
insights to quote here (I urge the reader to treat herself to the complete
essay). Eliot notes that the poetry of Donne (and to an extent that of
Marvell and Bishop King[7]), like that of Chapman, is *late Elizabethan*
in feeling: "a direct sensuous apprehension of thought, or a recreation
of thought into feeling." Others usually considered to be among The
Metaphysicals, including Herbert, Vaughan, and Crashaw (whose devo-

---

[4] In H. J. C. Grierson, *op. cit.*

[5] Kenneth Pitchford, "On Carew's Elegie for Donne," Oxford, 1956, unpub-
lished essay; quoted by permission.

[6] In *Selected Prose of T. S. Eliot,* edited with an Introduction by Frank
Kermode, Harcourt Brace Jovanovich/Farrar, Straus & Giroux, New York, 1975.

[7] Bishop King's *Exequy,* an elegy of longing and love for his dead wife, is
simply one of the finest poems in English.

tional poems, such as those to Saint Teresa, found an echo in the poems of Christina Rossetti) returned *through* the Elizabethan period to the early Italians for their influences, Eliot feels. But the not-coincidental tone set by Elizabeth Tudor and her Renaissance England informs and illumines to a considerable extent the work of all The Metaphysicals.

Eliot adds more pieces to the jigsaw puzzle of definition we are assembling on the metaphysical poets, each of which will be of use when we come to applying all this to the concept of metaphysical feminism. He finds rapid association of thought and a "telescoping" of images characteristic. (This is frequently accomplished with brilliantly witty puns.) He points out that "a thought to Donne was an experience; it modified his sensibility." This *unified sensibility* was almost a given among sixteenth-century poets and dramatists (in Elizabeth's reign); in the seventeenth century "a dissociation of sensibility set in, from which we have never recovered." Eliot sees this dissociation (of thought and feelings) as aggravated by Milton and Dryden, and he theorizes that Donne, Marvell, and the seventeenth-century poets up to the Revolution were "the direct and normal development of the precedent age," suggesting that the eighteenth-century Dr. Johnson may have overlooked this context for what he viewed, from his perspective, as such an aberrative group.[8]

In a related vein, and (all unaware) using terms ideally suited to a feminist context, J. B. Leishman characterizes Donne's poetry in particular as "the dialectical expression of personal drama."[9] One might use precisely the same phrase to describe feminism.

.   .   .

And Having Done That, Thou Hast Done

> "If, as I have, you also do
>   Virtue attir'd in woman see,
> And dare love that, and say so too,
>   And forget the He and She; . . ."
>
> —JOHN DONNE, "The Undertaking"[10]

---

[8] In a splendid paragraph from which I cannot resist quoting, Eliot places at least the potential for a unified sensibility at the center of the creative process: "When a poet's mind is perfectly equipped for its work, it is constantly amalgamating disparate experience; the ordinary man's experience is chaotic, irregular, fragmentary. The latter falls in love, or reads Spinoza, and these two experiences have nothing to do with each other, or with the noise of the typewriter or the smell of cooking; in the mind of the poet these experiences are always forming new wholes." T. S. Eliot, *op. cit.*

[9] J. B. Leishman, *The Monarch of Wit: An Analytical and Comparative Study of the Poetry of John Donne,* Hutchinson's University Library, London, 1955.

[10] In *The Songs and Sonnets of John Donne,* Introduction and Notes by Theodore Redpath, Methuen, London, 1956.

It is time we glanced briefly at the work of Donne himself. I can anticipate the distress of some readers in their confusion as to why a feminist should choose male poets as exemplary in any way for feminist politics. The answer is less complicated than even I would assume. I have not chosen "male poets" but a specific set of poets, (who happen to be male) and one poet in particular, Donne. I have in fact not "chosen" them. What they have come to represent has "chosen" me— they have been praised and damned for the very qualities I always have most loved, in art, in life and, I now realize, even in politics. Furthermore, I would with delight have used as my examples women poets, had we access to any who shared that period *and* poetic sensibility. Elizabeth Tudor, Mary Sidney Herbert, Isabella Whitney all wrote in an earlier time; only three books of poetry in English by women were published during the sixteenth century. During the seventeenth, Lady Elizabeth Carey published (under initials only) the first original play by a woman in England, and Mary Sidney Wroth, Rachael Speght, Lady Diana Primrose, and Dorothy Berry appeared in print. Later still, of course, there would appear "the matchless Orinda," Katharine Philips, as well as Margaret Cavendish, the Duchess of Newcastle. Yet none of these poets lived (or had access to publication) at that unique moment when the sensibility of the Elizabethan period was confronted with the special tension produced by the controversial new sciences— to unite in the art of The Metaphysicals before it became, in Eliot's phrase, "dissociated." The one possible exception is Lucy Harington, Countess of Bedford, who was a patron of Donne's; among the poems previously attributed to him is one that, according to Ann Stanford, was written by the Countess. This is a poem which begins "Death, be not proud," but proceeds as an elegy, unlike Donne's well-known sonnet. Ms. Stanford notes that manuscripts circulated freely at that time, and it is not now possible to discern which of the two poets used the opening phrase first.[11]

As for Donne himself, no feminist defense can or need be made for his biography—an eccentric one, to be sure, which ranged from a rather wild youth (he accompanied Essex to Cadiz in 1596 and to the Azores the following year) through a period of scholarship, an appointment as private secretary to the Lord Keeper of the Great Seal, and a defiantly romantic marriage, culminating in his taking orders and ending his life as the Dean of St. Paul's Cathedral (and author of the grand *Sermons*). During his life he underwent a controversial and probably politically induced (if not opportunistic) conversion from Roman Catholicism to the Anglican Church; he lauded Elizabeth, then de-

---

[11] *The Women Poets in English: An Anthology*, edited with an Introduction by Ann Stanford, A Herder and Herder Book, McGraw-Hill, New York, 1972.

nounced her when she executed his old leader, Essex, then mourned her eloquently in his great elegy for another Elizabeth (Drury), "The First Anniversarie." It is not surprising that a man of such contradictions (which vibrate throughout his poems) should span the excesses of misogyny and a pro-feminism which was daring even for his time (Ben Jonson called some of Donne's tributes to women "blasphemous"; Jonson, we must remember, wrote *Epicene: The Silent Woman*).

So the same Donne who wrote "No where/Lives a woman true, and faire,"[12] could also write "All measure, and all language, I should pass/should I tell what a miracle she was"—in his glorious love poem "The Relique," in which he staggers us with the unforgettable image of a love-token found in an opened grave: "a bracelet of bright hair about the bone." He can be bawdy: "License my roaving hands, and let them go/Before, behind, between, above, below";[13] exhortatory and praiseful: "Today put on perfection, and a woman's name";[14] defiant of those who would criticize his lover: "For Godsake hold your tongue, and let me love."[15] He can rail against woman's inconstancy, and, in a poem like "The Extasie,"[16] he can depict with breath-taking lyricism the synchronicity of divine and human love:

> ". . . Our soules, (which to advance their state,
>   Were gone out,) hung 'twixt her, and mee.
> And whilst our soules negotiate there,
>   Wee like sepulchrall statues lay;
> All day, the same our postures were,
>   And we said nothing, all the day."

A unified sensibility indeed.

.   .   .

Connections

A reflective interest in experience. A psychological curiosity about love and religion. Surely the former is a fitting description of the changing consciousness of any woman as she begins to examine her own life, with her own tools of expertise. Surely the latter could be an apt expression for the two-fold obsession of women through the ages: human and divine love. (Donne was, in fact, positively "womanly" in his pre-

---

[12] "Song" ("Goe, and catche a falling starre").

[13] "Elegie XIX, Going To Bed."

[14] "Epithalamion Made at Lincolnes Inne."

[15] "The Canonization."

[16] All of the lines quoted in this paragraph are from *The Poems of John Donne*, edited from the old editions and numerous manuscripts, with Introduction and Commentary by Herbert J. C. Grierson, 2 vols., Oxford University Press, London, 1912.

occupation with this two-fold love, seeing in human love the best approach to cosmic love, as women have done for centuries.

To go on: psychological curiosity, the desire to startle and to approximate poetic to direct, even colloquial speech, and above all, *the blend of passion and thought,* feeling and ratiocination. Psychological curiosity—and courage—is more required by the politics of feminist consciousness than by most political movements. The desire to startle is, naturally, experienced by all ignored peoples, but the desire to approximate poetic to colloquial speech seems especially and poignantly relevant to feminism. What else has our embryonic culture been attempting but to articulate in accessible terms that which previously has been unknowable or at least unspeakable? And that wonderful phrase "passionate thinking"—certainly this describes the electric leap of shared and connecting consciousness at its most intense. "Passionate thinking is always apt to become metaphysical, probing and investigating the experience from which it takes its rise." "The *dialectical* expression of personal drama."

When I think, then, of metaphysical feminism, I think not only of an all-encompassing feminist vision which goes literally beyond the physical (yet never leaves it behind) but which is in its very form related to those seventeenth-century English poets. An obsession with love has been at the heart of women's concerns—and in fact of feminists' concerns—for millennia, no matter how steadfast certain antithetical feminists remain, fixed in an anti-emotional polar response to what they see only as "feminine sentiment." How often have feminists called, too, for the "peculiar blend of feeling and ratiocination" in our battles against the patriarchal dichotomizing of intellect and emotion! It is the insistence on the *connections,* the demand for synthesis, the refusal to be narrowed into desiring less than everything—that is so much the form of metaphysical poetry and of metaphysical feminism. The unified sensibility.

But for the quintessential definition we must finally go to Dr. Johnson's wry and condemnatory essay in which he coined the name for the metaphysical poets. He didn't like them (Donne, Cleveland, and Cowley especially) for all the right reasons—which is to say that his definitions were most piercingly accurate precisely when most limited by his own brazenly affirmed prejudices. The standard practice of these poets, he huffed, was to create situations in which "the most heterogeneous ideas are yoked by violence together."[17] He

---

[17] Samuel Johnson, *Lives of the English Poets,* first published in 1779 and 1781. My reference edition is published in two volumes by Oxford University Press (Geoffrey Cumberlege), with an Introduction by Arthur Waugh, London 1906; 1952 edition.

used as an example of this violent yoking Donne's memorable image of "stiff twin compasses" to describe two lovers separated by geographical distance but still joined in spiritual and emotional unity.[18] Donne's astonishing image needs no defense any longer from anyone. We can concentrate therefore on Dr. Johnson's phrase—one which seems to me a strikingly appropriate metaphor for metaphysical feminism.

If by heterogeneous ideas we admit ambivalence, complexity, and the dialectic (philosophical and material); and if we understand "violence" to mean risked force, a defiance of stasis, a hazarding, a gamble with the greatest of stakes; *and* if by "yoked" we comprehend commitment held in balance by a discipline self-imposed—then we have in effect our own formula alchemized from the dear dross of Dr. Johnson.

The most heterogeneous ideas are yoked by violence together— such as struggle with the person one loves. Such as *contradiction* (the very element the proto-Marxist ideologue fears and would eliminate as quickly as possible). Such as these two at-first-glance utterly opposed concepts might be yoked together by the sheer *violence* of our desire:

(1) The idea of any meaning out there in the universe
(2) The idea of any freedom here for women

Normally the first statement would bring us up short at that old chestnut "If God is God he is not good; if God is good he is not God." But the violence of our desire regarding the second statement speeds us past, through, and into a self-created feminist metaphysic where there simply is no "out there" any longer. Because all that is out there is in here, and always was and always shall be, born of one's own actions renewingly, mystically, perpetually.

Microphotography of a blastula dividing in the womb divulges to our eyes a pattern and process identical to that enacted for us by interstellar radio waves "photographing" the expansion of a galaxy. This is a living metaphysically poetic image.[19] It is the third possibility.

The polarizing simplification that rejects the third way is impossible with metaphysical feminism. Impossible to drop out and "navelgaze" (which a muddled general definition of metaphysical thought might allow, but which our clarified analogy to the seventeenth-century poets does not permit). Impossible because the fantastic is rooted in the miracle of reality and flowers continuously within it. Equally impossible

---

[18] "A Valediction: Forbidding Mourning," *op. cit.*, note 10.

[19] "Immensity cloistered in thy dear womb"—from "Annunciation" in *The Holy Sonnets*, John Donne, *op. cit.*, note 16. For an exhaustive and stimulating examination of such images I recommend to the reader Rosemond Tuve's *Elizabethan and Metaphysical Imagery: Renaissance Poetic and Twentieth-Century Critics*, University of Chicago Press, Chicago, 1947. Ms. Tuve's scholarship on this period is as thorough as it is creative.

to settle for that reality alone, that "equal pay for equal work," when this damnably intrusive *passionate thinking* keeps leading us onward and inward.[20] It is only a fitting contradiction, then, that we encounter in John Donne and the other metaphysical poets of seventeenth-century England one excellent model for an approach to our own feminist metaphysic.

> "The ancient Church knew not, Heaven knows not yet:
> And where, what lawes of Poetry admit,
> Lawes of Religion have at least the same,
> Imortall Maide, I might invoke thy name . . .
> Thou art the Proclamation; and I am
> The Trumpet, at whose voice the people came."[21]

III: SPIRITUALITY

I OFFER YOU a feminist *koan* of my own devising:

Liberation and oppression can look much the same. Being unable to discern the difference between them—this is the meaning of oppression. (So much for at least one of the two definitions.) Or is this the ultimate definition of both?

In which case we might call it "grace."

But in which case?

. . .

Not the least devastating gesture of patriarchal power has been to cast the cosmos itself—the life force, energy, matter, and miracle—into the form of a male god. Feminists have already observed that this has had a less than salutary effect on women. We could spend fifty volumes delineating the destruction done in the names of such gods, and we can also look around us. At this writing, Christian armies and Moslem forces in Lebanon are slaughtering each other *and* civilians (for which read: women and children and the aged) in the streets of Beirut, even as Catholic and Protestant antagonists draft grammar-school children to snipe at one another across the blood-scummed cobblestones of London-derry in Northern Ireland. Both of these "religious wars" are misnomers in the political sense, but in a deeper sense they are perfectly named,

---

[20] "Oh, to vex me, contraryes meet in one:" XIX of *The Holy Sonnets*, *op. cit.*, note 16.

[21] From "The Second Anniversarie," in *Of the Progresse of the Soule*, by John Donne, *op. cit.*

since both are about the contest between the two great modern patri-archal religions: capitalism and communism. For it is not only the Judeo-Christian tradition which has shored up the patriarchy for five thousand years; it is every male-conceived and -dominated faith.

I confess to a particular antipathy for the Catholic Church, despite my loyalty to good theater wherever it can be found, and my long-standing passion for Gregorian chant.[22] I don't mean to let the rest of Christianity (or my own religion of origin from which I am so apostate, Judaism) off the hook easily. But it *is* hard to overlook or forget nine million women burned as witches over a period of three hundred years by Christianity, and largely by the Catholic Church.[23] Even today, in Catholic South and Latin America, illegal abortion and childbirth compete for the highest cause of death among women. In the United States, the church is financing Birch-Society-led campaigns to undo the moderate progress women have made in gaining self-determination over our own bodies. So much blood spilled on the cathedral steps, because that perfect microcosm of patriarchy—that hierarchy of octogenarian celibate males running around in drag—still thinks it can rule on the lives and bodies of millions of women, whatever our ages.

---

[22] This fondness extends itself to secular music of the Middle Ages, as well; nevertheless, I was gratified to learn that the structure of Gregorian chant is based on very old musical forms dating back to "pagan" matriarchal religious ritual. (See *Music in History*, McKinney and Anderson, American Book Company, New York, 1940). This comforts my conscience almost as much as the music delights my spirit.

[23] The New York *Post* of August 18, 1976, carried the Associated Press story of a twenty-three-year-old woman, Anneliese Michel of Klingenberg, Germany, who died after having undergone exorcism rites by two Catholic priests. *Time* magazine (September 6, 1976) also reported and expanded the story. It appears that civil authorities are now investigating the exorcism procedures, which were originally recommended by an eighty-one-year-old local priest who believed Ms. Michel was possessed of demons which sent her into violent seizures. With the permission of Bishop Josef Stangl, two exorcists—Fr. Arnold Renz and Fr. Ernst Alt—were called in. Fr. Renz, not one averse to publicity, claimed during a tele-vision appearance that Ms. Michel was possessed by six spirits, including Lucifer, Nero, Judas, Cain, and Adolf Hitler—a case of overkill, one would think. The exorcism rituals continued for ten months; Ms. Michel's seizures grew more frequent and intense and her weight dropped to seventy pounds. The priests called in no medical assistance. Finally she died, "of malnutrition and dehydration," according to the medical report. Bishop Stangl told the press that he was considering a church investigation into the "possible negligence" of the priests; he said his decision on this would be forthcoming upon his return from a health-resort holiday.

Bishop Stangl's diocese is Würzburg, where in one year alone during the seventeenth century, more than three hundred witches were burned alive for "trafficking with the devil."

Further medical background was uncovered about the dead woman, whose seizures had been diagnosed unmysteriously when she was in high school. Anneliese Michel suffered from epilepsy.

Which should not, I grant, keep us from justly condemning the gray, co-optative mask of modern Protestantism (clamped over the self-righteous expressions of Luther and Knox); the virulent woman-hatred in Fundamentalist Christianity; the woman-fear and woman-loathing rampant in Judaism to this day (as if the scars of that religion's matriarchal origin and its overthrow were still not eradicated from the Jewish collective unconscious); the female-as-temptress or the female-as-nonentity in, respectively, the exoteric and esoteric sophistries of Buddhist, Zen, or Western existential thought; the vitriol spewed on women for centuries in Moslem cultures. [24]

Very well. We do not exist or, since this is the choice, we are the devil's gateway, we are evil. What else, we may ask, is new? And for every female mystic who has somehow managed through her own genius, like Teresa, to reach her transcendence even through the labyrinth of patriarchal means—millions of us have stared with horror at the disbelievable reality of our own ankles stockinged in flame, have peeled open the parchment of our lips that the world might read the scream stuck in that throat. What else can we hear but that unspent scream—even if they did have anything to say to us now?

So we left their churches, and are still leaving. And the birth of what has been called female spirituality is a new phenomenon in the Women's Movement.[25] This has given me much personal joy—and at present it is worrying me sick. Because once again spirituality is becoming confused with religion—thus going nowhere near far enough. An anthropomorphized god has merely been replaced with a "gynemorphized" god, after all.

Earlier in this book I noted how, in the original WITCH group in the sixties (due to intellectual laziness and activist frenzy), we never quite got around to doing the research we meant to do. But by 1970 I had embarked on that research, later to compare notes with other women who were reading and working in the same area. Consequently

---

[24] The Associated Press recently reported from Istanbul that two orthodox Moslem villagers, Tahir Akcay and Mehmet Veysi, shot and killed their wives for their failure to uphold fasting traditions during the holy month of Ramadan. This was in September of 1976.

[25] Not as new as it might seem, perhaps. In a provocative paper entitled "Jane Lead: The Feminist Mind and Art of a Seventeenth-Century Protestant Mystic," Catherine F. Smith of Bucknell University suggests that the connections between feminism and a mystical tradition extend quite a way back, even though this linkage has been ridiculed, when recognized at all, by male-biased scholarship. She writes: "The patriarchal limitations of mystical thought are not the main point when women writers are concerned. Rather, mysticism has given women a voice, a literary form capable of describing both their reduced condition and their native powers. It has also provided them with an indirect language for protesting sexual politics." Quoted by permission.

when, in 1973, I affirmed myself publicly as a witch,[26] I did not mean it lightly. Still, I should not have been surprised when, at a press conference twenty minutes later, three other well-known feminists declared themselves instant witches. An act of solidarity? I wanted to believe so despite my own feelings of discomfort, which told me that I had been misunderstood and trivialized on the spot. Those initial misgivings were borne out in the following months and years, at times making me regret that I had ever discussed publicly my private beliefs.

It is of course very likely that feminists would have discovered matriarchal religion and particularly the importance of the Craft in that tradition all by themselves, quite without my having "popularized" this within the Women's Movement. Serious students of the origins of feminist culture had already begun investigating this subject. Nonetheless, I feel an itch of responsibility every time I hear of some new vulgarity perpetrated on the Craft in the name of "politics" or "life-style" —or on women in the name of the Craft. It's true that I feel an even greater pride when encountering women who are willing to juggle all the contradictions so complicatedly present in this area, but for each woman who seems desirous of doing some homework on such a subject, there appear to be two others who see the Craft as a "femology" or an excuse to smoke some grass, juice up, and lie around bare-breasted for six or eight hours under a gibbous moon. Recently, I came across a booklet written by a woman purporting to be both a feminist and a witch. The egotistical occult games repelled me. The booklet proposed that women might heal themselves of possibly malignant tumors by drinking certain herb teas and burning special candles (conveniently on sale at the author's shop). Still other herb teas, another page suggested, were a fine "natural" means of birth control. We can skip over the hundred less hazard-provoking inaccuracies in the pamphlet; we are still left with the author's stupendous lack of concern for responsible feminist politics, let alone for the serious medicinal tradition of the Craft. Least of all for *women's lives*.

To paraphrase Elizabeth Tudor, I have no wish to open windows into women's souls, but I do feel the need and the right to define my own terms for myself. What I have meant by a commitment to and affirmation of the Craft of the Wise is *synthetical* and, again, complicated. Nor is this the place to describe in detail what that involves. But I will say that I am an atheist who prays most commonly and devotedly through art. I am an initiated Wiccean priestess, true, but what that means to me and what it means to you, dear reader, may indeed be astral planes apart. I tend to be rude sometimes to those people who

---

[26] This happened at the end of the keynote speech at the Lesbian Feminist Conference in Los Angeles. The text of that speech begins on page 170 of this book.

dare not leave home in the morning without consulting their astrological charts, but I read a mean tarot—since the poetic symbolism resonating from its archetypes is pleasurable to me. I am intensely opposed to the notion of reincarnation, finding it an irritating, exhausting thought when I don't see it as a plainly silly one. (Have you ever noticed how everyone was either Cleopatra or Napoleon in their former incarnation—never Cleopatra's chamber-pot slave or Napoleon's foot soldier?) If, on the other hand, you view reincarnation as a *metaphor* for that mystically cellular transition in which the dancers DNA and RNA immortally twine themselves, then perhaps we can discuss it further. I identify strongly with the rich psychological and poetic symbolism of matri-archal religions, and with the experiential truths I, as a daughter and a mother, recognize. Again, these involve contradictions.

Is the only way to freshen thought, to clear out the eager misunder-standers and instant co-opters, to defend language from the violation visited daily on it—*silence?* Silence directed not only toward the patriarchy (which thought occurred to some of us long ago) but even more radically—toward women?

Yet I would sing. Is silence the only way to be *unsettling* to myself, and to those whom I would reach through our mutual vices and devices? How to make you realize the imperative of this moment? How to stretch out a hand and whisper, yes, here, step out over the edge, the drop is only magnetized toward your own density's grave center.

May your insurrection and your resurrection be the same.

The form, the fabric itself, is changing. If we could be aware of the cacophony in our silence, and the reverse. If we could be conscious of the simultaneity: as intolerable torture and as literal saving grace. If we could be aware, for more than a second at a time, for more than the flash before we fall asleep . . .

IV: JOURNAL ENTRY

2 August 1974
4:00 a.m.

AWAKE FROM another nightmare. The moon is full and it is the second day of my period. The time when women in lunatic asylums become uncontrollable, even now, in the twentieth century.

Today I learned that Elizabeth Gould Davis had shot herself, "dead of self-inflicted gunshot wounds." All day it was the first of August. Still I have written nothing, nothing in months. Seeking the grail of my art through the dragons of everyday living.

For months K. has been in his own despair. This time neither of us seems to have caused the other's depression; the world is sufficient motivation. I think of "King Zero."[27]

All month Blake has been sad, cranky about going to summer school half-days, missing us. All day Hektor has been vomiting periodically, from having licked his paws after walking over freshly varnished floors.

We try to talk with one another, K. and I. We pay extra attention to Blake: songs, special treats, long conversations. We cuddle Hektor and fill his water bowl with fresh milk.

Tonight I dreamt that Blake and Hektor both came downstairs where we (K. and I) were sitting, to let us know that something was wrong upstairs: Hektor meowing an unearthly guttural *rowrl* and Blake standing frightened, balancing on one foot, on the stairs. We pooh-poohed it all, then went up to find the top floor dense with smoke. There was no sensation of heat. There seemed to be no fire.

K. asked me (shouting above the smoke as if it were a din), "What's causing it? Where is it coming from?" He rushed to open the window in Blake's room, I to the windows in the front. For some reason, in dream-logic, this seemed an imperative thing to do. But I found that there were layers to open first: drapes, then curtains, then shade, then shutters, then screens, then at last I could fling up the sash and let in fresh air. But what billowed through instead, was the sound of sirens, loud and frantic.

I woke up. The sirens were real. Men's voices shouting in the street. Megaphones.

From the downstairs window I could see all the police cars—more than the twelve I managed to count, as they one by one backed up from their circle in the middle of the street and drove off. A threatened corner mini-riot perhaps, the way for our neighbors in this slum of a great city to pass a summer night. Was the fight between the blacks and Puerto Ricans, over turf? Or between the dealers and the pimps, the junkies and the bums? *Death to the Pimps* read the sidewalk graffiti defiantly stencilled by prostitutes trying to organize. Was management union-busting? I could see no more. But August has arrived on that street, living nightmare outside and in. My heart pounds with it. I know all the political reasons. They merely clarify the fear.

Back in bed, I lit a cigarette, really hoping to wake K. He stirred, asking only half-awake if anything was wrong. I told him I'd had a nightmare which was real. But he was too tired, too full of his own griefs this time to want to listen. He turned over, pretending to be reassured and reassuring, back to sleep. Oh my dear.

---

[27] "King Zero," a meditation on patriarchy in Kenneth's novel *The Beholding*, at this writing still awaiting publication.

Tomorrow—no, today, August 2, Elizabeth Gould Davis will be buried with no sheaf of wheat from me on her grave. She chose not to linger with lungs that would no longer breathe. But toward the end she had said that even the air was intelligible, could we but understand it. She cleaned her house. She found good homes for her cats. She had no children.

No sheaf of wheat from me on her grave. What have the child and the cat, saner animals than we, been trying to tell us about danger in this house, on this street, in this world?

Self-inflicted?

When I have a nightmare into whose bed can I crawl, like Blake, and be comforted? Into whose grail can I pour myself, if not my own? In what asylum can I seek to hide my fear, which will not lunify it? In whose grave can I rest except my own?

V: THE QUESTION

SOONER OR LATER we come to the question.

The question hides like a tick inside the casing of the most heavily armored of us, the most cynical, the most assured and embittered. It haunts those who know all the answers. Because sooner or later the rhetoric leaves one hungry for some truth, and in moments of crisis when the old wound runs and the adrenaline flows—then all the words like sexism and male supremacy and patriarchy and oppression compact into one word, as concisely felt as the shocked wail of a child: *unfair.*

What have we done to deserve this? The more radical a feminist one becomes, the less answerable the question appears—for if one believes that all other oppressions stemmed from the primary one, the subjugation of women by men, then the question becomes all the more imperative.

Some feminists reject theories of the existence of ancient matriarchal cultures (matriarchal in all senses, with women holding religious and secular power) mainly because it might then be required of them to explain what happened to *undo* such cultures? How did the "patriarchal revolution" come about? Or how did the matriarchies fall? What mistakes were made, and by whom? Why?

Some feminists may opt for a biologically deterministic analysis (which leads precariously toward a "final solution" of technologically induced mutation or the actual extermination of one sex by the other—whether the result be as gynocide or androcide). Others reassure themselves and one another that environment/culture is the sole culprit, and that a restructuring of it will solve the whole problem. A few have tilted out toward science-fiction theories of interplanetary colonization way back when. Some of us pretend to know—but wouldn't be caught alive saying. Some even pretend not to care any longer, claiming that our solutions must be more drastic than any analysis of the situation could help us devise. Meanwhile the question still hides like a tick inside our armor. And each of us hunches secretly within herself, like a hurt child, not understanding. *Unfair. What have I done to deserve this? What have I ever done?*

This is Wednesday. I was born on a Wednesday. Shall I give you the answer I sometimes think I know on Wednesdays?

VI: ANOTHER PARABLE

> *How can we love?*
> *How can we not love?*
> —The Three Marias,
> NEW PORTUGUESE LETTERS

THE SEA ORGANISMS crawled up onto the land to commit ecstatic suicide, to escape triumphantly from existing, to return to infinite pure energy, motionless.

But life forced itself to flow through even the gasps they drank in of what they assumed was death: air. Despite themselves, they became air-breathing organisms. Every step taken toward nonexisting brings us closer toward existing.

It is the fault of something Female.

Nature, we have heard, abhors a vacuum. Speaking then through male anguish at his own womb envy, Nature discovered existential despair. But male anguish expressed this despair as misogyny. What else to feel when faced with this female endless birthing, this repeated insistence on life and life-giving and life-re-creation? What *is* this maddening tendency to bear and bear and bear, as if each woman were somehow somewhere in herself singing "I never met a universe I didn't like"?

He only wants her to understand his wretchedness. He persecutes her to make her understand why death is the answer, he tortures her to raise her consciousness to the suicidal, to make her as truly aware as he is. She won't despair. She won't die. She creates agriculture, domesticates animals. Culture is born.

He appropriates her gods, her whole cosmic space, to the merciless, negative, bleak, terror-filled void in which he is trapped. She curses his gods—but does not die. She calls to him. She sees his beauty writhing, contorted in pain. He sobs with longing to share what she is, sees, owns, the whole earth as female, the solar system female, the universe female, all that he smells and touches and which holds him and bore him and will outlive him—female, eternally rutting and conceiving and laughing and producing.

For what? What is there to celebrate here, in this dimension? Is there no way to kill her out of this gross procreation? Can none of his entropy conquer her energy? If he cannot stop her, can he at least successfully pretend that he *insists* she do precisely what she is doing? Can he tell himself he *demands* she conceive? Rape is born, his own parthenogenic child. Laws are written controlling her body's freedom. She creates pottery, baskets, songs. She investigates the power of herbs. Art and science are born.

Is there no way to stop her? Is there no way to evade this inexhaustible deathless pursuing consciousness? He devises nirvanas of escape, Oriental philosophies which pretend she is illusion, Occidental philosophies which pretend she is existentially meaningless. And all the while she smiles and conceives. Children. Grapefruits. The thimble. Barnacles. The printing press. City squirrels.

He is more and more trapped into his systems. He invents new and efficient ways of murdering what she produces—wars, chemicals, political systems which destroy her creations or treat them as products. He is consumed with self-loathing for having become the weapon of himself and never the victim in his global attempt to commit suicide. She weeps for him and gives birth to a new star, hoping its nova will divert him from his misery.

He invents names for her creatures, deliberately mixed around. He calls the human ones insects, vermin, pigs, cows. Then he kills them, and their animal namesakes, too. He forgets what and who and why he is killing. He knows only where he came from—that womb of earth, and where he is going—that same insatiable womb with its infinite capacity for orgasm and for creation as it sucks him in and spews him out and laughs lovingly *lovingly* at him as if he were her plaything.

Only when he has totally forgotten who he is and why he hates her so; only when she herself has almost forgotten herself; only when his pain has at last infected her so that she almost has begun to listen, almost understand his message of nonexistence, his longing for peace and death and the silence of a collapsed nonwomb whose energy and matter are once and for all time separated—only then does she slowly rouse herself to remind him.

That time is now.

AFTERWORD: GOING

"**B**UT THEN, is metaphysical feminism something we do, or know, or experience, or understand, or practice? Is it a strategy, a perception, an invention? You have scolded us for getting lost but you have given us no maps to go by except the memory of some dead male poets and these damned impenetrable parables."

How do I tell you, how do I count the ways? How can I show you, how can you touch it on this flat, inanimate page—black letters white paper block printing *how can I curl through this page, this book in your hands, like smoke, and envelop you?*

Right now.

Right *now* our spaces intersect, your eyes moving right now over this line *there* caught you! moving focusing and refocusing *ah* you touched me no don't stop don't falter don't return to the start of the paragraph *good* do look and listen we are the woman in the mirror only you and I us private all alone you've always known that anyway haven't you so have I there's only ever been one of us and that's sufficient even just one so beautiful is the power of all this grace now can you understand *ah yes*. Look.

Far. No, *farther*. Simultaneously all at once and always happening in the same instant my lips cracking as I try to scream the flames have reached my ankles omigod my god somebody help me they're burning me alive. She whispers, "Be alert. It will be as you suspect, not as they reassure you, remember that." Freedom for everyone or freedom for no one. I must get to the bank before three tomorrow. I disown none of my transformations. The tree and the singing bird. Blake you are the honey in my life and K. the salt; he will explain this to you. The taste of coffee cartons and smell of plastic leaves at dawn. *Why*. Clara Wieck Schumann wrote some of his music but could not go mad for him. Wild hair flying, wild eyes staring, wild voices keening. So it seems I am going to marry K. after all. They murdered her with a broom handle rammed into her vagina and the women didn't do anything because no one was sure of her sexual preference. Elvira Shatayev died on the winter mountain with her all-woman team; her husband climbed in another storm to find her body. Elizabeth and Robert, Virginia and

Leonard, Cathy and Heathcliff. Brigid, Beltane, Lughnassad, Samhain. To be female and conscious is to be in a continual state of rage. My bright hair braceleted about your bone. We are a class, we are a caste, we are a colony, we are a people, *we are Vietnam*, we are the oceans and forests, we are a world, we are an idea. It's inherently female, there's nothing to be done about it. Various failures of me. All lists are helpful. The cleaners are closed on Saturdays in August. *What have they done to us?* No sheaf of wheat from me on her grave. We are women in a circle, I have been here before. Mary Wollstonecraft died in child-birth, in *childbirth*. The faces the voices the meetings the planes. Waiting for a love that will not happen. I am a proud atheist priestess, put that in your cauldrons and smoke it. She says she is sixty years old and was raped every night of her marriage for thirty-five years. The dialectic of personal drama. A good political movement can wear down stone, grain by grain. What grits in my teeth? Sand and Chopin. Uniplicity, duplicity, multiplicity. The proper study of womankind. *My cells remember this*. We are Harlem and China and Galesburg. My mother is dying. Her sister died. To understand this pain. If only we had changed the paper's name. Atalanta, Hippolyta, Medea, Clorinda. My madness protects me from their malignancy. We have been the model. *Why*. *What have we done?* Her endless proud laughing rutting. She will not die, she will not even cease giving birth to him, herself, worlds, universes, she will not even grant him that one mercy. My shoes are red; he is walking into the ocean. *Kneccht*. Growing older, knowing it wouldn't have had to be this way. "Remember the dignity of your womanhood." To rediscover the *words*. Self-inflicted. Into whose grave, whose grail can I pour myself if not my own? Good girls never get raped. Their malignancy protects me from my madness. Look, we have a conflict of life-styles here. Different voices but they sing for all of us. We may as well trust each other, they're going to try to burn us, anyway. Trust no one. No no no goodbye to all that. Getting ready to die. The hell with you, I'm going out for a walk. *And ye shall be free from all slavery*. Blake's perfect mouth, perfectly satisfied, at my perfect breast. You have no right to love your children, it only oppresses them and you. "I incite this meeting to rebellion." I shall never forget the leech's hiss, or what he said. I bless this study, I bless our bed, I bless the anguish that proved we would endure. A real bullet look lodged in the podium. How do we avenge our children, our children, as well as ourselves? Entropy and growth. *Contradiction*. She lay dying in the midst of gray filing cabinets, she was bourgeois. *What have I done, my son, my son, that you should hate me so?* Each breath a contraction, each exhalation a galaxy. Some Amazon tribes took women as prisoners and enslaved or massacred them—do not buy the cheapest model offered you, my sisters. *Greatness is simply a way of life*, and it must become so for everyone; that is the meaning of revolution. Charlotte Brontë vomited to death in pregnancy. How his knife gleams in the sun. *What if I cannot after all understand her?* No wonder Teresa was so cranky, organizing a whole order and levitating at the same time. Her silkworm soul, my spiderwebs, Penelope's revisions. We're almost out of milk. The icy Saskatchewan morning and the sultry flat clots of air in a Florida noon. Redwood-filtered sunlight, feeling only you. Something beneficent in the universe? *I stab him again and again and again.* The audience, the questions, the hotel keys. They have self-fulfilling prophecies; we have prophecies fulfilling self. Far, go farther. Rape exists anytime intercourse without *The right to a great love* the woman's initiation, initiated into madness, priestesshood. *I can see the taxi waiting.* A bomb is in the auditorium I'm afraid we must interrupt your speech. *Understand me,* know me. K. comes out of the bedroom in that dear summery sleep-potty way of his You may not love a man it is incorrect it is a contradiction. *For godsake hold your tongue and let me love.* And I love contradictions, they make life interesting, let all my contradictions blessedly be yoked by violence together. Together they bound such men with wood at the feet of the witch and called them faggots, only such faggots could kindle a fire foul enough to burn me in. *We will be torn from one another and ourselves.* The woman in the mirror. *You gave me life and now I've lost you, something female, your fault, your fault.* Susan B. Anthony's death-bed, Elizabeth's grave. Thou art the Proclamation and I am the Trumpet. She certainly is charming, with those yellow braids, but why does she carry that axe? The child and the cat understand. The Bach B-Minor Mass. As if the tears of women could save a world. *Know me.* She never mistakes it for the real thing and is therefore not degraded by it. She will not let him rest until he understands, beholding this, my one desire. He will torture her until she lets him die into rest. No no no. *Love is more complex than theory,* and all art is an act of frustrated love, all love an act of frustrated fear. I will find you, Little Kay. *To be beyond freedom.* If I love my people I owe them some truth, art being the harshest truth I can lovingly give them. *Thesis.* What are we becoming? Vengeance and patience. I never met a universe I didn't like, because in the end my madness protects me, their malignancy protects me, something beneficent? *Antithesis.* Dear Blake, welcome to the universe, dear dear Blake, goodbye. Endlessly birthing will she never die enough in childbirth will she never learn. We only as women are alone escaped to tell. My hair going too far silvery my face almost good grief *mature* how did this happen *why,* what have I done to them, whose hair is burning? Whose are those faces are they men killing a witch are they revolutionaries executing a poet *Why* we may as well trust each other. *Synthesis. Passionate thinking.* Phoenix from its ashes, my ashes, the grains of mytho-poetic-history *how can I reach you.* Do you understand now. *Breathe me in,* I am the smoke of your own flesh, the bracelet of bright flame about the ankle. If women are the cosmic work of art then men are our divine fallacy, the gap to let the soul out don't you see? Is not this the parable of love? If you are still afraid there must be within you a courage unique unto this moment. *I love you, K.* I am my people, *I am come into my power,* I am the mirror-blastula reflected in the newest nova. *I love you, Blake.* My son, my son. *If you are this afraid then farther.* Here is my hand. Breathe me in. We are dancing in the still-warm ashes of our burnt-away selves, *endlessly birthing.* Insurrection. *Resurrection.* Come along now, *you too,* don't you think it's time we started?

GERMINAL READING LIST

[Some of these books have been cited in the text; all of them have been important to the development of ideas expressed in *Going Too Far*.—R.M.]

Abbott, Sidney, and Love, Barbara. *Sappho Was a Right-On Woman*. New York: Stein and Day; 1972.

Ariès, Philippe. *Centuries of Childhood: A Social History of Family Life*, trans. by Robert Balick. New York: Random House; 1962.

Bachofen, Johann Jakob. *Myth, Religion, and Mother Right*, trans. by Ralph Manheim, Princeton, N.J.: Princeton University Press (Bollingen Series LXXXIV); 1967.

Barrett, Elizabeth. *The Complete Poetical Works of Mrs. Browning*. Boston: Houghton Mifflin (Cambridge Edition, which includes the complete "Aurora Leigh"); 1900.

Beard, Mary R. *Woman as Force in History*. New York: Collier Books; 1962.

Beauvoir, Simone de. *The Second Sex*, trans. and ed. by H. M. Parshley. New York: Alfred A. Knopf; 1952. Vintage Books edition, 1974.

———. *A Very Easy Death*. New York: Warner Paperback Library; 1973.

Benedict, Ruth. *Patterns of Culture*. New York: New American Library; 1959.

Bernikow, Louise, ed. *The World Split Open: Four Centuries of Women Poets in England and America, 1552–1950*. New York: Vintage Books; 1974.

Bird, Caroline, with Sara Welles Briller. *Born Female: The High Cost of Keeping Women Down*. New York: David McKay; 1968.

Bogin, Meg. *The Women Troubadours*. London and New York: Paddington Press; 1976.

Briffault, Robert. *The Mothers: A Study of the Origins of Sentiments and Institutions*. 3 vols. New York: Macmillan; London: Allen and Unwin; 1927.

————. *The Mothers: The Matriarchal Theory of Social Origins.* Abridged to one volume. New York: Macmillan; 1931. Grosset and Dunlap Universal Library Edition, 1963.

————. *The Troubadours,* ed. by Lawrence F. Koons. Bloomington: Indiana University Press; 1965.

Brownmiller, Susan. *Against Our Will: Men, Women, and Rape.* New York: Simon and Schuster; 1975.

Campbell, Joseph. *The Masks of God.* 4 vols. New York: Viking Press; 1969.

Catt, Carrie Chapman, and Schuler, Nettie Rogers. *Woman Suffrage and Politics: The Inner Story of the Suffrage Movement.* New York: Charles Scribner's Sons; 1923. Reissued with a new introduction by T. A. Larson; Seattle: University of Washington Press; 1969.

Chaplin, Dorothea. *Anthropological Bonds between East and West.* Copenhagen: Einar Munksgaard; 1938.

Chesler, Phyllis. *Women and Madness.* Garden City, N.Y.: Doubleday; 1972.

Cott, Nancy F., ed. *Root of Bitterness: Documents of the Social History of American Women.* New York: E. P. Dutton; 1972.

Daly, Mary. *The Church and the Second Sex.* New York: Harper & Row, Publishers; 1968. Reissued "With a New Feminist Postchristian Introduction by the Author," New York: Harper Colophon Books; 1975.

————. *Beyond God the Father: Toward a Philosophy of Women's Liberation.* Boston: Beacon Press; 1973.

Davis, Elizabeth Gould. *The First Sex.* New York: G. P. Putnam's Sons; 1971.

Diner, Helen. *Mothers and Amazons,* trans. and ed. by John Philip Lundin. New York: Julian Press; 1965.

Donne, John. *The Sermons of John Donne.* Selected and introduced by Theodore Gill. New York: Living Age Books/Meridian Books; 1958.

————. *The Songs and Sonnets of John Donne.* Introduction and notes by Theodore Redpath. London: Methuen; 1956.

————. *The Poems of John Donne,* edited, with commentary, by H. J. C. Grierson. 2 vols. London: Oxford University Press; 1912.

Ehrenreich, Barbara, and English, Deirdre. *Complaints and Disorders: The Sexual Politics of Sickness.* Old Westbury, N.Y.: The Feminist Press (Glass Mountain Pamphlet #2); 1973.

Eliot, T. S. *Selected Prose*, edited, with an introduction, by Frank Kermode. New York: Harcourt Brace Jovanovich/Farrar, Straus and Giroux; 1975.

Ewen, C. L'Estrange, ed. *Witch Hunting and Witch Trials*. London: Kegan Paul, Trench, Trubner & Co.; 1929.

Fanon, Frantz. *The Wretched of the Earth*, trans. by Constance Farrington. New York: Grove Press; 1968.

———. *Black Skin, White Masks*, trans. by C. L. Markmann. New York: Grove Press; 1967.

———. *A Dying Colonialism*, trans. by Haakon Chevalier. New York: Grove Press; 1965.

Firestone, Shulamith. *The Dialectic of Sex: The Case for Feminist Revolution*. New York: William Morrow; 1970.

Flexner, Eleanor. *Century of Struggle: The Women's Rights Movement in the United States*. New York: Atheneum; 1970.

Francoeur, Robert T. *Utopian Motherhood: New Trends in Human Reproduction*. Cranbury, N.J.: A. S. Barnes (A Perpetua Book); 1973.

Frazer, James G. *The New Golden Bough*, an abridgment, ed. by Dr. Theodor H. Gaster. New York: Criterion Books; 1959.

Fritz, Leah. *Thinking Like a Woman*. Rifton, N.Y.: WIN Books; 1975.

Fuller, Margaret. *Woman in the Nineteenth Century and Kindred Papers*. Reprinted, New York: Source Book Press; 1970.

Gardner, Helen. *Metaphysical Poets*. Baltimore, Md.: Penguin; 1957.

Gilman, Charlotte Perkins. *The Yellow Wallpaper*. Reprinted, Old Westbury, N.Y.: The Feminist Press; 1973.

———. *The Home: Its Work and Influence*. A reprint of the 1903 edition. Chicago: University of Illinois Press; 1972.

———. *The Man-Made World, or Our Androcentric Culture*. New York: Charlton Co.; 1911. Reprinted, New York: Source Book Press; 1970.

Goulianos, Joan, ed. *By a Woman Writt: Literature from Six Centuries By and About Women*. New York: Bobbs-Merrill; 1973.

Gransden, K. W. *John Donne*. London: Longmans, Green; 1954.

Graves, Robert. *The White Goddess*. New York: Farrar, Straus and Giroux; 1974.

———. *The Greek Myths*. 2 vols. Baltimore, Md.: Penguin; 1955.

Grierson, Herbert J. C., ed. *Metaphysical Lyrics and Poetry of the Seventeenth Century*. London: Oxford at the Clarendon Press; 1921.

Grimstad, Kirsten, and Rennie, Susan, eds. *The New Woman's Survival Sourcebook* (A Woman-Made Book). New York: Alfred A. Knopf; 1975.

Hamilton, Edith. *Mythology*. New York; New American Library; 1959.

Harrison, Jane. *Prolegomena to the Study of Greek Religion*. Cambridge, Eng.: Cambidge University Press; 2nd edition 1922.

Hays, H. R. *The Dangerous Sex: The Myth of Feminine Evil*. New York: G. P. Putnam's Sons; 1964.

Herberger, Charles F. *The Thread of Ariadne: The Labyrinth of the Calendar of Minos*. New York: Philosophical Library; 1972.

Howe, Florence, and Bass, Ellen, eds. *No More Masks! An Anthology of Poems by Women*. Garden City, N.Y.: Doubleday Anchor Original; 1973.

Iverson, Lucille, and Ruby, Kathryn. *We Become New: Poems by Contemporary Women*. New York: Bantam; 1975.

Jeffers, Robinson. *The Women at Point Sur*. Boni and Liveright; 1927. Reissued, New York: W. W. Norton; 1976.

Jenkins, Elizabeth. *Elizabeth the Great*. New York: Berkeley Medallion Books; 1972.

Johnson, Samuel. *Lives of the English Poets*. London, 1779 and 1781. Reissued in 2 vols. with an introduction by Arthur Waugh. London: Oxford University Press (Geoffrey Cumberlege); 1906 and 1952.

Johnston, Jill. *Lesbian Nation: The Feminist Solution*. New York: Simon and Schuster; 1973.

Jung, C. G. *Symbols of Transformation*. Volume V in the *Collected Works*. New York: Pantheon (Bollingen Series XX); 1956.

———. *Archetypes and the Collective Unconscious*. Volume IX in the *Collected Works*. New York: Pantheon (Bollingen Series XX); 1959.

Kaminski, Margaret, ed. *Moving to Antarctica: An Anthology of Women's Writing from Moving Out*. California: Dustbooks; 1975.

Kearns, Martha. *Käthe Kollwitz: Woman and Artist*. Old Westbury, N.Y.: The Feminist Press; 1976.

Koedt, Anne. "The Myth of the Vaginal Orgasm," in *Radical Feminism*, A. Koedt, E. Levine, and A. Rapone, eds. New York: Quadrangle/ The New York Times Book Company; 1973.

Koven, Anna de. *Women in Cycles of Culture*. New York: G. P. Putnam's Sons; 1941.

Kramer, Heinrich, and Sprenger, James. *Malleus Maleficarum*, trans. and with an introduction by Montague Summers. New York: Dover; 1971.

Leishman, J. B. *The Monarch of Wit: An Analytical and Comparative Study of the Poetry of John Donne*. London: Hutchinson's University Library; 1955.

Lerner, Gerda. *The Grimké Sisters*. New York: Schocken Books; 1971.

———, ed. *Black Women in White America: A Documentary History*. New York: Pantheon; 1972. Vintage Books edition, 1973.

Lévi-Strauss, Claude. *Totemism*. Boston: Beacon Press; 1963.

———. *Tristes Tropiques*. New York: Atheneum; 1963.

———. *The Elementary Structure of Kinship*. Revised edition. Boston: Beacon Press; 1969.

———. *The Raw and the Cooked*. Vol. I of *Introduction to a Science of Mythology*. New York: Harper & Row; 1969.

Lewinsohn, Richard. *A History of Sexual Customs*, trans. by Alexander Mayce. New York: Harper & Brothers; 1958.

Loyd, Dorothy Frances. *Women Counseling Women: An Art and a Philosophy*. Doctoral dissertation, University of Massachusetts; 1973.

Maddux, Hilary C. *Menstruation*. New Canaan, Conn.: The Women's Library/Tobey Publishing Co., Inc.; 1975.

Marias, The Three. *See listing for New Portuguese Letters.*

Martin, Del. *Battered Wives*. San Francisco: Glide Publications; 1976.

———, and Lyon, Phyllis. *Lesbian/ Woman*. San Francisco: Glide Publications; 1972.

Mead, Margaret. *Sex and Temperament in Three Primitive Societies*. New York: William Morrow; 1935; reissued 1963.

———. *Male and Female*. New York: William Morrow; 1949.

Memmi, Albert. *The Colonizer and the Colonized*. New York: Grossman Publishers; 1965.

Mernissi, Fatima. *Beyond the Veil: Male-Female Dynamics in a Modern Muslim Society*. Cambridge, Mass.: Schenkman Publishing Company; 1975.

Millett, Kate. *Sexual Politics*. Garden City, N.Y.: Doubleday; 1970.

———. *Flying*. New York: Alfred A. Knopf; 1974.

Moglen, Helene. *Charlotte Brontë: The Self Conceived.* New York: W. W. Norton; 1976.

Morgan, Elaine. *The Descent of Woman.* New York: Stein and Day; 1972.

Murray, Margaret A. *The Witch-Cult in Western Europe.* London: Oxford at the Clarendon Press; 1962.

———. *The God of the Witches.* London: Oxford University Press by special arrangement with Faber and Faber, Ltd.; 1970.

Mylonas, George E. *Eleusis and the Eleusinian Mysteries.* Princeton, N.J.: Princeton University Press; 1961.

Neumann, Erich. *The Great Mother: An Analysis of the Archetype,* trans. by Ralph Manheim. Princeton, N.J.: Princeton University Press (Bollingen Series XLVII); 1972.

New Portuguese Letters (The Three Marias: Maria Isabel Barreño, Maria Teresa Horta, and Maria Velho Da Costa), trans. by Helen R. Lane. Garden City, N.Y.: Doubleday; 1974.

Otto, Walter F. "The Meaning of the Eleusinian Mysteries" (1939) in *The Mysteries: Papers from the Eranos Yearbooks,* Princeton, N.J.: Princeton University Press (Bollingen Series XXX. 2.); 1955

Our Bodies, Ourselves, from the Boston Women's Health Book Collective. New York: Simon and Schuster; revised and expanded second edition, 1976.

Pankhurst, Emmeline. *My Own Story.* London: Eveleigh Nash; 1914.

Patterson, Rebecca. *The Riddle of Emily Dickinson.* New York: Houghton Mifflin; 1951.

———. "Elizabeth Browning and Emily Dickinson" in *Educational Leader,* July 1956.

Pitchford, Kenneth. *The Blizzard Ape: Poems.* New York: Charles Scribner's Sons; 1958.

———. *A Suite of Angels and Other Poems.* Chapel Hill: University of North Carolina Press; 1967.

———. *Color Photos of the Atrocities: Poems.* Boston: Atlantic–Little, Brown and Company; 1973.

———. *The Contraband Poems.* New York: Templar Press (Box 98, FDR Station, N.Y. 10022); 1976.

Plath, Sylvia. *Letters Home,* ed. by Aurelia S. Plath. New York: Harper & Row; 1975.

Power, Eileen. *Medieval Women.* New York: Cambridge University Press; 1976.

Reed, Evelyn. *Woman's Evolution: From Matriarchal Clan to Patriarchal Family*. New York: Pathfinder Press; 1975.

Rich, Adrienne. *Of Woman Born: Motherhood as Experience and Institution*. New York: W. W. Norton; 1976.

Schneir, Miriam, ed. *Feminism: The Essential Historical Writings*. New York: Vintage Books; 1972.

Sewell, Elizabeth. *The Orphic Voice: Poetry and Natural History*. New Haven: Yale University Press; 1960.

Sherfey, Mary Jane. *The Nature and Evolution of Female Sexuality*. New York: Random House; 1972.

Stanford, Ann, ed. *The Women Poets in English: An Anthology*. New York: A Herder and Herder Book, McGraw-Hill; 1972.

Stanton, Elizabeth Cady. *Eighty Years and More: Reminiscences 1815–1897*. Reprinted, New York: Schocken Books; 1971.

———. *The Woman's Bible*. Reprinted, New York: Arno Press, Inc.; 1974.

———, Anthony, Susan B., and Gage, Matilda Joslyn. *The History of Woman Suffrage*. Reprinted in 6 vols., New York: Source Book Press; 1970.

Stone, Merlin. *When God Was a Woman*. New York: Dial Press; 1976.

Stuard, Susan Mosher, ed. *Women in Medieval Society*. Philadelphia: University of Pennsylvania Press; 1976.

Tennov, Dorothy. *Psychotherapy: The Hazardous Cure*. New York: Abelard-Schuman; 1975.

Teresa of Avila. *The Interior Castle*, trans. and ed. by E. Allison Peers. Garden City, N.Y.: Doubleday (Image Books); 1961.

———. *The Way of Perfection*, trans. and ed. by E. Allison Peers. Garden City, N.Y.: Doubleday (Image Books); 1964.

Tillich, Hannah. *From Time to Time*. New York: Stein and Day; 1973.

Tuve, Rosemond. *Elizabethan and Metaphysical Imagery: Renaissance Poetics and Twentieth-Century Critics*. Chicago: University of Chicago Press; 1947.

Walsh, J. E. *The Hidden Life of Emily Dickinson*. New York: Simon and Schuster; 1971.

Weideger, Paula. *Menstruation and Menopause*. New York: Alfred A. Knopf; 1976.

Wilson, Joan Hoff. "Women's Studies and Feminism: Survival in the Seventies," in *Report on the West Coast Women's Studies Con-*

ference. KNOW, Inc. (P.O. Box 86031, Pittsburgh, Pennsylvania, 15221); 1974.

Wollstonecraft, Mary. *A Vindication of the Rights of Woman*. 1791. New York: W. W. Norton; 1967.

————. *Maria, or The Wrongs of Woman*. New York: W. W. Norton; 1975.

Woolf, Virginia. *A Room of One's Own*. New York and Burlingame: Harcourt, Brace & World; 1929.

————. *Three Guineas*. New York and Burlingame: Harcourt, Brace & World; 1938.

INDEX

[The legend § indicates that the name or title most closely preceding it occurs as a main entry in the Reading List.]

goddess-worship, 12, 72, 187–188; *see* matriarchy, Wicce
Goulianos, Joan, §
Graham, Alma, xii
Graham, Martha, 221, 282
grammar-school feminism, 6
Gransden, K. W., §
Graves, Robert, 233, §
Gregorian chant, 303
Grier, Barbara, 184
Grierson, H. J. C., 295–296, 299n, §
Griffin, Susan, 265
Grillo, Gilda, 202, 203n
Grimstad, Kirsten, §
Grove Press, 132–133
Guardian, 59, 73
guerrilla theater, 5, 63, 78, 80, 88, 101
"Gumbo," 130
gynarchy, *see* matriarchy
gynocide, 161, 186, 308; *see also* androcide, battery, death, violence
gynocracy, 187, 197; *see* matriarchy
Gypsies, 73, 139

Hacker, Marilyn, 265
hallucinogenic drugs, 242–245; acid (LSD), 51, 127, 243, 253; marijuana, 68, 77, 127, 194, 243; mescaline, 243; peyote 243
Hamill, Pete, 90
Hamilton, Edith, §
Hammer, Signe, 230n
Harington, Lucy, 298
Harlem, 225, 312
Harrison, Jane, 233, §
Hart, Lois,, 130
Haskell, Molly, 230n
Hawthorne, Nathaniel, 267
Hayden, Tom, 223, 224
Hays, H. R., §
health, 5, 11, 13, 15, 89, 138, 160–162, 198, 209; *see also* abortion, childbirth, contraception, Feminist Women's Health Centers, madness, midwifery, *Our Bodies Ourselves*, sexuality
Hefner, Hugh, 125
Hektor, 30–32, 56, 307–308, 313
Hellman, Lillian, 267
Herberger, Charles F., §
Herbert, George, 295, 296
Herbert, Mary Sidney, 298
Her Self, 177n
herstory, 10, 139, 220; coining of word, 121; *see* history (women's), women's studies
heterosexuality, 7, 14, 91, 156, 170, 174, 175, 176, 177, 178, 182, 183, 184, 185, 186, 187, 199, 234–235, 251,

279, 311, 312, 313, 314; Edenic potential of, 235n
Hetshapsut (Hatshepsut), 221
high-school feminism, 69, 92: on "home economics," 13, 69
Hinduism, 202
Hiroshima, 225
history, 91, 95, 103, 107, 122, 129, 162, 190, 197, 198, 205, 208, 233, 237–240, 272, 273, 274, 278, 288, 298, 312, 313, 314; women's, 21, 56, 62, 72, 77, 91, 96, 98–99, 156, 161, 175, 187, 190–191, 193, 194, 197, 198, 205–208, 225, 232, 237–240, 266, 288, 312, 313, 314; *see* Clio, Muse of, 268–289; *see also* herstory, matriarchy, mytho-history, women's studies
Hitler, Adolf, 288
Hoffman, Abbie, 125, 182
Hoffman, Anita, 125n, 130
Hoffman, Judge Julius, 124
Holliday, Billie, 206
homosexuality, 91, 171, 181, 232, 242; female, *see* lesbianism; male, 24, 84, 102, 232, *see also* faggot, gay
Horne, Lena, 285
Horney, Karen, 230
Horta, Maria Teresa, *see* Marias, The Three, §
hospital employees, 6
housewives, 6–7, 14, 59, 92, 94, 95, 96, 123, 148, 158, 186, 192, 195, 225, 242, 253; as feudal laborers, 196; average work week of, 196; unions for, 6, 92; wages for, 196; *see* housework; *see also* "runaway women"
housework, 3, 4, 6–7, 35–38, 43, 47, 83, 98, 99, 101, 102, 103, 111, 112, 124, 125, 138–139, 207, 209, 272, 311, 312; economics of as invisible labor, 196; wages for, 196
Howe, Florence, §
Hrovtsvitha, 285
humor, 125, 130, 210, 238, 281; Thalia, Muse of Comedy and the Pastoral, 268–289
hunger-strike, 200
Hutchinson, Anne, 206

Illinois, Galesburg, 222–226, 312
illiteracy, 21, 206; United Nations statistics on, 190
India, 6
Indonesia, 69
Inglis, Nancy, 17
inovulation (cloning), 11, 198
international feminism, 6, 15, 64, 65, 69, 76, 98, 108, 122, 155, 157, 170, 202–208, 215, 291, 313

ABOUT THE AUTHOR

ROBIN MORGAN compiled and edited the now-classic feminist anthology *Sisterhood is Powerful* (1970), and has written two books of poetry: *Monster* (1972), and *Lady of the Beasts* (1976). Her poetry and prose appear widely in literary and political journals. She is currently at work on a verse play, a third collection of poems, and a book of historical fiction on the lives of women accused of witchcraft. She lives in New York City with her husband, the writer Kenneth Pitchford, and their child, Blake Ariel.